TRAINING
CHRISTIANS
TO
COUNSEL

NORMAN WRIGHT

HARVEST HOUSE PUBLISHERS
Eugene, Oregon 97402

Training Christians to Counsel
Copyright © 1977 by H. Norman Wright
Published by Harvest House Publishers
Eugene, Oregon 97402

Edited by Samuel M. Huestis

CONTENTS

Introduction 1

PART I
TRAINING MANUAL

Advance Preparation 3

Session

  1. Introduction to Counseling 5

  2. Answers, Observations, and Goals of Counseling 8

  3. The Biblical Framework for Counseling 19

  4. A Model of Counseling, Part I 46

  5. A Model of Counseling, Part II 57

  6. A Model of Counseling, Part III 62

  7. Ministering to the Depressed Person, Part I 64

  8. Ministering to the Depressed Person, Part II 76

  9. Helping the Suicidal Person, Part I 84

 10. Helping the Suicidal Person, Part II 95

 11. Counseling Married Couples, Part I 100

 12. Counseling Married Couples, Part II 113

 13. Ministering to the Divorced Person, Part I 118

 14. Ministering to the Divorced Person, Part II 124

 15. Ministering to the Dying and Bereaved Person, Part I 133

 16. Ministering to the Dying and Bereaved Person, Part II 139

Alternate Session: Ministering to the Sick: Hospital Calling 147

Theological Teaching in Counseling 151

Bible Study in Counseling 153

Bibliography for Counseling 156

PART II
ARTICLES ON COUNSELING

Hazards to Effective Pastoral Counseling, Part I 163
  Maurice E. Wagner

Hazards to Effective Pastoral Counseling, Part II 167
  Maurice E. Wagner

Jesus' Style of Relating: The Search for a Biblical
View of Counseling 172
  David E. Carlson

Effective Counseling and Psychotherapy:
An Integrative View of Research 180
  Keith Edwards

Rapid Treatment for a Troubled Marriage 190
  Andre Bustanoby

Marriage Therapy 196
  Jay Haley

The Marriage Conference 203
  Raymond Corsini

The Growth Model in Marital Therapy 208
  Shirley Luthman

Group Procedures for Increasing Positive Feedback
between Married Partners 216
  Carl Clarke

Counseling the Homosexual 220
  Marriage & Family Resource Newsletter

PART I
TRAINING MANUAL

INTRODUCTION

Training Christians to Counsel is one of the first series of its kind. Hopefully other counselors and ministers will also recognize the need for training the layman (or the paraprofessional as he is called in the secular field) and develop further and more extensive materials. The first portion of this manual was designed to be used in 2-1/2-hour sessions for the purpose of equipping laymen to counsel and help others. Those who complete this training will hopefully be involved in helping and counseling others in their neighborhood, at the church, in community or church crisis centers, or wherever the Lord opens doors for them to serve Him in this capacity.

For many years secular clinics and schools have trained laymen to function as nonprofessional counselors. If anyone ought to have the opportunity to share in this helping ministry, it is the believer of a local church. "For just as we have many members in one body and all the members do not have the same function, so we, who are many, are one body in Christ, and individually members one of another. And since we have gifts that differ according to the grace given to us, let each exercise them accordingly: if prophecy, according to the proportion of his faith; if service, in his serving; or he who teaches, in his teaching; or he who exhorts, in his exhortation; he who gives, with liberality; he who leads, with diligence; he who shows mercy, with cheerfulness" (Rom. 12:4-8, NASB).

Giftedness must be considered in the selection of those who feel called to minister in this manner and those you feel ought to be involved. The field of counseling will undoubtedly interest some who are either curious or even seeking solutions to their own difficulties. This is not a therapy course. It should be limited to those who are settled and mature in their spiritual and emotional life.

The material contained in the first portion of this manual has been designed as a curriculum to be used in training others to counsel. However, it can easily be adapted for use in the following:

1. Sunday school classes — on the topic of ministering and helping others.

2. Retreats or conferences.

3. Preaching/teaching in morning or evening services — for the entire congregation.

The question may arise, How does one select persons to share in the ministry of counseling? Perhaps the idea could be discussed at the church board meetings or at various classes. You may want to personally approach some individuals or couples who you feel have the ability or interest to serve in this manner. Each person or couple should be interviewed personally concerning their own strengths and weaknesses and desires in this direction. It is important to explain that taking this course does not guarantee, in any way, that they would automatically be chosen to be used in a counseling ministry within the church following the course. Some will discover during the course that their gifts lie in other areas. You will probably have to suggest this to some. The need for counselors will help determine how many can be used in this capacity.

Before taking this course, those selected should take the Bible study course involving the Taylor-Johnson Temperament Analysis. This will help you to know more about each individual and will allow them to learn more about themselves and the teachings of scripture concerning many areas with which they will be confronted as they counsel others.

Prior to teaching this course, note carefully the subjects covered. Two additional areas of study and training not discussed in this manual should be covered: *evangelism*, of the basic steps involved in leading someone to Christ, and the counseling ministry of *premarital counseling and preparation*. It is recommended that you select some training materials or course on evangelism to present to the participants. Also obtain the series of training tapes, *Upon this Foundation*, Vol. I, *Premarital Counseling and Marriage Preparation*. The six hours of detailed information on the tapes and the accompanying workbook can be used to train others, but can be used on their own without being involved in a class setting. The material presented on these tapes is the same content taught at Talbot Seminary and the graduate program of Marriage and Family Counseling at Biola College. (All materials mentioned in this introduction and materials mentioned in the various session are found on the order form at the end of this manual.)

Because this course will reach a small segment of your congregation, here is another recommendation for you to consider. Every member of the body of Christ needs to develop some skills in helping and ministering to others.

The second portion of this book is a collection of articles I have found helpful on various topics and areas of counseling. Too often in purchasing books and journals on counseling (at considerable cost) I find only one or two chapters or articles of practical use. In order to eliminate buying several books to find the best chapters, they have been included in this resource for your own information and growth. Including them in this resource does not mean that I agree with every thought or concept, nor are you expected to do so. Yet much can be learned from the opinions and thoughts of those with whom we disagree as well as those with whom we agree.

The cost of purchasing some or all of the materials listed and conducting these training classes as well as marriage enrichment seminars, parent-teen seminars, and premarital training yourself, is less than the cost of outside speakers. Materials and tapes can be used again and again and in many different environments and class contexts. It is important that class members have their own copies of the booklets recommended in the various sessions and that they read them at the proper time.

Prior to teaching this series it is recommended that you read the following books for your own development in the area of counseling.

Egan, Girard. *The Skilled Helper.* Monterey, Calif.: Brooks/Cole Publishing Co., 1975.
Also read and complete the exercise in *Exercises in Helping Skills Workbook.*
Glasser, William. *Reality Therapy.* New York: Harper & Row, 1965.
Packer, J. I. *Knowing God.* Downers Grove, Ill.: InterVarsity Press, 1973.
Wright, Norman. *Christian Counseling—A Comprehensive Guide,* (Revised Ed.). Waco, Tex.: Word.
Wright, Norman. *Self Talk, Imagery and Prayer in Counseling,* Waco, Tex.: Word, 1986.

You should also read all of the articles in the second section of this manual and should listen to the tape series mentioned in the various chapters.

The minister who teaches this material should become proficient in his knowledge of counseling, the relevant scriptural teachings, and the creative methods necessary to assist adults in the learning process. *Before teaching any section of this course, spend one or two months acquainting yourself with the lessons and saturating yourself with the suggested books, tapes, and scriptures.* Read the Advance Preparation section as well as the lessons for each series well in advance of teaching the course.

When you are setting up your plans to teach the series in this manual, allow enough meetings to cover the material (one meeting for each session of the series). Also structure enough time for each session (as suggested in the instructions for the individual series). If you use this material for a Sunday morning, you may have to adjust the usual Sunday school hour. *Do not* cut down on the necessary time, and do not modify the suggested methods of teaching. This course is the result of several years of study, teaching, and experimentation; it has been carefully designed to produce the best possible results when used as instructed.

However, you will need to be flexible to a certain extent. Each learning activity in each session has a suggested time allotment. If students are deeply interested in a topic, you should let them pursue their study even if it takes more time than suggested. On the other hand, if class members complete a discussion or a study before the suggested time has elapsed, go on to the next activity.

You will need large charts or an overhead projector for each lesson. The contents for these charts or transparencies is found in the lessons. Patterns for some of the transparencies are found at the end of each section. If at all possible, use an overhead projector. Plan well in advance for the preparation of these visuals. If this kind of printing or preparation is difficult for you, enlist the services of someone who is gifted in this area. Be sure the words on the transparencies are large enough to be seen easily when projected. Try one or two ahead of time until you get the hang of it. If a chart or cartoon is suggested, you can place the film over the pattern in this manual and trace it, or you can make a photocopy of the pattern and make a transparency by using a thermofax machine.

Many materials are available for making transparencies. One of the most efficient and economical brands of transparency film is Projectofilm. This is produced in light and medium weight sheets by Ful-Vu Visuals Company. The address of their main office is P.O. Box

187, Blackwood, N.J. 08012. The Los Angeles address is P.O. Box 61035, Los Angeles, Calif. 90061. Use permanent ink marker pens with material.

The visuals are an essential ingredient in the presentation of these lessons. Do not try to get along without them.

You will need blank pieces of paper and pencils for every person in every session. Perhaps they can be stored in the classroom so that they will be available each time.

You will need to order books, tapes, and films for the various lessons. Some of the tapes will be used for more than one lesson. These materials may add an initial cost of twenty to forty dollars to the course, but in many instances it is a one-time cost, and the materials can be used over and over again. You may want to charge a fee for each person taking the course.

It is my hope that this material will help ministers and laymen assist others in their individual Christian growth and in their family relationships.

H. Norman Wright
Associate Professor of Psychology
Founder and Director of Christian
  Marriage and Enrichment, and
  Family Counseling and Enrichment
Tustin, California 92680

Additional copies of this manual can be ordered from Christian Marriage Enrichment, 17821 17th Street, Tustin, CA 92680.

ADVANCE PREPARATION

SESSION 1
Duplicate copies of the agree-disagree sheet.

SESSION 2
1. Prepare transparencies.
2. Order the tape *Damaged Emotions* by Dr. David Seamands.
3. Duplicate "Observations to Make During the First Session."

SESSION 3
Prepare transparencies.

SESSION 4
1. Prepare transparencies.
2. Duplicate the Bible Application Form.
3. Read (at least twice) the article in the second portion of this manual, "Effective Counseling and Psychotherapy: An Integrative Review of Research," by Keith Edwards.

SESSION 5
1. Prepare transparency.
2. Prepare a role-play demonstration.

SESSION 6
1. Secure extra copies of the "Bible Application Form" for those who may have forgotten to bring their form with them.
2. Arrange for the use of a tape recorder (any kind will do).

SESSION 7
1. Prepare transparencies.
2. Duplicate the questions concerning depression and the Holmes-Rahe Stress Test.
3. Order copies for each class member of *Beating the Blues* and *Uncovering Your Hidden Fears.* Each person should read the book on depression after session 8, to reinforce your presentation.

SESSION 8
1. Prepare transparencies.
2. Duplicate "Because God Loves Me."

SESSION 9
1. Prepare transparencies.
2. Duplicate the agree-disagree sheet and the case studies.
3. If you plan to use a film, order it weeks in advance.

SESSION 10
1. Prepare transparency.
2. If you plan to use a film, order it weeks in advance. See the list of suggested films in session 9.

SESSION 11
1. Prepare transparencies.
2. Duplicate "An Offended Wife's Responses" and the list of "Resources to Use in Counseling."

3. Read the articles in the back of this manual concerning marriage counseling and decide which of the materials you will share in your sessions. You will need to know thoroughly the information in the article "Rapid Treatment for Troubled Couples" as you will be sharing much of that material with your class.

4. Secure copies of the Marital Precounseling Inventory and the Marital Communication Inventory.

5. Secure copies of the tape series *Sex Problems and Sex Techniques in Marriage* and any other tape series you may want to recommend.

6. Order copies of *How to Speak Your Spouse's Language* and *The Pillars of Marriage*. Other helpful books for additional reading are *Why Marriage* by Edward Ford (Argus) and *No-Fault Marriage* by Marcia Lasswell and Norman Lobsenz (Doubleday).

7. For your own reading on the subject of marriage and family counseling, the following books would be helpful: *The Mirages of Marriage* by William Lederer and Don Jackson (Norton), *Conjoint Family Therapy* by Virginia Satir (Science & Behavior Books), and *The Dynamic Family* by Shirley Luthman (Science & Behavior Books).

SESSION 12
Duplicate the case studies.

SESSION 13
Duplicate the sentence completion and agree-disagree statements.

SESSION 14
1. Prepare transparency.
2. Duplicate the "Letter to a Couple on the Brink of Divorce."
3. Order a copy of *The Divorce Decision* for each class member. Distribute the books at the end of this session.
4. Invite guest speakers who have experienced divorce.

SESSION 15
1. Prepare transparency.
2. Duplicate the list of questions.
3. Order copies of *Recovering from the Losses of Life* by Norman Wright (available July 1991).

SESSION 16
1. Prepare transparencies.
2. Order the films *Though I Walk Through the Valley* and *Until I die*.
3. Duplicate copies of the "Bibliography of Death and Dying."
4. You may want to invite a guest speaker. See the alternate suggestion for this session.

ALTERNATE SESSION
1. Duplicate the true/false test.
2. Select, invite, and confirm the guest speaker for this session — either a medical doctor or hospital nurse.

INTRODUCTION TO COUNSELING

OBJECTIVES
— To verbalize reasons for taking this course of study.
— To identify and explain concepts of counseling.
— To analyze and clarify beliefs concerning counseling, mental conflict, and emotions.

ADVANCE PREPARATION
Duplicate copies of the agree-disagree sheet.

GETTING ACQUAINTED
Time: 5-8 minutes.

Welcome the class members. Divide them into groups of four and have each one share within the small groups why he is taking this course and what he hopes to change and to develop into by the end of the course.

DEFINITION OF COUNSELING
Time: 10-15 minutes.

Ask class members to take a piece of paper and write their own definition of counseling. Then ask them to write what they believe distinguishes Christian counseling from the secular approach. Ask for several responses from the group for both questions. Share with the group your own definition of counseling.

CASE STUDIES
Time: 30-35 minutes.

Read each case study to the group. After each one ask the class to write their responses to the actual statement. You could introduce the series of statements by saying: "Here are several actual cases or statements which people have expressed as they have come for counseling. As I read each one to you, immediately write what you think you would say in a similar situation. I will make the statement once and will not repeat it, for in counseling we have to be able to respond to a person immediately without an opportunity to go to a textbook to determine the correct response."

After you have read each statement and given the group an opportunity to write their responses, go back to the beginning of the list and read each statement again, asking for several responses from the group for each one. You may find different answers but do not spend much time analyzing them at this point. A few may want to disagree with one another over their response but this time is designed to expose them to statements they might hear and to increase their awareness of their need for this course. You may want to give some of your own responses to these actual counseling situations. Following this activity take a brief break.

1. A teen-ager comes in to see you, sits down, and says, "I hate my parents! They stink. And I don't care what happens to them!"

2. A wife in counseling says, "I just separated from my husband. I'm emotionally involved with another man. I'm not sure that my husband and I can work it out. I know what my beliefs are, but I'm not sure what to do."

3. A man is sharing and says, "I'm so depressed I can't work; I can't think. I just sit there all day. Nothing gets done."

4. For the twelfth time a woman in counseling says, "I reached out and gave him love for sixteen years — first through his alcoholism then through his seven-year affair. I have nothing more to give. I can't trust him and I can't forgive him."

5. You have been called to see a man in the hospital. Before you go in to see him you find out through talking with the doctor that the man is terminally ill. You go into the room and the man says to you, "I want to ask you something. Am I going to die? Do you know? Can you tell me? Am I going to die?"

6. A husband is talking to you and says, "You know, I've got all this guilt. Every time I sleep with this other woman I feel so guilty. What can I do about it?"

7. You are calling on a person in the hospital. While you are there one of the nurses recognizes you and asks you to stop in and see an older woman who was just brought into the hospital with a stroke. You enter the room and the woman is strapped to the bed and has an oxygen mask over her face. She is moving very restlessly upon the bed, her eyes frantic with fear.

8. A housewife was at home with her four children one morning. While she was upstairs bathing the infant twins in the bathtub, a child downstairs pulled over a boiling pot of water upon herself and was seriously injured. The mother hearing the screams left the children and rushed downstairs to help this child. While she was down there the twins drowned in the bathtub. When the mother discovered this after she returned upstairs, she screamed at the remaining ten-year-old to get some help. The child without looking rushed across the street and was struck by a car. The mother hears the accident, looked out, and saw the child lying under the car. At this point the mother collapsed. In due time the father is called home and is told what has happened. You arrive on the scene and it is your responsibility to speak to and minister to the father.

9. For the last case, ask for a volunteer from the group to come up in front and role play a situation with you. He will be the counselor and you will be a suicidal caller. Position the chairs back to back as this more closely resembles a phone call structure in which you cannot see the other person. You should make up your own situation but the call should be fairly serious. Let the person work with you for 8-10 minutes and then abruptly hang up the phone to simulate a caller hanging up in the middle of a helping situation. You may want to ask for some immediate feedback from the group, for their evaluation and suggestions.

AGREE-DISAGREE STATEMENTS

Time: 50-60 minutes.

Distribute an agree-disagree sheet to each person and then give the following instructions: "Each of you has been given an agree-disagree sheet. On this form you will find several statements concerning counseling and life problems. Individually and without talking to anyone else, read each statement and decide whether you agree or disagree with each statement as it is presented there. Read it carefully and decide what you think. If you agree, place a check in the appropriate blank marked 'agree.' If you disagree, place a check in the blank marked 'disagree.' You will be given enough time to answer the statements. Please work individually and as quickly as possible."

Give the group enough time to complete their work. When everyone has finished, thank them for completing the sheet. Ask all those who agree with statement number one to raise their hands. Then ask how many disagree with statement number one. Proceed to statement number two and repeat the process for each of the statements without stopping to discuss any of them. After you have finished, divide the class into small discussion groups of five to eight. They should discuss the statements, sharing not only their answers but their reasons as well. What was the basis for their answer? They do not have to discuss all of the statements thoroughly, but may discuss those they are most interested in or those that produced the most differences of opinion. As a teacher-leader of this group, you should circulate from group to group and listen to the interaction of the members. Allow enough time for the groups to become involved in their discussion.

HOMEWORK ASSIGNMENT

Ask class members to search the four Gospels and develop their own suggested model of counseling based upon Jesus' interactions with others. Ask them to be prepared to share it with the group at the next session.

Conclude with prayer.

AGREE-DISAGREE STATEMENTS

Agree   Disagree

_____   _____   1. Confrontation in counseling means to point out another's errors to him and help him see where he is wrong.

_____   _____   2. The Bible teaches more of a confrontational model of counseling than a helping model.

_____   _____   3. Depression is a sin.

_____   _____   4. Listening as a counseling method is enough for some types of problems.

_____   _____   5. Giving advice is a poor counseling procedure.

_____   _____   6. Scripture is our only legitimate source of information about counseling.

_____   _____   7. Every Christian is competent to counsel others.

_____   _____   8. It is possible for a highly neurotic person to be healed through prayer and Bible reading without having to go to a psychologist or psychiatrist.

_____   _____   9. A severely disturbed person has come to you for help. There are psychologists and psychiatrists locally, but they aren't Christians. It would be best for you then to go ahead and attempt to help this person or refer him to your pastor.

_____   _____   10. Mental illness is caused by a person having engaged in a sin of some kind.

_____   _____   11. If a person's emotional life is stable, then his spiritual life will be stable.

_____   _____   12. The concept of "praising God for everything" teaches us to deny and suppress true honest feelings.

_____   _____   13. If your spiritual gift is "mercy," you will find counseling to be a natural ministry.

_____   _____   14. Since God gives different spiritual gifts to His people, some ministers should *not* be counseling.

Duplicating Pattern
Session 1

ANSWERS, OBSERVATIONS, AND GOALS OF COUNSELING

OBJECTIVES
— To identify and explain biblical teaching concerning problems and conflicts.
— To identify and express the goals and objectives of counseling.
— To develop a procedure for evaluating the counselee and his perception of the problem during the initial interview.

ADVANCE PREPARATION
1. Prepare transparencies.
2. Order the tape *Damaged Emotions* by Dr. David Seamands.
3. Duplicate "Observations to Make During the First Session."

ANSWERS TO AGREE-DISAGREE STATEMENTS
(Lecture presentation)
  Time: 45-55 minutes.
  Many of the statements will be answered throughout the remainder of this course, especially those pertaining to the actual counseling procedures. However, several should be answered at this time, for the statements pertain to basic and important principles in the Christian life.
  Perhaps the thoughts expressed here will clarify some of the questions that many of our counselees will have concerning what is taking place in their life.
  Many individuals, when difficulty and problems confront them, ask the question, Why? Why me? Perhaps this question comes from the inner expectation that events which are tragedies or just upsetting should not happen to us because we are children of God — Christians. Perhaps this stems from a belief that as Christians we should have peace and smooth sailing at all times.

When people accept Christ as Lord and Savior they unrealistically hope to receive a cure for every problem they have at that time whether it be physical, psychological, or spiritual. In heaven we are promised freedom from pain and unhappiness (Rev. 21:4) but the scripture does not promise us freedom from all difficulty here on earth. In this life we will have problems and difficulties (John 16:33; 2 Tim. 3:12).
  Paul did and Jesus did as well. Paul was sorrowful yet he learned to rejoice and to accept circumstances (2 Cor. 6:10; Phil. 4:11-13). There were times when Jesus did not have perfect peace of mind and was distressed (John 11:33, 38; Matt. 26:37,39). We can, however, expect God to help us resolve or endure the problems and difficulties we experience. The teaching of scripture is not that we will be problem free, but God will enable us and assist us in going through the difficult times (1 Cor. 4:9-13; 12:9; Heb. 4:16; see Isa. 43:1).
  Dr. Marion Nelson, a Christian psychiatrist, has given an interesting observation and analysis of our response to conflict and illustrated it with an example from the life of Jesus:
  "Psychological conflicts, with their associated nervous symptoms, are not sinful. But failure to make a valid, effective attempt to resolve a conflict and end the suffering is sinful. Why? Conflict reduces our efficiency as instruments of God (II Cor. 4:7), because our usefulness to God is hindered by anything that disturbs our physical or psychological or spiritual health. We are obligated to keep the vessels of God as healthy and clean and pure as we can (II Cor. 7:1; I John 3:3) so that He may use us in service more effectively (Rom. 6:13,19; 12:1). It is neither wise nor spiritual for a Christian to continue suffering nervous symptoms due to psychological conflict,

refusing to accept psychiatric or pastoral counsel. This is just as illogical as a Christian developing a physical illness and refusing to let a physician treat him. He reduces his efficiency as a servant of Christ.

"My proof that conflict is not sinful is the fact that Christ Himself experienced severe conflict over the Cross experience and suffered several emotional symptoms until He resolved the conflict. Yet He never sinned (John 8:46; II Cor. 5:21; Heb. 4:15; I Peter 2:22; I John 3:5). What was the conflict and how did He resolve it?

"Christ, being without sin, regarded the idea of death which involved His bearing the sins of everyone (I Peter 3:18) and the associated temporary state of alienation from God the Father (Matt. 27:46) as horrible. He shrank from it as a normal reaction. But He also wanted to please and obey God the Father, who had sent Him for this very purpose (Matt. 20:28; John 18:11).

"From time to time during His earthly life Christ was troubled by this conflict (John 12:27). It reached a peak in the Garden of Gethsemane the night before He died on the cross. There Christ, emotionally upset, expressed this conflict to God in prayer. His words to the Father were: 'My Father, since it is possible, let this cup pass away from me at once. Nevertheless, not as I desire but as You (desire)' (literal, expanded translation of Matt. 26:39). In this one sentence are expressed the two sides of the conflict. Christ wanted to avoid the cross, but He also wanted to obey God the Father.

"The gospel writers use vivid words in describing His emotional state during this conflict (the following quotations are all excerpts from literal, expanded translations): 'afflicted with grief,' 'distressed' in Matthew 26:37; 'distressed,' 'terrifyingly amazed' in Mark 14:33; 'exceedingly sorrowful' in Matthew 26:38 and Mark 14:34; 'My soul is encompassed with grief, so much so that I am close to dying' in Matthew 26:38; 'having entered a state of an agonizing struggle, He kept on praying more fervently. And His sweat became like clots of blood, repeatedly falling down upon the ground' in Luke 22:44.

"This phenomena mentioned by Luke of bleeding through the sweat glands of the skin has been observed several times and is recorded in medical literature. It is a sign of great psychological distress and tension.

"Christ did not remain in conflict and suffering. He resolved the conflict by giving up hope for one of His wishes — escaping the cross (Matt. 26:42). When his conflict was resolved, the psychological distress was ended. His nervous symptoms disappeared and He was once again at peace within His soul. Here we have a clear illustration of the proper way to resolve a psychological conflict.

"Christians are not only subject to the same kind of conflicts experienced by non-Christians, but also the additional conflicts of the new nature and the old nature. The goals of the Spirit often clash with the desires of our human nature (Gal. 5:17)."[1]

NOTE: At this point you may want to ask the class for their response or reaction to what Dr. Nelson has suggested.

Some have asked the question, What are the reasons for having problems? Here are four suggestions:
1. To achieve purification of our Christian life (2 Cor. 7:9,11)
2. To produce patience (literally, endurance) (Rom. 5:3; James 1:3)
3. To produce humility (2 Cor. 12:7-10)
4. To produce dependence upon God (2 Cor. 1:8-9)

What attitudes and responses can we have toward life's problems and those events which some call senseless tragedies? It is very true that we cannot always choose our circumstances, for there are many factors which bring about the reality of life. However, we can choose our attitudes toward those circumstances. And it is this basic point that much of counseling focuses upon — helping people sort through their attitudes toward their circumstances.

It is quite common for the following attitudes to develop in light of problems:

1. A person may decide that life is cruel and hard and thus develop anger toward God for either causing or allowing something to happen.

2. He may close himself to the rest of life and allow the current problems to so embitter him toward others that he develops a protective cocoon. The person believes that such "protection" keeps away the problems of life, but it also keeps away the joys of life as well.

3. The anger which comes about as part of one's reaction can be turned inward and thus an individual will blame himself and even punish himself.

4. One may decide that life does not have any meaning and that there is no God.

5. Another reaction is looking at what has happened and saying, "It is not what I had planned and not what I asked for, but it is here. What can I learn from this and how can I grow through it? How can God be glorified through this experience?" We essentially move ahead and

experience the resources that God has for us. We can experience through this event the comfort, healing, and encouragement which God has for us. But it is a matter of faith and trust.

Here is what faith is in the midst of life:[2]

1. When a person is living a life of faith, a crisis is a signal to stop and listen. It could be that one has become so preoccupied with plans, projects, and other things of life that the real focus has been lost. This is a time to take stock of oneself and one's resources, goals, and direction of life. When our world begins to crumble we do have someone who can give us stability. Sometimes in the midst of a crisis we learn once again who it really is who can give real and lasting stability to life. Read Isaiah 41:10; 43:1-3.

2. When a person lives a life of faith, as crisis comes he looks for God's alternatives to the despair and futility. The answer may not come immediately, but some answers will be discovered or a peace to accept that which cannot be discovered and known can be found.

3. Faith enables a person to see that nothing in his experiences of life will be wasted. Faith does not always give reasons or answers to our questions but does give strength (Rom. 8:28). Perhaps we discover that in this life the whole story cannot always be found. This comes later.

Dr. Dwight Carlson, in his book *Living God's Will*, has given a concise and helpful explanation to the questions being asked.

"God doesn't mind the sincere, honest question 'Why did this misfortune happen to me?' In fact, that's the question He wants us to ask so that we will evaluate our lives and be sure we are following His will. But having done that we must be very careful that we don't linger at this point too long, for then we are probably becoming bitter and resistive individuals, blaming God or others. Job deliberately avoided accusing God, an example we should follow (*see* Job 1:21,22; 38-41).

"At times you may still be perplexed and you don't have to feel alone. Paul states in 2 Corinthians 4:8, 'We are pressed on every side by troubles, but not crushed and broken. We are perplexed because we don't know why things happen as they do, but we don't give up and quit' (LB). Now we see through a 'glass, darkly' but someday we will totally understand (*see* 1 Corinthians 13:12 KJV). His ways are higher than our ways and our minds just don't understand the mind-working of an infinite God (*see* Isaiah 55:8,9). Periodically the proverb (20:24) must be applied which states: 'Since the Lord is directing our steps, why try to understand everything that happens along the way' (LB). In some Christian circles there is a tendency to 'manufacture' some spiritual reason for everything that happens — this may be unwise. We don't have to explain to ourselves or to others why everything happens to us.

"In the final analysis, our attitude toward difficulties has a much greater effect on us and others than the actual circumstances. Brother Lawrence *(The Practice of the Presence of God)*, a monk in the seventeenth century said, 'The sorest afflictions never appear intolerable except when we see them in the wrong light.' God is more concerned about our response than the problem. The right attitude is often the first step to the solution. Our response to what happens may actually determine whether or not there is a solution. Job had to be willing to actually pray for his falsely accusing friends in order that they might come into a right relationship with God. As an incidental result, God restored Job's wealth and happiness! In fact, the Lord gave him twice as much as before (*see* Job 42:10).

"We praise God in adverse situations, not necessarily because we feel like it, but because it's commended. We rejoice, not for the evil done, but that God will see us through it and ultimately triumph. We are told, 'Always be joyful . . . No matter what happens, always be thankful, for *this is God's will* for you who belong to Christ Jesus' (1 Thessalonians 5:16-18 LB author's italics).

"We can be assured that God will help us in every difficult situation: 'For God has said, "I will never, *never* fail you nor forsake you." That is why we can say without any doubt of fear, "The Lord is my Helper and I am not afraid of anything that mere man can do to me" ' (Hebrews 13:5, 6 LB; *see also* 1 Peter 4:12-19; Psalms 34:19; Psalms 112 LB).

"With each problem we are assured that God will find a way to use it to His glory and our good. He promises, 'And we know that all that happens to us is working for our good if we love God and are fitting into His plans' (Rom. 8:28 LB)."[3]

The two passages of scripture which are so important in giving strength and stability to those who are struggling are James 1:2-3 and Romans 8:28.

James 1:2-3 (NASB): "Consider it (or count it) all joy, my brethren, when you encounter various trials; knowing that the testing of your faith produces endurance (or patience)."

What do these words actually mean? "Consider" or "count" means an internal attitude of heart and mind that causes the trial and circumstance of life to affect us adversely or beneficially. The verb tense here means a decisiveness of action — not passive. We do not just give up and say,

"That's it. There is nothing else I can do." We purposely direct our thinking toward this end. It is possible that this phrase could be translated, "Make up your mind to regard adversities as something to welcome or be glad about." Again it reflects an attitude. The wording here can also imply that it is also a manner of looking forward or thinking forward.

"Trials" in this verse means outward trouble, stress, disappointments, sorrow, or hardship. These are the kinds of problems with which the person experiencing them had no part in their occurrence. These are all of the various sorts of trouble that people encounter in their human life.

"Endurance" or "patience" means fortitude. It can mean to stabilize, remain alive, or to be permanent. It is a picture of being under pressure and instead of trying to escape, standing firm. Patience can mean to bear under. The picture here could be of one who is under a terrific load.

It may appear strange for joy to be commended as the accompaniment of trouble and difficulty. Here it is not the ending of grief that brings joy but the beginning of grief. It is also a joy which follows a particular trial.

Romans 8:28 (NASB): "And we know that God causes all things to work together for good to those who love God, to those who are called according to His purpose."

Unfortunately too many people glibly quote this verse without ever considering the depth of what it is saying, or they react to it as being unrealistic or as a catch-all and reject it. They question how all things can be good. How can you believe that all things work together for good if you look around you? There are four truths which, if understood, grasped, and applied, can refocus one's attitude.

First, Paul said in this passage that all things *work* together for good. He did not say that every event or experience of life becomes or is good. He did not say that by chance eventually some good is achieved. He said all things work, with an emphasis upon the work. This is similar to Ephesians 11: God accomplishes or works all things according to the "counsel of His will." Even tragedies can turn out for good because God is at work in the entire process. And He can make all things work together for good whether we can see that or not.

Second, we see that all things work *together* for good. Experiences when taken separately can be seen as bad but, when taken together, the good can be discovered. It is similar to a cook taking the elements of a pie. By themselves they may not be too good, but eventually the final product is excellent. Genesis 50:20: 'And as for you, you meant evil against me, but God meant it for good in order to bring about this present result, to preserve many people alive.' "

(You may want to give the background of this story of Joseph.)

Third, all things work together for *good*. How do we define good? We equate material holdings with good and freedom from sickness with good, and believe success is the same as good. But this is from our perspective and not necessarily God's. Goodness is really Christlikeness. God is working to have us form our lives to the image of Christ. His goal is conformity to the image of His own Son.

The last portion of this verse indicates who it is speaking of: those who love God, those who know Christ as their Savior.

One of the other very important statements on the agree-disagree sheet concerns our emotional and spiritual life. The statement reads, "If a person's emotional life is stable, then his spiritual life will be stable." Most people do not agree with this statement. However, we do find many who do let the emotional or feeling part of them influence and affect their spiritual life instead of the other way around. Many come into the Christian life with emotional upset and disturbance and instead of allowing the Holy Spirit and the application of scripture to work through these areas of their life and free them from what is binding them, they take their subjectivity or emotional bias or disturbance and superimpose it upon their new faith and thus begin to warp the teachings of scripture and theology. Not only do they intensify some of their emotional ills through the spiritual distortion, but, because they feel they have the truth of the teaching of the Word of God, they become set and even more defensive about their life and beliefs and are quite resistant to help. This is unfortunate. Others believe that even though they have been born again, what went on before has so influenced and crippled them that they will be bound or controlled by it the rest of their life. Concerning this attitude Dwight Carlson has said:

"I may have some scars from being out of God's will in the past, but despite the scars He wants to make me into a beautiful person. Satan would just love to have me think that because of the scars (depicting sin or time lost in the past) I am utterly useless for the rest of my life. I am a second-rate citizen and bound to be unhappy and unsuccessful. This attitude is dead wrong. It is true that scars leave their permanent effects. Yet God's recreative powers are tremendous. He may not erase every last scar, but He will make me into an attractive person who will be satisfying to me and Him.

"Let's look further in the Scriptures for some examples of those whom God used after they 'blew it.' Abraham used deceit in Genesis 20, yet he was esteemed one of the highest patriots of old. Moses was a murderer, yet was chosen by God to be the great leader of Israel. Rahab was a prostitute and a liar. Yet she was physically saved and praised in the Hall of Faith in Hebrews II without mention of her years of debauchery. King David won favor in God's eyes and yet committed more infamous acts than some of our recent leaders. He not only committed adultery but also murder. Yes, some scars were left as a result of this, but he still is mentioned as a man after God's own heart (*see* Acts 13:22).[4]

"Emotional development begins at birth, perhaps even prior to birth. As the image we have of ourselves begins to form we learn how to trust or not to trust. We experience fear, jealousy, anger, sadness, joy, elation, happiness, and other emotional reactions. Our emotions grow and develop in different ways. One person may develop a balanced emotional life, another an imbalance. For some, emotional control is easier than for others.

"Our emotions play a large part in making our lives meaningful or miserable. C. B. Eavey, in his book *Principles of Mental Health for Christian Living*, suggests:

Nothing in us so defiles and destroys the beauty and the glory of living as do emotions; nothing so elevates, purifies, enriches, and strengthens life as does emotion. Through our emotions we can have the worst or the best, we can descend to the lowest depths, or we can rise to the highest heights. Every normal human being has a longing for the overflowing of natural emotion. Without capacity to experience emotions suitable to the situations we meet, we would not be normal. Emotions of the right kind, expressed in the proper way, make life beautiful, full, and rich, rob it of monotony, and contribute much to both the enjoyment and the effectiveness of living.[5]

"Our emotions are a gift from God for we were created as emotional beings. Because of the fall, man's emotional life often becomes distorted. But our emotions as such should never be despised, expelled, ignored, or even neglected. 'If we try to drive out any one of them,' adds Eavey, 'we simply intensify its activity. When we let them go without guidance and control, they cause confusion and riot in our lives. If we try to suppress them, they produce destruction in our personalities.'

"A non-Christian can experience emotional balance to a limited degree and appear quite well adjusted. A Christian, however, has the *potential* and *means* available for complete emotional balance.

"Some people think that once a person accepts Jesus Christ as Savior, emotional balance comes about immediately and automatically. It does neither! An emotionally stable person will have more to build upon initially in his Christian life than the unstable. The emotionally damaged person and the emotional infant do not become emotionally mature or healed by regeneration. Growth in the Christian life is a process and part of that process is emotional growth. It is not the fault of Christianity or the teachings of Scripture if a Christian does not achieve this control. *But for those who are willing to turn their emotions over to God, control is possible.*

"The goal of our emotional development is found in the emotions or attitudes expressed in the Fruit of the Spirit of Galatians 5:22,23 NASB. *But the fruit of the Spirit is love, joy, peace, patience, kindness, goodness, faithfulness, gentleness, self-control; against such things there is no law.* Here we find the healing emotions of life such as faith, hope, joy, peace, self-control, and love."[6]

Our emotional life can be transformed. Dr. Lloyd Ogilvie has expressed it so well:

"It is on the emotional level that most of us are blocked. Some of us have emotional malnutrition as a result of an inadequate experience of love in our childhood or present families and find it difficult to give what we have not experienced. Others of us have felt rejection or the excruciating pain of broken relationships. Still others are racked with the memory of past failures, the inability to forgive ourselves and try again. And then, all of us at times feel the turbulent emotions of anger, impatience, fear, and frustration. Often we don't know what to do with these feelings. Repression results in depression. Explosion results in confusion. There must be some alternative.

"Getting our feelings sorted out is crucial not only for ourselves, but for all the people around us. It's not a simple matter. Only God can do it, and that brings us to the foot of the cross. It is there that the love, forgiveness, security, and hope we so desperately need flow in limitless, unreserved power. Charles Spurgeon once said that 'there are some sciences that may be learned by the head, but the science of Christ crucified can only be learned by the heart'."[7]

God works through the body of Christ. He works through laymen and ministers alike and He works through the process of the ministry of counseling to bring about wholeness.

GOALS AND AIMS OF COUNSELING

Time: 5 minutes.

When someone comes for counseling, what are we attempting to accomplish in his life? What are some of the goals and aims of the initial stages of counseling? (Ask for several responses.) Here are a few just to stimulate your thoughts about some of the purposes. (Use the overhead transparencies.)

1. To understand the counselee's current situation.
2. To understand how he has tried to handle his problem.
3. To understand his view of the problem.
4. To understand his reasons and motivation for seeking counseling.
5. To understand his emotional reactions.
6. To estimate tentatively the counselee's strengths.
7. To evaluate the total problem.
8. To help him clarify his life situation and problem.
9. Others, including Christian growth and presentation of the Gospel.

Some other goals and objectives which may be accomplished in counseling are to assist in reducing undue tension, resolve conflicts, improve insight and self-understanding, release some of his inner strengths, provide information, encourage continued growth, make realistic choices, improve interpersonal relationships, mature in his Christian life, and for some, accept Jesus Christ as Lord and Savior.

OBSERVATIONS TO MAKE DURING THE FIRST SESSION

Time: 10-15 minutes.

(Distribute a copy of these guidelines to each person before presenting them.)

As you counsel a person in a scheduled counseling session, consider these questions:[8]

1. Observe the kind of person the counselee seems to be. How did he respond to you? How did he begin the interview? What were his beginning words in the interview? What seem to be his feelings at this point?

2. Did this person have some motivation for coming for counseling or was it suggested by someone else? Will he probably have enough motivation to make use of counseling?

3. What precipitated the counselee's seeking an appointment here at this time? Usually some event has brought the person to seek help.

4. Has the counselee made previous efforts to obtain help for his problems? If so, what were the circumstances and what was the outcome?

5. How has the counselee hoped or expected counseling would benefit him?

6. What does he see as his problems? How does he describe them? Are these problems of recent origin? When did he recognize that he had the problems?

7. If the counselee is currently under medical treatment, has the doctor referred him, or does the doctor know about his coming for counseling? If not, is the counselee willing for the counselor to refer him to a physician if necessary? Note any significant health, economic, social, or cultural factors.

8. If the counselee is married, did he discuss his desire to obtain marriage counseling with his spouse? Does the spouse wish to see a counselor also? If the counselee wishes the counselor to see the spouse, what is his expectation or hope? Are parents or families of either of the marriage partners (or premarital couple) involved in the problem? What is the attitude of these persons toward the marriage or proposed marriage?

9. At the close of the first interview, carefully evaluate your impression of the person and the situation. In particular you should note:

a. Whether the person has been able to delineate his problems so that he has defined that with which he wishes to have help.

b. What factors seem to have contributed to the emergence of the problem in this particular relationship?

c. Is the person more concerned with the relationship or with his own personal problems?

d. How has the counselee reacted and how is he now reacting to his situation? Do these reactions appear to be appropriate to the real situation?

e. What is your evaluation of the person's strengths? Is he going to be able to make good use of counseling?

f. What is your conclusion at this point concerning whether the problem should be handled by marriage counseling?

THE COUNSELEE'S NONVERBAL BEHAVIOR

Time: 15 minutes.

Many things provide clues to the needs and feelings of a counselee. This includes, of course, his stated purpose which usually includes his feelings. Some nonverbal clues can substantiate, emphasize, or correct his stated feelings. (Ask class members to write down what they would look for and what it would mean to them. Ask for several responses.) None of the following should be considered definitive in and of themselves but, when taken together and evaluated with other factors such as the interview and tests, reveal important information about the counselee.[9]

1. *Physical symptoms* may be observed by the counselor or mentioned by the counselee. Moist hands, dry mouth, palpitations of the heart, muscle tension, and insomnia are all evidences of anxiety.

2. *Frequent body movdments,* such as crossing and recrossing the legs, drumming the fingers, rising up from the chair, pacing the floor of the counseling room, increasing intensity of movement, or cessation of movement, can be indications of anxiety.

3. The *voice* reflects a person's emotional state. Tenseness of the voice, shrillness, rapid speech, stuttering, or pauses in speaking are evidences of anxiety.

4. *Dress* also reflects a person's attitudes, and may be an unconscious means of communication. In the past few years styles have changed considerably, so this may not be as significant a factor as it used to be. Striking, inappropriate dress may be evidence of a narcissistic person, often with dependent demands and wishes. Flashy dress or exaggerated makeup often indicates a poor self-image. Slovenly dress, especially if it is a change from the usual, may mean depression. Poor or cheap clothing may not mean poor economic standing, and attractive clothing may not mean economic security.

5. *Slowness* of action or slowness of speech, if different from the person's normal responses, may indicate depression.

6. *Seductive behavior* — in dress, actions, manner of sitting, conversation, or looks — could indicate insecurity or sexual maladjustment, sometimes frigidity in women. In men it signifies insecurity, maybe homosexuality. It is usually an evidence of strong transference feelings that should be considered.

7. *The location of the counselee* — where he sits in a counseling room — indicates his relationship to the counselor and the counseling situation. If he takes a chair some distance from the desk, hesitation and resistance are indicated. If he moves the chair closer or seeks to move closer, he may either be afraid or rejection or desire closeness. The desk may frequently be used as a barrier by the counselee. They way the person sits is also significant. Sitting on the edge of the chair, rigid and upright, indicates tension and anxiety.

8. *Laughter* is a good indication of a person's state of mind. Nervous laughter or giggling indicates tension. Inappropriate laughter, that is, laughter at the wrong things, indicates maladjustment. Free and easy laughter, especially at oneself, is a sign of good adjustment.

9. When a person is consistently *late or habitually breaks appointments*, he may be resistant. (Or perhaps he simply could not find a place to park.) When a person is *early*, anxiety may be indicated.

Dr. A. Mehrabian, in his book *Silent Messages*, discussed the importance of our nonverbal behavior. His research has indicated that our messages include those conveyed in the content of our verbal message, our tone of voice, and our nonverbal behavior. The impact of our facial expression and body language is greatest (55%), then our tone of voice (38%), and finally the words themselves (7%). There are times when we would respond to the tone of voice rather than the actual words, for the tone may be saying something contrary to the words. We listen to the entire message and the context in which it is presented. Sometimes the nonverbal element carries more of an emotional message.

Here are several factors about body posture which are important in the counseling process:

1. *Posture.* Face the counselee squarely. This posture says that you are available to him. Maintain an open posture. Arms not crossed and legs not crossed convey to the person an involvement on your part. It is a nondefensive posture. Lean toward the counselee. This too is a sign of involvement.

2. *Eye contact.* Look directly at the person. The expression of the face can help the counselee feel that he is not being stared at or stared down.

3. *Relaxation.* Remain relaxed. This assists the interaction of the two and at the same time can assist the counselee in relaxing as well.

TERMINATION OF COUNSELING

Time: 10-15 minutes.

(Ask the class to pair off with another person and for two minutes to discuss the question, How and when should counseling be terminated? Show the question on the overhead projector as you introduce it. Ask for several responses.)

Some counselors, prior to the first visit, make a commitment with the counselee for four to six interviews, at which time an evaluation is made and a decision reached as to whether counseling has been complete or if there is a need to refer or to continue. This provides a natural and agreed-upon point at which to discuss the issue.

If the counselee feels the problems have been resolved but the counselor feels other problems exist that need to be faced, the counselor should indicate this fact and suggest continued counseling. If the counselee still feels it unnecessary, he may be asked to check back with the counselor once more for an evaluation, or may be informed that he can always return if he desires.

If the counselor feels the problems have been resolved but the counselee wishes to prolong the relationship, the whole situation should be evaluated to determine whether there are more problems that the counselor has recognized (or wished to recognize), or whether the counselee — because of dependency feelings or other reasons — is unnecessarily prolonging the experience. If so, the procedure would be the same as for the counselee who desires to terminate counseling too early.

Long-term counseling cases should be periodically evaluated with a supervisor to determine whether there are factors that are prolonging the procedures unnecessarily.

When a counselee or a counselor feels that progress is unsatisfactory or that progress is not being made and that the problems still exist, every effort should be made either to transfer the counselee to another counselor or to refer him to another agency.

When it is necessary to terminate a relationship because a counselee is leaving the community, the counselor should reinforce the gains that have been made, prepare the counselee for problems he may be expected to face, and suggest that he find further counseling in the new community if the problems are rather difficult. There may be occasions when the pastor will help to locate another counselor by mail or phone.

When the counselor anticipates that termination is approaching, he should prepare the counselee by suggesting that in one more session or so they should be able to complete the process or that counseling will no longer be necessary.

In the closing stages of counseling one may prepare for termination by going from one session a week to one every two weeks, or even once a month. This gives the counselee a chance to gain confidence by going on his own, but also to have a chance to continue if he feels a need.

Termination, for whatever reason, should be positive but realistic. The counselee should be made to feel, even if he is disappointed in the results, that it was significant for him to make the effort. He should recognize, no matter how successful counseling has been, that other problems may present themselves and he can return to counseling if need be.

(Original source unknown.)

HOMEWORK

Ask class members to listen to the tape *Damaged Emotions* by Dr. David Seamands. Give the copy you ordered to one individual or couple and ask them to pass it along to the others as soon as possible. You may want to take an hour during one of the sessions, or add an extra session, to play it for everyone.

REFERENCES
1. Marion H. Nelson, *Why Christians Crack Up* (Chicago: Moody Press, 1960), pp. 92-94.
2. Adapted from *Coping with Tough Circumstances* pp. 166-70.
3. Dwight Carlson, *Living God's Will* (Old Tappan, N.J.: Fleming H. Revell Co., 1976), pp. 74-76.
4. Carlson, p. 19.
5. C. B. Eavey, *Principles of Mental Health for Christian Living* (Chicago: Moody Press, 1957), quoted in H. Norman Wright, *The Christian Use of Emotional Power* (Old Tappan, N.J.: Fleming H. Revell Co., 1974), pp. 19-20.
6. Wright, pp. 29-30.
7. Lloyd Ogilvie, *Loved and Forgiven* (Glendale, CA : Regal Books, 1977), pp. 32-33.
8. Adapted from Dean Johnson, *Marriage Counseling*, pp. 80-81.
9. Adapted from Gerard Egan, *The Skilled Helper* (Brooks Cole: Monterey, CA, 1975), pp. 65-66.

GOALS AND AIMS OF THE
EARLY STAGES OF COUNSELING

1. To understand the counselee's current situation.
2. To understand how he has tried to handle his problem.
3. To understand his view of the problem.
4. To understand his reasons and motivation for seeking counseling.
5. To understand his emotional reactions.
6. To estimate tentatively his strengths.
7. To evaluate the total problem.
8. To help him clarify his life situation and problem.
9. Others, including Christian growth and presentation of the Gospel.

NONVERBAL BEHAVIOR

1. Physical symptoms
2. Frequent Body Movements
3. Voice
4. Dress
5. Slowness
6. Seductive Behavior
7. Location of the counselee
8. Laughter
9. Late or early

THE COMPLETE MESSAGE

**NONVERBAL
COMMUNICATION
55%**

**TONE OF
VOICE
38%**

**ACTUAL
WORDS
7%**

THE BIBLICAL FRAMEWORK FOR COUNSELING

OBJECTIVES
— To explain the biblical teaching concerning helping and counseling others.
— To identify specific methods of ministering to others based upon the life and teachings of Jesus.
— To define and apply the following principles of counseling: listening, confrontation, empathy, encouragement, etc.
— To develop one's own model of counseling based upon the biblical teaching concerning God and man.

ADVANCE PREPARATION
Prepare transparencies.

LECTURE PRESENTATION
Time: 2-2½ hours.
(You will need to decide when to take a break.)

INTRODUCTION

The struggle and desire to develop a biblical system of counseling has been coming to the forefront more in the past several years than ever before. Some counselors have attempted to develop their model of counseling by taking a psychological theory of counseling and attempting to super-impose it upon biblical teaching. In some instances there appears to be a correlation but in others the biblical teaching is distorted as authors have attempted to mold it to fit their preconceived ideas. Other counselors begin with a biblical perspective and use it to screen psychological theories of counseling.

The various attempts will probably continue for several years and perhaps there never will be an absolute standard of counseling reflecting integration between psychological theories and biblical teaching. In the meantime, however, it is possible to find indications from the scriptures of how to minister to, relate to, and help others.

THE NATURES OF GOD AND MAN

The starting place for developing a method of counseling or helping others is not the consideration of specific techniques but rather a focus upon the nature of God and the nature of man. (Use the transparency pattern.) What we believe about God — who He is, His attributes, and what He desires for mankind — certainly influences how we respond to the people with whom we have contact and to whom we have been called upon to minister. How we view man — who he is, his potentials and his defects — certainly influences how we respond to individuals within the context of counseling. A. W. Tozer said that a right conception of God is basic not only to systematic theology but to practical Christian living as well.

As we look at who man is, several facts must be remembered. Man was created by God and was made in the image of God, but because of the Fall, a distortion has occurred in the image of God within man. Man is a sinful being, yet he is very, very worthwhile and worth redeeming. A counselor may see man as being totally good with no problems or defects and will respond to individuals in counseling in a manner reflecting this belief. Another counselor may see man as totally lost, totally deficient, with no good or worth or potential within him whatsoever and will respond in a different manner. But if we see the individual as made in the image of God and yet sinful but with potential, perhaps the balance we are seeking in our counseling can be found.

As we approach man in counseling, perhaps one of the very first matters a counselor must consider is man's need. What is his basic need? One suggestion is the regarding of himself as a worthwhile human being. This has nothing to do with *feeling* worthwhile; it is an examination of the evidence and realization and conclusion that one is worthwhile regardless of his feelings.

Dr. Maurice Wagner described this in his book, *The Sensation of Being Somebody.* He summarized what individuals are looking for. They want to know Who am I? What am I? and Why am I? When satisfactory answers are found, a sense of being somebody, a sense of being worthwhile, is realized. This is called self-concept. It can be realistic or very unrealistic. This feeling of belongingness is an awareness of being wanted, accepted, of being cared for and enjoyed.

Another feeling is worthiness in the sense of "I am good, I count, I am right." A third feeling is competence — the feeling of adequacy, courage, hopefulness, and strength or ability to do what needs to be done. To show how these feelings are related, Dr. Wagner said, "Belongingness rests on the voluntary attitude of others as they display their acceptance. Worthiness rests on the introspective attitude of self-approval. Competence rests on the evaluations received in past relationships and on one's present sense of success."[1]

Using this philosophy as a background for counseling, that is, knowing who God is and an understanding of man, what then would be the goal of counseling? There are actually several goals of counseling and some of these depend upon the status of the counselee. For those who have never entered into a relationship with Jesus Christ, new birth is definitely a goal. Another goal, prior to the new birth experience or for one who has been a Christian for some time, is a greater understanding of who God is. A teaching ministry concerning the attributes of God would be appropriate. For one who is already a Christian, Christ-likeness as expressed in Ephesians 4:13 is a goal of counseling.

Because the self-concept is at the heart of so many difficulties, helping a counselee develop a positive self-concept is a major objective. This is accomplished through an understanding of the extent of God's acceptance which leads to one's own acceptance and healthy self-concept.

Earlier it was mentioned that belongingness, worthiness, and competence were important factors in the development of a healthy self-concept. In a relationship with God the Father, a person is assured of belongingness. This is seen in passages such as Matthew 6:9; Ephesians 1:6; John 3:16; and Romans 8:15-17. As Dr. Wagner said, "He is pleased to call us His son. This gives us a position with Him in His family. We know we are somebody to God. We have been redeemed from being a nobody. The idea of being a nobody

never again will have any validity. When it threatens us we can firmly reject it in the reassurance of God's promises."[2] In one's relationship with Jesus, the Son of God, a person is assured of worthiness (John 3:36; 2 Cor. 5:18; 1 John 1:9). Dr. Wagner also said that a person gains a secure sense of competence as he relates to the Holy Spirit, who is the Comforter, the Guide, and the source of great strength. The Holy Spirit, directs a person's attention to Christ. "He shall testify of Me" is stated in John 15:26. We see this also in John 14:26. The Holy Spirit imparts the love of God (Rom. 5:5), imparts hope (Rom. 15:13), and gives joy (Rom. 14:17; Gal. 5:22; 1 Thess. 1:6).

So many people who come for counseling focus their attention on their incompetence and unworthiness and their distortions. The counselor's role is encouraging and helping the counselee see himself as being in the image of God instead of focusing upon the distortions in his image. In helping a counselee obtain a feeling of worth and adequacy, a counselor could share the thoughts expressed by Dr. Lloyd Ahlem in his book *Do I Have to Be Me?*

"The writers of the Scriptures are careful to point out that when God looks at you in Jesus Christ, He sees you as a brother to His own Son. Because of the work of Christ, all the ugliness of humanity is set aside. God has absolutely no attitude of condemnation toward man. You are worth all of God's attention. If you were the only person in the whole world, it would be worth God's effort to make Himself known to you and to love you. He gives you freely the status and adequacy of an heir to the universe."[3]

Another way of assisting a counselee in coming to an understanding of God's acceptance is helping him realize that God also knows who he is and, since He does, what this can mean to his sense of adequacy. Dr. J. I. Packer, in his book *Knowing God*, put it better than anyone else: "What matters supremely, therefore, is not, in the last analysis, the fact that I know God, but the larger fact which underlies it — the fact that *He knows me.* I am graven on the palms of His hands. I am never out of His mind. All my knowledge of Him depends on His sustained initiative in knowing me. I know Him, because He first knew me, and continues to know me. He knows me as a friend, one who loves me; and there is no moment when His eye is off me, or His attention distracted from me, and no moment, therefore, when His care falters.

"This is momentous knowledge. There is unspeakable comfort — the sort of comfort that energizes, be it said, not enervates — in knowing that God is constantly taking knowledge of me in love, and watching over me for my good. There is tremendous relief in knowing that His love to me is utterly realistic, based at every point on prior knowledge of the worst about me, so that no discovery now can disillusion him about me, in the way I am so often disillusioned about myself, and quench His determination to bless me. There is, certainly, great cause for humility in the thought that He sees all the twisted things about me that my fellow-men do not see (and am I glad!), and that He sees more corruption in me than that which I see in myself (which, in all conscience, is enough). There is, however, equally great incentive to worship and love God in the thought that, for some unfathomable reason, He wants me as His friend, and desires to be my friend, and has given His Son to die for me in order to realise this purpose."[4]

THE BIBLICAL APPROACH

In counseling a person, what approach should a counselor take to achieve these goals? Not only must the question of technique be considered, but as we look at the counselee's life, we must also decide upon the area to stress. Do we deal just with his thoughts? Do we deal just with his behavior? Do we deal just with his feelings? Or is there an area that should be ignored, left out, or even played down?

In any kind of counseling approach or system one rarely finds an emphasis on all three of these. Some, such as Reality Therapy, emphasize behavior. Rational Emotive Therapy or Cognitive Therapy deals specifically with thought processes. The nondirective or client-centered approach deals basically with the feelings of the person and makes little attempt to analyze one's thoughts or behaviors. The scripture itself speaks of all three — feelings, thoughts, and behaviors.

We see the examples of many within the scripture, including Jesus Himself, and the effect and extent of their emotions. In the life and ministry of Jesus we see occasions on which He was sensitive to the feelings of others. At other times He emphasized rational thinking. On still other occasions He focused on behavior. It appears that the scriptures specifically talk more about behavior and thinking than feelings.

Some of the passages in the scriptures that emphasize the thinking process or the thought process are Genesis 6:5; 8:21; 1 Chronicles 28:9; Proverbs 15:15; 16:2; 23:7; Isaiah 26:3; Romans 8:6-7; 12:2; Ephesians 4:23; and 1 Peter 1:13.

There is a strong interrelationship between thoughts, feelings, and behavior. Many of our emotions or feeling responses come from our thought life; what we dwell upon, what we think about, can stimulate feelings. The words "think," "thought," and "mind" are used over three hundred times in the scriptures. Often a person's behavior can create both feelings and thoughts. Then once a person has certain feelings, those feelings can intensify or reinforce a particular thinking pattern and can also influence one's behavior.

In the New Testament there is quite an emphasis upon specific behaviors as well as emotional responses. This emphasis is usually described in terms of putting off certain negative behaviors, attitudes, and emotional responses, and putting on their opposites. The following is a suggested sampling of what is presented in the New Testament.

(Use the overhead transparency, "Put On — Put Off.")

Is there a biblical method of counseling? As we look at scripture, what can we learn about the way in which we are to respond or relate to the people who come to us with difficulties and problems?

"The principles, or absolutes, are given in Scripture, but the process of applying these absolutes is not detailed. There is no one scriptural method of counseling; there are only scriptural absolutes that must be recognized and honored whatever method is used.

"In looking at Christ's life and Paul's letters, it appears that each adapted his method of personal contact to the individual's needs. Jesus talked personally with people. He touched some; He cried with some; He rebuked some; He confronted some; He was direct with others; and He never wrote any letters! Paul shared his life with many (1 Thess 2:8); admonished some; taught some; and wrote letters to many. Possibly Paul detailed his methodology in 1 Thessalonians 5:14, 'And we urge you, brethren, admonish the unruly, encourage the fainthearted, help the weak, be patient with all men.'

"For the Christian counselor there are scriptural absolutes, but certain freedoms in application and methods . . ."[5]

The word "counsel" is not used much in scripture. In the Old Testament we find the word used with three different Hebrew words. Here is a listing of these words within the context of Scripture. (Make your own transparencies for this section or use the chalkboard.)

THE USE OF "COUNSEL" IN SCRIPTURE

Three Hebrew words translated "counsel" are defined below in an attempt to further understand what scripture means by "counsel."

Yaw-ats' =	to deliberate, resolve, advise (well), guide, devise, determine, purpose (Exod. 18:19)
yaw-sad' =	to sit down together, settle, consult, found, establish, instruct
ay-tsaw' =	advice, plan, prudence, advisement, counsel, purpose

1. Word (dabar)
   Numbers 31:16: The counsel of Baalam was the agency for the trespass of Israel against the Lord. Counsel is a word of advice.
2. To counsel (yaats)
   2 Chronicles 25:16: Amaziah at the rebuke of God's prophet asked him if he had been appointed a royal counselor. Counsel is giving advice or direction.
3. Counsel (melak)
   Daniel 4:27: Daniel counseled Nebuchadnezzar to break away from sins by doing righteousness and from iniquities by showing mercy to the poor. Counsel is direction which exposes problems and gives specific procedures for their elimination.
4. A sitting, session, assembly (sod)
   Psalm 55:14: In his prayer to God regarding his treacherous friend, David indicated that the friend was one with whom he had sweet counsel. Counsel is sharing among equals which is sweet but may be betrayed.
   Psalm 83:3: In prayer Asaph indicated that God's enemies made counsel against His people. Counsel is planning together to achieve a specific purpose.
5. Counsel, advice (eta)
   Daniel 2:14: Daniel answered with counsel. Counsel is discretion.
6. Counsel, advice (etash)
   Deuteronomy 32:28: In the song of Moses, Israel is seen as a nation lacking in counsel and understanding. Counsel is necessary for understanding and discernment of the future.
7. To give counsel (yaats)
   Exodus 18:19: Jethro urged Moses to listen to him and he would give counsel. Counsel is wise advice for action. The leader Moses had to receive counsel in this situation.
8. To be counseled (yaats)
   1 Kings 12:9: Rehoboam asked the young men for counsel.

2 Chronicles 10:6: Rehoboam asked the elders for counsel.
9. To counsel together or fully (sumbou)
   John 18:14: Caiaphas counseled the Jews that it was expedient for one man to die on behalf of the people.
10. To have a foundation laid (yasad)
    Psalm 2:2: The rulers took counsel together against the Lord and His anointed.

Two Greek words commonly translated "counsel" are defined below. These terms speak of advice and planning together to gain some direction or solve a problem. The terms do not require God to be a part of the counsel; however, God's advice is to be sought (James 1:5).

bouleuo =	to advise, deliberate, counsel (to be a member of the Sanhedrin)
sumbouleuo =	to consult, advise, counsel together, to give or take advice jointly

One can approach a scriptural model of counseling in several ways. One way is to look at the entirety of scripture and draw from it principles of counseling or helping others. Another way is to focus upon the life and ministry of Jesus, noting His style, method, and technique of ministering to others. Each of these models of counseling is presented with two possible variations.

Dr. Frank B. Minirth, a Christian psychiatrist, suggested 1 Thessalonians 5:14 as a basis for counseling:

"There are five variations of biblical verbs on counseling. They are: *Parakaleo, Noutheteo, Parmutheomai, Antechomai,* and *Makrothumeo.*

"These five Greek verbs are used in 1 Thessalonians 5:14 mentioned above. The first is *parakaleo.* Paul used this counseling verb himself as he began his statement on the different types of counseling. It means to beseech or exhort, encourage or comfort. It is used in a milder sense than the next verb which means to admonish. In the original Greek text, this next verb is found in Romans 12:1,2, Corinthians 1:4, and Romans 15:30 quoted respectively below:

I beseech you therefore, brethren, by the mercies of God, that ye present your bodies a living sacrifice, holy, acceptable unto God, which is your reasonable service.

Romans 12:1

Who comforteth us in all our tribulation, that we may be able to comfort them which are in any trouble, by the comfort we ourselves are comforted of God.

II Corinthians 1:4

Now I beseech you, brethren, for the Lord Jesus Christ's sake, and for the love of the Spirit, that ye strive together with me in your prayers to God for me;

Romans 15:30

It is an active verb. It is the verb on which Paul Morris bases his counseling known as 'love therapy'.

"The next Greek verb is *noutheteo*. This verb can be used in a broad context in counseling, but in the new testament (*sic*) it usually means to put in mind, to warn, and to confront. One admonishes the unruly, the undisciplined, or the impulsive. It is found in the verses quoted respectively below:

And concerning you, my brethren, I myself also am convinced that you yourselves are full of goodness, filled with all knowledge, and able also to admonish one another.

Romans 15:14 NAS

I am not writing this to shame you, but to warn you, as my dear children.

I Corinthians 4:14 NIV

Let the word of Christ richly dwell within you; with all wisdom teaching and admonishing one another with psalms *and* hymns *and* spiritual songs, singing with thankfulness in your hearts to God.

I Corinthians 4:14 NAS

"It is also an active verb. It is the verb on which Jay Adams bases his Nouthetic counseling.

"The third counseling verb is *parmutheomai*. It means to cheer up, to encourage. One encourages the fainthearted or discouraged. It is found in the original Greek text as follows:

just as you know how we *were* exhorting and encouraging and imploring each one of you as a father *would* his own children.

I Thessalonians 2:11 NAS

"The fourth counseling verb is *antechomai*. It means to cling to, to hold fast, to take an interest in, to hold up spiritually or emotionally. It is a passive verb.

"The fifth Greek verb is *makrothumeo*. It means to be patient or to have patience. It is found in Matthew 18:26, Matthew 18:29, James 5:7, and Hebrews 6:15. It is also a passive verb.

"Thus, there is not just one biblical verb on counseling, but there are several, a fact which proves that a person needs balance in his counseling approach.

"Christian counseling is *unique* in its ability to provide this balance."[6]

As we look at the model of counseling as seen in the life and ministry of Jesus, two suggested approaches are considered. One approach was shared by David Carlson, a professor at Trinity College. His approach has been called "Jesus' Style of Relating: The Search for a Biblical View of Counseling." The following is an explanation of his approach.

"I began my exploration of the question, What is Jesus' style of counseling? by searching the Gospels to observe how Jesus approached people. What I found is this: Jesus' style of relating to people was varied, not monistic. While it is true that Jesus used confrontation, it is equally accurate to describe Jesus' technique of relating as comforting. Jesus' approach is multivaried, that is, He taught from Scripture, listened, drew pictures, asked questions, told stories from which He asked His listeners to draw their own conclusions, etc. As we take the whole counsel of God into consideration we begin to see that Jesus was not limited to one style of relating.

"Reviewing Jesus' dealings with people, an interesting relationship appears between the role Jesus chose to play and His style of relating. For example, when Jesus assumed the role of prophet, He preached, taught, confronted, and called for repentance. When He assumed the role of priest, He listened, forgave, mediated, and called for confession. When He assumed the role of king, He paraded, ruled, and called for the establishment of the kingdom. When He chose the role of lamb, He sacrificed, accepted ridicule and rejection, and called sinners to be healed by His stripes and bruises. When He submitted to the role of servant, He washed feet, served food, gave of Himself, and called for humility. When He played the role of shepherd, He fed His flock, nurtured, protected, and called the lost to be found.

"If we attempt to model our counseling or relating after Jesus' example, then like Jesus we should play a variety of interventive roles as we relate redemptively to hurting people. I submit that the biblical view of counseling is a multivaried one. It seems to me that if my analysis of Scripture is correct, then it is a mistake to claim one style of relating as distinctively Christian or biblical. It is a mistake in at least two ways — first, because it is based on selective reading and interpretation of Scripture and second, because it limits the mobility of responses essential for helping ...

"A dichotomous view of Christian counseling then is unacceptable. But so is an eclectic view which tends to ignore paradox and conflict. I would like to suggest a biblical view of counseling which is continuous rather than dichotomous, integrative rather than eclectic. The model of counseling which I believe is more accurately descriptive of Jesus' style of relating than either the dichotomous or eclectic views can be conceptualized on a status-role continuum. Notice that roles and technique are intimately related but technique is not exclusively limited to one role. Also notice that I have added a third descriptive term which I believe is a necessary conclusion from the biblical data. (Use the overhead transparency pattern, "Jesus' Style of Counseling.")

"By this model I am suggesting that our interventive roles can be professional (functional) specializations as well as personal capability to carry the range of therapeutic responses. As you can see from this continuum of status and roles, therapists have many interventive role possibilities. Whatever our primary counseling role, whether it be prophetic, pastoral, or priestly, I see the need for us to expand our repertoire of interventive roles and therapeutic responses to include all three role models if it is to be correctly a biblical style of counseling.

"What can we learn from Jesus' multirole ministry? First, therapeutic role integration is possible when one takes into consideration the whole counsel of God. Specific roles can be differentiated and distinguished from each other, but they cannot be logically or biblically segregated from each other. There are many interventive roles from which the Christian counselor can choose. Jesus' roles were not mutually exclusive, but they did have relative importance based on both who and why He was relating to a person. Jesus demonstrated role flexibility and variability. The implications of this for our Christian counseling are rooted in the observation that Jesus related to people where they were. Jesus was never in a dichotomous bind, having to choose between prophetic, pastoral, or priestly roles. The Christian counselor, for example, can be both directive and nondirective. He does not need to choose a directive approach which is dogmatic, that is, to the point of not being able to listen to where and why people hurt. He can be a listener without excluding teaching. The Christian counselor may be prophetic but not at the expense of the needs of the hurting person for a priest. He may reprove, correct, and instruct, but like prophets in Scripture, he must at times be the bringer of a message of consolation and pardon.

"Second, we can learn from Jesus' style of relating that one can 'know' what the problems and solutions are and yet be willing to listen and understand. Having knowledge does not preclude a willingness to listen and understand nor does it suggest that a counselor must ignore his preconceived ideas of what the client needs. However, it does mean that one can be explorative without excessive explaining, and he can be confrontive without unnecessarily challenging or raising the person's defenses.

"Third, Jesus' style of relating suggests that a counselor can be authoritative without being authoritarian. A danger of prophetic counseling is not the style of counseling as much as the personality needs of the counselor. The prophetic approach lends itself to be used by persons who need their counseling to be evidence of their authority.

"Fourth, Jesus' style of relating indicates that one can be right without having to demand that the counselee accept and recognize the counselor's rightness. For example, most of the prophets were not heard but that is not evidence that their message was incorrect.

"Fifth, Jesus' style of counseling raises the issue of the counselor timing his confrontations and interpretations. Jesus shared ideas, advice, and solutions without demanding that his audience hear these before they were ready. The prophetic style counselor is often a person who expects he can change others by saying the right words regardless of their preparation and readiness.

"And last, we learn from Jesus' style of relating that the role of counselor-priest is to mediate between the divine and the human. He is man's representative to God.

"Therefore, Jesus' style of relating is based more on *who* Jesus is than on *what* Jesus says or does. Whatever role Jesus plays — prophet, priest, pastor, king, savior — He is Christ. Whatever Jesus' approach to hurting, sinful people, He is Christ. Whatever role or approach we use in counseling, let us above all imitate Jesus' Christlikeness more than His techniques. Moreover, let us depend on 'Christ in us' (Col. 1:27) as we counsel.

"Jesus' style of relating provides a model for us today, but it does not necessarily provide a norm. There are no commands in Scripture to imitate Jesus' style of counseling. But there are commands to be like Jesus. 'So if there is any encouragement in Christ, any incentive of love, any participation in the spirit, any affection and sympathy, . . . Have this mind among yourselves, which you have in Christ Jesus' (Phil. 2:1-5)."[7]

JESUS' STYLE OF HELPING OTHERS

Before looking at the techniques which Jesus employed in helping others, we should know the purpose of His coming. The following verses present the purpose:

"The Spirit of the Lord (is) upon Me, because He has anointed Me (the Anointed One, the Messiah) to preach the good news (the Gospel) to the poor; He has sent Me to announce release to the captives, and recovery of sight to the blind; to send forth delivered those who are oppressed — who are downtrodden, bruised, crushed and broken down by calamity." (Luke 4:18, Amplified).

" 'For the Son of Man has come to seek and to save that which was lost' " (Luke 19:10, NASB).

"The thief comes only in order that he may steal and may kill and may destroy. I came that they may have and enjoy life, and have it in abundance — to the full, till it overflows" (John 10:10, Aplified).

(T)he one who practices sin is of the devil; for the devil has sinned from the beginning. The Son of God appeared for this purpose, that He might destroy the works of the devil" (1 John 3:8, NASB).

(Use the transparency patterns, "Jesus' Style of Helping Others," for this part of the presentation.)

Jesus' ministry was that of helping people achieve fullness of life, assisting them develop an ability to deal with the problems and conflicts and burdens of life. Perhaps what is really important for the counselor, professional or layman, is to consider why Jesus was able to be successful in His ministry. As we look at His own personal life, perhaps the answer will be evident. We see first, Jesus was obedient to God His Father. There was a definite connection and a relationship between Him and His Father and obedience was the mainstay of His life.

" 'For I did not speak on My own initiative, but the Father Himself who sent Me has given Me commandment, what to say, and what to speak' " (John 12:49, NASB).

" 'I glorified Thee on the earth, having accomplished the work which Thou hast given Me to do.' " (John 17:4, NASB).

Another reason why Jesus' ministry was effective was that He lived a life of faith and was therefore able to put things in proper perspective and see life through God's eyes. The example of the ruler of the synagogue's daughter in Mark 5 and Jesus' response to his statement that his daughter was dead shows the faith of Jesus.

The third source of Jesus' power was His prayer life. The example of His prayer life indicates that prayer is a very important element in one's ministry.

"But so much the more went there a fame abroad of him; and great multitudes came together to hear, and to be healed by him of their infirmities. And he withdrew himself into the wilderness, and prayed . . . And it came to pass in those days, that he went out into a mountain to pray, and continued all night in prayer to God. And when it was day, he called unto him his disciples; and of them he chose twelve, whom also he named apostles" (Luke 5:15-16; 6:12-13; KJV).

Many counselors have found it helpful to pray either at the beginning or at the end of their counseling sessions. Others do not, but prayer is still as much a part of their counseling ministry as it is for the one who prays verbally prior to or following the session. Some have developed the practice of praying specifically for each counselee each day and letting the counselee know that this is their practice. Some have also asked their counselees to pray for them that God would give them the wisdom and insight as they minister to the counselee.

One pastor shared that it is his practice, when he is completely stymied in a counseling session and does not know what to do next, to openly share this fact with the counselee and state that he would like to just pause for a moment and ask God to reveal to him what should be done next, what should be said, and the direction that he should take. This pastor said that on many occasions, as soon as he had completed praying, it was very clear to him what needed to be done or said next.

Another source of power available to Jesus was the authority by which He spoke. This is seen in Matthew 7:29: "For he taught them as one having authority, and not as the scribes" (KJV). Jesus was very conscious of His authority. Those who know Christ and are called to a ministry of helping in counseling have the authority of God's Word.

Caution must be expressed at this point, though, because some want to become authoritarian rather than use the authority of the scripture. Some want to simply pull out a scriptural passage and apply it to any problem without hearing the full extent of the difficulty and knowing whether scripture is necessary at that particular time. Some individuals who are unwilling or fail to examine the problems in their own life but attempt to counsel and use scriptural authority might misapply scripture or distort it because of their own difficulty.

Another reason for the success of Jesus' ministry was His personal involvement with the disciples and with others. He was not aloof; He was personal, He was sensitive, He was caring.

Jesus' ministry was effective because it was done through the power of the Holy Spirit. Some have called this an anointing of the Holy Spirit. We see how His ministry began with receiving the power of the Holy Spirit in Luke 3:21-22: "Now when all the people were baptized, it came to pass, that Jesus, also, being baptized, and praying, the heaven was opened, And the Holy Ghost descended in a bodily shape like a dove upon him, and a voice came from heaven, which said, Thou art my beloved Son; in thee I am well pleased" (KJV). Chapter 4 indicates that Jesus was full of the Holy Spirit and led by the Spirit and states that the Spirit of the Lord was upon Him.

Luke 5:17 states that the power of the Lord was with Him to heal: "And it came to pass on a certain day, as he was teaching, that there were Pharisees and doctors of the law sitting by, who were come out of every town of Galilee, and Judea, and Jerusalem; and the power of the Lord was present for him to heal them" (KJV).

William Crane, in his book *Where God Comes In — The Divine Plus in Counseling*, talked about the influence and the ministry of the Holy Spirit in the lives of the counselor and counselee. He said, "The Holy Spirit has access to all the materials that other psychotherapists know and use. In addition, he has direct access to the inner thoughts and feelings of the counselee. When the counselor becomes counselee in the presence of the Wonderful Counselor and sincerely seeks the honest reproval, correction and training in righteousness which the Holy Spirit promises, then he may find it. Many have."[8]

In discussing the counselor's need to trust the counselee, Crane talked about the effectiveness of the ministry of the Holy Spirit: "He needs to trust his counselee, but how can he trust one who is so false, deceptive, and insincere? Actually, he cannot. Nevertheless, he must learn to trust his belief in a knowledge of his counselee's need for help. Above this he must have an unfailing trust in the presence and the power of the Wonderful Counselor The Holy Spirit who is ready and willing to change the counselee from an untrustworthy person to a person of integrity and honor through the instrument of the counselor."[9]

As we look at the technique of Jesus we find that it is a model for all of us. It is important to remember, however, that technique alone is not effective. Who the counselee was and who Jesus was were really the most important considerations. When Jesus counseled or ministered to others it was not just an appointment when someone came in for a few minutes and then left. Jesus worked with people through a process. He spent time helping them with their life's difficulties, helping them work through their problems in an in-depth manner. He did not see people with just a problem. He saw them with their potentials and their hopes as well.

Jesus was one who had compassion — sorrow for the suffering of other individuals. We see this expressed in Mark 8:2: "I have compassion on the multitude, because they have now been with me three days, and have nothing to eat" (KJV). Mark 1:41: "And Jesus, moved with compassion put forth his hand, and touched him, and saith unto him, I will; be thou clean" (KJV). Mark 6:34: "And Jesus, when he came out, saw much people, and was moved with compassion toward them, because they were as sheep not having a shepherd, and he began to teach them many things" (KJV). His concern was to alleviate suffering and the pain and meet the need of the people.

Second, Jesus accepted others. We see this in John 4, John 8, and Luke 19. In John 4 — the case of the woman at the well — we see Jesus accepting her as she was and not putting upon her restrictions, hostility, or judgment. He accepted the woman caught in adultery and Zacchaeus the tax collector as well.

Third, Jesus gave worth to the individual. He put individuals first by giving them His personal attention. He looked to the need rather than to the rules and regulations the religious leaders had constructed. He became involved in the lives of people who were considered the worst of sinners, and He met the people where they had a need.

The fourth point is responsibility. Jesus sought to have people accept the responsibility for their actions. In John 5 He responded to the man at the pool of Bethesda by saying, Do you really want to get well? Do you want to be healed? Do you want to change? By these questions He was asking the man to accept the responsibility for what he wanted. In another instance He asked a blind man, What do you want me to do for you?

Jesus also gave hope, encouragement, and inspiration. Jesus' method was a positive approach. He saw and gave hope to the people to whom He ministered. Mark 10:26-27: "And they were astonished out of measure, saying among themselves, Who, then, can be saved? And Jesus, looking upon them, saith, With men it is impossible, but not with God; for with God all things are possible" (KJV). Matthew 11:28-30: "Come unto me, all ye that labor and are heavy laden, and I will give you rest. Take my yoke upon you, and learn of me; for I am meek and lowly in heart; and ye shall find rest unto your souls. For my yoke is easy, and my burden is light" (KJV). John 14:27: "Peace I leave with you, my peace I give unto you;

not as the world giveth, give I unto you. Let not your heart be troubled, neither let it be afraid." (KJV).

Jesus emphasized the peace of mind that people could have. He stressed hope for the future and strength for their present life. William Crane talked about the use of inspiration. Inspiration is more than just encouragement. Inspiration is an element which provides the counselee with hope and with the desire to change and to receive.

We can also see that Jesus helped to reshape or refashion people's thinking. He helped them redirect, in a sense, their attention from the unimportant things of life to the important. Luke 2:22-25: "And when the days of her purification according to the law of Moses were accomplished, they brought him to Jerusalem, to present him to the Lord (As it is written in the law of the Lord, Every male that openeth the womb shall be called holy to the Lord), And to offer a sacrifice according to that which is said in the law of the Lord, A pair of turtledoves, or two young pigeons. And, behold, there was a man in Jerusalem, whose name was Simeon; and the same man was just and devout, waiting for the consolation of Israel; and the Holy Ghost was upon him" (KJV).

Matthew 19:4-9: "And he answered and said unto them, Have ye not read that he who made them at the beginning, made them male and female; And said, For this cause shall a man leave father and mother, and shall cleave to his wife, and they twain shall be one flesh? Wherefore, they are no more twain, but one flesh. What, therefore, God hath joined together, let not man put asunder. They say unto him, Why did Moses then command to give a writing of divorcement, and to put her away? He saith unto them, Moses, because of the hardness of your hearts, suffered you to put away your wives, but from the beginning it was not so. And I say unto you, Whosoever shall put away his wife, except it be for fornication, and shall marry another, committeth adultery; and whosoever marrieth her who is put away doth commit adultery."

Teaching is a definite part of counseling and we see over and over again how Jesus taught. He taught through direct statements. He also taught with many questions. Luke 14:2-6: "And, behold, there was a certain man before him who had the dropsy. And Jesus, answering, spoke unto the lawyers and Pharisees, saying, Is it lawful to heal on the sabbath day? And they held their peace. And he took him, and healed him, and let him go; And answered them, saying, Which of you shall have an ass or an ox fallen into a pit, and will not straightaway pull him out on the sabbath day?

And they could not answer him again to these things." (KJV).

Luke 6:39: "And He also spoke a parable to them: 'A blind man cannot guide a blind man, can he? Will they not both fall into a pit?' " (NSAB). Luke 6:42: " 'Or how can you say to your brother, "Brother, let me take out the speck that is in your eye," when you yourself do not see the log that is in your own eye? You hypocrite, first take the log out of your own eye, and then you will see clearly to take out the speck that is in your brother's eye' " (NASB).

Another technique Jesus used was expressing Himself with authority. He was not hesitant, backward, bashful, but He spoke as one having authority. Matthew 7:29: "for He was teaching them as one having authority, and not as their scribes" (NASB).

Notice how Jesus admonished and confronted individuals. Matthew 8:26: "And He said to them, 'Why are you timid, you men of little faith?' Then He arose, and rebuked the winds and the sea; and it became perfectly calm" (NASB). Matthew 18:15: " 'And if your brother sins, go and reprove him in private; if he listens to you, you have won your brother' " (NASB). John 8:3-9: "And the scribes and the Pharisees brought a woman caught in adultery, and having set her in the midst, they said to Him, 'Teacher, this woman has been caught in adultery, in the very act. Now in the Law, Moses commanded us to stone such women; what then do You say?' And they were saying this, testing Him, in order that they might have grounds for accusing Him. But Jesus stooped down, and with His finger wrote on the ground. But when they persisted in asking Him, He straightened up, and said to them, 'He who is without sin among you, let him be the first to throw a stone at her.' And again He stooped down, and wrote on the ground. And when they heard it, they began to go out one by one, beginning with the older ones, and He was left alone, and the woman, where she had been, in the midst." We see the admonishment given to the woman caught in adultery in verse 11.

Another characteristic or technique of Jesus' ministry is His seeing the needs of individuals and speaking directly to them regardless of what they might have brought to His attention. We see that in the example of Nicodemus.

The very words Jesus used were important. Sometimes Jesus spoke directly, even harshly. Other times He was soft-spoken. Sometimes He conveyed His feelings nonverbally as in Mark 3:5: "And after looking around at them with anger, grieved at their hardness of heart, He said to the man, 'Stretch out your hand.' And he stretched it out, and his hand was restored." (NASB).

Jesus also emphasized right behavior in the lives of those to whom He ministered: " 'Everyone who comes to Me, and hears My words, and acts upon them, I will show you whom he is like: he is like a man building a house, who dug deep and laid a foundation upon the rock; and when a flood arose, the river burst against that house and could not shake it, because it had been well built. But the one who was heard, and has not acted accordingly, is like a man who built a house upon the ground without any foundation; and the river burst against it and immediately it collapsed, and the ruin of that house was great' " (Luke 6:47-49, NASB).

One of the ways in which Jesus gave worth to individuals was showing them their value in God's eyes by comparing God's care for other creatures as seen in Matthew 10:29 with God's care for them: " 'Are not two sparrows sold for a cent? And yet not one of them will fall to the ground apart from your Father' " (NASB). We also see that Jesus related to people according to what they needed at the particular time and did not use the same approach or the same method or technique with every person. Gary Collins shared this so well in his book *How to Be a People Helper:*

"Jesus not only dealt with people in different ways, but He also related to individuals at different levels of depth or closeness. John was the disciple whom Jesus loved, perhaps the Master's nearest friend, while Peter, James, and John together appear to have comprised an inner circle with whom the Lord had a special relationship. Although they were not as close as the inner three, the other apostles were Christ's companions, a band of twelve men who had been handpicked to carry on the work after Christ's departure. In Luke 10 we read of a group of seventy men to whom Jesus gave special training. Following the resurrection He appeared to a larger group of five hundred people, and then there were crowds, sometimes numbering in the thousands, many of whom may have seen Christ only once and from a distance."[10]

One further method of studying the counseling ministry of Jesus is to examine a present-day, secular counseling model which has proven very effective to see if there is a relationship between this model of counseling and biblical teaching. Here is what Gary Collins has said about such a model of counseling in comparison with a biblical model:

"All of these helping techniques describe what the counselor-helper does in his counseling, but equally important is the question of goals. Where is the counseling going and what does it seek to accomplish? All of this refers to the process of helping.

"This is a big topic of debate among professional counselors. Some see counseling as a highly complex procedure, but more recent writers have simplified the process considerably. Egan, for example, lists four stages: attending to the counselee and building rapport; responding to the counselee and helping him to explore his feelings, experiences, and behavior; building understanding in both counselor and counselee; and stimulating action which subsequently is evaluated by counselor and counselee together.

"A psychologist named Lawrence Brammer has a longer but similar list: opening the interview and stating the problem(s); clarifying the problem and goals for counseling; structuring the counseling relationship and procedures; building a deeper relationship; exploring feelings, behavior, or thoughts; deciding on some plans of action, trying these out, and evaluating them; and terminating the relationship.

"To a large extent what we do in counseling will depend on the type of problem involved, the personalities of the helper and helpee, and the nature of their relationship. Building on the suggestions of Egan and Brammer, I would suggest that the counseling process has at least five steps, all of which are clearly illustrated in the Bible. (Use the overhead transparency.)

    a. *Building a relationship* between helper and helpee (John 6:63; 16:7-13; 1 John 4:6).

    b. *Exploring the problems,* trying to clarify issues and determine what has been done in the past to tackle the problem (Rom. 8:26).

    c. *Deciding on a course of action.* There may be several possible alternatives which could be tried one at a time (John 14:26; 1 Cor. 2:13).

    d. *Stimulating action* which helper and helpee evaluate together. When something doesn't work, try again (John 16:13; Acts 10:19,20; 16:6).

    e. *Terminating the counseling relationship* and encouraging the helpee to apply what he has learned as he launches out on his own (Rom. 8:14).

Much of this is beautifully illustrated by Jesus on the road to Emmaus.

"When He met the two men, Jesus used a variety of techniques to help them through their crisis and period of discouragement . . .

"In Luke 24 we see that *Jesus first came alongside* the men and began traveling with them.

Here was rapport-building . . .

"As they walked *Jesus began asking some very nondirective questions* . . .

"As they traveled along, *Jesus spent a lot of time listening.* He surely didn't agree with what the men were saying, but He listened, gave them opportunity to express their frustrations, and showed them the love which sent Him to die for sinners in the first place.

"After a period of time, *Jesus confronted* these men with their logical misunderstandings and failure to understand the Scriptures. The confrontation was gentle but firm, and it must have begun to process of stimulating the men to change their thinking and behavior . . .

"At the end of the journey, *Jesus got close* by accepting an invitation from the two men to eat a meal together . . .

"Then an interesting thing happened. It is something that every helper dreams of doing with some of his helpees — especially the more difficult ones. Jesus 'vanished from their sight!' In so doing *Jesus left them on their own and spurred them on to action.* This is the ultimate goal of all helping — to move the helpee to a point of independence where there is no longer any need to rely on help from the helper."[11]

PRINCIPLES OF COUNSELING

An approach which uses more than one passage and relies upon the entire scripture is the following counseling technique. The basic premise for this approach to counseling is that we are called, as members of the body of Christ, to become involved in the lives of one another. The scripture teaches that when one member of the body suffers, we all suffer. We are called upon in the scripture to reach out, to assist, and to help. The body concept is part of the foundation of this scriptural approach to counseling. Waylon Ward said:

"Christian counselors have the resource of the Body of Christ for reinforcing and aiding in the counseling process. As a counselee experiences warm, loving Christian relationships within the Body of Christ, this will foster emotional and spiritual growth in his life. The Christian counselor is one member of many within the Body, so he, too, can experience the encouragement and aid of the Body in his counseling practice . . .

"As a Christian counselor learns to work with a local church fellowship, he opens the door for many new possibilities for ministry, both within the Body and through the Body. If a Body fellowship were correctly implementing and living by the "one-another" concepts in the New Testament, much of the need for a professional counselor could be eliminated. God's ideal appears to the Body members ministering to one another daily."[12]

(Use the transparency pattern "Helping and Counseling Involves . . ." for the following presentation.)

One basic principle of counseling is knowing when to speak and when to keep silent. If there is one problem of counseling with which people have the most difficulty, it is knowing when to keep silent. There is a tendency in the ministry of counseling to want to talk or speak. But one does not know what to say unless he has listened. The very first principle of counseling is that of listening.

Listening is one of the paramount qualities of a good counselor. Paul Tournier stressed the need for listening; "How beautiful, how grand and liberating this experience is, when people learn to help each other. It is impossible to over emphasize the immense need humans have to be really listened to. Listen to all the conversation of our world between nations as well as those between couples. They are for the most part dialogues of the deaf."[13]

As we look into the scripture, we see God as our model for listening. (Read Psalms 34:15-18; 116:1-2; Jeremiah 33:3.) The scripture has much to say about the importance of listening as we see in these passages. James 1:9 (Amplified) says that we are to be "a ready listener." (Read the following verses to the group: Proverbs 15:31; 18:13,15; 21:28.)

It is also important to note the difference between hearing and listening. "Hearing" is the gaining of information for oneself. "Listening" is caring for and being empathic toward others. In listening we are trying to understand the feelings of the other person and we are listening for his sake. "Hearing" is determined by what goes on inside of *me*, what effect the conversation has on me. "Listening" is determined by what is going on inside the other person, what my attentiveness is doing for him. We interpret and try to understand what we have heard.

(At this time divide the class into groups of two. Ask each person to talk to the other for four minutes about anything they would like to talk about. During the four minutes the listener should do just that — listen. He cannot ask any questions or make any comments, nor take any notes. At the end of four minutes he should repeat back to the other what he heard the other saying and what he thought the other was feeling. When this has been done, reverse the roles and let the other one talk about any subject for four minutes while the other listens.

After this ask for their feelings and reactions to what they just experienced. Allow several to express what they felt. Then ask what they feel they could do to improve their listening skills.)

There are three parts to true listening:

1. Listening means that when another person is speaking we are not thinking about what we are going to say when he stops talking.
2. Listening is complete acceptance without judgment of what is said and how it is stated.
3. Listening is the ability to restate accurately both the content and the feeling of a message.

One of the reasons we have listening problems is that physiologically we can listen five times as fast as we can speak. Thus, if the person you are counseling is speaking at 120 words per minute and you can listen at 600 per minute, what do you do with the extra time? Full attentiveness is needed.

There are many other elements in counseling. In Proverbs 3:5-6 we are instructed to "Lean on, trust and be confident in the Lord with all your heart and mind, and do not rely on your own insight or understanding. In all your ways know, recognize and acknowledge Him, and He will direct and make straight and plain your path" (Amplified).

Another similar thought is in Proverbs 15:28: "The mind of the (uncompromisingly) righteous studies how to answer, but the mouth of the wicked pours out evil things" (Amplified). With all the years of training and experience there are many occasions every week when counselors wonder what they should do or what should be said. This experience forces the Christian counselor to go back to the Lord and ask Him, "Lord, what should I do now? What does this person need?" If we begin to assist and help people out of our own strength, mistakes are made. We need to rely upon the power and wisdom of God.

Another basic requirement in helping others is genuine interest and love. We can listen to the person, we can rely upon the power of God for knowing how to counsel, but we must also have a genuine interest and love. Proverbs 27:9: "Oil and perfume rejoice the heart; so does the sweetness of a friend's counsel that comes from the heart" (Amplified). Sometimes a counselor will "flip off" an answer that is superficial and does not meet the counselee's need. It does not deal with the problem, and thus the person is disappointed. We have to ask ourselves the question, How do I really feel about this counselee who is coming to me? Am

I genuinely concerned? If not, maybe I should pray about my own attitude.

A fourth principle of counseling is knowing when to speak and when to be quiet, when enough has been said. Ecclesiastes 7 emphasizes this principle. Proverb 10:19 further emphasizes it: "In a multitude of words transgression is not lacking, but he who restrains his lips is prudent" (Amplified). The Living Bible is very graphic: "Stop talking so much. You keep putting your foot in your mouth. Be silent and turn off the flow!" Proverbs 11:12: "He who belittles and despises his neighbor lacks sense, but a man of understanding keeps silent" (Amplified). Proverbs 17:27: "He who has knowledge spares his words, and a man of understanding has a cool spirit" (Amplified). This is a sign of an individual who has knowledge. He chooses his words well. "Even a fool, when he holds his peace, is considered wise. When he closes his lips he is esteemed a man of understanding" (v. 28).

Proverbs 29:20: "Do you see a man who is hasty in his words? There is more hope of a (self-confident) fool than of him" (Amplified). Hastiness means you just go ahead and blurt out what you are thinking without considering the consequences, without considering the effect it will have upon others. When you are ministering to a counselee and he shares something that shocks you, don't feel that you have to respond immediately. Take a few moments to pray, asking God to give you the words. Then try to formulate what you want to say.

If you don't know what to say, one of the best things to do is ask for more information: "Tell me some more about it" or "Give me some more background." This gives you more time. You do not have to come right out and say something. There may be times when you say to a person, "I need a few seconds to go through what you said and decide what to share at this time." This takes the pressure off you and also off the counselee.

Timing is yet another principle. Proverbs 15:23: "A man has joy in making an apt answer, and a word spoken at the right moment, how good it is!" (Amplified). The right answer, the correct answer, the word spoken at the right moment.

Keeping confidences is the sixth principle. Can you keep a confidence when somebody shares something with you? The keeping of confidences is a trait of a trustworthy individual. Proverbs 11:13: "He who goes about as a talebearer reveals secrets, but he who is trustworthy and faithful in spirit keeps the matter hidden" (Amplified). Proverbs 20:19: "He who goes about as a tale-bearer reveals secrets; therefore associate not with him who talks too freely" (Amplified). If you have a friend who is a gossiper, who can't keep something hidden, the scripture is saying, Watch out! Don't associate with that person too much. Proverbs 21:23: "He who guards his mouth and his tongue keeps himself from troubles" (Amplified).

Undoubtedly, most of us, when we have had things shared with us, have had the temptation to share it with others. Some respond with, "Wait until you hear what I heard this week." People love to use that as a vehicle to conversation with somebody else. But such conversation is a violation of trust and a violation of friendship, and much damage can be done. What we must do as Christians and as counselors is ask God to help us bury confidential information deep inside or give it away to the Lord so that it will not come out on purpose or through some unconscious motivation.

Another principle we find in scripture is the saying of the right words and giving of advice. Advice-giving, in the proper manner, is a part of counseling. Proverbs 12:18: "There are those who speak rashly like the piercing of a sword, but the tongue of the wise brings healing" (Amplified). The word "rashly" means blurted out hastily and recklessly.

There are occasions when we really don't know what to say. We might say to the counselee, "I'd like to think for a moment before I respond to what you have said because I need to collect my thoughts and ask the Lord for wisdom at this time." Proverbs 15:23, which has been emphasized already, states: "A man has joy in making an apt answer, and a word spoken at the right moment, how good it is!" (Amplified). Proverbs 16:24: "Pleasant words are as a honeycomb, sweet to the mind and healing to the body" (Amplified).

Another passage which reflects the idea of understanding is Proverbs 25:20: "He who sings songs to a heavy heart is like him who lays off a garment in cold weather and as vinegar upon soda" (Amplified). Being merry, joyful, happy around the person who is deeply hurting and suffering, making inappropriate comments or jokes or even statements, "Oh, you really don't feel that way, come on out of it; let me tell you this story I heard ——," is inappropriate. This person is hurting so much he is unable to focus on what is happening. Inappropriate statements or jokes can be very, very burdensome to the person who is deeply hurt. On some occasions light conversation can help lift a person.

The question arises, How do you give advice? It is possible to receive wrong advice. In fact, there are probably many occasions on which we have struggled and Christian friends have given us advice. But their advice was not what we needed at that particular time. In fact, it is possible that we would receive several different viewpoints. Then we wonder, What in the world do I do now?

If you give suggestions, give tentative ones. "What if you did —?" "Have you considered —?" "What possibilities have you come up with?" A safety factor we can employ if we are going to give advice is to give several alternatives. Don't say to a person, "This is exactly what you need to do." If we do, we are assuming the responsibility for the solution and if our suggestion doesn't work, he may come back and say, "You really gave me a stupid idea. It didn't work. It's your fault." Giving several tentative suggestions not only is safer for you, but causes the person to think it through. Most people have the ability to resolve their problems but need the encouragement to do it.

Another principle we find in the Word of God is helping and edifying. Some of these passages might be familiar to you. Galatians 6:2 teaches the concept of bearing one another's burdens. Romans 14:19 reads: "So let us then definitely aim for and eagerly pursue what makes for harmony and for mutual upbuilding (edification and development) of one another" (Amplified). The word "edify," which is part of helping, means to hold up or to promote growth in Christian wisdom, grace, virtue, and holiness. Our counseling includes edification. Helping means assisting a person do something for his betterment. We have to ask ourselves, Is what I'm sharing with that person going to cause him to grow in the Christian life and assist him to be strong? A person might come to you and say, "I really want you to help me." What does he mean by "help"? He might mean agreeing with his point of view, especially if it is a marital dispute, or even taking sides. That is where a counselor gets into difficulty — taking sides.

Another way of helping others is encouragement. Proverbs 12:25: "Anxiety in a man's heart weighs it down, but an encouraging word makes it glad" (Amplified). First Thessalonians 5:11: "Therefore encourage (admonish, exhort) one another and edify — strengthen and build up — one another, just as you are doing" (Amplified).

Encouragement means to urge forward, to stimulate one to do what he should be doing. It is like saying to the person, "I believe in you as an individual. I believe that you have the ability and the potential to follow through in doing this. Now, can we talk about this together so that you would feel a little more competence in yourself?"

Involvement and empathy are scriptural basics for counseling. Empathy is one of the most important commodities for effective counseling but, unfortunately, the word "empathy," like so many others, has many meanings to many people. What does empathy mean in the counseling relationship? The word comes from the German word *einfulung* which means to feel into or to feel with. It is as though we are in the driver's seat of the other person and feeling and sensing with him. It is viewing the situation through his eyes, feeling as he feels. The scriptural admonition to bear one another's burdens in Galatians 6 and to rejoice with those who rejoice and weep with those who weep in Romans 12:15 is what we call empathy.

Girard Egan has said that empathy involves discrimination — to be able to get inside the other person, to look at the world through his perspective or frame of reference, and to get a feeling for what his world is like. Not only is it the ability to discriminate, but also to communicate to the other person this understanding in such a manner that he realizes we have picked up both his feelings and his behavior. We must be able to see with his eyes what his world is like to him. It is like being able to see another person's joy, to understand what underlies that joy, and to communicate this understanding to the person.

What is the function of empathy? "It serves us in two ways. First, it helps us to understand the other person from within. We communicate on a deeper level and apprehend the other person more completely. With this kind of communication we often find ourselves accepting that person and emerging into a relationship of appreciation and sympathy. In another sense, empathy becomes for us a source of personal reassurance. We are reassured when we feel that someone has succeeded in feeling himself into our own state of mind. We enjoy the satisfaction of being understood and accepted as persons. It is important for us to sense that the other person not only understands our words but appreciates the person behind the message as well. We then know that we are recognized and accepted for the particular kind of person we are. When friends fail to empathize, we feel disappointed and rejected. When empathy is lacking, our self-awareness and self-respect are diminished. We then experience ourselves more as objects and less as persons."[14]

"Love is the capacity to involve oneself, unselfconsciously, in the lives of other men — without using these relationships primarily to minister to oneself. To understand their weaknesses, to suffer with them, to hate the things that hurt them, to grieve over their hard-heartedness — these are manifestations of the kind of relationships which contribute to new life in those whose lives have been so touched."[15]

William Crane, in his book *Where God Comes In: The Divine Plus is Counseling*, described empathy in this way: "The person who practices the presence of the Holy Spirit and learns to love God through focusing upon His demonstration of love in the gift of His only Son becomes increasingly mature and capable of ministering to the needs of others. As Dr. Reuel Howe and others have said, nothing will take the place of love in the heart of the counselor for his counselee. This kind of love is more concerned with giving than with getting; it is the basic factor in establishing an empath(ic) relationship between counselor and counselee. True empathy must have its roots in agape love, for only this kind of self-giving concern is capable of entering into the deeper areas of the counselee's problems.

"For a better understanding of the meaning of this 'larger love' in empathy, let me quote from J. B. Phillips' translation of I Corinthians 13:4-8: 'This love of which I speak is slow to lose patience — it looks for a way of being constructive. It is not possessive: it is neither anxious to impress nor does it cherish inflated ideas of its own importance.

"'Love has good manners and does not pursue selfish advantage. It is not touchy. It does not keep account of evil or gloat over the wickedness of other people. On the contrary, it is glad with all good men when truth prevails.

"'Love knows no limit to its endurance, no end to its trust, no fading of its hope; it can outlast anything. It is, in fact, the one thing that still stands when all else has fallen.'

"First of all, there can be no empathy when one loses patience quickly with a troubled person. This can happen when one is more concerned about his own affairs than about his counselee's interests or needs. Lack of patience may destroy any possibility of empathy; it can easily be detected by the counselee whether through words or through actions and attitudes.

"Sometimes the counselor shows his impatience by 'pushing' the counselee too fast to get on with his problems, so that, presumably, the counselor may begin *his* 'important work.'

"The basic love from which empathy springs 'is not touchy.' 'Touchy' implies a degree of oversensitivity on the part of the counselor, which really means that he is more concerned about receiving the counselee's praise and approval than he is of giving his attention to the counselee's needs. Here is an area where lack of insight and failure to be aware of the counselor's own emotional blocks may cause trouble and destroy empathy or make it impossible to establish empathy in the first place.

"A touchy counselor is one who listens primarily for things that might reflect upon his own character or worth rather than seeking for constructive ways to be helpful to the counselee. A neurotic counselor is inclined to become extremely touchy and to be thrown on the defensive by any slight, word, or act on the part of the counselee which would insinuate that the counselor is not as important as the counselee.

"Love also refuses 'to keep an account of evil or gloat over the wickedness of other people.'

"Rather than having a judgmental attitude, the counselor is 'glad with all good men when truth prevails.' This is to say that the counselor is responsive to the counselee wherever he sees in him potential for good and evidence of truth. The counselor's joy is a contributing factor in the deepening and strengthening of empathy.

"There is an ongoingness in love which 'knows no limit to its endurance.' The counselor must learn to endure all sorts of things in his counselees.

"But the next factor is even more difficult at times. Love knows 'no end to its trust.' Every counselor and especially every pastoral counselor has people who come to him clothed in hypocrisy, insincerity, and falsehood. Their neurotic problem makes them need to test the sincerity of the pastoral counselor by their very insincerity.

"The smiling face, smooth words, and overly pious attitude which some counselees bring to their counseling relationship with their pastors may be deceptive for a while. Eventually the real nature is discovered — and then the counselor has a real problem. He needs to trust his counselee, but how can he trust one who is so false, deceptive, and insincere?

"Actually he cannot. Nevertheless he must learn to trust his belief in and knowledge of his counselee's need for help. Above this he must have an unfailing trust in the presence and power of the Wonderful Counselor, the Holy Spirit, who is ready and willing to change the counselee from an untrustworthy person to a person of integrity and honor, through the instrument of the counselor. This basic personality change is impossible without the work of the Holy Spirit within the heart, but the pastoral counselor need never

doubt it is an unfailing possibility and a desirable result in the counseling relationship."[16]

"And concerning you, my brethren, I myself also am convinced that you yourselves are full of goodness, filled with all knowledge, and able also to admonish one another" (Rom. 15:14, NASB).

The word "Confrontation" is used frequently in discussions of counseling techniques. What is confrontation? When should it be used? Confrontation is really part of everyday life and it can be used effectively when we are involved in helping another individual. Confrontation is not an attack on another person for his "own good." Such a negative and punitive attack would be detrimental to the counselee.

William Crane has said, "A judging confrontation, unprepared for, may end any relationship which would make counseling possible. The person already feels guilty and ashamed, and to be judged and condemned rather than understood and accepted is nothing less than absolute rejection. A person laden with guilt already feels cut off and rejected by all that stands for rightness and justice; he surely does not need to be condemned more by the one to whom he goes seeking help."[17]

Girard Egan has suggested that confrontation at its best is an extension of advanced, accurate empathy. That is, it is a response to a counselee based on a deep understanding of his feelings, experiences, and behavior that involves some unmasking of distortion and the client's understanding of himself and some challenge to action.

William Crane has suggested that "Only when empathy is established is the climate ready for confrontation; until then it is neither wise nor helpful."[18] The relationship between confrontation and empathy is very important and yet so many have never attempted to link the two together and have failed to see the relationship between the two. A counseling confrontation has been defined as an act by which a counselor points out to the counselee a discrepancy between his own and the counselee's manner of viewing reality. Bates and Johnson have said that counseling confrontations are "acts of grace." Girard Egan has defined confrontation as "a responsible unmasking of the discrepancies, distortions, games, and smoke screens the counselee uses to hide both from self-understanding and from constructive behavioral change."[19] It also involves challenging the undeveloped, the underdeveloped, the unused, and the misused potentialities, skills and resources of the client with a view to examining and understanding these resources and putting them to use in action programs.

Confrontation is an invitation by the helper to the client to explore his defenses, those that keep him from understanding and those that keep him from action.

Our purpose in confronting a person should be to help him make better decisions for himself, to become more accepting of himself, and to be more productive and less destructive in his life. There are times when professional and nonprofessional alike hesitate in confronting because it involves a commitment and there is also the risk of the possibility that the counselor could be wrong or the other might misunderstand and feel rejected. In confronting the person we also need to be careful that even though the confrontation is given with proper intentions, it does not work against what we are actually trying to accomplish in the counselee's life.

When is confrontation appropriate? Earlier it was mentioned that empathy must be a part of the relationship. The quality of the relationship between counselor and counselee is very important. Generally speaking, the stronger the relationship, the more powerful and intense the confrontation can be. A confrontation must come about because the counselor cares about the counselee. If we do not care about him or his improvement, confrontation can be harmful. Another factor involved in confrontation is the ability of the counselee to understand and see what we are saying. Does he have the ability to accept the confrontation? Can he follow through with what we are suggesting?

How should confrontations be given? A confrontation should be given with empathy. The caring approach is so vital, for when care is expressed and perceived by the counselee, he can accept the confrontation much more readily. Confrontations can be made in a tentative manner with statements such as "I wonder if —," "Could it be —," "Is it possible —?" "Does this make sense to you?" and "How do you react to this perception?"

How might a client or counselee respond when confronted? Again, Girard Egan has suggested several different responses. The counselee might try to discredit the counselor. He could do this by attacking the counselor, showing that he knows better than anyone else. If this occurs, it could mean that we have been wrong in our confrontation and have not been perceptive. A counselee might attempt to persuade the counselor to change his views. He might employ reasoning. He might try to show the counselor that he is really not that bad or that he is being misinterpreted. He might also try to minimize the importance of the topic being discussed in the form of rationalizing. As often happens in pastoral counseling, the counselee might seek support for his own views from others.

Romans 15:14 states: "And concerning you, my brethren, I myself also am convinced that you yourselves are full of goodness, filled with all knowledge, and able also to admonish one another" (NASB).

Often a counselee will agree with the counselor. His agreement could be valid or it could be a game. He could agree in order to get the counselor to back off. If the agreement does not lead to behavioral change, the sincerity of the counselee should be questioned. Our goal in confrontation is not necessarily to have the person agree with us, but to have him reexamine his behavior so that he can understand himself better and act in a much more effective manner.

One example of a direct confrontation in scripture is in 2 Samuel 12:7-14. Nathan confronted David with his sin against Uriah and his wife Bathsheba. David openly admitted his sin and Nathan responded by saying, " 'The Lord has also taken away your sin; you shall not die. However, because by this deed you have given occasion to the enemies of the Lord to blaspheme, the child also that is born to you shall surely die" (NASB). Because of the wrong that David has done — to Uriah, to his position as king of Israel, to Bathsheba, and to the unborn child — David had to be confronted with the total picture. William Crane noted that "the judgment placed upon David for his sin was not without an expression of the love and mercy of God in providing pardon and forgiveness. When Nathan was able to say, 'The Lord has also put away your sin; you shall not die,' he was giving reassurance to David of his acceptance by God and his pardon as a result of his true repentance. Had David not been confronted by Nathan in this way it is doubtful that he would have come to recognize or admit the fact of his sinfulness and need for forgiveness."[20]

It is important to share the concepts in 1 Thessalonians 5:14 because when you work with people you cannot use the same approach every time. You must be sensitive to their needs. Adaptability is important. In 1 Thessalonians 5:14 it is stated: "And we earnestly beseech you, brethren, admonish (warn and seriously advise) those who are out of line; encourage the timid and fainthearted, help and give your support to the weak souls (and) be very patient with everybody — always keeping your temper" (Amplified).

How do you confront a person when he is doing something wrong? In John 5 Jesus asked the man at the pool, Do you really want to be healed? Do you really want to change? When I work with people I am asking that question in one way or another. In John 8 Jesus responded to the woman who was caught in adultery by saying: "Let him who is without sin cast the first stone."

Honesty is yet another part of counseling. Proverbs 28:23 states: "In the end people appreciate frankness more than flattery" (TLB). In Proverbs 27:5 we read: "Open rebuke is better than love that is hidden."

Finally, acceptance is involved in helping others. Galatians 6:1: "Brethren, even if a man is caught in any trespass, you who are spiritual, restore such a one in a spirit of gentleness; looking to yourself, lest you too be tempted" (NASB). John 8:7: "But when they persisted in asking Him, He straightened up, and said to them, 'He who is without sin among you, let him be the first to throw a stone at her'" (NASB). (Note: Illustrate the way in which God accepted the responses of Moses and Elijah in Numbers 11 and 1 Kings 19.)

REFERENCES

1. Maurice Wagner, *The Sensation of Being Somebody* (Grand Rapids: Zondervan Publishing House, 1975), p. 37.

2. Wagner, p. 164.

3. Lloyd H. Ahlem, *Do I Have to Be Me?* (Glendale, Calif.: G/L Publications, Regal Books Division, 1973), p. 71.

4. J. I. Packer, *Knowing God* (Downers Grove, Ill.: InterVarsity Press, 1973), p. 37.

5. Waylon O. Ward, *The Bible in Counseling* (Chicago: Moody Press, 1977).

6. Frank B. Minirth, M.D., *Christian Psychiatry* (Old Tappan, N.J.: Fleming H. Revell Co., 1977), pp. 23-25.

7. From David Carlson, Jesus' Style of Relating: *The Search For a Biblical Model of Counseling.*

8. William Crane, *Where God Comes In: The Divine Plus in Counseling* (Waco, Texas: Word Books, 1970), p. 28.

9. Crane, p. 36.

10. Gary Collins, *How to Be a People Helper* (Santa Ana, Calif.: Vision House, 1976), p. 37.

11. Collins, pp. 51-53.

12. Ward.

13. Paul Tournier, *To Understand Each Other* (Richmond, Va.: John Knox Press, 1967), p. 29.

14. Joshua Loth Liebman, *Peace of Mind* (New York: Simon & Schuster, 1946), pp. 7-8, reprinted by permission of the publisher.

15. Donald C. Houts, "Sensitivity, Theology and Change: Pastoral Care in the Corinthians Letters," *Pastoral Psychology*, Vol. 20, No. 193 (April, 1969), p. 25.

16. Crane, pp. 31-36.

17. Crane, p. 57.

18. Crane, p. 60.

19. Girard Egan, *The Skilled Helper* (Monterey, Calif.: Brooks/Cole Publishing Co., 1975), p. 158.

20. Crane, p. 56.

A BIBLICAL BASIS OF COUNSELING FOUNDATION BASED UPON . . .

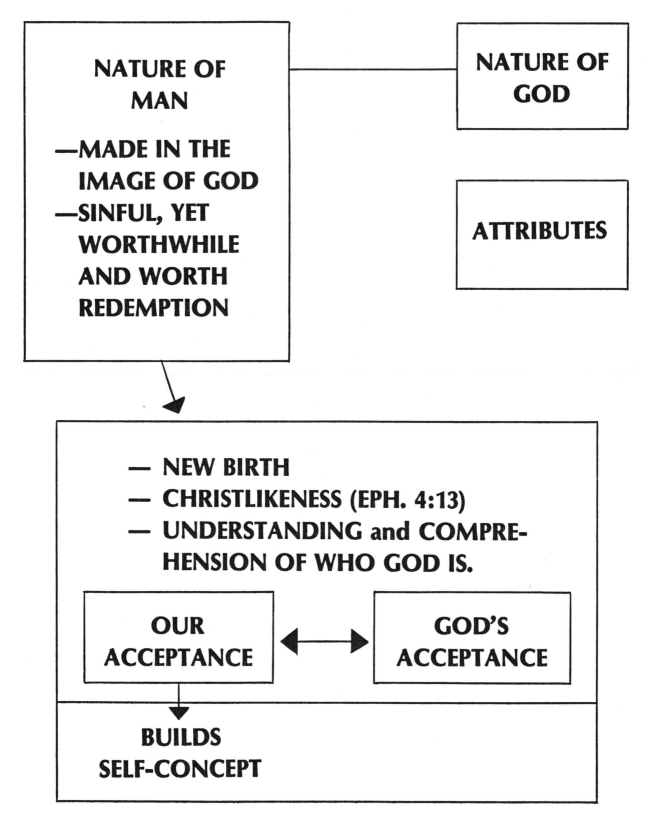

NATURE OF MAN

—MADE IN THE IMAGE OF GOD
—SINFUL, YET WORTHWHILE AND WORTH REDEMPTION

NATURE OF GOD

ATTRIBUTES

— NEW BIRTH
— CHRISTLIKENESS (EPH. 4:13)
— UNDERSTANDING and COMPREHENSION OF WHO GOD IS.

OUR ACCEPTANCE ◀▶ GOD'S ACCEPTANCE

BUILDS SELF-CONCEPT

"PUT ON — PUT OFF"

" . . . Lay aside every weight, and . . . sin" (Heb. 12:1-2).

"PUT OFF"	SCRIPTURAL INSIGHT		"PUT ON"	
1. Lack of love	1 John 4:7-8,20	John 15:12	Love	
2. Judging	Matt. 7:1-2	John 8:9; 15:22	Self-examination	
3. Bitterness	Heb. 12:15	Col. 3:12	Tenderhearted	
4. Unforgiving spirit	Mark 11:26	Matt. 6:14	Forgiving spirit	
5. Pride	Prov. 16:18	James 4:6	Humility	
6. Selfishness	Phil. 2:21	John 12:24	Death of self	
7. Boasting (conceit)	1 Cor. 4:7	Prov. 27:2	Humility	
8. Stubbornness	1 Sam. 15:23	Rom. 6:13	Submission	
9. Lack of submission and/or disrespect	2 Tim. 3:6	Matt. 6:10	Broken will	
10. Rebellion	1 Sam. 15:23	Joel 2:12-13	Submitting—Jesus, Lord	

"PUT OFF"		SCRIPTURAL INSIGHT		"PUT ON"
11.	Disobedience	1 Sam. 12:15	Heb. 5:9	Obedience
12.	Ungratefulness	Rom. 1:21	Eph. 5:20	Thankfulness
13.	Impatience	James 1:2–4	Luke 21:19	Patience
14.	Discontent	Phil. 4:11–13	Heb. 13:5	Satisfaction
15.	Covetousness	Exod. 20:17	Col. 3:5	Yielding rights
16.	Murmuring	Prov. 19:3	1 Cor. 10:10	Gratefulness
17.	Complaining	Jude 15–16	Heb. 13:5	Contentment
18.	Sassing	John 6:43	Eph. 5:21	Respect for authority
19.	Irritation to others	Prov. 25:8	Phil. 2:3–4	Preferring in love
20.	Jealousy	Prov. 27:4	1 Cor. 13:4	Trust, preferring others
21.	Strife	James 3:16	Luke 6:31	Esteem of others
22.	Losing temper	Prov. 16:32	Rom. 5:3–4	Self-control

Transparency Pattern
Session 3

"PUT OFF"	SCRIPTURAL INSIGHT		"PUT ON"
23. Bodily harm	Prov. 16:29	1 Thess. 2:7	Gentleness
24. Anger	Prov. 14:17	Gal. 5:24-25	Self-control
25. Wrath	James 1:19-20	Gal. 5:24-25	Self-control
26. Hatred	Matt. 5:21-22	1 Cor. 13:3	Love or kindness
27. Murder	Exod. 20:13	Rom. 13:10	Love
28. Gossip	1 Tim. 5:13	Rom. 14:19	Speaking with praise
29. Lying	Eph. 4:25	Zech. 8:16	Speaking truth
30. Bad language	Eph. 4:29	1 Tim. 4:12	Edification
31. Profanity	Ps. 109:17	1 Tim. 4:12	Edification
32. Idle words	Matt. 12:36	Prov. 21:23	Bridle the tongue
33. Evil thoughts	Prov. 23:7a	Phil. 4:8	"Think on these things"
34. Bad motives	1 Sam. 16:7	Ps. 19:14	Meditation on God

"PUT OFF"		SCRIPTURAL INSIGHT		"PUT ON"
35. Complacency	James 4:17		Col. 3:23	Diligence
36. Hypocrisy	Job 8:13		Eph. 4:25	Honesty
37. Other gods	Deut. 11:16		Eph. 4:6	Jesus first place
38. Lost first love	Rev. 2:4		1 John 4:10,19	Meditate on Christ
39. Lack of rejoicing always	Phil. 4:4		1 Thess. 5:16	Rejoicing
40. Worry (fear)	Matt. 6:25-32		1 Peter 5:7	Trust
41. Doubt (unbelief)	1 Thess. 5:24		Heb. 11:1	Faith

JESUS' STYLE OF COUNSELING
A STATUS-ROLE CONTINUUM

PROPHETIC   PASTORAL   PRIESTLY

critic preacher teacher interpreter comforter mediator confessor

corrector caller to repentance preacher proclaiming truth

affirming

convictor lecturer advice-giver burden bearer listener

urger to change requestor encourager consoler pardoner

admonisher advocate helper invitor reprover warner exhorter

sustainer supportive forgiver

JESUS' STYLE OF HELPING OTHERS

I. THE PURPOSE OF HIS MINISTRY

LUKE 4:18 (AMPLIFIED)   JOHN 10:10 (AMPLIFIED)
LUKE 12:20-21 (TLB)   LUKE 19:10
                               JOHN 3:8

II. HIS EXAMPLE FOR THE COUNSELOR

OBEDIENCE
JOHN 12:49; 17:4

INVOLVEMENT WITH DISCIPLES AND THOSE WHO CARE

PRAYER
LUKE 5:15-16;
6:12-13

ANOINTING
LUKE 3:21-22;
5:17

AUTHORITY
MATT. 7:29

FAITH

III. HIS TECHNIQUE — HIS MODELING FOR US

A Process — He spent time with people working through their problems in an in-depth way.

1. **Compassion (Mark 1:41; 6:34; 8:2)**

2. **Acceptance (Luke 19; John 4,8)**

3. **Worth to others (Mark 2:27; Luke 9:11)**

4. **Responsibility (Luke 5:24; 6:10; John 5)**

5. **Hope, encouragement, inspiration (Matt. 11:28-30; Mark 10:26-27; John 14:27; 16; 17)**

6. **Redirected thinking — refashioning people's thinking (Matt. 19:4-9; Luke 7:3-50; 8:22-25)**

7. **Teaching others (Luke 6:39,42; 14:2-6; 20:28)**

   Positive authority (Matt. 7:29)

8. **Admonishment and confrontation (Matt. 8:26;**

9. **18:15; John 8:3-11)**

10. **Seeing needs of others (example: Nicodemus)**

11. **His words (soft-spoken, harsh, His look of anger)**

12. **Emphasis upon right behavior (Luke 6:47-49)**

13. **Example of John 17.**

FIVE STEPS OF
BIBLICAL COUNSELING

1. **Build a relationship.**

2. **Explore the problems.**

3. **Decide on a course of action.**

4. **Stimulate action.**

5. **Terminate the counseling relationship.**

HELPING AND COUNSELING INVOLVES KNOWING WHEN TO SPEAK AND WHEN TO KEEP SILENT (ECCL. 3:7).

1. **Listening (Prov. 18:13; James 1:19)**
2. **Relying upon the power of God for knowing how to counsel (Prov. 3:5-6; 15:28)**
3. **Maintaining genuine interest and love (Prov. 27:9)**
4. **Knowing when to speak and when to be quiet (Eccl. 3:7; Prov. 19:19; 11:12; 17:27; 29:20; James 1:19)**
5. **Timing (Prov. 15:23)**
6. **Keeping confidences — being a trusted person (Prov. 11:13; 20:19; 21:23)**
7. **Saying the right words, giving advice (Prov. 12:18; 15:23; 16:24; 25:20)**
8. **Helping and edifying (Rom. 14:19; Gal. 6:1-2; Heb. 3:13)**
9. **Encouraging (Prov. 12:25; Rom. 1:12; 1 Thess. 5:11)**
10. **Being involved and empathic (Rom. 12:15; Gal. 6:2; 27:9)**
11. **Teaching and admonishing — confronting things that are wrong and need warning (Rom. 15:14; Col. 3:16; 1 Thess. 5:14)**
12. **Being honest (Prov. 28:23; 27:5)**
13. **Accepting the counselee (Gal. 6:1; John 8:7; Num. 11; 1 Kings 19)**
14. **Modeling**

A MODEL OF COUNSELING, PART I

OBJECTIVES
— To outline the basic principles of Reality Therapy and demonstrate their use in counseling.
— To outline the basic principles of Cognitive Counseling and demonstrate their use in counseling.
— To explain (or defend) the importance of homework in counseling and match appropriate assignments to case study problems.
— To become acquainted with the Bible Application Form demonstrating a functioning model of using the Bible in counseling and for homework.

ADVANCE PREPARATION
1. Prepare transparencies.
2. Duplicate the "Bible Application Form."
3. Read (at least twice) the article in the second portion of this manual, "Effective Counseling and Psychotherapy: An Integrative Review of Research," by Keith Edwards.

LECTURE PRESENTATION
Time: 45-60 minutes.

Counseling to bring about change focuses upon feelings, thoughts, and behavior. The main emphasis, however, rests upon the counselee's behavior and thoughts. Here is a suggested format of counseling based upon both Reality Therapy and Cognitive Therapy. The presentation of this model presupposes, however, that the lay counselor will also use, integrate, and emphasize the previously taught techniques such as listening and empathy. This model is simply a suggested progression of procedures or a framework of counseling. Within this framework many different techniques, comments, and questions can be utilized. (Be sure to take questions as they arise during your presentation. Use the transparency patterns.)

In any approach to counseling another person, an attitude of caring, warmth, sympathy, and concern is essential. This is sometimes called *involvement*. In Reality Therapy it has been suggested that the way in which we become involved in the life of the other person is by being concerned about his personal life and his present concerns with his present behavior. This can be done by a sharing of ourself with him and him with us as we endeavor to get acquainted. We can ask, "What is going on in your life right now and how can I help?"

We can show an interest in all areas of his life and we can also expand the counselee's range of interest. One of our objectives in helping the person is to make him aware of life and possibilities beyond his difficulties. Often the person is so bound by his difficulties that he fails to see any hope or accept any help. Through gentle questioning or comments he can begin to see new possibilities. Statements or comments such as, "Isn't it just as possible ——" of "Perhaps there are other possibilities we haven't explored yet ——" may help him become aware of the alternatives.

After we have become involved we need to bring the person to the point where he will *evaluate his present behavior*. He will not do so unless he feels that you care and are involved. He needs to make a value judgment about what he is doing with his life right now. "Are you happy about your life or would you like to change? Is this a negative thing for you or positive? Do you feel good or bad about this? Would you like this to continue or would you like to see a change?"

We also want to have him consider his thought life as well. What is it like? Is it a positive, constructive approach or is it basically negative? Does he feel good about his pattern of thinking or could it be better? There are many questions which could be used to bring him to a point of evaluation. He must make a value judgment or he will not progress in the counseling. Jesus asked the woman at the well, "Do you want to be healed? Do you want to change?" Once a person answers affirmatively, the way is clear for progress.

By having counselees do outside homework or projects such as reading books or listening to tapes, you can see if their response to these projects matches their verbal assent to change. If their behavior is consistent with what they have said, we can assume they would like to grow and develop. But if they do not follow through, then their motivation to change might not be as strong as they have said it is.

Waylon Ward, in *The Bible in Counseling*, has suggested the following purposes of homework. (Make your own overhead transparency of these points.)

"... Homework assignments can be effectively used to improve the counseling experience and to accomplish more in the same amount of time ...

"1. Homework will help to *reprogram* the counselee's mind (Rom 12:1-2). The counselee must come to view life, himself, his problems, and his needs from God's perspective ...

"2. Homework enables the counselee to *gain new insights into his life, his problems, and his relationships* ...

"3. Homework *reinforces insights and knowledge* the client has gained in the actual counseling session ...

"4. Homework helps to *establish a God-dependency in the counselee* instead of a counselor-dependency ...

"5. The *comfort and support offered in the counseling session can be spread over the entire time period* between counseling sessions through the homework concept ...

"6. Homework assignments make it possible for the counselor to *communicate more information in a shorter amount of time* ...

"7. Counseling homework helps to enable the client to *establish good habits and reprogram his use of time* ...

"8. The counselee's performance on the assignments can often be a *gauge of both his attitude and his progress* ...

"9. Homework can be used for evangelism ...

"10 Homework can also be used to establish good relationships and communication in interpersonal conflicts ...

"11. Certain types of homework can be used to gain new information about the counseling problem ..."[1]

Part of our counseling ministry is helping people make a decision to change. After this is done your work will be helping them effect this change.

We are also emphasizing their present behavior and focusing upon the future. Many people like to talk about their past and all that has happened and how they were misused, but it is impossible to change past events. We can help people react differently to what is affecting them from their past. If they want to talk about the past, find out what they were doing when they were successful. This would be far better than hearing about all of the mistakes and blunders or problems. If they can learn from their mistakes and see what they did wrong and how they can improve, then perhaps there would be some benefit in looking at a past situation. But the past must always be linked to the present.

The next step is helping them select some alternatives to what they are doing or the way in which they are thinking. One possible statement or question we could use is, "Since your behavior (or your thought life) is your own, what can you do to change your behavior? What plans can we make?" We need to place the responsibility for the future and present success upon the person himself. The emphasis must be upon his own responsibility for what he is doing and what or how he is thinking. We are responsible for what we think and do. Others may influence us or manipulate us and put pressure upon us, but their efforts are not successful unless we cooperate with them. People choose to act ot think in a particular way. Sometimes we discover the reason behind their decisions.

If people continue to choose behavior which backfires on them or they choose to remain with a low self-concept, we might try to discover the advantage or payoff the person receives from it. We don't hit them over the head with these statements, but at the same time we must express concern. We could say, "I know you are hurting or suffering but is it possible that there is some advantage? It seems that this is your choice so I wonder if you are not getting something from hanging on to this? What might it be?" or "What do you think about the suggestion I have just made? Does it make any sense to you? Had you

47

thought about it in this way before? What alternatives could you suggest at this time?"

After they suggest some alternatives we explore them together. You may find someone who says, "I can't think of any. That's why I came to see you." Another may say, "I don't know. You tell me what to do." Be careful that you don't tell them what to do for this takes away their responsibility and puts you in a difficult position, especially if your suggestions do not work.

If people react by saying, "I can't change, it's impossible," or "I can't do anything. I'm just stuck," we might suggest that perhaps it is not a matter of not being able to change but perhaps they haven't yet learned how. Through talking together they can discover some ways of changing. Some have found it helpful with the proper tone of voice and timing to suggest, "Is it a matter of not being able to change or at this point in your life really resisting change — not wanting to change?" If you do suggest alternatives, give several in a tentative manner and have them select the one they would like to pursue. As we work with the person we need to focus on responsible behaviors and thought patterns and de-emphasize irresponsibility in behavior and negativism in thinking.

After the counselee has decided upon an alternative, it is important to ask him to make a commitment to follow through upon what he has decided. This is the real work of counseling — assisting him make a detailed plan so he will be able to carry through and be successful. We help him choose an alternative and construct a plan which is attainable through the use of small steps. Sometimes we ask him, "What are you going to do?" or "I'd like you to tell me what you are going to do this week." (This is an example of taking a question and changing it into a statement.) "How are you going to do it? When are you going to do it?" Ask him to consider the possible consequences of his new choice — positive and negative. How will he handle either?

When the counselee returns we can ask, "What changes have taken place this week?" If he has not followed through in his commitments, we spend time helping him construct a plan in which he will be successful. It is important not to spend time going over the excuses for why the plan didn't work. We work toward the next week. (At this point distribute a copy of the Bible Application Form to each person and explain its use. This form has been used in counseling, either as a resource by the counselor or as a work sheet by the counselees to assist them in bringing about change in their life.)

At the same time we are working with a person's behavior we seek to help him with his thought life as well. The technical term for this method is "Cognitive Counseling" or "Therapy." This means that attention is focused upon the person's thought life. This approach assumes that a person's problems are derived largely from distortions of reality based on erroneous thinking, such as false premises and assumptions. As people learn certain patterns of behavior they learn certain patterns of thinking as well. A counselor helps the counselee evaluate and unravel his distortions and discover and learn alternative and more realistic ways of thinking. Here we are suggesting a combination of focusing upon behavior and thoughts. A person's thoughts and behavior bring on his feelings, so to correct his feelings we help him develop better patterns of behaving and better patterns of thinking. By correcting erroneous thought patterns, inappropriate emotional responses can be changed. In helping a person reconstruct his thoughts we must remember the following.

1. He must be aware of what he is thinking.
2. He must recognize that some of his thoughts are not accurate.
3. He must learn to substitute accurate thoughts and judgments for inaccurate ones.
4. He needs feedback to inform him whether his changes are correct. The counselor can provide feedback.

People develop what we can call "maladaptive" thoughts or systems of thinking. If any thought interferes with a person's well-being, then we call it a maladaptive thought. These thoughts produce inappropriate or excessive emotional reactions. Sometimes this is also called self-talk, for most people engage in some form of self-talk whether it be positive or negative. (Some of these concepts are discussed in the sessions on depression as well as here.)

One description of self-talk is derived from a system of counseling called Rational Emotive Therapy. This system suggests a simple way of analyzing a person's progression of thinking.

When we are criticized or someone becomes angry with us, we react to the person with either rejection or anger. Many people believe that the criticism or the anger of the other person brought on our feeling of rejection or anger. But in reality it did not. Prior to our reaction something happened with our own thoughts. These thoughts could be called our attitudes or beliefs. Such beliefs could be, "It's terrible to be rejected. He has no right to get angry at me. I am worthless. This should not have happened." The thoughts we have at this point create the reaction we have to whatever happens to us. The model for this kind of thinking may be described as follows: (Use the transparency pattern.)

A. The event (such as anger toward us or rejection).

B. Our belief or attitude (our thinking reaction).

C. The emotional reaction (We could feel anger, rejection, or depression.)

(At this point ask class members to work together with another person for two minutes in developing some other examples which fit into this format. Ask for several examples. Then ask them to work together again in suggesting ways to break this thinking pattern. Ask for several suggestions. Then share the following suggestions with them.)

Steps D and E are essential in the process of counteracting thoughts such as these. Step D is questioning, disputing, or challenging our own thoughts and beliefs. For example, "Why is it awful to be rejected? Does being rejected make me worthless? Why should their anger make me angry?" This process is a matter of challenging and questioning our thoughts toward the situation or rejection.

Step E is answering some of our own questions which were asked in step D. For example, "Why is it awful to be rejected? It isn't awful to be rejected. I prefer not to be treated in this manner but is it really all that important? Can I learn through this experience? Can I apply James 1:2-3 to this experience? Why must I feel bad if someone becomes angry at me? I prefer that he did not become angry but my life does not have to stop because of it. His anger does not make me worthless. I can look at what he is angry about and see if I did make an error. If so I can learn to correct what I have done. If not then I can clarify this for him and we can both learn through this experience."

Another example of this kind of self-talk is illustrated by a young man and a girl he had dated for two years. Suddenly she broke up with him with very little explanation.

A. The event in this case was the girl breaking up with the young man.

B. His thinking reaction or self-talk contained the following: "Life is terrible. I can't go on. I must be worthless if she does not want me anymore. What is wrong with me? Why am I so terrible that she does not care for me? This should not have happened to me."

C. In this case the emotional reaction included rejection, depression, withdrawal, anger, and confusion of thinking.

D. In questioning or challenging the thoughts and self-talk he could ask, "Where is the evidence that all of life is terrible? Who says I can't go on? Where is the evidence that anything is wrong with me? Why does it mean that I am terrible? Where are the facts for all of my questions? Why should this not have happened to me?"

E. This final step is answering the previously asked questions: "All of life is not terrible. This is an upsetting, unexpected event and I was shocked, but much of life is still very worthwhile. I am hurt and feel a great loss. I can go on even though I hurt. Her breaking up with me does not mean there is anything wrong with me. If I have done something that is wrong I can correct it. She chose to break up and it is her decision. I am not a terrible person. Somehow through this I will learn and grow and perhaps change."

(Read the following examples to the group one at a time, giving time in between each one for them to respond, and ask them to discuss with another person what this individual could say to himself to counter his present thoughts.)

1. A young woman had a straight-A average during her first two years of college. When other students were asked for their comments in class she would think, "Why didn't the teacher call on me? He must think I don't have the answer and that I'm dumb. He probably won't call on me again."

2. A pastor saw several people yawning during his sermon and several going to sleep or looking bored. Following the service he noticed that a number of them were not overly friendly in response to him as they left the church. His thoughts were, "That sermon was one of the worst I have ever given. No wonder they are not friendly. They must think it's time for a new pastor, and they may be right. I guess my message was pretty bad. I don't think I can improve either."

3. A young man asked an attractive girl at school for a date but she turned him down. He thought, "I must be unacceptable to her. It's sure a let-down to get a refusal like that. I'm not going to ask anyone for some time. It's not worth getting turned down like that."

4. A husband became upset because his wife was very quiet and withdrawn and snapped at him for several days. He thought, "Perhaps there is something wrong with me. What if she doesn't love me anymore? Perhaps she is interested in someone else. This is terrible. How can I handle this?"

Several kinds of thinking can help to bring on a negative thinking pattern which perpetuates more negative thinking. If this kind of thinking is engaged in long enough, it can lead to depression. Some of these patterns are described below. (Ask the class for an example of each.)

1. Arbitrary inference — making a conclusion without evidence to support it or even in the face of evidence to the contrary.
2. Selective abstraction — focusing upon details taken out of context. The basic idea is separated from the whole picture and eventually becomes warped.
3. Overgeneralization — making a conclusion based upon a single incident.
4. Magnification or minimization — underestimating one's own ability or performance, or exaggerating the intensity of one's problems.
5. Inexact labeling — describing an event inaccurately, which results in an emotional reaction to the label rather than to the significance of the event itself.

There are several other steps which can be employed in the process of helping a person analyze his thought life. As we counsel individuals our task is helping them learn to recognize and identify the thoughts and value judgments they express to themselves. They should also realize that many of these thoughts are automatic — they just pop into our mind because of past experiences and years of practice. The next step is learning to distinguish between ideas and facts. Just because a person thinks something does not make it true nor does it mean that he should believe it. After he discovers that a particular thought is not true, he should state precisely why it is inaccurate or invalid, preferably in writing. Putting the reasons into our own words helps in three ways:

1. The frequency of reoccurence of the idea is reduced.
2. The intensity of the idea is decreased.
3. The feeling or mood that the idea generates is lessened.

The final step is considering alternative explanations to the event.

COUNSELING PRACTICE

Time: 60 minutes.

The concluding activity for this session is practicing the principles of Reality Therapy and Cognitive Counseling. Here are three suggestions for the practice sessions.

1. Demonstrate this method of counseling in front of the entire group or ask for a volunteer to do this demonstration.
2. Divide the class into groups of three so that each person can role play the parts of counselee, counselor, and observer. In one hour each one should play each role and also have his counseling analyzed by the other two.
3. Divide the class into larger groups and ask just a few to demonstrate or practice this approach while the others observe and offer suggestions. Conclude with prayer.

BIBLE APPLICATION FORM

1. Describe the behavior or attitude you want to change (for example, anger, anxiety, quarreling, yelling).

2. List several very personal reasons for giving up this behavior or attitude.

3. Motivation to change is very important. From your reasons for giving up the behavior or attitude select the most important reason.

4. How could you change your behavior if you wish to succeed?

5. Adopt a positive attitude. What has been your attitude toward changing this in the past? Indicate what attitude you are going to have now. How will you maintain this new attitude?

6. Whenever you eliminate a behavior or attitude that you dislike, often a vacuum or void remains. Frequently a person prefers the bad or poor behavior to this emptiness so he reverts to the previous pattern. In order for this not to happen, substitute a positive behavior in place of the negative. Describe what you can substitute for the behavior or attitude you are giving up.

7. Read the scriptures suggested for this problem area. List the positive behavior or attitude that the scripture suggests in place of the negative. How do you see yourself putting this scripture into action in your life? Describe specific situations in which you will do what the scripture suggests. Describe the results of thinking or behaving in this new way.

BIBLE APPLICATION FORM (cont.)

Here is a passage of Scripture to use as an example for practice. (Many have found this passage very applicable to their lives and circumstances.)

Scripture: Ephesians 4:31-32

Behavior or Attitude to Stop	**Results of this Behavior** (Give several for each one.)

bitterness
(resentfulness, harshness)

Anger
(fury, antagonism, outburst)

Wrath
(indignation, violent anger,
boiling up)

Clamor
(brawling)

Slander
(abusive speech)

Positive Behavior or Attitude to Begin	**Results of this Behavior** (Give several for each one.)

Kindness
(goodness of heart)

Tenderheartedness
(compassion)

Forgiveness
(an action)

8. In which practical ways do you see yourself acting as suggested in the scripture?

9. When and how will you begin and what results do you expect? Be very specific.

10. Now take the scripture that pertains to your problems or concern and complete this procedure as outline in number 7 above.

ONE METHOD OF ASSISTING A COUNSELEE REDUCE IMPULSIVENESS AND DEVELOP SELF-DISCIPLINE

Impulsiveness means that a person may be hasty in making decisions, vacillates, has a poor ability to plan, tends to take chances, has an inability to break bad habits, jumps from one thing to another, has poor control, and is not persistent in sticking with activities or programs that may help him. Sometimes an impulsive person tends to be nervous, depressed, subjective, and critical.

There are many reasons why people are impulsive. Some have never learned how to plan their activities or lives, either because they have been too dependent upon others, or simply because it was easier and less of a struggle not to follow through with plans. Often this person is giving in to immature desires and drives, and has not learned how to postpone fulfillment of his immediate needs or desires. These people often live for the moment, and because of this infringe upon the needs and feelings of others. (For an excellent description of this problem read pages 125-29 of *Your Inner Child of the Past* by Hugh Missildine.)

It is important to understand and realize that a person who is impulsive brings this impulsiveness with him even when he is trying to improve in this area. This means that it will be more difficult for him to stick to any program or plan of change because of his tendency to jump around.

Suggestions for improving in the area of impulsiveness:

1. Make a complete list of the areas of your life or the goals of your life in which you would like to see improvement or achievement. Stick with making the list until you have finished it. Sit down and do this; do not let anything take you away from completing this assignment.

2. For each item on your list, give two or three suggestions as to how you could improve that area of your life.

3. Pick one of the simpler tasks or areas of improvement, and make a specific, step-by-step plan for accomplishing the improvement. Make it simple and realistic, but commit yourself to follow it until completed.

4. Before you make any decision, be sure that you have thought it through. Do not make any decision on the spur of the moment. Make a list of the pros and cons. Avoid snap judgments.

5. Plan your day's work in advance. Do not try to do too much; what you plan should be realistic and within reach. Tackle the hardest job first and get it over with. This way your day should get easier and easier. Stop at intervals during the day and evaluate how you are doing.

6. When a difficult task is facing you, don't skirt around the edges of it; plunge right into it.

7. If you find, at the end of a day or a week, that you have continued to jump around and that you are not following through, you need to make a chart or a time schedule. This will help you keep track of how you spend your time, what you do that gets you off the task at hand, and why you choose to leave what you were doing originally.

8. In learning to become a more disciplined person, do not be discouraged by setbacks. Learn to profit from these, and do not repeat the same mistakes.

9. If you fall back into your old pattern, ask yourself these questions:
   a. Is this what I really want?
   b. What will this accomplish?
   c. Why did I go back to the old pattern?
   d. How soon will I go back to my new way or new program of being more disciplined?
   e. What can I do this time to help keep me from reverting again to my old pattern?

10. Make a list of the ways in which you are efficient and a list of the ways in which you are inefficient. Begin making necessary changes.

11. Look at all the activities of your life and decide if you have a proper balance between work, exercise, recreation, self-improvement, and rest.

12. Take a hard look at the reasons why you were impulsive in the past. Were any justifiable? Are there any present situations which bring you embarrassment or discomfort because of your impulsive behavior?

13. Read, study, and memorize the following scripture. Write in your own words what these verses mean for you in light of being impulsive.
   Proverbs 15:28
   1 Corinthians 14:40; 15:58
   Philippians 4:13
   James 1:4

A MODEL OF COUNSELING

Step 1. Involvement

Step 2. Evaluation of present behavior and thought life

Step 3. Selection of alternatives
(People choose their behavior and their thoughts.)
What plans can be made?

Step 4. Commitment to follow through
(Construct a plan which will be successful.)
What will you do?
When will you do it?
How will you do it?

Step 5. Follow-up
What changes occurred this past week?
What needs to be done now?

COGNITIVE COUNSELING

A. The Event
B. Our Belief or Attitude
C. The Emotional Reaction
D. Questioning and Challenging
   the Thought or Belief
E. Answering the Questions or Challenges

A MODEL OF COUNSELING, PART II

OBJECTIVES
— To identify the specific types of questions and comments which can be used to help counselees.
— To demonstrate an ability to recognize and use these questions and comments in the counseling process.

ADVANCE PREPARATION
1. Prepare transparency.
2. Prepare a role-play demonstration.

ROLE-PLAY DEMONSTRATION
Time: 15 minutes.

Ask class members to observe the questions and comments you will be using with the counselee. For 10 minutes role-play a counseling situation with another person. Then ask for observations from the class.

LECTURE PRESENTATION
Time: 45-55 minutes.

Use the transparencies and present the various kinds of questions and comments. Stop after each one and ask the class how they felt about the question or comment. Ask in what situation they think it should be used.

ASKING QUESTIONS

Asking questions of a counselee should be a purposeful venture. Counseling is not a mere social conversation. The client is the focus of conversation. All questions and comments and even the listening employed by the counselor are directed toward accomplishing a definite purpose. A minister or lay person wants to be of assistance to the counselee, and he knows that he can do so only if he constantly tries to understand what the counselee is thinking and feeling concerning himself, his spouse (if it is marriage counseling), and their relationship. A counselor thus becomes aware of the strengths of the counselee and helps him to make better use of the positive factors in himself and in his environment. There are several types of questions and comments one may use. They are the following. (Use the transparency pattern.)

1. *The Clarifying Question.* This kind of question that asks for clarification of the information given may be used effectively to help the counselee become more aware of his thoughts about what he is telling the counselor. Many people are confused as to just where the problem lies. Until this is clarified, they are unlikely to be able to work toward adequate solutions to their difficulties.

Counselor: Well, where shall we begin?

Counselee: I don't know exactly. I suppose what worries me most is whether I ought to go back to my husband or not. You see, he's begging me to come back to him and that keeps me all upset. I left him two weeks ago and now I'm living in my own apartment.

Counselor: How did that come about?

Counselee: Well, he told me to get out. He said he never wanted to see me again. He was mad, and I guess he didn't really mean it, but at the time he certainly acted like he meant it.

Counselor: Why was he so angry?

Counselee: Oh, I guess he had reason to be. I had gone out with some friends of mine and he doesn't like them and won't have anything to do with them and so he was just real mad about it.

2. *The Reflective Question.* This kind of question helps a client decide whether what he has just said is really what he means. By reflecting the part of the counselee's comments

that seems improbable, the counselor encourages him to become somewhat more objective about his situation.

Counselee: I know that part of the trouble is my mother. My wife doesn't like her. Never has. Of course, we lived with her when we were first married and I guess that was the wrong thing to do. But my mother has always been good to us. Oh, she's not the easiest person in the world to get along with. I know that. But she's old and she won't be here always. I just can't neglect my mother. But my wife hates me for it.

Counselor: Hates you?

Counselee: I believe she does. Oh, I guess she doesn't really. But there are times when I feel like she absolutely despises me. Like the other night I got off work and I thought, well, I haven't been by Mom's for a couple of days, so I went over there. She was so glad to see me and all, I hated to leave right off, but I looked at my watch and I knew my wife would be mad if she had to wait supper on me. So finally I just called my wife and told her I wouldn't be home for supper.

Counselor: You felt you had to choose between disappointing your mother and making your wife angry?

Counselee: Well, yes . . . only, I guess really I couldn't stand to feel in myself that I had hurt my mother's feelings by leaving so soon. And if I didn't leave and get home, then my wife would look at me like I was a worm. And then I'd feel bad about that, too.

3. *Connecting Questions.* Frequently a counselee can be helped in seeing his difficulty more clearly if interrelated facts or occurrences are connected by a question that makes this relatedness quite apparent.

Counselee: I don't know what's the matter with us. We used to be happy together but now we just don't seem to have anything in common. It's all just faded out.

Counselor: How do you think the fading out came about?

Counselee: I don't know, really. It just seems like we had everything in our marriage and then we didn't.

Counselor: You had everything . . . until?

Counselee: Until . . . well, right up to the time our first baby came.

Counselor: You think there is some connection between the coming of the baby and the difference in your relationship.

Counselee: There must be, because we were just real happy up to that time. Then . . . but, of course, we loved having the baby. Only, I think it sort of shocked us when I got pregnant right off again.

4. *Information-Gathering Questions.* If a counselor is to succeed in gaining enough understanding of a counselee's personality, his life situation, and his difficulties, certain facts must be held clearly in mind. Most counselors probably keep some kind of record about the persons they interview so they can review pertinent facts prior to each counseling session. But however valuable these records may be, at times in counseling one forgets facts and has to ask about them again in order to fully understand what the counselee is concerned about at the moment.

In addition, the counselee may talk about persons, things, or occurrences as if the counselor were quite familiar with the concomitant facts whereas, in reality, the counselor may be completely unaware of them. Under these circumstances, the counselor should ask for the needed and lacking information. If he does not ask, he cannot fully understand. Moreover, failure to ask such questions may later be recognized by the counselee, who may then assume that the counselor was not really interested in trying to understand what was being said.

Counselee: My brother once told me that I'd never be able to get along with this girl, but I was so sure.

Counselor: Let's see now . . . which brother was this?

Counselee: (Name). He's the one, you know, who always tried to tell me what to do. We never got along at all.

Counselor: Mmhm. And you and he talked about (wife) before you were married?

Counselor: Yeah. He didn't want me to get married. He said she would always keep me broke and we'd never have a dime because she would spend every cent I made. Well, I guess he was right on that. But I don't like people telling me what to do, especially him. It wasn't any of his business and I wanted to tell him so, but I couldn't. That's another thing — when somebody says something like that I just take it. Oh, I think things, but I don't say 'em. I just act like it's all right . . . That's one thing about my wife. She will say something I don't like and I may feel real hurt about it, but I just let it go and say nothing.

Counselor: What do you do?

Counselee: Oh, I just walk off and leave her. Sometimes I just go get in the car and drive around. You know, something like that.

5. *Confronting Questions.* Confrontation (helping a person to examine the meaning of his actions) may validly be used in counseling when a

counselee is unable to recognize that his behavior is leading him into further confusions, conflicts, or dilemmas. But this technique should be used sparingly and preferably when other and usually less threatening techniques have proved ineffective.

Counselee: Well, I've just about decided to get a divorce. He says he'll fight me on it unless I give him the children, but I guess that's what I'll do, just let him take them.

Counselor: Is that what you want?

Counselee: No, I don't want that. I love my children and that's the last thing I'd do, but what else can I do? If I don't, he won't give me the divorce. Oh, I don't know what to think. He said last night that he still loves me, and he says he can overlook what I've done and pick up and go on. But I just laughed at him.

Counselor: You laughed at him? Why was that?

Counselee: Why, the poor guy. Doesn't he know that if he did what I've done, I'd leave him in a minute?

Counselor: How do you think he felt when you laughed at him?

Counselee: Hurt, I guess. He just looked at me and then left.

Counselor: Do you think you wanted to hurt him?

Counselee: No, of course not . . . well, maybe I do. Anyway, I guess I did hurt him.

MAKING COMMENTS

Just as a counselor purposefully listens and asks questions in his endeavors to understand and help counselees, he also makes comments or statements in response to what is being said. As a general rule, one should avoid making statements with an air of finality, either in tone of voice or in the content of the statements.

1. *Reflective Comments.* When a counselee is attempting to sort out his thoughts and feelings about his problems, the counselor may give some assistance by restating what the client has said. This reflective technique can be very effective in helping psychologically minded people clarify their problems and decide upon an appropriate course of action.

2. *Empathic Comments.* The counselee's perception of the counselor as an understanding person is one of the most potent forces in the counseling process. While sympathy is seldom helpful and, in reality, rarely desired, empathy is indispensable for effective counseling. Unlike sympathy, which tends to be more emotional and often an identification with the counselee, empathy is largely an intellectual process in which the counselor, with minimal emotional involvement, attempts to put himself momentarily in the counselee's frame of reference.

Counselee: (Sobbing) Then he told me . . . he said, I've just lost all the love I ever had for you.

Counselor: (Pause while client continues weeping) . . . That's pretty rough for you.

Counselee: (Nodding) It . . . I just feel like I can't bear it.

3. *Puzzling Comments.* Counselees who would become threatened by direct confrontation can frequently be helped to move toward more adequate and satisfying courses of action when the counselor exhibits a puzzled or quizzical attitude. In effect, puzzling comments tend to evoke "soul searching" on the part of the client without the defensiveness that often results from direct confrontation.

Counselee: My wife thinks I'm having some kind of affair with another girl, but I'm not. Oh, I'll date one now and then, but that's all. It doesn't mean a thing to me, but she gets upset over it. But that's no problem. I don't think we really have any problem.

Counselor: You know, it seems a bit strange that you feel there's no problem when your wife is so upset over it.

Counselee: Well, yes . . . yes, I guess from her viewpoint it's a problem all right.

Counselor: I wonder how you see that.

Counselee: Well . . . she . . . I mean, I guess maybe she's afraid I'll leave her for one of these other girls, but that's silly. I'd rather have her than any girl I ever saw and I've told her so. But she gets all upset about it.

Counselor: Since it upsets her so, it looks as if it would be a problem for you, too. I wonder . . .

Counselee: Well . . . it is, in a way. I know the answer is to stop doing it. I don't see much wrong in it, but still, if she did the same thing I sure wouldn't like it either. I . . . I don't know why I get involved that way with other girls. I've got a good wife. She's a wonderful mother and wife and all that. I . . . I don't know. (Pause) It just bolsters my male ego, I suppose.

4. *Enabling Comments.* When a counselee is attempting to verbalize thoughts and feelings and cannot quite succeed in putting them into words, the counselor can help by making a comment that enables the counselee to continue his verbalizations. This kind of comment is helpful in two ways: It facilitates counselee production and it increases rapport through

reassurance that the counselor understands what is being said and meant.

Counselee: I don't know what's the matter. I love my wife and I'm so fond of the children, but still, I . . . I don't know, I don't know why it is that I . . . Well, I just don't respond to her as I should . . . in little things, I know what I should . . . I don't know . . .

Counselor: You seem to feel that somehow something keeps you from responding.

Counselee: Yeah, like I know what I want to do or say, and still, I don't do it. Like the other day . . .

5. *Connecting Comments.* Although counseling is not designed to reveal to counselees underlying (unconscious) reasons for their behavior and reactions, it must be concerned with specific attitudes and actions. Many persons, far from understanding why they behave as they do, are not even aware of the behavior itself. Undoubtedly, this is one of the reasons for much of the marital conflict we observe. If, for example, a husband engages in a kind of behavior that constantly provokes his wife to respond with anger, he probably will not attempt to alter his actions unless he can clearly recognize what he is doing to disturb the marital relationship.

Counselors can frequently assist the people with whom they work by helping them to see some connection between one situation and another or between one set of actions and another. Sometimes this involves connecting the past with the present in order to help the person see the continuity of his behavior. This technique should be used with caution, however, and the counselor should be certain that a similarity actually exists between one situation and another before any connection is made. Moreover, a connecting comment should be a tentative comment so that the counselee can, without embarrassment or excessive defensiveness, reject the connection if it does not seem accurate to him.

Counselee: One thing we don't agree on is the children. My wife think I'm too strict with them, and I think she's too easy-going with them. But I don't want them to be like the little delinquents on our street. She says I expect too much of them. Maybe I do. But I was brought up to toe the line, and I expect my children to do the same. Of course, I didn't like it too well when I was growing up . . . I don't know.

Counselor: Apparently you see a similarity between what was expected of you and what you expect of your children.

Counselee: Yes . . . yes, I do. And I feel like it's right, but then I don't want my children to feel toward me the way I felt about my father. I never could please my dad, no matter what I did. Never. I always had to feel that no matter how I tried, he was always disappointed in me.

Counselor: You felt you just couldn't meet his expectations.

Counselee: That's right, I just couldn't measure up. And I don't want my kids to have to feel that way.

Counselor: I guess you wonder if perhaps you expect more than they can comfortably produce. Is that it?

Counselee: Yeah, Well, it's funny. Looks like I'm doing to them just about what my dad did. And Lord knows I don't want them to feel as I did. (Pause) You know, I wonder if I do the same way with my wife . . .

6. *Confronting Comments.* A confronting comment is one that tends to bring a counselee face to face with some aspect of his problem or behavior that he has not recognized, or at least not verbalized. This technique should be used with caution. A good rule of thumb for beginning counselors is to use other and less threatening techniques before attempting to confront a counselee. Here, again, patience is a virtue. Techniques previously discussed will be sufficient for many people to begin to move toward solution to their problems.

(Original source unknown.)

COUNSELING PRACTICE

Time: 45-60 minutes.

Divide the class into groups of three. Each member of the group should play each role — counselor, counselee, and observer. While a person is playing the part of an observer, he should listen for and note the kinds of questions and comments which have just been presented. Each role-play should last for 8-10 minutes. This exercise was designed to help the participants become familiar with both identifying these questions and comments and using them as well.

ASKING QUESTIONS

1. Clarifying
2. Reflective
3. Connecting
4. Information-Gathering
5. Confronting

MAKING COMMENTS

1. Reflective
2. Empathic
3. Puzzling
4. Enabling
5. Connecting
6. Confronting

A MODEL OF COUNSELING, PART III

OBJECTIVES
— To identify and verbalize one's own feelings and emotions.
— To identify, analyze, and respond realistically to the feelings and emotions of a counselee.
— To apply the Bible Application Form properly in a counseling situation.

ADVANCE PREPARATION
1. Secure extra copies of the "Bible Application Form" for those who may have forgotten to bring their form with them.
2. Arrange for the use of a tape recorder (any kind will do).

IDENTIFYING AND RESPONDING TO FEELINGS
Time: 45-60 minutes.

It is important in counseling not only to identify feelings, but also to be able to accurately describe them. In order to help a counselee fully describe feelings it is important for the helper or counselor to be in touch with his own feelings and be able to describe them. In the book *How Do You Feel*, edited by John Wood (Prentice-Hall), the authors discuss their own experience of a variety of emotional states. What they have said can be of use in this training program. Listed in front of you on the chalkboard are a variety of emotional states. Write down your descriptions, as many as possible, and then pair off with another person and take turns responding to the various emotional states. (Write the words in advance and cover them with paper.) Describe what you feel when you experience these emotions. Describe in as much detail and as concretely as possible.

Here is one example: When I feel accepted, I feel . . .
. . . good inside
. . . freed up to be me
. . . safe and like I can open up
. . . comfortable
. . . like life is all right
. . . more alive and productive.

You should try to picture yourself actually experiencing these emotions. Here are the various emotions.

1. acceptance	11. guilt
2. affection	12. jealousy
3. fear	13. joy
4. anger	14. loneliness
5. anxiety	15. love
6. boredom	16. rejection
7. confusion	17. sadness
8. defensiveness	18. shyness
9. disappointment	19. suspicion
10. frustration	20. trust

Here is another exercise to help you identify feelings. Several statements will be read to you. Based upon the words and the tone of voice, please write down several possible feelings that you derive from what has been presented. (While you are reading these statements, tape record them. When you have given all of them turn off the tape recorder, rewind the tape, and then play each of your statements one by one and ask for their evaluations after each one. Be sure that you explain what you were trying to convey through each statement.)

1. "Boy! After dating for three years I've finally found a gal who seems to have it all put together. I can care about her and feel free enough to express it to her. I really feel comfortable with her. Maybe marriage is in the future."

2. "I just walked into this group today and I don't know what to expect. I don't know anyone here and I guess I wonder what is going to happen. I guess I'm kind of concerned about being accepted at this point."

3. "My wife left me the other day. (pause) I was shocked and yet I guess I knew that it was coming. (pause) I am wondering what to do at this point. If she divorces me, I just don't know . . ." (voice trails off)

4. "Did I have a time with my boss the other day! You can't believe how much of a fool he makes of himself. In fact, I got so fed up I walked out on him and just left him standing there. I don't know what he thought but that's the way it is."

You may want to go back and use two or three of the statements shared during the first session and continue the discussion.

Take a break at this point.

BIBLE APPLICATION FORM

Time: 45-60 minutes.

Review once again how to use this form. Divide the group into pairs and have them practice helping a counselee take a passage of Scripture and apply it to his life. They should use the step-by-step principles and guidelines on the form as their model and answer each stage or question in detail, taking the person through the application form. Each group of two should come up with their own problems and scripture which they would like to try to apply.

Conclude the session by having each group of two pray for each other.

MINISTERING TO THE DEPRESSED PERSON, PART I

OBJECTIVES
— To define depression.
— To diagnose the cause for a person's depression.
— To identify the proper methods of counseling a depressed person.

ADVANCE PREPARATION
1. Prepare transparencies.
2. Duplicate the questions concerning depression and the Holmes-Rahe Stress Test.
3. Order copies for each class member of *Beating the Blues* and *Uncovering Your Hidden Fears*. Each person should read the book on depression after session 8, to reinforce your presentation.

SENTENCE COMPLETION AND AGREE-DISAGREE STATEMENTS
Time: 15 minutes.

Write the following sentence completion and agree-disagree statements on transparency. Ask each person to complete the sentences and write down whether he agrees or disagrees with the statements. Reveal the statements one at a time.
1. Depression is . . .
2. When I am depressed I usually . . .
3. The Bible teaches that Christians should not be depressed. Agree or disagree?
4. Depression is a sin. Agree or disagree?
5. The greatest cause of depression is . . .
6. Joy is the opposite of depression. Agree or disagree?
7. A passage of scripture that I would share with a depressed person is . . .
8. A good way to help a depressed person is to pity him. Agree or disagree?

9. Depression can be a healthy response. Agree or disagree?

Ask your class to divide into groups of three and spend the remainder of the time discussing and sharing their answers to these questions and statements. Leave the statements on the screen so they can refer to it if needed.

THE DEFINITION OF DEPRESSION
Time: 20-25 minutes.

Who are the depressed?

Emotional depression is probably the most common symptom in our country today. It has been called the social disease of the seventies. Some have said that if the fifties were the age of anxiety, the seventies are the age of melancholy or depression. The number of cases of depression has risen to the level of a national epidemic. One out of eight Americans can be expected to require treatment for depression in his lifetime. In any one year it is estimated that between four and eight million are depressed to the extent that they cannot effectively function at their jobs or they must seek some kind of treatment.

At some time in our lives depression affects each of us. No one is immune, not even the Christian. Some will experience it mildly and others severely. The psalmists reflected these deep feelings of sorrow. "The Lord is close to those who are of a broken heart, and saves such as are crushed with sorrow for sin and are humbly and thoroughly penitent" (Psalm 34:18, Amplified). "O Lord, the God of my salvation, I have cried to You for help by day; at night I am in Your presence. Let my prayer come before You and (really) enter into Your presence; incline Your ear to my cry! For I am full of troubles, and my life draws near to (sheol) the place of the dead. I

64

am counted among those who go down into the pit (the grave); I am as a man who has no help or strength — a mere shadow; Cast away among the dead, like the slain that lie in a (nameless) grave, whom You (seriously) remember no more, and they are cut off from Your hand" (Psalm 88:1-5, Amplified).

Writers in ancient times described depression as melancholia. The first clinical description of melancholia was made by Hippocrates in the fourth century B.C. He also referred to swings similar to mania and depression (Jelliffe, 1921).

Aretaeus, a physician living in the second century A.D., described the melancholic patient as "sad, dismayed, sleepless . . . They become thin by their agitation and loss of refreshing sleep . . . At a more advanced state, they complain of a thousand futilities and desire death."

Plutarch, in the second century A.D., presented a particularly vivid and detailed account of melancholia: "He looks on himself as a man whom the gods hate and pursue with their anger. A far worse lot is before him; he dares not employ any means of averting or of remedying the evil, lest he be found fighting against the gods. The physician, the consoling friend, are driven away. 'Leave me,' says the wretched man, 'me, the impious, the accursed, hated of the gods, to suffer my punishment.' He sits out of doors, wrapped in sackcloth or in filthy rags. Ever and anon he rolls himself, naked, in the dirt confessing about this and that sin. He has eaten or drunk something wrong. He has gone some way or other which the Divine Being did not approve of. The festivals in honor of the gods give no pleasure to him but fill him rather with fear or a fright" (quoted by Zilboorg, 1941).[1]

Who gets depressed?

Depression affects everyone — both sexes, people of all ages, the rich and the poor. Just because a person is successful he is not protected from the possibility of depression. Artists, movie stars, politicians, people who are in the public spotlight, creative and sensitive people, high achievers, and celebrities are no more depression-prone than others. These people are just more visible than others; if depression hits, the whole world seems to know about it.

One type of person who may be a bit more vulnerable to depression than most is the one who has experienced nothing but success from early childhood. One who has never tasted of defeat may crumble at the first setback.

Depression often affects people who are reliable, capable, and conscientious. In fact,

depression is more frequently seen in adults who were expected to be this way as children!

Are women more prone to depression than men? Women are treated for depression two or three times more often than men. But this evidence is based upon visits to clinics; and clinics are mostly open in the daytime when men are at work. Also, our society traditionally allows women to admit weaknesses or problems and to seek help, but insists that men maintain stability and put up a brave front. Unfortunately males in our culture have been taught not to admit weakness and not to reveal inner feelings. It is interesting to note that male alcoholics outnumber female alcoholics somewhat; and the rate for successful suicides is three times higher for men than for women. Men, perhaps, deal with their depression differently than do women.

Ninety-five percent of even the severely depressed can be totally cured — if the condition is identified early enough. The everyday, minor depressive episodes can certainly be overcome. But it is important to heed the *early* warning signs of depression and act immediately.

How long does a bout of real depression last?

Dr. Aron Beck of the University of Pennsylvania has said that an episode of depression usually "bottoms out" within three weeks; after that the person begins to improve. But unless the problem is diagnosed and help is sought, either from family members or a physician or a counselor, the depression could become worse than it has to. Dr. Floyd Estess of Stanford University Medical School Psychiatry Clinic has estimated that a person with one *untreated* attack of depression runs a 50:50 risk of a second attack within three years.[2] This ought to be reason enough for a person to seek help.

What is depression? What are the characteristics? (Use the transparency.)

1. A person feels hopelessness, despair, sadness, and apathy. It is a feeling of overall gloom. A move toward depression is a move toward deadness.

2. When a person is depressed he loses perspective. The way you experience your life, your job, and your family is colored when you are depressed. As one man said, "There's a real difference between being unhappy and being depressed. When my wife and I have an occasional argument, I'm unhappy about it. I don't like it. But it's a part of living. We make up in a fairly short time. I may be concerned over it, but I can sleep all right, and I still feel in good spirits. But when I'm depressed, that's a different matter. It hurts all over; it's almost something physical. I

can't get to sleep at night, and I can't sleep through the night. Even though there are still times when I'm in pretty good spirits, the mood comes over me nearly every day. It colors the way I look at everything. If my wife and I have a fight, our marriage seems hopeless. If I have a business problem, which I would normally react to with some tension and frustration but which I deal with promptly and appropriately, I feel as though I'm a lousy businessman and I battle with the problems of self-confidence instead of dealing with the issues in front of me."[3]

3. The depressed person experiences changes in physical activities — eating, sleeping, sex. Sexual interest wanes, and some men find that they cannot perform. This reinforces their feelings of worthlessness. A lessening of sexual interest should always raise the question of depression. Some lose interest in food while others attempt to set a world record at gorging themselves. Some sleep constantly; others cannot sleep.

4. There is a general loss of self-esteem. The person feels less and less positive about himself and questions his own personal value. Self-confidence is very low.

5. There is a withdrawal from others because of a groundless fear of being rejected. Unfortunately the depressed person's behavior could bring on some rejection from others. The depressed person cancels favorite activities, fails to return phone calls, and seeks ways to avoid talking with or seeing others.

6. There is a desire to escape from problems and even from life itself. Thoughts of leaving the home or running away as well as the avoidance of others enters in. Suicidal thoughts and wishes arise because of the feeling that life is hopeless and worthless.

7. A depressed person is oversensitive to what others say and do. He may misinterpret actions and comments in a negative way and become irritable because of these mistaken perceptions. Often the person cries easily because of misinterpretations.

8. The person has difficulty in handling most of his feelings — especially anger. Anger can be misdirected toward oneself and others. The anger at oneself is based upon feelings of worthlessness and a lack of knowing how to deal with the situation; often this anger is directed outward.

9. Guilt is usually present at a time of depression. The basis for the guilt may be real or imagined. Frequently guilt feelings arise from the assumption that the depressed person is in the wrong somehow or that he is responsible for making others miserable because of the depression.

10. Often depression leads to a state of dependence upon other people. This reinforces feelings of helplessness; then the person becomes angry at his own helplessness.

It is important to remember that once a person starts becoming depressed, he usually behaves in a way that reinforces the depression.

After sharing the following questions, give each person in the class a copy.

Here are some questions[4] a person could ask himself to determine if he is manifesting the characteristics of depression. These questions may assist you in determining the extent of an individual's depression.

1. Are you tired even when you have had enough sleep?
2. Do you have difficulty getting yourself into action in the morning?
3. Do you accomplish less than you want?
4. Are you restless?
5. Have you lost interest in life such as family, work, sex, etc.?
6. Are you unable to make decisions?
7. Are you continually angry and resentful?
8. Do you often have feelings of dread? Do you expect something awful to happen?
9. Are you a chronic complainer?
10. Are you critical of yourself and do you feel inferior or inadequate?
11. Do you spend much time daydreaming?
12. Does your mood fluctuate? Do you have some weeks that are "up" and some that are "down"?

All of the above are common symptoms of low-grade chronic depression.

Severe or clinical depression is often indicated by positive responses to the following questions.
1. Do you cry often?
2. Have your sleeping habits changed so it takes you longer to fall asleep or you wake up much earlier?
3. Do you sleep more than you used to?
4. Have you lost weight without dieting? Does the thought of food almost make you sick?
5. Do you have a lot of guilt?
6. Do you think of ending your life?
7. Do you feel as though you are in a fog and things are unreal?
8. Are you unable to concentrate and do you go over certain thoughts?

66

COUNSELING PRACTICE

Time: 15-20 minutes.

Decide in advance whether to use role playing or a demonstration. Ask the individuals in the class to pair off. One of them should play the role of a depressed person and the other should attempt to counsel him. Or put on a demonstration in front of the group of how to counsel a depressed person. Be sure to use a combination of what to say and do and what not to say and do. Ask for their evaluation following the demonstration.

You may take a break after the discussion.

THE CAUSE OF DEPRESSION

Time: 30-40 minutes.

In a 1971 issue of *Science Digest*, a study by Dr. Eugene S. Pakyel was reported. Three hundred seventy-three people were asked to rate the most "upsetting" events in their life. The twenty-five most distressing events (and those which can induce a depressive reaction), in order of importance, were

1. Death of a child
2. Death of a spouse
3. A jail sentence
4. An unfaithful spouse
5. Major financial difficulty
6. Business failure
7. Being fired
8. A miscarriage or stillbirth
9. Divorce
10. Marital separation due to an argument
11. A court appearance
12. Unwanted pregnancy
13. A major illness in the family
14. Unemployment for a month (Additional studies indicated that four out of five marriages end in a divorce when the man is out of work for nine months or more.)
15. Death of a close friend
16. A demotion
17. A major personal illness
18. Start of an extramarital affair
19. Loss of personally valuable objects
20. A lawsuit
21. Academic failure
22. Child married without family approval
23. A broken engagement
24. Taking out a large loan
25. Son drafted

Men might respond to some of these differently than women, but these were the most significant events as described by the people in the study.

(List twelve of these on a transparency or the chalkboard prior to class. Ask class members to rank the items listed in order of importance. Ask several for their list and then share with the group this list of twenty-five using a transparency. Remind class members that this chart appears in the book they will read after Session 8, *Beating the Blues*.)

We must realize also that a person can undergo just so much change or stress at one time before it begins to affect him. Even moving from one house to a nicer house might bring on a brief time of depression. Some have said that they could not understand why they had become depressed after having moved a thousand miles away, received a promotion, or purchased a larger house. However, they left familiar surroundings, friends, church, and social activities. All of these changes constitute a loss in some way and a natural response may be sadness or depression for awhile.

(To further illustrate the results of change and stress, consider the Holmes-Rahe Stress Test which has been developed by the medical profession. Use the transparency to show the class the test and read them the significance of it. Then distribute a copy to each person and ask them to go through the test for themselves.)

According to the two doctors, Holmes and Rahe, if your score is under 150 stress units, you have only a 37 percent chance of getting sick within the next two years. If your score is between 150 and 300, the probability rises to 51 percent. And if your score is over 300, the odds are 4 to 5 (80 percent) that you will be sick during the next two years. This test is widely used, especially in the military, to predict whether one will be sick during the subsequent two years.

(Use the transparency in discussing the following causes of depression.)

When one thinks of depression it is important to distinguish between the various kinds that plague people. Such a simple thing as not eating properly or not getting proper rest can cause depression. The person who does not eat regular meals or get sufficient sleep may find himself becoming depressed because he is cheating his body of the food and rest it needs to keep functioning properly. College students often suffer from this type of depression. The cure is simple and obvious: eat right and get enough sleep.[5] This principle is in keeping with the scriptural teaching that the believer's body is the temple of the Holy Spirit. Eating the right type of food and eating it regularly honors the Spirit. See Romans 12:1.

Reactions to certain drugs can affect a person's moods. Medications administered to correct a physical disturbance may cause a chemical change in the body that brings on the blues. All drugs affect the body and the mental processes in some way. If a drug results in brain or nervous system toxicity, extreme depression could be the result. If a person takes too much of a drug or sedative over an extended period of time, he may be a candidate for toxic depression. The symptoms are listlessness, indifference, and difficulty in concentrating. Often the person evidences odd and illogical thought patterns which interfere with his normally good judgment. In many cases the depression and drug toxicity will clear up in a day or so after the drug is no longer in the system.[6]

If a person who is taking any kind of medication becomes depressed, whether the medication was prescribed by a doctor or not, he should seek his physician's advice. The doctor may want to change the dosage or the medication. It is unwise to prescribe medication for oneself.

There are many physical causes for depression. Infections of the brain or nervous system, generalized body infections, hepatitis, and hypoglycemia can cause depression. Glandular disorders, a low thyroid condition, hyperthryoidism, excessive ovarian hormonal irregularities, and an imbalance of secretions from the adrenal or pituitary glands also cause a type of depression. Usually other symptoms and bodily changes are also in evidence.

Repressed anger turned inward upon oneself will lead to depression. In fact repressed anger is commonly used as a synonym for depression. This type of anger has been turned from its original source to the inner person.

Reactive depression, usually called grief depression, immediately follows the loss of a loved one, a job or some important opportunity. The intensity of this type of depression is greater immediately after the loss and lessens as the weeks go by. During this time the person's usual functions of living may be impaired but he can still operate within normal limits. There is a sense of emptiness because of the loss. For the most part, however, his feelings about himself and his self-esteem remain the same. We expect this type of grief depression when a person loses a loved one or even a close friend. Grief is very important in helping a person regain his full functioning capabilities.[7]

Jesus Himself experienced the depth of these feelings when He was in the garden: "And talking with Him Peter and the two sons of Zebedee, He began to show grief and distress of mind and was deeply depressed. Then He said to them, My soul is very sad and deeply grieved, so that I am almost dying of sorrow . . ." (Matt. 26:37-38).

Another major type of depression is biochemical or endogenous — generated internally. It is caused by a disturbance in the body's chemical system. Depression results when the brain and part of the nervous system become disorganized and no longer function normally.

Today more and more researchers and writers are emphasizing the role of our thought life in causing depression. Faulty and negative thinking is at the root of much depression. The thinking pattern discussed here is that found in the person who has a low self-concept or self-image. This low self-esteem leads to depression; then, when the person is depressed, the low self-image is reinforced and intensified; and that feeds the depression.

To best describe the thinking process of a depressed individual, consider these three faulty patterns of thought which distort the individual's total view of life. We will call this pattern the *Depressive Triad.* (Use the transparency pattern.)

The first part of the Depressive Triad is concerned with a person looking at his experiences in a negative manner. This gives him a negative view of the world. He interprets (whether right or wrong) his interactions with the world as representing defeat, disparagement, or deprivation. All of life is filled with burdens and obstacles and these detract from the person. *Negative thinking can lead a person into depression. And when he is depressed he continues to think more and more negatively, which reinforces the depression.*

The person with a negative view of the world interprets his experiences as actually detracting from himself. Even neutral experiences are interpreted in a negative manner. A neutral attitude on the part of a friend is seen as rejection. A neutral comment is interpreted as a hostile remark. His thinking pattern is clouded by reading into the remarks of others that which fits his previously drawn negative conclusions. He makes assumptions and selective abstractions, generalizes, and magnifies events and remarks way out of proportion. He is so predisposed to negative thinking that he automatically makes negative interpretations of situations.

Depression is a form of coping. When a person has intolerable feelings of self-hatred, he can become depressed to obscure the pain. This coping is like playing dead emotionally. Depression can serve to keep feelings from tearing us apart with grief, despair, and rage. The depression is helpful to overcome this but the cost is high, for depression depresses everything.

Perhaps another variation of the negative thinking problem is the unrealistic expectation cause for depression. Some have an expectation called the *perfect self*. They have thoughts such as "I must be the perfect mother, the perfect wife. I must say all of the right things. I must have a perfect house," etc. But unfortunately no person alive is perfect. When one fails to be the perfect self, he becomes the *despised self*. And when he feels like the despised self, he is totally despicable and unacceptable. This individual may feel despised by others but in all truth it is he who despises himself.

The authors of *The Book of Hope* suggested that when a person's perfect self fails to meet the standards of how one should perform, he becomes his despised self. When these feelings become too painful, he may choose an automatic numbing process — a novocaine reaction — to relieve the pain. This is depession. But this cure may be as damaging as the cause.

When the person becomes the despised self, he becomes angry at himself, which creates a feeling of anxiety. Quite often when the anxiety sets in, the person begins to seek the approval of others to save his feelings. If approval is not forthcoming, the feeling of being despicable may intensify. And the endless circle goes round and round.

Excessive self-pity will also lead to depression. In fact, an overabundance of self-pity indicates a poor self-concept. Most of us have felt sorry for ourselves at one time or another. That is normal; but to wallow in it is an invitation to depression.

Another common cause for depression has to do with our behavior. If the way you are acting is contrary to your moral standards or your value system, depression could be the result. A Christian man who has a high standard of morality but gets involved in an affair could experience depression. A parent who does not live up to his understanding of the scriptural pattern in dealing with his children could wonder why he is depressed; the answer could be in the conflict between the standard and the actual behavior. When behavior is violating scriptural teaching and depression results, then we may honestly say that sin is the cause for the depression.

Have you ever considered that achieving success could bring on depression? It can happen. One who has worked hard and strived for a position finally attains the goal. And much to his amazement he becomes depressed. It could be that all of the emotional and physical energy he exerted has left him depleted. Or it could be that

in the new position he feels inadequate and uncertain; the demands for a higher level of performance could be threatening to his confidence and self-esteem. His newly won level of success is not just an achievement, but a new challenge and more work!

The common thread that underlies much of depression is loss. Whenever a person experiences a real or an imagined loss, depression may result. That is why in counseling we search to discover if there has been some loss. Many losses are perceived as a threat to security or self-esteem, since the object or person lost is viewed as vital for one's existence or day-to-day functioning. It is common for adolescents to undergo bouts of depression as the normal developmental process presents teenagers with many real losses and threats to their self-esteem. They want independence, and yet the loosening of ties to parents and the making of decisions creates anxiety and insecurity.

Yet another kind of depression has been called the *"four-day blues"* or *postpartum blues*. This form of depression is usually experienced by a mother after the birth of a child. Many husbands have difficulty handling this kind of depression because they cannot understand why it occurs. There could be several reasons why a mother experiences this depression. Hormonal disturbances or drugs which the woman has taken could contribute to depression.

Physical exhaustion could also be a contributing factor. A woman who is a perfectionist may have difficulty adjusting to the arrival of a noisy, dirty, and demanding child. She would like to be the perfect mother with the perfect child and finds it difficult to cope with reality.

Perhaps the wife has had an idealized picture of what it would be like to have a child and the responsibility begins to weigh heavily upon her. Now that she has a home, a husband, and a child, she may begin to question her ability to handle all of these responsibilities. All of these new responsibilities may also bring about a change in her self-concept. Uncertainty can contribute to this state too.

Another aspect of this problem may be that she thinks a mother should feel pride and satisfaction at the birth of a healthy child, and when she does not, she begins to question herself and consider herself a failure or a poor mother.

Is depression in itself a sin? No! It is an indication of some other disturbance occurring in a person's life. In fact, the only healthy reaction to many life situations is depression. Becoming depressed is a common psychological response to stress. We cope with the stresses of life on both a physical and a psychological level; every thought and feeling can produce a change in the chemistry of the nervous system. When we look at the numerous causes for depression you will see the extent of this relationship.

Dr. Frederic Flach has suggested that most people in our society are very well defended against knowing themselves. And any event or change in a person's life that forces him to break any of his defenses can be painful. To experience acute depression can be an opportunity for a person to become more whole than he was before.

Dr. Theodore Rubin has stated that being depressed is a signal that a change is indicated. This can be one of the most constructive times in a person's life if he responds to the signals. It can clear the air and help a person rid himself of years of accumulated anger and hurt. By doing this the depressed person can move toward feeling warmth and love, and can re-evaluate how he is thinking and responding.

Elizabeth Skoglund, in her book *The Whole Christian*, said, "Many Christians seem to think that they are always to be the opposite of depressed, that is, happy and joyful. The rightness or wrongness of that viewpoint lies in one's definition of those words. A light sort of continued 'up' feeling is not, in my opinion, what God expects of us; and to teach that this is a necessary characteristic of a good Christian is to cause great discouragement and guilt. What God does give to a Christian is a settled sense of contentment. One person who has suffered greatly said with tears: "I am glad God has used my pain to bring something good into this world, and if I could choose to change it all and lose the good, I would not change even the pain. But I did not like the pain nor do I like it now.' She was content but not masochistically happy over suffering. At times she had been depressed and frightened, but never had she lost that deep sense of God's control and strength in her life. Such an attitude reminds one of Paul's words: 'We are troubled on every side, yet not distressed; we are perplexed, but not in despair; persecuted, but not forsaken; cast down, but not destroyed' (II Cor. 4:8,9 KJV)."[8]

In many cases depression is the healthiest response to what a person is doing to his life. Depression is a normal reaction to what is happening to him psychologically and physically. Depression is a scream, a message to him that he has neglected some area of his life. He should listen to his depression, for it is telling him something that he needs to know. *Depression is a signal that something in his life is not right;* he ought to respond to the message.

As we look at the scripture, both Moses and Elijah give us clear examples of some of the causes of depression that we have just been considering. They especially illustrate the kind of thinking pattern evident in depression. Read Numbers 11:10-15.

Moses was complaining to the Lord: "Why me? Why must I have this burden?" He actually believed he was carrying the burden himself; at the same time he was reflecting his feelings of inferiority (see vv. 14-15). It is interesting that men can be reluctant to relinquish tasks or authority to others even though the amount of work they place upon themselves is unbearable. Because of this inability to delegate, everything looms out of perspective. God dealt with Moses in a very simple manner — He divided up the labor among the elders of Israel. There are times when people wouldn't have to experience depression if they would quit attempting to do it all themselves and would call for help.

Elijah is a classic example of the tortures of depression. Elijah's despondency moved him to the point of wanting to die (1 Kings 18-19). Elijah was an example of a man who misinterpreted a situation and saw only certain elements of it. He had misconceptions concerning himself, God, and others. This happened partly because of his tremendous emotional and physical exhaustion.

Elijah had an intense emotional experience in the demonstration of the power of God. Perhaps he expected that everyone would turn to the true God, and was disappointed when Jezebel was still so hostile. He was physically exhausted because of the encounter on Mount Carmel and his twenty-mile race before the king's chariot. When Jezebel threatened his life he became frightened. He probably spent time dwelling upon the threat (and forgetting about God's power which had just been demonstrated). Fearing for his life, he left familiar surroundings and cut himself off from his friends. All of these factors led to the depression. The distortion of his thinking is evident in his idea that he was the only one left, the only one who was faithful to God. He was convinced that the whole world was against him. Possibly he had some self-pity which helped him to lose perspective.

But the graciousness of the Lord is evident in this account. Nowhere did God berate Elijah for being depressed, or tell him to confess his depression as a sin! Instead He sent an angel to minister to Elijah. The prophet slept and was given food. God allowed Elijah to "get everything

70

off his chest." The prophet told God his complaint and concern. Then God did two things: He pointed out to Elijah the actual reality of the situation; and He asked Elijah to get into action — He gave him an assignment. This account of Elijah helps us see the various causes of depression; it also gives us an insight as to how God responds to a depressed person.

Depression does not have to be the end of the world, even though to the depressed individual it appears that way. There are ways to cope and ways to counteract the causes of depression. This can be an opportunity for change and growth as the causes are pinpointed and steps are taken to rebuild the areas of life that are causing problems.

STATEMENTS AND QUESTIONS TO USE WHEN HELPING A DEPRESSED PERSON

Time: 5-10 minutes.

Ask class members to write down questions and statements they would use in helping a depressed person. These could be opening statements or questions to use throughout the counseling session. Ask several to share their responses.

Close with prayer.

REFERENCES
1. H. Norman Wright, *The Christian Use of Emotional Power* (Old Tappan, N.J.: Fleming H. Revell, 1974), p. 76.

2. "When the Blues Really Get You Down," *Better Homes and Gardens*, January, 1974.

3. Frederic F. Flach, *The Secret Strength of Depression* (New York: J. B. Lippincott Co., 1974), p. 15.

4. Adapted from Helen Do Rosis and Victoria Pellegrima, *The Book of Hope: How Women Can Overcome Depression* (New York: Macmillan Co., pp. 17-19. Used by permission.

5. Wright, *The Christian Use of Emotional Power*, p. 77.

6. Ibid., p. 78.

7. Ibid., pp. 84-85.

8. Elizabeth R. Skoglund, *The Whole Christian* (New York: Harper & Row, 1976), p. 12.

CHARACTERISTICS OF DEPRESSION

1. Hopelessness, despair, sadness, apathy

2. Loss of perspective

3. Changes in physical activities

4. Loss of self-esteem

5. Withdrawal

6. Desire to escape

7. Oversensitivity

8. Anger

9. Guilt

10. State of dependence

CAUSES OF DEPRESSION

1. Insufficient rest

2. Food

3. Reaction to drugs (toxic depression)

4. Physical causes

5. Repressed anger

6. Reactive or grief depression

7. Biochemical or endogenous

8. Self-pity
9. Faulty and negative thinking
   (poor self-concept)
   Unrealistic expectations:
   Perfect self
   despised self
   novocaine
   depression
   reaction

10. Faulty behavior

11. Loss

DEPRESSIVE TRIAD
Thinking Patterns
A Negative View Of

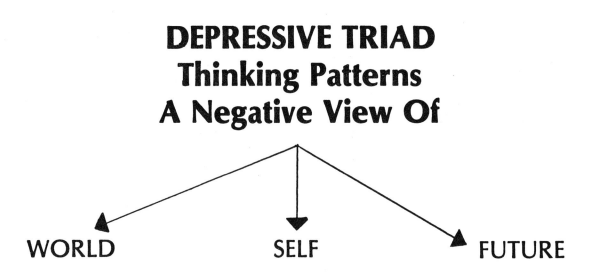

WORLD

Construes experience in a negative way. Sees defeat, deprivation, or disparagement.

SELF

Regards self as deficient, inadequate, unworthy. Sees self with a defect — then regards self as undesirable and worthless — then rejects self.

FUTURE

Anticipates that current difficulties will continue. Sees a future life of hardship, frustration, and deprivation.

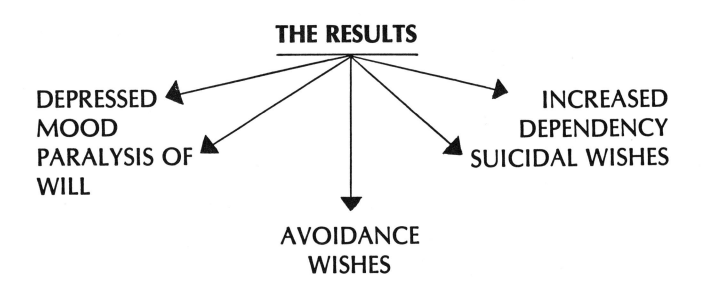

THE RESULTS

DEPRESSED
MOOD
PARALYSIS OF
WILL

INCREASED
DEPENDENCY
SUICIDAL WISHES

AVOIDANCE
WISHES

HOLMES-RAHE STRESS TEST

In the past 12 months, which of these have happened to you?

EVENT	VALUE SCORE
Death of spouse	100 ___
Divorce	73 ___
Marital separation	65 ___
Jail term	63 ___
Death of close family member	63 ___
Personal injury or illness	53 ___
Marriage	50 ___
Fired from work	47 ___
Marital reconciliation	45 ___
Retirement	45 ___
Change in family member's health	44 ___
Pregnancy	40 ___
Sex difficulties	39 ___
Addition to family	39 ___
Business readjustment	39 ___
Change in financial status	38 ___
Death of close friend	37 ___
Change in number of marital arguments	35 ___
Mortgage or loan over $10,000	31 ___
Foreclosure of mortgage or loan	30 ___
Change in work responsibilities	29 ___

EVENT	VALUE SCORE
Son or daughter leaving home	29 ___
Trouble with in-laws	29 ___
Outstanding personal achievement	28 ___
Spouse begins or starts work	26 ___
Starting or finishing school	26 ___
Change in living conditions	25 ___
Revision of personal habits	24 ___
Trouble with boss	23 ___
Change in work hours, conditions	20 ___
Change in residence	20 ___
Change in schools	20 ___
Change in recreational habits	19 ___
Change in church activities	19 ___
Change in social activities	18 ___
Mortgage or loan under $10,000	18 ___
Change in sleeping habits	16 ___
Change in number of family gatherings	15 ___
Change in eating habits	15 ___
Vacation	13 ___
Christmas season	12 ___
Minor violation of the law	11 ___
TOTAL	___

MINISTERING TO THE DEPRESSED PERSON, PART II

OBJECTIVES
— To outline the thinking process of the depressed, apply scriptural teaching concerning the control of one's thought life, and help a depressed person learn to control his thoughts.
— To demonstrate an ability to use proper methods of counseling a depressed person.

ADVANCE PREPARATION
1. Prepare transparencies.
2. Duplicate "Because God Loves Me."

PRINCIPLES OF HELPING AND COUNSELING A DEPRESSED PERSON
Time: 35-45 minutes.

Depression is a complex state, the causes of which are many. There are some practical and simple guidelines which can be followed so that one can help a depressed person. (Be sure to remind the students to read the section in their text, *Beating the Blues*, on helping a relative, spouse, or friend who is depressed. Many are looking for this kind of assistance.)

Dr. Louis Jolyon West, writing in the book *The Nature and Treatment of Depression*, suggested "four r's" which depressed person needs. The first of these is *rapport*. It is even more important that rapport is established with a depressed person. He needs a person who cares and is willing to express his care and concern for him. We can establish rapport with a person by becoming involved in his life. This means talking with him about his family, his business, friends, hobbies, personal background. Rapport is best established by one who is quiet, warm, accepting, firm, and objective. An assertive, aggressive, boisterous person is not always appreciated nor is the passive, noncommittal, noninvolved person.

The second "r" which the depressed person needs is *reassurance*. This person appears to have a tremendous need for reassurance, but often it does not appear to do him any good. Naturally the tendency is to give up and not provide further reassurance, but his need is genuine and it should be expressed again and again in a calm manner. We can also let the person know that we understand his inability to take much comfort from our reassurance. At this point passages from the Word of God may make a difference in the person's life (e.g., Isa. 40:28-31; 41:19; 42:3; 43:1-4; Phil. 4:4-9). Ask him to take a copy of "Because God Loves Me" and read it out loud each day. (Give each member of the class a copy of this form.)

The third "r" is *revelation*. As a person talks with you and you assist him in looking at his life, he begins to learn more about himself and the cause of the depression. These revelations may be positive or negative. One must be aware that both can occur. It is important to assist the depressed person to look at all sides of these revelations, for he may have the tendency to put them into a negative state because of being depressed.

The final "r" that Dr. West has suggested is *reorganization*. A depressed person will reorganize his life style and in some way his personality. As his mood lifts, time will be spent reviewing with the person what happened to him — the causes of his depression as well as what he might do the next time in a similar situation. Actually, the two most important features that can be covered at this time are a thorough understanding of what caused the depression and the construction of an even stronger self-concept than he had prior to his depression.

These four principles are simply an overview or theoretical background. The major question is,

What specifically can I do to assist a person who is depressed? Keeping the first four principles in mind, here are some procedures to follow:

1. As a person shares with you either formally (as in counseling) or informally (as a friend to a friend), it is important to help the person begin to look at the cause of the depression. This could be done immediately or as you progress in the conversation. The various causes presented to you earlier are important to remember and perhaps discuss with the person. Often having him read the book *Beating the Blues* assists him in pinpointing the cause. Perhaps even going through the chart of life changes to determine the amount of stress in his life could be helpful.

2. You may want to ask the person, "As you think about your life at the present time, can you think of anything that you might be doing that could be causing your depression?" This is a helpful way to discover causes. The question or statement, depending upon how you word it, should not be said in an accusing manner but with a concerned tone of voice. It is important to remember too that a depressed person usually begins to behave in such a way that he reinforces his own depression.

3. Another question you may want to ask is, "What have you been thinking about that might have contributed to the depression?" or "In what way might you have been thinking that might have helped to bring on the depression?" You may want to show him the chart on the depressive triad of thinking. Many depressed individuals identify with this chart because it describes them so well.

4. Another question that can be asked is, "If you were not depressed, what would you do when you leave here today?" You may find the person saying, "Well, the department store has a sale on and I could stop by there. And when I get home I could do the dishes which have stacked up for two days. And a friend of mine called and wanted to have me help her with her sewing and I could go over there for an hour. And I think I could fix my husband a better meal than he has been getting for the past few weeks," and so forth. When the person has finished sharing these things, you could suggest that this is what you would like him to do when he leaves. There is probably very little that would keep him from doing these things. If he agrees, work out the specific details with him of how to proceed with these new tasks.

Ask questions such as "How long will you spend at the department store? What will you look for? What are you interested in buying? What do you want to spend? What is the first thing you will do when you arrive home? How will you do the dishes? What will you wash first?" etc. This may sound trite and overly detailed, but it is very necessary to help construct a detailed plan so the person will be successful in carrying out this new pattern of behavior.

Here are some other specific suggestions you could make to the person.

Suggestions for the depressed person:

1. Try to keep up your daily routine. If you work outside the home, try to go to work each day. It is more beneficial for you to get up in the morning, get dressed, have breakfast, go to your place of work and go through the motions of working than to remain home in bed with your discomforting thoughts.

2. If your work is in the home, the same procedure may be followed. Consider your daily chores important. You may feel that "It doesn't matter what I do." But it does.

3. Try to get out of the house, even for very short periods of time. You might go out for the paper in the morning after breakfast or to a shop or for a walk around the block. Try to go to a favorite place or store.

4. If you can push yourself to do it, try to see family members and friends as much as possible, but for *very short periods of time*. Don't try to entertain in your own home, but visit others informally and briefly. Try to do things spontaneously.

5. Deliberate physical activity is very important for overcoming depression. Involvement in any kind of physical activity you ordinarily might like is helpful. It is difficult to remain depressed when you are singing, swimming, bicycle riding, jogging, playing tennis, and so on.

6. If it is difficult to talk to the people you live with, write a note. Explain briefly, for example, that it is of no use to you if they try to lift your spirits by kidding you, however well intentioned they may be.

7. If your friends and family are the kind of persons who think that you will be strengthened by being scolded and criticized, tell them they are mistaken. You need encouragement, support, and firmness.

8. Let your partner know what you are feeling and that your performance is not as it usually is.

9. Remember that severe depressions usually end. Accept this whether you feel like it or not. Each day might be easier to get through.

10. In all depressions, have a person you can trust (a family member or a friend) to whom you can complain and express feelings of anger. Find one — and let your feelings out!

11. If your appetite is poor and you are losing weight, try very hard to eat frequently small amounts of food.[1]

Help the person come to the place where he can follow and practice these suggested questions:

For now, say this to yourself: "Okay, I am depressed. There are reasons why I'm depressed, and they are valid reasons.

"My depression is telling me that something is bothering me about the way I am living my life. While it is very painful, it may help me to understand myself better."

When you feel "down" on yourself, tell yourself, "I'm going to learn something from this experience. And I *am* going to feel better." Say this to yourself as many times a day as you need to.

The reason for these suggestions is to meet one of the goals of counseling a depressed person. He needs to have his self-esteem and self-confidence fostered and restored. His motivation to do and succeed must be reinforced and he must be encouraged to develop purpose and interest in life. It is important to remember that in most cases it is easier to make changes in the behavior of the depressed person first and then begin to modify the thought life and thinking pattern of the person.

The thought life of any person is very crucial to how we respond to life and everyday events. One of the features of the Christian life is the fact that it is possible to control our thoughts.

(Note: This next section of material[2] could be shared with a depressed person at an appropriate time. He may not be ready to accept or believe that it is possible in his life, so timing is important. It should not be shared in such a manner that it increases his guilt.)

When a person becomes a Christian, God gives him a new life through the new birth (see John 3). He becomes a new creation (see 2 Cor. 5:17) and receives a new *capacity* of mind, heart, and will. Many Christians struggle along with their previous pattern of thinking and do not avail themselves of the new freedom and discipline available to them. By activating his new mind and following the scriptural pattern for thinking, a person will have the emotional freedom he seeks. This scriptural pattern is found in several passages.

In Ephesians 4:23 Paul said to be *renewed in the spirit of your mind.* This is allowing the spirit of the mind to be controlled by the indwelling Holy Spirit. The spirit of the mind is that which gives the mind the discretion and content of its thought. The renewal here is basically an act of God's Spirit powerfully influencing man's spirit, his mental attitude, or state of mind.

Romans tells us *Do not be conformed to this world, but be transformed by the renewal of your mind . . .* (see Rom. 12:2). This passage is talking about a renovation, a complete change for the better. The word *renewal* here means *to make new from above.* Man's thoughts, imaginations, and reasonings are changed through the working of the Holy Spirit. As Dr. Bernard Ramm puts it, "The Spirit establishes the direct connection from the mind of God to the mind of the Christian."

The *first step* in controlling your thoughts comes from the ministry of the Holy Spirit in your life. This reflects, however, upon *your own willingness* to let the Holy Spirit work in your life and to stop trying to run your life by yourself. Renewal of the mind brings about a spiritual transformation in the life of the Christian.

The second step in the process is to consider the direction of your thought-life itself. What do you think about? As suggested by Proverbs 23:7, *What a man thinks in his heart, so is he.* As we build up storehouses of memories, knowledge, and experiences, we seem to retain and remember those things which we concentrated upon the most. We are largely responsible for the things we let our minds dwell upon. We are told in Philippians 4:8 just what we are to think about. "Finally, brethren, whatever is true, whatever is honorable, whatever is just, whatever is pure, whatever is lovely, whatever is gracious, if there is any excellence, if there is anything worthy of praise, think about these things" (RSV).

The *third step* is to realize that the Christian *does not* have to be dominated by the thinking of the old mind, the old pattern. He has been set free. *God has not given us the spirit of fear, but of power, and of love, and of a sound mind* (see 2 Tim. 1:7). Soundness means that the new mind can do what it is supposed to do. It can fulfill its function.

The *fourth step* is to let your mind be filled with the mind of Christ. There are three scripture passages that place definite responsibility upon the Christian in this regard. In Philippians 2:5 Paul commanded, *Let this mind be in you, which was also in Christ Jesus* (KJV). This could be translated, *Be constantly thinking this in yourselves* or *Reflect in your own minds, the mind of Christ Jesus.* The meaning here for the words *this mind be* is "to have understanding, to be wise, to direct one's mind to a thing, to seek or strive for" (see Wuest's *Word Studies in the Greek New Testament* for explanation). The main thrust here is for the Christian to emulate in his life the virtues of Jesus Christ as presented in the previous three verses. "Complete my joy by being of the same mind . . . Do nothing from selfishness or conceit, but in humility count others better than yourselves. Let each of you look not only to his own interests, but also to the interests of others" (Phil. 2:2-4, RSV).

In verses 6-8, another example of Christ is given — that of humility. This humility came about through submission to the will of God. The mind of Christ knew God and submitted to Him. A Christian following Jesus Christ must give his mind in submission to God.

A second passage, 2 Peter 1:13, tells us to *gird up your minds*. The words refer to mental exertion, putting out of the mind anything that would hinder progress in the Christian experience. Thoughts of worry, fear, lust, hate, jealousy, and unforgiveness are to be eliminated from the mind. Nowhere in scripture does it say we are to get rid of these thoughts *if we feel like it* or tell someone else to get rid of them. The responsibility is upon the individual. It takes effort, determination, and a desire to be rid of these emotions or thoughts. When the desire is there, the ministry of the Holy Spirit is available to assist. Through the work of the Holy Spirit a person can exert his will over those thoughts that work against the Christian life.

Herman Gockel wrote in *Answer to Anxiety* about this process:

"There is much more to this whole business than merely getting rid of negative or unworthy thoughts. In fact, the concept of 'getting rid' is itself a sign of negative thinking. We shall succeed in this whole matter, not in the measure in which we empty our minds of sinful and degrading thoughts, but rather in the measure in which we *fill* them with thoughts that are wholesome and uplifting. The human mind can never be a vacuum. He who thinks he can improve the tenants of his soul simply by evicting those that are unworthy will find that for every unworthy tenant he evicts through the back door several more will enter through the front (see Matthew 12:43-45). It is not merely a matter of evicting. It is also a matter of screening, selecting, admitting, and cultivating those tenants that have proved themselves desirable."[3]

This is the pattern set forth in Philippians 4:6-8 which tells us what to *stop* thinking about and what to *begin* thinking about.

Many Christians fail to bring into their minds the proper thoughts. Others hold onto the old pattern of thinking while they attempt to bring in the new pattern of thought. The result is conflict.

A third passage, 2 Corinthians 10:3-5, talks about *casting down every vain imagination* and *bringing every thought captive*. Imagination is the deduction of man's reason. Every thought that would be contrary to the Christian way of life is to be eliminated. Every thought should be brought into subjection to Jesus Christ.

The *fifth step* is this: In order to sustain the new thinking pattern it is important for the Christian to fill his mind with those thoughts and resources which will help him. Scripture itself fills this need.

"How can a young man keep his way pure? By guarding it according to thy word. With my whole heart I seek thee; let me not wander from thy commandments! I have laid up thy word in my heart, that I might not sin against thee" (Ps. 119:9-11, RSV).

We are also told to *desire the sincere milk of the word, that you may grow* (see 1 Pet. 2:2). The Word of God is the safeguard against sins of the mind. Solomon said to commit your works upon the Lord. *(He will cause your thoughts to become agreeable to His will) so shall your plans be established and succeed* (see Prov. 16:3, Amplified). An attitude of yielding and dependence upon God is a first step.

A person who reads, studies, and memorizes the Word of God will find it easier to think and act according to the pattern it sets forth, as Webb Garrison wrote in "The Joy of Memorizing Scripture":

"A 'mind set' is slowly molded by Scripture that is memorized and often repeated. Anyone who devotes as much as fifteen minutes a day to this process for several years undergoes subtle changes. Most of them occur so gradually that he is hardly aware of them"[4]

Counseling that focuses upon a person's thought life is called *cognitive counseling*. As we work with a person, we must follow several steps to correct his thinking disorders. First, we must help him become aware of what he is thinking. Then we must help him recognize which of his thoughts are distorted. Third, we must help him substitute accurate thoughts and judgments for the inaccurate thoughts. Then he needs to have some kind of feedback to inform him whether his changes are correct or not.

Another way of explaining the process of thinking that brings on emotional reactions is illustrated by the following example.

A 17-year-old girl was very upset and depressed because her boyfriend at church stopped dating her and began going with another girl. She felt angry, worthless, rejected, and depressed. She was so depressed at times that she stayed home from school and was making life miserable for everyone at home.

If you were to talk to her about the reason for her depression, she would say that it was because of the rejection. This is called the *event*. She states that the next step was her *emotional reaction*, which was anger, depression, etc. However, in counseling and helping her it would be important to help her realize that she has left out an element between the event and her emotional reaction. This missing element is actually the *thought* or *series of thoughts* she had in reaction to her rejection. As she now thinks about her reaction, we can discover some of the reasons for her depression.

She said, "It isn't fair that he did that to me. It was awful. That shouldn't happen to me. I didn't do anything to deserve being treated like that. I feel worthless. Other kids will know about him dropping me and who will want to go out with me now? I probably won't get another boyfriend for months, if ever." What do her thoughts tell you? Actually many of her thoughts are irrational and not really true. But unfortunately they are causing the emotional reactions.

The next step involved in the process of counseling is to help her *evaluate these thoughts* and challenge them. For example, "Why was it awful that it happened? It was unfortunate, but not the end of the world. Where does it say that the only time that we should be treated like that is when we deserve it? Does being dropped by a boy make you a worthless person? Where is the evidence that others will not like you or want to date you just because you were dropped by this boy?"

Taking a person through these steps and helping him challenge and counter his original thoughts will bring a greater balance into his perspective. The person doing the counseling spends time gently challenging these thoughts.

Several other approaches may be used in helping a person with his depression. Aaron Beck has given five other practical suggestions which can be very effective.

1. *Success Therapy or Graded Task Assignment.* The purpose of this approach is to give the person some task to accomplish in which he can be successful in accomplishing it and thus achieve a success. A simple assignment is given at first which is within the person's capability. One person might be given the assignment of boiling an egg for breakfast one morning and working up gradually to an entire meal for himself, and then for the family. Each time the person completes an assignment there is a sense of success and accomplishment which counters his feelings of depression.

2. Another approach has been called *Mastery and Pleasure Therapy* (or M & P Therapy). The depressed person is asked to keep a list of his activities and mark down an "M" for each mastery experience and a "P" for each pleasure experience. A depressed person is blind to the fact that he can accomplish some things and is also blind to satisfaction that he receives. This person's recall is limited and even though he may have experienced something worthwhile or achieved a task, he does not remember it and says, "I can't do anything anymore." By recognizing, labeling, writing down, and recalling mastery experiences, a person is able to see that he is capable and he can achieve satisfaction. He discovers that he has many more pleasure experiences than he thought.

You may help the person list some activities that he was able to accomplish prior to being depressed to show that he has been capable. The same can be done for pleasurable activities. Sometimes a person is asked to keep a running account of his activities hour by hour so he can see the events in greater detail.

3. Another method that has been successfully is to *schedule activities* with the person. Since this person probably sees himself as being ineffective, he needs to be active in order to see himself as potentially more effective. This type of schedule helps him to structure his day. But remember, depressed persons tend to resist attempts to get them to be "busy." You can suggest that being busy will perhaps relieve some of his unpleasant feelings to a degree.

4. *Alternative Therapy.* This method contains two different parts. One is to consider alternative explanations for his experiences, which may help him see the bias in his interpretations. The other is to consider alternative ways of dealing with his problems. By doing this, problems that he thought were unsolvable may seem obtainable to him at this time.

5. In the technique called *cognitive rehearsal*, the counselor helps the person deal with what he feels are the problems keeping him from carrying out his plans or achieving his goals. The person is asked to imagine himself going through the steps necessary to reach his goal and report the various obstacles that he expects and the conflicts which these bring about. All of these conflicts and obstacles can be discussed and actually overcome through the discussion which frees up the person to begin to work again.

A final approach is to give the person *homework* assignments which counteract his depressive symptoms. Often the person is asked to write down on one side of a page some of his automatic negative thoughts and in another column a rational response.

The results of these approaches, which can be expected in the depressed person, are as follows. the person's self-concept can be changed as he now sees himself as being more masterful and he also becomes more optimistic. He is distracted from his painful depressive thoughts and feelings because of his new work and activity. Others' responses become more positive and he sees them as being more positive. He begins to enjoy what he is doing and thus can feel better.

Here is an example of how these can be put to use in a person's life. A depressed person has come to see you. He states that his problems are those of withdrawal and he also avoids others. He has begun a life style of inactivity. Now he begins to give some reasons for not trying. He may say that he is too tired or weak to try and it is really pointless to try to change. He also feels that he will feel worse if he is active and he will fail at anything that he tries.

If you were helping this person, you could ask some questions such as "What do you have to lose by trying? Has being inactive done you any good? Most people do feel worse if they are passive. How do you know that you will fail at anything that you try?" These questions thoughtfully posed and discussed may penetrate his defenses against trying. You could then work out with this person some of the techniques such as activity schedules, graded task assignments, and cognitive rehearsals.

ROLE PLAYING

Time: 1 hour.

This is an opportunity for each member to practice some of the principles which he has just heard. Divide the class into groups of three with a counselor, counselee, and observer. Ask them to try specifically to implement the methods they have just learned. Each person will have the opportunity to be the counselor, counselee, and observer. When a person role plays the part of the counselee, he should play the part of a fairly depressed person.

Conclude your session with prayer.

REFERENCES

1. Adapted from De Rosis and Pellegrima.

2. H. Norman Wright, *The Christian Use of Emotional Power* (Old Tappan, N.J.: Fleming H. Revell Co., 1974), pp. 39-40, 42-45.

3. Herman Gockel, *Answer to Anxiety* (St. Louis: Concordia Publishing House, 1965), p. 156.

4. Webb Garrison, "The Joy of Memorizing Scripture," as quoted in *The Christian Use of Emotional Power*.

HELPING THE DEPRESSED PERSON

THE FOUR "R'S"

1. Rapport

2. Reassurance

3. Revelation

4. Reorganization

OTHER APPROACHES

1. Success therapy or Graded Task Assignment

2. Mastery and Pleasure Therapy

3. Scheduled Activities

4. Alternative Therapy

5. Cognitive Rehearsal

6. Homework Assignments

BECAUSE GOD LOVES ME
I Corinthians 13:4-8

Because God loves me He is slow to lose patience with me.

Because God loves me He takes the circumstances of my life and uses them in a constructive way for my growth.

Because God loves me He does not treat me as an object to be possessed and manipulated.

Because God loves me He has no need to impress me with how great and powerful He is because *He is God* nor does He belittle me as His child in order to show me how important He is.

Because God loves me He is for me. He wants to see me mature and develop in His love.

Because God loves me He does not send down His wrath on every little mistake I make of which there are many.

Because God loves me, He does not keep score of all my sins and then beat me over the head with them whenever He gets the chance.

Because God loves me He is deeply grieved when I do not walk in the ways that please Him because He sees this as evidence that I don't trust Him and love Him as I should.

Because God loves me He rejoices when I experience His power and strength and stand up under the pressures of life for His Name's sake.

Because God loves me He keeps on working patiently with me even when I feel like giving up and can't see why He doesn't give up with me, too.

Because God loves me He keeps on trusting me when at times I don't even trust myself.

Because God loves me He never says there is no hope for you, rather, He patiently works with me, loves me and disciplines me in such a way that it is hard for me to understand the depth of His concern for me.

Because God loves me He never forsakes me even though many of my friends might.

Because God loves me He stands with me when I have reached the rock bottom of despair, when I see the real me and compare that with His righteousness, holiness, beauty and love. It is at a moment like this that I can really believe that God loves me.

Yes, the greatest of all gifts is God's perfect love!

(Dick Dickinson, Interface Psychological Services, Los Alamitos, California)

HELPING THE SUICIDAL PERSON, PART I

OBJECTIVES
— To identify facts and myths concerning suicide.
— To identify the risk factor of the suicidal person.

ADVANCE PREPARATION
1. Prepare transparencies.
2. Duplicate the agree-disagree sheet and the case studies.
3. If you plan to use a film, order it weeks in advance.

INTRODUCTION
Time: 5-10 minutes.

What does the word suicide mean to you? What kind of mental pictures come to mind when you hear someone mention the word *suicide*? Many people do not like to talk about the subject. For some it is very threatening, either because of the apparent unpleasantness of the subject or because of having had a friend or relative attempt to commit suicide. Some are uncomfortable because of their own thoughts about suicide at one point in their life. But it must be talked about because it is a problem, and we must be equipped to help the person at the time he or she is considering this action. Here are some facts to consider. (Make your own transparency for these facts.)

1. Approximately 25,000 people commit suicide each year in the United States. Probably 10,000 to 20,000 more deaths a year are suicidal although the facts are not conclusive.[1]

2. The World Health Organization estimates that throughout the world at least 1,000 persons commit suicide each day. It is difficult to obtain accurate statistics because a number of self-destructive deaths are included in other categories. Because of the social stigma attached to suicide, and economic and other factors, some coroners exercise discretion in stating that a death was a suicide.[2]

3. There are 23 percent more deaths in the United States by suicide than by murder.[3]

4. Once every minute someone in our country attempts suicide.[4]

5. Among males between 50 and 60 years, one attempt out of two is successful.[5]

6. Eight times the number who commit suicide each year make serious attempts.

7. Suicide is among the first ten causes of death in our country and the third killer after accidents and cancer among your age groups.[6]

Remember too that 42 percent of those who are emotionally disturbed and want help seek out a minister first. This is one of the reasons why we all need to be aware of the problem, for if people associate us with the church, they may come to us too.[7]

AGREE-DISAGREE STATEMENTS
Time: 25 minutes.

After each person has had the opportunity to answer each statement, ask them to share their answers in groups of three. You will not be asking for a show of hands or spending time in an extensive discussion with this particular form. It is to stimulate their thinking and further activate the questioning and answer-seeking processes on the part of the trainee.

LECTURE PRESENTATION
Time: 30-35 minutes.

WHO ARE THE PEOPLE
WHO COMMIT SUICIDE?

Are suicidals in a particular class of persons? The following estimates can give us a better picture of this group. (Use the transparency pattern.)

1. 10 percent of the people who commit suicide do so for no apparent reason.

2. 25 percent are classified as mentally unstable. They have a variety of motivations, justifications, and rationalizations for their action. If a person states that he has been under psychiatric care or confined in a hospital, it is helpful to ask if the doctor prescribed medication for him. It is not uncommon for a person under the care of a physician to forget to take his medication, and this can contribute to his state of confusion.

3. 40 percent commit suicide on an impulse, during a period of emotional upset. They are experiencing some kind of stress, pain, emotion, defeat, etc. It is when the stress is momentarily overwhelming that they decide to commit suicide. These individuals are most likely to call for help and are the easiest to help. They will need to be supported, understood, and helped through the stress or crisis situation which they are experiencing. They will also need some assistance to handle their problems and crisis so they will not again turn to suicide as an option.

4. 25 percent commit suicide after giving it quiet consideration and weighing the pros and cons of living and dying. They decide that death is the best option. It may seem strange to us that there are people who actually feel that death is the best option and who choose this alternative. Perhaps this factor can motivate us who know the Good News of life to share it with those who have no hope.

Is there a particular kind of person who is most prone to suicide? Doman Lum reported in his book, *Responding to Suicidal Crisis*, that "Suicidologists have characterized the suicidal person as a 'dependent-dissatisfied' individual who continually demands, complains, insists, and controls; who is inflexible and lacks adaptability; who succeeds in alienating others with his demands; who needs reassurances of self-worth in order to maintain his feelings of self-esteem; who eventually sets himself up for rejection; and who is an infantile personality who expects others to make decisions and perform for him."[8]

In the scriptures we do not find any biblical judgments on suicide, but we do find several instances of suicide which were recorded as historical facts. In the Old Testament we find the following mentioned: Abimelech (Judges 9:54), Samson (Judges 16:28-31), Saul (1 Sam. 31:1-6), Saul's armor bearer (1 Chron. 10), Ahithopel (2 Sam. 17:23), and Zimri (1 Kings 16:18). (Take some time and expand on these incidents telling about the person, his life, events, etc.) In the New Testament we have the account of Judas Iscariot (Matt. 27:3-10). There are many extra-biblical accounts of suicide. Perhaps the most familiar account is the mass suicide of those at Masada who had held out for several years against the attackers.

WHAT ARE THE COMMON MYTHS ABOUT SUICIDE?

An understanding of some of the common myths will help us in understanding what suicide is and what it is not. (Use the transparency pattern.)

Myth 1: Suicide and attempted suicide are in the same class of behavior. Suicide is committed usually by one who wants to die, whereas attempted suicide is carried out usually by one who has some desire to live. Attempted suicide has been called a cry for help.

A few people do not plan their attempts carefully and die not really wanting to. One wife attempted suicide about once every six months in an attempt to control and manipulate her husband. She would turn on the gas shortly before he was to arrive home, and he would find her just on the verge of unconsciousness. Naturally she received much attention from him after that, but it would slowly dissipate until she would again perform her act. One time, however, her husband was two hours late in arriving home. Her miscalculations led to her death.

Myth 2: Suicide is a problem of a specific class of people. Suicide is not the curse of the rich nor the disease of the poor. Suicide is no respecter of persons in socioeconomic class, race, etc. There appears to be a slightly higher rate among white males as compared to black males. Males outnumber females in committed suicides, whereas females make many more attempts. At age 15 there are 64 attempts for each girl actually committing suicide. There are less than 6 attempts for each 15-year-old boy who commits suicide.

Myth 3: People who talk about suicide don't commit suicide. About 80 percent of those who take their own life have communicated their intention to someone prior to the act. Any threats or hints about suicide must be taken seriously for most acts are preceded by a warning. Unfortunately, many warnings have gone undetected or have been ignored because some people had not wanted to believe that the other person was serious about his intention.

Myth 4: Once a person is suicidal, he is suicidal forever. This is not true. Many who have thought of or attempted suicide have discovered the answers to their problems and they no longer remain suicidal.

Myth 5: Suicide is inherited or runs in families. If another family member has committed suicide, this fact could cause a person to be fearful of his own future behavior. Although suicidal tendencies are not inherited, the family environment and examples of others may be influencing factors.

Myth 6: If a person is a Christian, he will not commit suicide. This, unfortunately, is not true. Some have said that if a person commits suicide he is not really a born-again person; a true believer could never become so unhappy that he would think of such an act. Christians do experience all kinds of physical and emotional disorders in their life, and because of the many factors that could cause a person to consider suicide, we need to remember that none of us are immune.

Myth 7: Suicide and depression are synonymous. Most people who attempt suicide are experiencing stress, and yet others experience stress without thoughts of suicide. The statement, "I can't understand why he did this, he didn't seem unhappy or depressed," indicates the belief that suicide occurs only when there is unhappiness or depression. Depression is not a sign of suicidal thoughts. Many who are depressed do not entertain such thoughts. However, whenever a person is depressed we should be on the lookout for any thoughts or indications of this possibility.

Myth 8: Improvement after a suicidal crisis means that the risk of suicide is over. Studies by the Los Angeles Suicide Prevention Center indicate that almost half of the persons who were in a suicidal crisis and later actually committed suicide did so within three months of having passed through their first crisis. The period of time immediately following a suicidal crisis appears to be critical. If a person immediately states that his problems are solved and seems overly happy, we ought to be wary and concerned.

THE CHURCH'S ATTITUDE TOWARD SUICIDE

For several centuries the church did not say much about suicide. Augustine was one of the first to speak about it. Augustine felt that suicide was generally unlawful and indicated a weak mind. Thomas Aquinas, in the thirteenth century, stated that the commandment, "Thou shalt not kill," refers to the killing of oneself as well as the killing of others. In the year 452 the Council of Arles was the first to condemn suicide. The Second Council of Orleans in 533 ordered that offerings or oblations be refused for suicides. The Council of Brage, in 563, denied religious rites at the burial of suicides. The Council of Toledo, in 693, punished attempted suicides with exclusion from the fellowship of the church for two months. During the middle ages, civil law began to follow the teaching of the church and prohibited suicide. Desecration of the corpse of a suicide was standard practice among civil authorities. Bodies of suicides were dragged through the street. Stakes were driven through the heart of the victim and they were sometimes left unburied at a crossroads for animals and birds to consume. They were hung on gallows and allowed to rot there. Superstition and fear were in evidence at the death of a person by suicide. If the death took place in a house, the body could not be carried out through a door but through a window, or a portion of a wall had to taken down. In Scotland it was thought that if the body of such a person were buried within sight of the sea or cultivated land, it would be disastrous to fishing or agriculture. In England the last body to be dragged through the streets and buried at a crossroads was in 1823. In 1882 Britain ordered that suicides could have normal burials. The strong feeling and reaction toward death in this manner has lingered for many centuries.

WHO IS A HIGH RISK?

As has been indicated, it is sometimes difficult to obtain accurate statistics on suicide rates. It could be that the actual rates are twice as high as we know them. However, here are some statistics that may show who is a high risk. (Use the transparency patterns of Figures 1 and 2.) Figure 1 shows that the suicide rate is much higher for men than for women at all ages. In fact, at age 65 the rate is over 3 times higher for men than it is for women. Figure 2 shows the rates for married and divorced people. The rate is significantly higher for the divorced group. At age 65, almost 75 percent who committed suicide were divorced. The rate for single or widowed adults is also significantly higher than for the married group. Both Figures 1 and 2 show that the rates rise as a person gets older.[9] The most suicidal individual is a divorced male over the age of 40 who has not remarried.

THE SIGNS OF SUICIDAL INTENTION

In working with counselees or through contact with individuals in our everyday life, it is important to be aware of the verbal and nonverbal hints people give about their suicidal thoughts.

1. The Suicidal Attempt is the most clear and dramatic cry for help. One who has attempted suicide needs immediate help and support.

2. The Suicidal Threat. Any kind of threat should be taken seriously. The majority of those who talk about suicide do attempt it.

3. The Suicidal Hint. Some individuals who consider killing themselves are unclear in communicating their intent. They may make statements such as, "You would be better off without me," "Life has lost all meaning for me," or "It's just that I hate to face each day more and more." Some who express keener-than-usual interest in suicide may be hinting at suicide. A Christian may ask, "Does a person who commits suicide lose his salvation?" or "What does God really think of a person who takes his own life?"

4. Suicidal Activity. There are many kinds of suicidal activity. Making sure all the bills are paid, making out a will, and making arrangements as though the person were going to take a long trip could be clues that the person is considering suicide. It is important, however, not to be analyzing every person's activities and seeing suicides behind every bush!

5. Suicidal Symptoms. A long serious illness could bring a person to the point of despair, especially if there is no immediate hope or if the illness is terminal. Another symptom is sudden changes in personality, such as becoming very easily upset, moody, anxious, or agitated. Remember too that among alcoholics there is a high incidence of suicide. Agitated depression is one of the most serious signs, as this person is prone to take his life. The depressed person who becomes withdrawn by staying indoors for long periods of time and keeping to himself and cutting off contact from others may be a definite risk. A person thinking of suicide may be bothered by physical symptoms such as loss of appetite, sexual drive, weight, etc.

6. Recent Crisis. Many suicides have been in response to some immediate and specific stress. Each person evaluates stress in a different manner. A crisis might be the death of a loved one, failure at work or school, marital or home problems, loss of a job, a broken romance, financial reversal, divorce or separation. (See the listing of the most upsetting events in one study cited in the chapter on depression.)

Take a break at this point.

CASE STUDIES

Time: 40-45 minutes.

Distribute a copy of the case studies to each person. Ask them to meet in groups of four to discuss the risk value of each phone contact and to suggest what ought to be done. They must do this based only upon the information given in each case. Each group should complete their discussion of all the cases in the time allotted and be prepared to give their reasons for their answers. They should also discuss what they would say or do to help this person. If they are going to share scripture, which passages would they select? Allow 35 minutes for their analysis, then spend 5-10 minutes in open discussion of the cases.

REFERENCES

1. Doman Lum, *Responding to Suicidal Crisis* (Grand Rapids: Wm. B. Eerdmans Publishing Co., 1974), p. 14.

2. Lum, p. 14.

3. U.S. Department of Commerce, *Statistical Abstract of the United States*, Bureau of the Census, 96th annual ed. (Washington: Government Printing Office, 1975), p. 154. In 1973 the homicide rate was 13.3 per 100,000 and the suicide rate was 16.3 per 100,000.

4. KNXT-TV in cooperation with the Los Angeles County Medical Association, . . . *and I'll Talk to You Tomorrow* (Los Angeles: KNXT-TV, 6121 Sunset Blvd., Los Angeles, CA 90026, n.d.).

5. Farberow, *The Cry for Help* (New York: McGraw-Hill Book Co., 1961), p. 25. Multiply the percentage by sample size for a comparison of the groups.

6. Lum, p. 15.

7. Lum, p. 13.

8. Lum, p. 119.

9. U.S. Department of Health, Education, and Welfare, *Suicide in the United States 1950-1964*, Public Health Services Publication No. 1000, Series 20, No. 5 (Washington: Government Printing Office, 1967), pp. 16, 32-33.

FILMS FOR SESSIONS ON SUICIDE

You may wish to show one of the following films during your training.

The Cry for Help — a series of dramatic cases of ambivalent and suicidal persons involving the role of the police in suicide intervention, particularly the case of a desperate police officer who faces the curtailment of his job and is rescued by his fellow officers. For police training, hospital staffs, mental health workers, clergymen, and other gatekeepers. Distributed by the National Medical Audiovisual Center, U.S. Public Health Service, Atlanta, Georgia, 1963. Free loan; 33 minutes.

Point of Return — the progression of despair in the life of a young man and the prodromal signs of a desperate person approaching a suicidal decision. A panel of discussants point out the clues to suicide. For general audiences to stimulate public thinking and discussion on suicide and on the need for a community suicide-prevention facility. Distributed by International Film Bureau, 333 S. Michigan Avenue, Chicago, Illinois, 1964. Rental $7.50; 24 minutes.

The Number Ten Killer — a report on the Los Angeles Suicide Prevention Center and the history of its inception from the investigation of a coroner's cache of suicide notes to the establishment of the center. Designed to explain a newly accepted aspect of community-based suicide-prevention centers. Available on loan from The Los Angeles Suicide Prevention Center, 2521 West Pico Blvd., Los Angeles, California; 25 minutes.

Daywatch — the story of the gradual breakdown of an elderly widow, interwoven with the training of a new volunteer in a suicide-prevention center. A good introduction to telephone crisis intervention and recruitment of volunteers. Distributed by Crisis Clinic, Inc., 905 East Columbia, Seattle, Washington. Rental $7.50; 37 minutes.

SUICIDE STATISTICS*

National Average
12 out of every 100,000

MEN

65-74	38 out of every 100,000
75-84	57 out of every 100,000
85 & older	60 out of every 100,000
85 & older in California	103 out of every 100,000

TEENS

1960	3.5 out of every 100,000
1985	10 out of every 100,000

Los Angeles Times, March 16, 1989. "Suicide, Retired Professor Chooses Death," Part V., p. 1 and 10.
The American Family Under Siege, Logos Research Institute, 1989, Family Research Institute.

MENTAL STATE OF THOSE WHO COMMIT SUICIDE

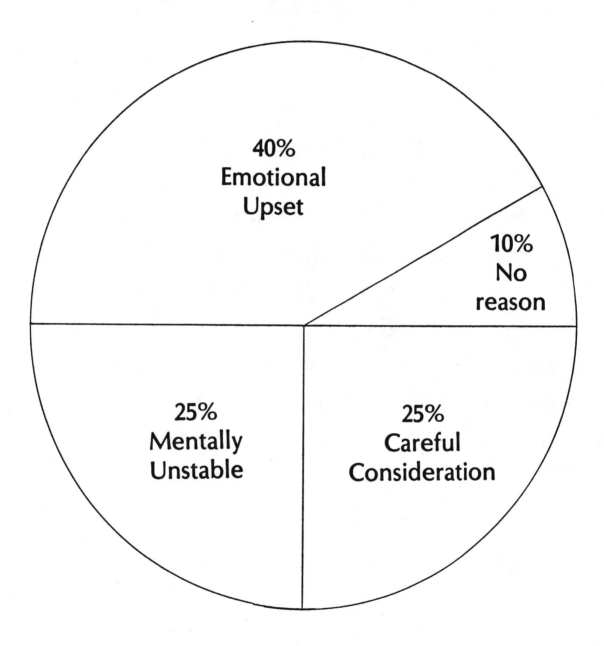

MYTHS ABOUT SUICIDE

1. Suicide and attempted suicide are in the same class of behavior.
2. Suicide is a problem of a specific class of people.
3. People who talk about suicide don't commit suicide.
4. Once a person is suicidal, he is suicidal forever.
5. Suicide is inherited or runs in families.
6. If a person is a Christian, he will not commit suicide.
7. Suicide and depression are synonymous.
8. Improvement after a suicidal crisis means that the risk of suicide is over.

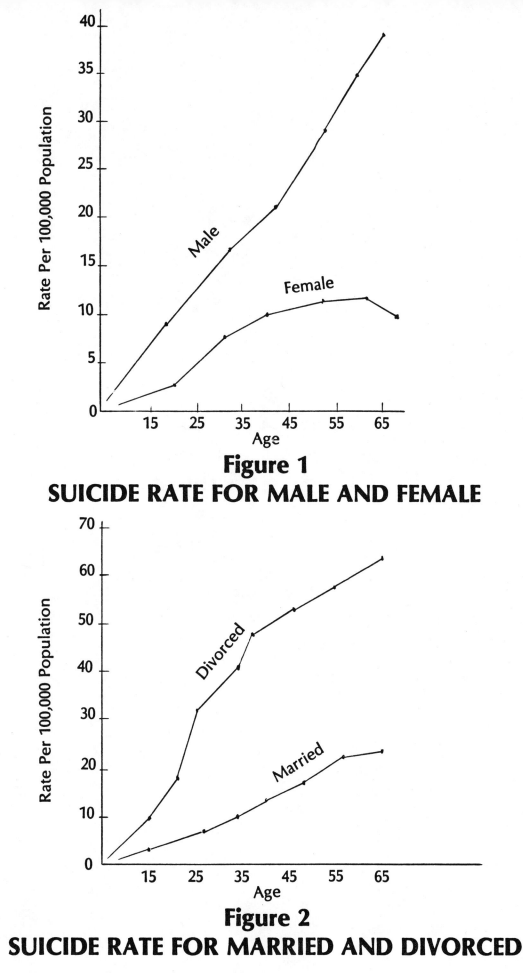

Figure 1
SUICIDE RATE FOR MALE AND FEMALE

Figure 2
SUICIDE RATE FOR MARRIED AND DIVORCED

SIGNS OF

SUICIDAL INTENTION

1. The Suicidal Attempt

2. The Suicidal Threat

3. The Suicidal Hint

4. Suicidal Activity

5. Suicidal Symptoms

6. Recent Crisis

AGREE-DISAGREE STATEMENTS

Agree	Disagree	Statements
_____	_____	1. The Bible teaches that suicide is a sin.
_____	_____	2. Even if the Bible doesn't say anything about suicide, we would still say that it is a sin.
_____	_____	3. People who talk about suicide do not usually make an attempt upon their life.
_____	_____	4. Women are more prone to commit suicide than men, but men make more attempts upon their life.
_____	_____	5. If a person talks about suicide, it is best to challenge and attempt to shame him out of that kind of thinking.
_____	_____	6. If a person is suicidal, he is also depressed.
_____	_____	7. The tendency toward suicide does run in families.
_____	_____	8. A true Christian would not commit suicide.
_____	_____	9. When a suicidal crisis is over, we should not relax, for if another attempt is made, it will be done within the next three months.
_____	_____	10. The person most likely to take his life is an older single male.
_____	_____	11. Talking with a suicidal person about the details of his plan could motivate the person to act upon the plan.
_____	_____	12. In counseling a suicidal we should attempt to bring in the love of God and the person of Jesus Christ as soon as possible.

CASE STUDIES FOR DETERMINING THE SUICIDAL RISK FACTOR

The following cases are examples of calls that you could receive by working on a help line or in a clinic or even within the church. As you read each case, decide whether you feel the caller is a low risk, medium risk, or high risk. You are to indicate also what you think ought to be done to help this caller. Be sure you have reasons to back up your decision. You will be discussing these cases in your group.

CASE 1

A woman between 30 and 40 years old calls one evening saying that she doesn't understand why she feels so depressed. She says that she is alone, complains of not being able to sleep, and her thoughts bother her. She feels that she needs to talk to someone. She states that she has had some suicidal thoughts over the past few months. She cries while she is talking to you. She even appears demanding and wants to know what can be done to help her right at this moment. In talking with her you discover that she has had some similar episodes before.

CASE 2

A woman between 40 and 55 calls about herself and complains that she is very depressed, feels tired and lonely, and feels that no one is interested in her. She states that her husband does not pay enough attention to her. She describes many physical and medical problems at length and says that she feels that her doctors don't care that much about her. She feels that her life is over, and there is no point in continuing to live.

CASE 3

A man between 20 and 30 calls and sounds quite upset on the phone. He is evasive and refuses to give his name. He has a problem but he is hesitant to identify it. He says that the only reason that he is calling is that the only solution that he can think of is killing himself. He states that he has a personal problem over which he has a great deal of guilt. He talks about going out and buying a gun tonight or driving his car over a cliff or into a bridge.

CASE 4

A man calls who is recently divorced from his wife. He says that he is a Christian and wants to do the Lord's will. His wife is living with another man and also has the children with her. He starts talking about what the Bible says about suicide. He states that the only thing that has kept him from taking his life is that he feels that he would go to hell if he did it. He also feels, however, that it would be better to be out of this life, and he doesn't want his children to be with his wife who is wicked nor have to go through what he has in life. He states indirectly that it would be nice to have them with him wherever he goes.

CASE 5

A man about 60 calls and sounds depressed and discouraged. He apologizes for calling and troubling you. He is alone and has some physical problems which keep him from working. He doesn't want to be a burden upon anyone. When asked about his suicidal plans you find they have been worked out very specifically.

CASE 6

A family member calls about a person who is depressed, withdrawn, and has undergone some personality change. He feels that the other person is thinking of suicide and wants to know what he should do at this point.

HELPING THE SUICIDAL PERSON, PART II

OBJECTIVES
— To identify the steps involved in counseling the suicidal person.
— To demonstrate an ability to minister to the suicidal person.

ADVANCE PREPARATION
1. Prepare transparency.
2. If you plan to use a film, order it weeks in advance. See the list of suggested films in session 9.

LECTURE PRESENTATION
Time: 35-45 minutes.

HOW TO MINISTER TO THE SUICIDAL PERSON

Many individuals who are contemplating suicide call a friend or church or agency for assistance. Thus the procedure shared here focuses upon a plan to minister to those who call. The same principles can be used in face-to-face contact with someone who in the midst of his counseling session indicates suicidal thoughts or intentions.

Step 1: Establish a relationship, maintain contact with the person, establish rapport, and obtain information.

For many people suicide is a gradual process while under stress. They begin to seek solutions to their problem and they try alternative 1, then alternatives 2, 3, 4, and 5, and perhaps several others, all without success, and then arrive at the solution of suicide. Many struggle against this alternative and again seek other alternatives, but if their way is blocked, they return to this last choice as their solution. Remember that a suicidal person is ambivalent toward life and death. He wishes to kill himself and is tired of what is going on in his life. At the same time, he wants to be rescued by someone. When this person calls, it is important to begin to develop a positive relationship. This relationship could be the reason that he decides to stay alive. Several statements could be shared with the person who calls.

1. You did the right thing by calling.
2. I'm glad you called.
3. I think there is help for you.

These statements are important because they assure him that he made a right decision and that someone else cares for him. This verbal approval could be a way of getting through to him the message that he can make other right decisions. This person needs you to talk calmly, confidently, and with a voice of authority (but not authoritarian), and in such a manner that he will not feel challenged. As you talk with him it is important to find some common ground upon which you and the caller can agree.

A common ground upon which to start is the fact that the caller has a problem and wants help, and you want to help him. Sometimes when a caller is unclear and ambivalent, it takes more work to discover a common ground. It is important to use the word "help" frequently in different contexts. It is important also to show interest in the caller and attempt to discern his feelings. A relationship of trust needs to be developed. This can be done by giving straight-forward, unevasive answers to questions. You should not be fearful of identifying yourself and your relationship with the church or organization if asked. If asked if you have ever helped a person in a similar situation and you have not, be honest but also let him know that you feel that you have the resources and training to help such a person.

In establishing the relationship, identify yourself and try to get the person's name, phone number, and address. These questions should be spaced throughout the conversation so the person is not unduly threatened by them. If there is a reluctance to give his name, do not pressure the caller at that point. You could ask, "Could I know your first name so I have something to call you by? I would feel more comfortable with that." If he will not give an address, you could ask what part of town he is from. If he gives you a general area, you could respond by saying, "Oh, that's out near ——." This statement will perhaps invite him to give more information.

You may find that a person asks you to promise not to tell anyone that he called. A professional counselor and minister have the right to keep some information confidential. However, some state laws (e.g., California) require the counselor to contact authorities when someone threatens to kill himself or someone else, and you cannot make a promise not to do so. But you can assure the person that you will do nothing to harm him.

In the conversation you should also attempt to obtain the phone number of other significant individuals who could help this person, such as relatives, neighbors, physicians, etc.

Step 2: Identify and clarify the problem.

Hear the person's story with as few interruptions as possible. Encourage him to tell you (1) what has led him to where he is now, (2) what is bothering him right now, and (3) what he has tried before to cope with his situation. Do not challenge what he is saying. Statements such as "You should feel that way" or "Things are not as bad as they seem" are setbacks to the person, and they do not really help him. Focus on what the person is feeling and assist him in clarifying his feelings. If he has difficulty expressing his feelings, help him to label them. Try to reflect what you think he is thinking and feeling, as this will help him to pinpoint the problem. His overwhelming helplessness can now be broken up into specific problems, the solutions to which may be more easily seen. He should be helped to see that his distress may be impairing his ability to assess his life situation. When he can see the problems, he can begin to construct a specific plan for solving them.

If a person calls and just talks about being down or depressed, statements such as the following may help: "You seem to be depressed much of the time." "How much have you been depressed over the past few weeks?" "When do you get depressed?" "Have you ever thought that life just isn't worth living?" "Have you thought of ending it all?" Statements such as these can help a hesitant person put his feelings into words. The actual threat of suicide needs to be out in the open for you to help the person!

When a person has trouble talking about suicide he is usually relieved to find that you are not afraid to talk about it openly. This can at times relieve him of the trapped feeling. Suicide should be discussed in an open and nonmoralistic manner. Suicide is not a moral issue for the suicidal person. It is the result of stress for the most part. Many are already struggling with guilt feelings and if a discussion of suicide as an immoral act occurs, it can add to this burden and cause discouragement.

Step 3: Evaluate the suicidal potential or lethality. A number of factors are involved in making this evaluation. As you listen to the person, you will be receiving pieces of information that will assist you in making this determination.

1. Age and sex. Remember that the suicide rate rises with age and that men are more likely than women to follow through. Older single males are more vulnerable. Younger females are less likely to carry out their plan.

2. History of the suicidal behavior. It is important to try to determine if this is the first attempt or if this is one of a series. The more recent the onset of suicidal behavior, the better the chance is to prevent it. But at the same time the need is greater for active intervention. An extensive pattern of suicidal behavior will require long-term therapy from professionals. If the person has repeatedly attempted suicide, he will probably at some time succeed and kill himself. The job of both the paraprofessional and the professional is to help break this suicidal circuit and help the person develop a plan for living.

3. Evaluate the suicide plan. There are three parts to the plan.

a. How lethal is it? When a person has admitted planning to end it all, you can ask, "How are you thinking of killing yourself?" Sometimes the harsh words can bring home the reality of the situation. Shooting and hanging are considered the most lethal methods, with barbiturates and carbon monoxide poisoning second. The lethality of a method is measured by how abruptly the point of no return is reached. People also use explosives, hanging, knives, poisoning, and drowning.

b. How available is it? If a gun or bottle of pills is at hand, the risk is greater. We can ask what kind of pills and where they are. If he plans to use a gun, ask, "Do you have a gun? Where is it? Do you have shells for it?"

c. How specific is the plan? If he has worked out the details very well, the risk is higher. If the person says, "I have 100 pills here and I am also going to turn on the gas. I have covered the cracks around the door and windows so the gas will stay in," etc., this is very specific. But if he says that he has to go out and buy the pills or the gun or a hose for the car exhaust, the risk is lower.

Remember that even if you are talking with a person who has a well-worked-out plan and has the means, he still called, which indicates that some small seed of desire to live still remains. If a person is in this situation and will not say who he is (or if he has already started the process of taking his life), you may need to work out some system of getting the attention of a co-worker. The co-worker should notify the police department who will trace the call.

4. Stress. This must be evaluated from the caller's point of view. To you it may not seem significant but to him it is. If he has experienced losses, reversals, or even successes, it could be creating stress or strain.

5. Symptoms. What are the symptoms in this person's life? Is there depression? Alcoholism? Agitation? Is the person psychotic? Remember that agitated depression is the worst symptom. It stress factors and symptoms are high, your actions must be fast.

6. Resources. What resources does this person have available to help him? Are friends or relatives available? Are counseling services available to him in the community or at work? Does he have a place to stay? A lack of resources makes the risk factor higher. If the person is remaining at his home, which is a sick environment, it would be better for him to be cared for elsewhere. He may need to be away from a parent or spouse who is contributing to his problem. An individual living in a depressogenic environment would be better off to be out of its influence.

7. Life style. What is his life style? If it is unstable, such as a history of changing and or losing jobs, changing living locations, history of drinking, impulsive behavior, etc., the risk is higher.

8. Communication with others. Has the person cut himself off from other people, including friends and family? If so, he could be a higher risk. If he is still in touch with others, you can use them to help.

9. Medical status. If there are no physical problems, the risk is less. If there is some illness or injury, talk about it and find out how serious it is. Is it really the case, or is it merely in the person's mind? Has he seen a physician? Some who have a terminal disease may think of suicide as a way of eliminating the pain for themselves and the expense for their own family.

There is only one single criterion that should be alarming by itself: having a lethal and specific plan for suicide.

Step 4: Formulate a plan to help the caller. It is important to find out what part of the plan he has put into action and to get him to reverse it. If he has turned on the gas and sealed the windows, have him reverse the procedure. Do not let him promise to do it when you hang up. Give specific instructions and stay on the phone while he carries them out. Ask him to open the door and windows as well. If he has a gun, have him unload it. If it is an automatic, have him take the clip out and the shell out of the chamber, and take the shells out of the clip. Place the shells in a drawer and put the gun somewhere difficult for him to find in a hurry. If the person has pills, you might ask him to flush them down the toilet. If he does not want to reverse the plan, continue talking until your relationship is built to the point that he can trust you.

Then get a commitment from him. Ask him to promise to call you if he has any other difficulty or if he is tempted again to take his life. Professionals have found that this is quite effective. The person may let other obligations go, but he will keep his promise to call you. Your word of encouragement on the phone may keep the person alive.

One professional counselor stated that on one occasion when he was out of town, a counselee called and asked for him. He was very depressed that night and later on it was discovered that he was planning to kill himself that same night. The counselor's wife replied by saying, "My husband is not here tonight but I know that he wants to talk to you. I will have him call you as soon as he gets back and I would also like you to call back again yourself. I will let him know, and thank you for calling." Later when the counselor saw this person, he said that those very words kept him alive that night.

Help the person determine his strengths and resources. If he has committed himself to you and agreed not to do anything, help him widen his view of his problem and discover the resources that he has lost sight of during his crisis. Perhaps there are some other people who can help him. Perhaps you know of some agencies from which he can obtain the food he needs, or the job he needs, or the professional or legal assistance he is seeking. Perhaps there is a neighbor who can stay with him or give him emotional assistance. Be sure to convince him that there are various positive alternatives to suicide. He may not be able to see them right now but working together, the two of you can discover them.

Before concluding the call, your last task is to get the person personally involved with someone. You may want to have him come into the church for counseling or to an agency that you know can help. You could say, "I could see you tomorrow at 11:00 or I could have you see our pastor. Can you come over then?" Let him know that you are looking forward to seeing him or working with him. Let him know that he can find further help by coming in to see someone personally.

In this type of counseling, it is important to convey to the person that you care. It is also important to carefully work in the fact that God cares as does His Son Jesus Christ. In some cases you may feel led to share this during the first telephone conversation. At other times it may be best to share this face to face. Be careful that your approach and tone do not take on a preaching air. This should be shared naturally and honestly with a direct leading of the Holy Spirit for the right time.

Summary: Three elements are crucial to this phone counseling approach. The person calling must feel:

1. Activity. He needs to feel that something is being done for him right at this time. This assurance can relieve his tension.

2. Authority. The counselor must set himself up as an authoritative figure who will take charge. The caller is not capable of taking charge of his life at this time, so someone else must step in.

3. Involvement of others. If the caller realizes that others are now involved and caring for him, he will be more apt to feel that he is being cared for and will respond.

BARRIERS TO HELPING THE CALLER

In order to be of the best possible help to a caller, it is important to be aware of our own defenses which may hurt this ministry of help. Dr. Paul Pretzel, of the Los Angeles Suicide Prevention Center, outlined the following barriers to communication with individuals contemplating suicide.[1]

1. Anxiety on the part of the listener which makes him uncomfortable (and less of a listener).

2. Denying the significance or meaning of previous suicidal behavior which the caller has not made totally clear or the listener has failed to determine.

3. Rationalizing verbal and nonverbal suicidal cues. This is like saying to oneself, "That isn't what he really means."

4. An aggressive reaction to suicidal hints or threats.

5. Fear, which immobilizes the helper and prevents him from really talking about the situation. It could also be a fear of becoming too involved with the responsibility demanded by another person.

6. Manipulating a suicidal person who has "cried wolf" too many times and is no longer listened to by others.

ROLE PLAY

Time: 45 minutes.

The last part of this training exercise is devoted to helping the trainees begin to practice their skills using this new information. Divide the class into groups of two or three. If you use groups of three, one person is the counselor, one the suicidal person, and one the observer. If you divide them into groups of two, one is the counselor and the other the suicidal counselee. In either case, divide your time properly so each person can be involved in each role. The counselee should role-play the part of a suicidal person calling for help. He should make up the situation and then proceed. Have the counselor and counselee sit back to back as this best creates a situation similar to a phone call. After each brief experience the counselor and counselee should discuss what happened and the feelings involved. You may wish to expand this time segment. You may also ask them to practice during the week with each other.

Conclude your session with prayer.

REFERENCE

1. Paul Pretzel, *Understanding and Counseling the Suicidal Person* (Nashville: Abingdon Press, 1972), pp. 93-95.

STEPS IN HELPING THE SUICIDAL PERSON

Step 1: Establish a relationship, maintain contact with the person, establish rapport, and obtain information.

Step 2: Identify and clarify the problem.

Step 3: Evaluate the suicidal potential or lethality.
1. Age and sex
2. History of the suicidal behavior
3. Evaluate the suicide plan
   a. How lethal is it?
   b. How available is it?
   c. How specific is the plan?
4. Stress
5. Symptoms
6. Resources
7. Life style
8. Communication with others
9. Medical status

Step 4: Formulate a plan to help the caller.

THREE CRUCIAL ELEMENTS

1. Activity
2. Authority
3. Involvement of others

COUNSELING MARRIED COUPLES, PART I

OBJECTIVES
— To become acquainted with and develop the skill of using the marital evaluation tools.
— To learn how to begin a counseling session with a married couple.
— To identify procedures in using a model of marriage counseling.

ADVANCE PREPARATION
1. Prepare transparencies.
2. Duplicate "An Offended Wife's Responses" and the list of "Resources to Use in Counseling."
3. Read the articles in the back of this manual concerning marriage counseling and decide which of the materials you will share in your sessions. You will need to know thoroughly the information in the article "Rapid Treatment for Troubled Couples" as you will be sharing much of that material with your class.
4. Secure copies of the Marital Assessment Inventory from Christian Marriage Enrichment, and the Marital Communication Inventory from Family Life Publishers, Box 427, Saluda, N.C. 28773.
5. Secure copies of the tape series *Sex Problems and Sex Techniques in Marriage* and any other tape series you may want to recommend.
6. Order copies of *How to Speak Your Spouse's Language* and *The Pillars of Marriage*. Other helpful books for additional reading are *Why Marriage* by Edward Ford (Argus) and *No-Fault Marriage* by Marcia Lasswell and Norman Lobsenz (Doubleday).
7. For your own reading on the subject of marriage and family counseling, the following books would be helpful: *The Mirages of Marriage* by William Lederer and Don Jackson (Norton), *Conjoint Family Therapy* by Virginia Satir (Science & Behavior Books), *The Dynamic Family* by Shirley Luthman (Science & Behavior Books), *Therapy for Couples* by Billie Ables (Jossey-Bass).

HOMEWORK ASSIGNMENT
At the beginning of this session, distribute to each class member copies of the Marital Precounseling Inventory and the Marital Communication Inventory. Each person (unless attending with his spouse) should receive two copies of the Marital Precounseling Inventory and Forms F and M of the Marital Communication Inventory. Ask them to complete these forms as a couple and then discuss them together. By completing these forms the class members and their spouses will enhance their own communication and also understand the materials to be used in marriage counseling. They will also learn what areas to discuss in marriage counseling.

Ask class members to listen to the series of tapes by Dr. Ed Wheat on *Sex Problems and Sex Techniques in Marriage*.

LECTURE PRESENTATION
Time: 15-20 minutes.

Marriage counseling is a process of helping both the individuals within a marital relationship and the marital relationship itself. Marital disruption is often a symptom of individual problems or lack of ability to adjust to a "different" person.

You will find couples sharing many different problems including some of the following: in-laws, communication, finances, work, children, remarriage adjustments, self-concept, violence, unfaithfulness, time, and religion. In this particular series of sessions some basic principles of marital counseling and help will be shared. But it is important to remember that you will probably encounter many marital and family problems which are so intense that you will need to refer them to a professional counselor.

One question that must be answered is whether marriage counseling really works. If so, what are the best conditions? Based on the latest research, here are the indications.

Conjoint therapy (nonbehavioral counseling in which the couple is seen together) has been found superior to conjoint plus individual therapy, programmed communication-enhancing methods, group therapy, concurrent therapy, and individual therapy.

Marital therapy has been demonstrated to produce at least a moderately positive therapeutic effect across a heterogeneous sample of patients, therapists, and treatment procedures and counseling methods.

Almost all studies of marital therapy have dealt with therapies of short duration. Thus, the finding of a 76-percent improvement rate over an average of roughly four months of treatment suggests that noteworthy clinical gains may often be observed with a relatively modest investment of professional time and at rather reasonable expense to patients.[1]

There will be occasions on which you will counsel just one marriage partner, usually the woman. Eight of every ten individuals who seek marriage counseling are women. They are more open to seeking help. Men are more resistant, proud, and unwilling to admit that they are in need of assistance. As soon as possible you should try to see both parties. In fact, some counselors refuse to see just one party and insist upon seeing both. Others will agree to see the one person for one visit and then must see both.

If you see just one person, here are some guidelines to follow.

COUNSELING ONE PARTNER ONLY[2]
A. Definition
   Unilateral counseling is broadly defined as counseling one person with the view to its effect upon other persons important in his life, as well as upon himself.
B. Problems or Disadvantages
   1. The counselor must be objective, for he has only one story to go by. He must constantly check and recheck the counselee's story and evaluate the results or effects upon the mate or others involved.
   2. In drawing conclusions the counselor must consider bias and/or masculine and feminine differences.

3. Both partners (or both people involved) should (but frequently do not) feel equal responsibility in creating a successful marriage, or in solving problems.
4. Little or no rapport may be built between the counselor and the other person(s); in fact, antagonism often exists until results begin to show.
5. What may be a crucial problem to one person (e.g., a spouse) may be of little importance to the other, or the other may never learn of the problem.
6. The complaining partner may be unable to reveal the true nature of the other person's problem if the other has a problem.
7. Only the other person may be able to add significant details that the counselor needs to know, e.g., the mate may be involved in an affair of which the counselee is unaware.

C. Advantages
   1. It is often the "offended" person who seeks counsel.
   2. He has failed to get along with the other person and feels the need to learn how to do so.
   3. He is motivated to do something about his problem. This is 50 percent of the work done.
   4. The counselor doesn't have to hear two "contradictory" stories or act as arbitrator.
   5. The counselee will have to learn cooperation (marital or otherwise) at some time.
   6. The counselee is forced to view the problem objectively, his side and that of another person.

D. Methods of Counseling
   1. Hear the story, This is of cathartic value to the counselee as in any other counseling. In the meantime, the counselor should determine:
      a. impressions of the counselee's personal strengths,
      b. how much damage has been done,
      c. the counselee's motivation to work on his problem,
      d. his objectivity and clarity of thinking, and
      e. the counselee's general health.
   2. Get test results for general good profile.
   3. Assess his personal, social, and situational handicaps.
   4. Help the counselee first resolve and reduce those problems which are a direct result of his own behavior. In other words, he can stop throwing gasoline on the fire.

5. Attempt to reduce his antagonism toward his spouse or other person(s).
6. Plan the extent of the spouse's cooperation. Use tests to get the other person(s) to come in, or to elicit his interest in helping the one who is actively seeking help.
7. Work on helping the counselee to try to understand his spouse or the other person. Explain his role in unilateral counseling and what he can expect to get from it.
8. Increase his objectivity in other areas, e.g., on his job, socially, with his neighbors, etc.
9. Help the counselee to understand or even counsel the spouse or other person(s) involved.

Often you will see one person whose spouse has been unfaithful. The American Institute of Family Relations in Los Angeles has suggested that the following problems may occur if the wife is the offended party. (See "An Offended Wife's Responses" in the resources for this session.) You may want to have this form available to share with the woman so she does not fall into the typical trap of reacting in this manner.

(After you read these to the class, remind them that you have a copy prepared for them to take with them following the session.)

(After reading "An Offended Wife's Responses," distribute copies of the Marital Communication Inventory, Forms F and M, and two copies of the Marital Precounseling Inventory. Ask them to spend a minute or two looking over the forms. Ask them to take these forms home to complete, and then to discuss them with their spouse (who has also completed the form) and bring back their questions and reactions for the next session.)

The Marital Assessment Inventory is used in marriage counseling and is given to couples prior to their first visit. As the counselor reads them, he gains a wealth of information about the couples and their difficulties. The information obtained from these forms saves several hours of counseling. (Many counselors use the Taylor-Johnson Temperament Analysis as well for the same reasons and to discover possible emotional difficulties and areas of differences. Special training is available on how to use the TJTA. Write to Christian Marriage Enrichment for details.)

The use of the Marital Communication Inventory will be shared later.

HOW TO BEGIN WITH A COUPLE
Time: 10 minutes.

One of the frustrations of a beginning counselor, professional or layperson, is how to begin the session. What questions or statements could be shared? (Ask class members to write down two suggested statements or questions they would use with a couple. Ask for several responses.) Naturally we try to help the individual or couple feel comfortable and let them know something about us. Then several approaches can be used. The following are only suggestions. You may want to change or expand them. (Use the transparency.)

(You may want to spend time discussing with the class what these questions would reveal and why they are being used. Ask how they would change them.)

1. What brings you here and which one was concerned about coming?
2. Often when people come for counseling they are experiencing some kind of pain. What is the pain that you are experiencing in this relationship?
3. Who do you feel is contributing to this pain and in what way? (If they say only others contribute, you might ask if they think that any of the others feel that they are contributing to the pain. Or ask, In what way might you be contributing to this pain?)
4. What efforts have been made to eliminate this pain and what has happened?
5. Describe what you want to have in your marriage.
6. How much time do you have to work on your marriage?
7. What is your dream that you had for your marriage when you got married and what has happened to it?
8. What would it take for you to be satisfied with your spouse? What would it take for him/her to be satisfied with you?
9. If your marriage were really good tomorrow, how would you know?
10. What do you want from your marriage and what are you willing to do to get there?
11. If I were to ask you the question, What are you doing to mess up this marriage? after you recover from the shock of such a direct question, what would you say?
12. In what way do you complement each other? (Use comments that emphasize the positive side of the relationship.)
13. What are your needs? Is your spouse aware of how to meet them?
14. Let's think about the goals you have for counseling. What would it be like if the counseling were completely successful?

15. What is the worst possible thing that could happen in counseling? What do you fear the most?

16. After one person has made a statement, but before the other replies, ask, What do you hope your spouse will say in response to your statement?

LECTURE PRESENTATION

Time: 40-60 minutes.

(At this point in your session you will be presenting a model of counseling which is simple but effective. This model was designed by Andre Bustanoby and called "Rapid Treatment for a Troubled Marriage." It includes some additional material and suggestions. The article by Mr. Bustanoby is in the resource section of this manual. You will need to read it several times before making your own presentation.)

RAPID TREATMENT FOR A TROUBLED MARRIAGE

ASSUMPTIONS: The couple is committed to make the marriage work and is willing to accept reponsibility for making it work.

THE FOUR STEPS — AN OVERVIEW
I.   Communication
II. Diagnosis
III. Negotiation for Change
IV. Follow-Up

Many counselors make a commitment with the couple for a given number of sessions such as four or six. At the end of these sessions they evaluate their responses to see if more are needed or if it is possible to terminate.

THE FOUR STEPS IN DETAIL
I.   Communication
     A. Marital Communication Inventory
     B. Revolving Discussion Sequence

In discussing this section with your class members, you may want to present these three additional suggestions.

(1) You may want to teach the class how to use the Corsini's Marriage Conference approach.

(2) Encourage them as they counsel to draw out the positive comments and side of the couple's relationship which they are overlooking and to also redefine the situation differently than they are doing. (This is explained in the article on "Marriage Therapy" by Jay Haley.)

(3) Present the following material which will enable them to teach couples how to communicate more effectively. Some of this information will be reinforced as they read *How to Speak Your Spouse's Language.*

A MODEL FOR RESOLVING CONFLICT IN MARRIAGE

1. Recognize conflict issues. No one has to look for conflicts, but if a disagreement arises, accept it as an opportunity to gain understanding of yourself and the other person. Consider it a time of growth. Your attitude toward the problem is determinative. Your pessimism or optimism will influence conflict resolution.

2. Listen carefully to the other person. (See Prov. 18:13; James 1:19.) Any changes desired by either spouse have to be heard and understood. If we listen to another, we soon notice that he begins to take us seriously and listen to us. If you are a true listener, others will begin to invite you as a guest into their life. Listen to others as you would have them listen to you. Perhaps you would want to try the summarization sequence. In order for couples to ensure that each spouse is being heard accurately, they sometimes find it helpful for one to summarize the content of what the other has said before responding to his statement. This process can encourage a person to say what he really wants his spouse to hear. When the emphasis is on listening and understanding, accusations and insults tend to be replaced by positive statements.

3. Select the most appropriate time. (See Prov. 15:23.) It is very important to select a time that will allow for the greatest understanding and cooperative effort. If you are hungry, physically exhausted, emotionally upset, or have a limited time before an appointment, real problem solving should be postponed.

Be sure, however, that the subject or issue is defined so you both know what it is that you need to talk about, and be sure that both of you understand when it is that you will get together to discuss it.   The word *later* is not sufficient, because each person has a different conception of when later is. By setting a time you will have time to practice what you want to say, how you want to say it, and to reflect upon your feelings and basic needs before trying to seek a solution to the problem.

4. Specifically define the problem or conflict issue. Look for the relationship between the problem as you see it and the underlying basic psychological need from which it might have arisen. Put your feelings down in writing. This may take time and energy, but it produces a much better understanding of how the problem relates to unfulfilled needs. As you define the problem, consider both your own and the other person's behavior, and the situation or environment in which the behavior occurs. How do *you* define the problem? How do you think the other person defines the problem? In your opinion, what behaviors contribute to the conflict? What behaviors do you think the other person sees as contributing to the conflict? What are the issues of agreement and disagreement in this conflict? The more narrowly the conflict is defined, the easier conflict resolution will be.

5. Identify your own contribution to the problem. This step was briefly considered above. In resolving a conflict you are basically saying to another person that *"we"* have a problem. You may think that he is part of the conflict, but he might not think so. The way in which you approach him and the words that you use will be very important here. If you believe that "we" have a problem, then you are probably contributing to it. *When you accept some responsibility for a problem, your partner perceives a willingness to cooperate and will probably be much more open to the discussion.*

As you consider what you are going to say to the other person, here are some practical steps to follow:

• Choose one word that best indicates what you want to talk about.

• State the word or subject that you want to talk about in one complete sentence. Be precise and specific. Try not to blame, ridicule, or attack your partner, and do not overload him with too much information all at once.

• Take responsibility for the problem, and tell your partner the reason that you are bringing this matter up for discussion. For example, "I have a problem. I have something that is a little difficult for me to talk about, but our relationship is very important to me, and by talking about it I feel that we will have a better relationship. I feel that —— is the problem, and this is what I am contributing to it ———. I would like to hear what you think and how you feel about it." Any statement similar to this is a very healthy way of expressing yourself and approaching what otherwise might be an explosive confrontation.

If your partner approaches you in this manner, respond by saying, "Thank you for telling me. If I understand what you feel, the problem is ———. I can agree that you feel this way." Restate the problem to make sure you have correctly understood your partner.

The conflict may be the result of a specific behavior of the other person. Take, for example, a husband who does not pick up after himself. His wife approaches him with a typical response: "Time after time I've asked you to pick up your things. Good grief! You couldn't be this sloppy at

work or you wouldn't keep your job. I'm sick of this. I'm not picking up one more item around here after you. What kind of example are you giving to the children?"

Contrast her response to the wife who selects a proper time and approaches her husband by saying, "Dear, I have a problem, and I feel that I need to talk to you about it, as it does involve our relationship. Perhaps I have not shared my real feelings with you, but I am bothered by our differences in neatness around the house. I would feel better toward you and less resentful if I felt you were helping by picking up your clothes in the morning and putting your work away from the night before. If this were done, I would feel better and actually have more time to ———. How do you feel about it?"

Most of us are not prepared for a calm, timed, rational approach to problem solving. And yet conflicts are a part of daily life, and we can learn procedures and statements such as this so they can be resolved. Remember, these statements are just suggestions. You must use your own words. However, be sure to incorporate these guidelines and follow the communication principles given earlier.

As you discuss the problem, you must state as explicitly as possible what the other person's behaviors are that you find difficult to accept. You must also state as explicitly as possible your behaviors that the other person probably finds unacceptable.

6. Identify alternate solutions. Once each spouse has identified his contributions to a problem or conflict, it becomes clear that a behavioral change would be to everyone's advantage. The next step — the solution of the problem — is not always clear, however. Now is the time for individual and joint brainstorming. Each should think of as many solutions to the problems as possible. These should be behavioral changes both for yourself and for the other person. It is important to propose more than one alternative, as the greater the number of possible solutions the more likely you will find one that both will respond to and accept. Posing alternatives also helps you to become more flexible and avoid the tendency to think in terms of either/or, which hinders problem solving. As you look for alternatives, be sure to consider those which meet both your own needs and the needs of the other person.

7. Decide on a mutually acceptable solution. After identifying all of the alternatives you have listed, evaluate them and make a choice. If you evaluate each alternative as it is mentioned, you may fail to identify others which may be more feasible. Your evaluation of each alternative should include (1) the steps in implementation and (2) the possible outcomes. What will be required for each person to effect a change by implementing a given alternative? How will the change affect the behavior of both individuals and their relationship?

If one spouse likes an alternative but the other finds it unacceptable, discuss the reasons. Mutual sharing can promote growth and prevent feelings of rejection on the part of the one who suggested the alternative.

8. Implement new behaviors. Concentrate on your own behavior.changes and allow your spouse to work on his own changes.

After you have made the behavior changes mutually agreed upon, evaluate their effect on your relationship.

You may be thinking that all this is too highly structured and artificial to be of any possible value to you, but couples have found that it works. As married couples learn to resolve conflicts and model this approach in front of their children, they too may learn a new method of problem solving. Parents of teens have found this approach very effective too.

Resolving conflicts is not a matter of winning or losing. By using this problem-solving approach, both husband and wife find a creative solution in which both are satisfied.[3]

Step II. Diagnosis (how to identify what's happening)
   Identify the fight issues:
   A. Distance
   B. Power Struggle
   C. Trust
   D. Defense of self-identity
   E. Sex
   F. Centricity
   G. Unrealistic illusions
      and expectations
   H. Territorial aggression
Step III. Negotiation for Change
   A. Identify the feelings
      Negotiate contracts for change
      There are two kinds of contracts:
      1. Learning contracts
      2. Action contracts (time
         limited and specific)
A basic principle here is change the behavior in yourself that is creating bad feelings in others, and you will change their feelings. When their feelings are changed, they will be disposed to change their behavior too.

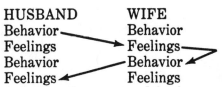

HUSBAND   WIFE
Behavior   Behavior
Feelings   Feelings
Behavior   Behavior
Feelings   Feelings

A suggestion from a model of counseling developed by Dr. Richard Stewart could be employed at this point. Dr. Stewart has developed what he calls a Caring Days model of counseling. This model of counseling involves using the Marital Precounseling Inventory, setting up six mandatory counseling sessions, helping couples rethink their role responsibilities, developing new styles of communication, and increasing the amount of caring acts performed toward each other. This method has proved extremely successful. Follow-up results on this method of counseling have indicated the following:

Seven hundred couples have been involved with this approach. Out of 200 studied, in 87 percent of the couples at least one spouse met the initial behavior change objectives, and in 81 percent those objectives were met by both partners. This resulted in increased commitment to the marriage by one spouse in 84 percent of the couples and by both in 77 percent. One year after treatment there were five divorces with 84 percent of the still-married couples reporting that their commitment to the marriage remained high. Five years later the number of divorces increased fivefold (16) and 89 percent of the couples who were still married reported a continued high level of commitment to their marriages.[4]

In the Caring Days portion of this model of counseling, each person in the marriage writes down between 10 and 20 positive actions which he would like to see his partner perform toward him. These are not negative actions which he would like to see eliminated, but positive, loving, caring actions. They exchange their list with each other. Each person, without telling the other of his plans, selects one day during the week and endeavors to perform as many of these caring acts as he can during that day. They may end up choosing the same day or their selected days may be different. The basic thinking behind this approach is twofold: (1) providing positive behaviors toward each other decreases the negative behaviors; (2) by producing positive behaviors toward the other person the one performing these actions will personally derive more benefit from these behaviors than the negative ones and thus be more inclined to continue to perform them and eliminate the negative behaviors. There is also the likelihood that the other person will begin to respond with more love and care as he experiences these caring acts. Here is a sample of a couple's list of caring behaviors which they desired the other to perform toward them.

SAMPLE REQUEST LIST FOR CARING DAYS

Wife's Requests

1. Greet me with a kiss and a hug in the morning before we get out of bed.
2. Bring me pussywillows (or some such).
3. Ask me what record I would like to hear and put it on.
4. Reach over and touch me when we're riding in the car.
5. Make breakfast and serve it to me.
6. Tell me you love me.
7. Put your things away when you come in.
8. If you're going to stop at the store for something, ask me if there is anything that I want or need.
9. Rub my body or some part of me before going to sleep, with full concentration.
10. Look at me intently sometimes when I'm telling you something.
11. Engage actively in fantasy trips with me — e.g., to Costa Rica, Sunshine Coast, Alaska.
12. Ask my opinion about things which you write and let me know which suggestions you follow.
13. Tell me when I look attractive.
14. Ask me what I'd like to do for a weekend or a day with the desire to do what I suggest.

Husband's Requests

1. Wash my back.
2. Smile and say you're glad to see me when you wake up.
3. Fix the orange juice.
4. Call me at work.
5. Acknowledge my affectionate advances.
6. Invite me to expose the details of my work.
7. Massage my shoulders and back.
8. Touch me while I drive.
9. Hold me when you see that I'm down.
10. Tell me about your experiences at work every day.
11. Tell me that you care.
12. Tell me that I'm nice to be around.

Step IV. Follow-Up

The final stage of this counseling program is Follow-Up.

REFERENCES

1. Alan Gurman and David Rice, *Couples in Conflict* (New York: Aronson, 1975), pp. 414, 421-22.

2. Adapted from the American Institute of Family Relations.

3. H. Norman Wright, *Communication and Conflict Resolution* (Elgin, Ill.: David C. Cook Publishing Co., 1977), pp. 11-13.

4. David Olson, *Treating Relationships* (Lake Miles, Iowa: Graphic Press, 1976).

SUGGESTED QUESTIONS
First Interview With Married Couple

1. What brings you here and which one was concerned about coming?

2. Often when people come for counseling they are experiencing some kind of pain. What is the pain that you are experiencing in this relationship?

3. Who do you feel is contributing to this pain and in what way?

4. What efforts have been made to eliminate this pain and what has happened?

5. Describe what you want to have in your marriage.

6. How much time do you have to work on your marriage?

7. What is your dream that you had for your marriage when you got married and what has happened to it?

8. What would it take for you to be satisfied with your spouse? What would it take for him/her to be satisfied with you?

9. If your marriage were really good tomorrow, how would you know?

10. What do you want from your marriage and what are you willing to do to get there?

11. If I were to ask you the question, What are you doing to mess up this marriage? after you recover from the shock of such a direct question, what would you say?

12. In what way do you complement each other?

13. What are your needs? Is your spouse aware of how to meet them?

14. Let's think about the goals you have for counseling. What would it be like if the counseling were completely successful?

15. What is the worst possible thing that could happen in counseling ? What do you fear the most?

RAPID TREATMENT FOR A TROUBLED MARRIAGE

ASSUMPTIONS: The couple is committed to make the marriage work and is willing to accept responsibility for making it work.

THE FOUR STEPS — AN OVERVIEW

     I. Communication
    II. Diagnosis
   III. Negotiation for change
   IV. Follow-up

THE FOUR STEPS IN DETAIL

Step I. Communication
  A. Marital Communication Inventory
  B. Revolving Discussion Sequence
    1. Recognize conflict issues.
    2. Listen carefully to the other person.
    3. Select the most appropriate time.
    4. Specifically define the problem or conflict issue.
    5. Identify your own contribution to the problem.
    6. Identify alternate solutions.
    7. Decide on a mutually acceptable solution.
    8. Implement new behaviors.

Step II. Diagnosis (how to identify what's happening)
  Identify the fight issues:
  A. Distance
  B. Power struggle
  C. Trust
  D. Defense of self-identity
  E. Sex
  F. Centricity
  G. Unrealistic illusions
     and expectations
  H. Territorial aggression

Step III. Negotiation for Change
  A. Identify the feelings
  B. Negotiate contracts for change
    1. Learning contracts
    2. Action contracts
       (time limited and specific)

Step IV. Follow-Up

RESOURCES TO USE IN COUNSELING

I. FINANCES

Burkett, Larry. *Your Finances In Changing Times*. (6 tapes) Christian Financial Concepts Services.
Burkett, Larry. *Debt-Free Living*. Moody Press, 1989.
Crosson, Russ. *Money and Your Marriage*. Word Books, 1989.

II. DISCIPLINE AND CHILD REARING

Briggs, Dorothy. *Your Child's Self Esteem*. Garden City, N.Y.: Doubleday, 1970.
Dobson, Jim. *Hide or Seek*. Old Tappan, N.J.: Fleming H. Revell Co., 1974.
Narramore, Bruce. *Help! I'm a Parent*. Grand Rapids: Zondervan Publishing House, 1972.
    Also use the workbook that accompanies this book. A tape series by the same title is also available from Christian Marriage Enrichment.

III. SEX ADJUSTMENT

Wheat, Ed and Gail. *Intended for Pleasure*. Old Tappan, N.J.: Fleming H. Revell Co., 1977. (Available from CME)
Wheat, Ed. *Sex Problems and Sex Techniques in Marriage*. Tustin: Christian Marriage Enrichment.
    This two-cassette series is the best material available.

AN OFFENDED WIFE'S RESPONSES

*HOW A WIFE MIGHT RESPOND
IF SHE FINDS THAT HER HUSBAND
HAS BEEN UNFAITHFUL*

The indignant wife is likely to handle the problems as badly as possible. Here are ten mistakes she may make when she discovers that her husband has been unfaithful:

1. She denounces him, thereby increasing the alienation.
2. She tells his relatives and friends what he has done. This will make it more difficult for him to come back to her because his pride has suffered a blow.
3. She gets relatives and friends to plead with him or to denounce him.
4. She refuses him further intimacies, thereby sometimes virtually throwing him into the other woman's arms.
5. She goes to see the other woman and pleads with her. Such pleas will not work; if the other woman were a person of sensitivity, she would not be involved.
6. She denounces and denigrates her husband and the other woman. Oddly enough, in many cases she is probably right; the other woman could be an inferior person. But the moment the wife attacks, the husband will have to try to justify himself.
7. She starts a campaign to "make him suffer."
8. She orders him to leave their home.
9. She tells the children of their father's evil ways.
10. She files suit for divorce.

Adapted from the American Institute of Family Relations.

COUNSELING MARRIED COUPLES, PART II

OBJECTIVES
— To demonstrate an ability to counsel and help married couples.
— To pinpoint and verbalize marital difficulties.
— To describe and share with others a model for resolving conflict in marriage.

ADVANCE PREPARATION
Duplicate the case studies.

ROLE-PLAY DEMONSTRATION
Time: 20-40 minutes.

Prior to this session arrange with couples in the class or others from the church to come and be available for some demonstrations. During this time it will be important for you to be willing to demonstrate your ability to counsel a couple so others can observe and learn. Ideally the couple should present several different kinds of problems so you can illustrate several approaches to solving their problems.

Another suggestion is to invite several couples from a couples' class in the church to serve as counselees and role-play some problems so every person in the class could have the opportunity to practice his counseling skills. When they have practice sessions such as this, hold a debriefing session. During this time they can share their feelings and frustrations and learn answers to their questions. Those who role-played the part of the troubled couples should have the opportunity to share their insights and observations with the one who was the counselor. If at all possible each class member should bring a tape recorder with him to tape their session and then play it back later to learn from the experience first hand.

Another suggestion you may want to use is to share with the class some of the thoughts from Jay Hayley in his section on "Marriage Therapy." You may also want to put some of the verbatim interviews from the article by Shirley Luthman, "The Growth Model in Marriage Therapy," on an overhead transparency. On many occasions this has been used to help prospective counselors learn how to respond to feelings. Each statement is revealed a step at a time on the overhead and before showing the counselor's response each class member is asked to write down what he would say if he were counseling. By doing this, prospective counselors can develop a greater level of sensitivity.

CASE STUDIES
Time: 60-80 minutes.

During this period of time the class members may meet in groups and discuss together how they would resolve the problems presented in these cases. Give each person a copy of the cases with any questions he needs to answer. Ask them to work out their answers in their groups and have one member role-play the person in the case with another member counseling. The other members could be of assistance as they observe and make their own suggestions and observations.

Conclude this session by asking several to pray briefly.

HOMEWORK ASSIGNMENT
This homework assignment is very important for the growth and development of the counselor. It will take some effort and planning on the part of the students. Ask each one to find a couple during this next week who would be willing to role-play a marital counseling problem with them. This session should be tape recorded. The couple cannot be recorded unless they agree to it in advance. If they refuse another couple could be found to participate in this learning activity. Following the counseling, the counselor should listen to the tape and write an analysis of his counseling. Positive and negative points should be discussed and the person should indicate how he would approach a similar problem the next time. He should also listen to his tone of voice as well as his comments and questions. This type of learning activity has been very helpful. Even though some class members might be hesitant or say they would have difficulty finding a couple or a tape recorder, they should be encouraged to follow through with the assignment.

CASE STUDIES

CASE 1

Sally and Ronald grew up together. They came from the same neighborhood in a small town, went to school and church together, and started going steady in high school. When the time came they went off to the same college. By the time they were juniors they decided that they could no longer wait to be married. After the wedding Sally quit going to school and took a job as a typist so that Ron could complete his education.

In due course Ron was graduated from college and admitted to medical school. Sally and Ron moved into a small housing project originally designed for low-income families. Sally, of course, continued to work, but she resented that. Besides typing for eight hours a day, the household chores were largely her responsibility as well. In the few hours that Ron was home, he usually had some studying to do. Sally sometimes suspected that he could have done his studying at school, but then he would have missed the cafeteria conversation and the occasional bridge games with the other students.

Finally the great day came and Ron was graduated from medical school and accepted as an intern at a nearby hospital. There was still very little money to spare, so Sally continued to work, but at long last she persuaded Ron to start a family. Before his internship was complete, they had a child. Sally quit her job and seemed to be very happy with her new life. Getting started in practice meant more lean years. Moreover, another baby was born. With two in diapers and a house to take care of, Sally was always tired. But she loved Ron and she believed Ron loved her.

Within a few years Ron's practice began to prosper. In fact, before long Sally and Ron had money for all the material things they wanted. At first Ron worked very hard to pay off the debts and to build up an investment income. After a while, however, he began to take an increasing amount of time off to play golf at the country club. Sally went to the country club once or twice, but she was a smalltown girl and felt out of place there. The women there talked about golf and bridge, neither of which she played. Ron kept urging her to try, but finally he gave up. With increasing frequency he went to the country club by himself.

Meanwhile two more children had arrived and Sally was even busier with homemaking activities. At the country club Ron met a great many people, including some attractive young divorcees who had grown up in the atmosphere of the country club. Sophisticated and charming, they had gone to elite Eastern women's colleges and seemed able to anticipate exactly what Ron wanted even before he realized it himself.

One day Ron came home and, in effect, said to Sally: "I have found that the women at the country club meet my needs better than you do. I've changed. I need someone who is gay and sophisticated. I am sure you wouldn't want to have me spend the rest of my life with you, knowing that I didn't love you. You are a good woman and would make some other man a good wife, but you and I no longer have common interests. I will always take care of you and the children financially, but I want a divorce."

What should Sally do? What should she have done? Would you advise Ron to press for a divorce, or should he be forced to stay with his wife?

1. What will probably be Sally's first reaction?
2. Could Sally do anything now to meet Ron's needs? What?
3. For what reason might Sally not be able to change?

4. Could Ron accept a change in Sally?
5. Would Ron's needs really be met by a more sophisticated woman than Sally?
6. What are Ron's needs? How have they changed?
7. What are Sally's needs? How have they changed?
8. What would you see as a solution?

CASE 2

"If my mother-in-law makes one more comment on my cooking or house-keeping I think I will scream. She has nothing to do at all so she drops in two or three times a week and tells me what's wrong with my recipes, why I should change furniture polish, how the plant won't grow in that corner, and why I shouldn't spend money on having laundry done. There's never a word that comes out of her mouth that isn't some direct or implied criticism.

"I keep telling Larry to shape her up on this matter. He says he knows his mother can sometimes be a pain but that I am too sensitive too. Besides, he adds, I'm a big girl and can fight my own battles. What do you suggest?"

1. Describe what you feel is the basic problem between the couple.
2. Is the wife objective about this problem? What are the indications?
3. What do you feel are the mother-in-law's needs and how could they be met?
4. What do you feel the husband could do in this situation?
5. Describe what you feel would be three possible alternatives that might help this problem.
6. Describe a way in which the wife could share her concerns with Larry in a more constructive manner.

CASE 3

"All Don thinks about is business and golf," Elsie told the counselor. "We've been married for twenty-six years now, and for the last twenty-five he hasn't paid much attention to me at all. He stays away from home many nights when I know that he could be here if he wanted to. He says his business needs him, but I think that they could get along without him. He spends every minute thinking about the business anyway, though, so he might as well be there. And when he isn't at the plant he's out playing golf. Almost every weekend he's down on the golf course or in the clubhouse with the other men.

"I thought growing older together was going to be different. Now the children are all gone; the last boy went off to college last year. We have three sons, and he should be very proud of them. I think he is, although you'd never hear it from him. He hasn't paid much attention to them since the day the first one was born.

"I need more attention from him now. When the boys left home I suddenly felt deserted and very alone. I turned to him for some of the companionship we had when we were first married. But he doesn't seem to want to be bothered with me now. He only takes me some place when I force him to. He doesn't really fight with me about it; sometimes I wish he would. He just gets that resigned, hangdog look on his face.

"This isn't the way I thought it would be after the children were gone. When I thought about it at all, I just had a sort of nebulous picture of gay contentment, traveling to Europe and to the Orient, and doing all those things I've always wanted to do. Now I'm just terribly lonely and unhappy. I wish you would tell him that he should pay more attention to me."

Don did indeed seem to be resigned when he talked to the counselor. "Yes," he said, "I know that Elsie is my responsibility, that I have an obligation to take care of her. I always will. But we don't have anything in common any more. I don't enjoy talking with her because we don't have anything to talk about — not even the boys, now.

"I remember what happened, and it wasn't exactly the way Elsie said. When the first boy was born, she suddenly turned completely away from me. She gave all her attention to the child; at least that's the way it seemed to me. Sure I was jealous. I knew I was jealous even then. But what could I do about it? After all, he was my son and I wanted him to have his mother's love. So I just kind of pushed it down inside myself and tried to get more interested in my business. That wasn't hard, because I had a lot of problems and a great opportunity to make something out of it. Now my firm is one of the best in the field, and it's that way because I give it a lot of time. I handle every problem personally, and I know all the men and all their troubles. Sure, I like to play a little golf on the weekends. I'm one of the best they've got at the country club now.

"It isn't as if I don't take Elsie out once in a while. Every time she asks me to go some place I take her. And it isn't as if there were any other women. I know a lot of fellows play around but I'm proud of the fact that I've been faithful. Why should I want any more? I'll provide a home for Elsie for the rest of her life. What more should she want?"

I. Note the facts.
   A. They have been married twenty-six years.
   B. Don spends much time at business and golf.
   C. All the children are grown and away from home.
   D. Don never did pay much attention to the children.
   E. Elsie feels the need for attention.
   F. Elsie thought that after the children left her life would be filled with trips, etc.
   G. Don resignedly takes Elsie places.
   H. Elsie wants the counselor to tell Don to pay her more attention.
   I. Don feels that Elsie is his responsibility.
   J. Don said that Elsie turned all her attention to the children and that he was jealous at first.
   K. Don made his business the *best*. He said he was *best* in golf too.
   L. Don says there is no other woman; he has enough trouble with one.

II. Answer these questions.
   A. Don and Elsie made no attempt to adjust to the problem of having to be husband and father and wife and mother at the same time. Elsie turned to her children and away from her husband. What was her reason?
   B. When the children were gone, Elsie had nothing on which to base her relationship with her husband. They had made no plans. They had not kept up a relationship in which the two of them were the featured persons. What could they have done?
   C. Don faced the problem of Elsie's turning to the children with much accommodation. He still faces her in the same way — resignedly taking her places and accepting her as his obligation. Why did Don choose to solve the problem this way? Yet why was he very active in solving the problem of getting ahead in business? What should Elsie have done for Don when the children were small?
   D. Don kept saying that his business was *best* and his golf game was one of the *best*. Does this mean he had to be the whole show? Is this why he could not deal with the problem of Elsie and the children? Could he not adjust to sharing love and attention in a mature way?
   E. The adjustment in the empty-nest stage is harder because there is no romance to help. Also, they have set up a pattern of not meeting the problem of being together. How can romance return?

F. Don apparently now has the least interest in continuing the relationship and therefore is apparently making no effort to understand. Elsie, though, needs some attention and is very interested in reviving the relationship. Will her asking the counselor to *make* Don pay more attention to her be the solution?

III. Empathize with each person.
  A. Elsie had three sons and a husband who wanted all the attention. She was brought up in a world that didn't teach her to be both wife *and* mother. It emphasized being a good mother above all else. She was not prepared for the empty-nest stage because it wasn't publicized as much as the role of mother. She does at least realize she needs her husband now.
  B. Don wanted to be a part of Elsie and the children but she ignored him. He needed someone to want him and need him, and Elsie didn't take the opportunity. He turned to other people who did need him and gave them all he had. He resents Elsie's turning to him now because she pushed him away before.

IV. Make assumptions; review facts.
  A. Assuming that Elsie really wants to renew the relationship, should she begin to do things that interest Don?
  B. Assuming that Don does like to be best, should Elsie begin to look for ways in which she can show him he is also "best" at home?
  C. Assuming that Don would also like his marriage to be best, would he react favorably to attention now?

CASE 4

"My wife is Mrs. Clean. She's forever dusting, mopping, and straightening. Use an ash tray and she immediately swoops down to clean it. Any spill, rip, tear, or wrinkle is a crisis.

"Now, I've always thought of myself as a neat person. But, if I skip a shoeshine or a shave on a weekend, wear shorts or socks two days running, leave a match on the floor, miss using enough deodorant, or drop a jacket on a chair instead of hanging it up — it's war! I'm all for comfort. There are a lot of things in life more important than cleanliness. Whoever said 'Cleanliness is next to Godliness' was a heretic! How can I straighten her out?"

1. Describe the husband's attitude concerning his wife.
2. What are some of the reasons for his wife's concern for the home reflecting such a clean and neat image.
3. If you were counseling both husband and wife, what questions would you ask each of them?
4. What positive suggestions would you make to each of them?
5. What needs do you feel the husband is not having fulfilled in his own life? What are her unfulfilled needs?

*Case studies adapted from *Marriage and Family Relationships* by R. Klemmer. Marriage: Discoveries and Encounters, The Cava Conference of Chicago, pp. 11, 12.

MINISTERING TO THE DIVORCED PERSON, PART I

OBJECTIVES
— To identify and clarify personal attitudes and beliefs about divorce and the divorced person.
— To define the feelings and adjustments that a divorced person must make during and following a divorce.

ADVANCE PREPARATION
Duplicate the sentence completion and agree-disagree statements. Please check with your own county for updated information on divorce and remarriage in your area and in the United States.

INTRODUCTION
Time: 5-10 minutes.

(Make your own transparency patterns or write some of this information on the chalkboard.)

Many have been overwhelmed and saturated with facts and statistics about divorce. Yet, here are some more! The National Alliance for Family Life reported in the late 1970's that:

"Throwaway marriages" have become part of the fabric of American society. Today, 21 percent of all married couples have divorce somewhere in the background of one partner or the other or both."

The number of divorces in 1974, according to the National Center for Health Statistics, was 970,000. If each divorcee represented a family of three breaking up, the number would exceed the population of Los Angeles.

In 1974, there were over 2,647,000 divorced women in the labor force.

If you were married in 1974, your chances of being divorced or separated by 1976 were one in two.

The most recent report concerning Los Angeles and Orange Counties in California is as follows (note the comparative figures):

	L.A. COUNTY 1974	L.A. COUNTY 1989	ORANGE COUNTY 1974	ORANGE COUNTY 1989
Licensed Marriages	55,000	41,326	13,000	3,888
Confidential Marriages	—	32,066	—	6,079
Divorces filed	48,000	41,332	13,232	13,530
Divorces completed	40,000	42,284	10,000	16,123
Nullity	—	300	—	—
Separate maintenance	—	456	—	—

A report from the U.S. Department of Health, Education, and Welfare stated the following:

"The total number of marriages and divorces increased considerably during the 100 years from 1867-1967 due to both increases in population and changes in rates. Increases in regional and divisional totals were also influenced by the distribution of the unmarried or married population in various parts of the country as well as the location of marriage and divorce 'mills' (places where many out-of-state people are married or divorced). The increase was more pronounced for divorces than for marriages: In 1967 there were more than 50 times as many divorces in the United States as in 1867 (10,000 to 523,000) but only 5.4 times as many marriages (357,000 to 1,927,000). During the 100 years annual marriage totals increased in 70 of the years, declined in 29, and once remained the same for two consecutive years. For divorces, the comparable figures were 70, 20, and 10. The lowest observed marriage total was 345,000 in 1868, the highest 2,291,000 in 1946 — a ratio of 1 to 6.6. Divorce totals ranged from 10,000 to 610,000."

ATTITUDES AND BELIEFS ABOUT DIVORCE

Time: 20-25 minutes.

Class members should be aware of their own ideas and attitudes toward divorce. The use of a sentence completion form is one way of getting an honest response. Distribute the forms and ask each person to complete it. Following this the participants could either meet in small discussion groups to share and discuss some of their responses or turn them in so you as a leader could get a feel of the attitudes and beliefs of the group.

1. The word divorce means . . .
2. I feel that divorce . . .
3. When I am around a divorced person I feel . . .
4. The scriptures teach that divorce is . . .
5. Remarriage for a divorced person is . . .
6. The children of a divorce are . . .
7. The greatest problem that a divorced person faces is . . .
8. The church's attitude toward divorce is . . .
9. If I were to go through a divorce my friends would . . .
10. The person most likely to experience a divorce is . . .

AGREE-DISAGREE DISCUSSION

Time: 60 minutes.

Distribute copies of the agree-disagree sheet found in the resource section for this session. Follow the usual procedures for using this discussion form. Divide the class into groups of four to six individuals. Ask them to formulate their reasons for the answers to these statements.

Take a brief break following this activity.

LECTURE AND SUMMARY PRESENTATION

Time: 20-30 minutes.

Share the information given here concerning the facts of divorce and divorced individuals. You may want to spend some time speaking to the question of the biblical teaching on divorce. The book by Guy Duty, *Divorce and Remarriage*, will be a helpful resource as you prepare your own presentation on this subject. Remember, however, that the main objective of these sessions on divorce is not to answer whether it is right or wrong. It is a fact that people are divorced and we need to know how to best help through the difficult readjustment period.

From a course in Marriage and Family, a student's report based upon research indicated the following effects upon family life:

1. The children are utterly confused as to where their loyalties belong.
2. They must adjust to living with one parent and seeing the other only at stated intervals.
3. Children know or feel they have been let down by both parents.
4. Things are made even more difficult for them when their divorced parents "use" them. For example, a mother says to the child after a visit with her father, "When you saw Daddy on Saturday did he say anything about Mrs. Smith?" (Mom heard through the grapevine that Dad has been seeing Mrs. Smith.)
5. The divorce rate is higher for second marriages than for first ones. (a) 25 percent of all marriages in one year involve at least one person who has been previously married. (b) After divorce — by the end of two years for men, three for women — 50 percent of men and women have remarried. (c) Divorced people get married faster than widowed people, more easily than single people. (d) 70 percent of divorced people remarry. (e) Remarried people usually marry people who have been previously married.
6. Comparisons with former partners crop up constantly, though they are often unvoiced except in quarrels. For example, John states, "Look at the collars on these shirts — you call that ironing?" Thought: Patty wasn't any ace as a housekeeper, but she took darn good care of my clothes.
7. The divorced man who has a first wife and children to provide for now has two family units to consider. This can be added financial burden

and it can cause increasing resentment as he sends his first wife the monthly check.

8. A divorced woman/mother may feel her children are a burden. They now demand so much more from her because their own world has been toppled.

9. When there are children remarriage becomes even more complex. Children are not things you hand from one family to another.

10. Emotional climate: widow gets help, sympathy, and emotional support for herself and her family in their bereavement because most people feel she was dealt an unfair blow. Divorcee (bereaved also): too often onlookers feel "she got what she deserved." There are many ways to make her feel she has done something wrong or scandalous.

Conclude with prayer.

sentence completion

1. The word divorce means _____
   _____

2. I feel that divorce _____
   _____

3. When I am around a divorced person I feel _____
   _____

4. The scriptures teach that divorce is _____
   _____

5. Remarriage for a divorced person is _____
   _____

6. The children of a divorce are _____
   _____

7. The greatest problem that a divorced person faces is _____
   _____

8. The church's attitude toward divorce is _____
   _____

9. If I were to go through a divorce my friends would _____
   _____

10. The person most likely to experience a divorce is _____
    _____

AGREE-DISAGREE STATEMENTS

Agree Disagree

_____ _____ 1. Moses allowed divorce in the Old Testament because of the hardness of the wives' hearts (i.e., submission problem).

_____ _____ 2. The scriptures teach that all divorce is wrong.

_____ _____ 3. The rising rate of divorces today means that there are greater problems within marriages today than fifty years ago.

_____ _____ 4. The biblical teachings on divorce and remarriage are designed to bring pressure to bear on couples to make their marriages work.

_____ _____ 5. God hates divorce but loves divorcees. If you agree, why does God hate divorce?

_____ _____ 6. Marriages kept together "for the sake of the kids" rarely benefit the children.

_____ _____ 7. When a divorce occurs there is no such thing as an "innocent party."

_____ _____ 8. The scriptures teach that a divorced person should not hold a place of service in the local church.

_____ _____ 9. Divorce is a tragedy, but there are times when it is preferable to an unhappy marriage.

_____ _____ 10. A married couple experiencing trials and conflict is an indication that God is *not* at work in their lives.

_____ _____ 11. Christians today are usually judgmental and exhibit less grace than God allows to divorced couples.

_____ _____ 12. If there is to be a remarriage of a divorcee it is best that he/she marry a divorced person.

_____ _____ 13. Separation may be used in a marriage to bring the offending mate around to his senses, with the door *open* for reconciliation.

_____ _____ 14. Divorce, even a wrongful divorce, can be forgiven through Christ's gracious and redemptive provision on the cross.

_____ _____ 15. The scriptures allow for divorce in some instances but does not allow for remarriage.

——— ——— 16. Desertion is a legitimate ground for divorce.

——— ——— 17. Adultery permanently destroys the marriage union.

——— ——— 18. Divorce is mandatory when infidelity (adultery) is involved.

——— ——— 19. The innocent partner is free to seek divorce if his/her mate is unfaithful.

Adapted from Roger Moore, *Marriage Enrichment Class Teacher Notebook* (Aptos, Calif.: Twin Lakes Baptist Church, n.d.); H. Norman Wright, ed., *Marriage and Family Resource Newsletter.*

MINISTERING TO THE DIVORCED PERSON, PART II

OBJECTIVES
— To define the feelings and adjustments that a divorced person must make during and following a divorce.
— To identify needs of the divorced person in order to minister to these needs.

ADVANCE PREPARATION
1. Prepare transparency.
2. Duplicate the "Letter to a Couple on the Brink of Divorce."
3. Order a copy of *The Divorce Decision* for each class member. Distribute the books at the end of this session.
4. Invite guest speakers who have experienced divorce.

INTRODUCTION
Time: 10-15 minutes.

Ask the group to spend three minutes discussing any of the statements or information presented in the prior session. Then complete any of the session material from the previous week that you may not have covered. Answer any of the questions the group may have at this particular time.

LECTURE PRESENTATION
Time: 20-30 minutes.

(Use the transparency pattern to accompany your presentation.) Divorce involves a loss, an adjustment, a reorientation of one's entire life. Who can best describe the ordeal but one who has experienced it? Amy Ross Young shared her experience in her book, *By Death or Divorce — It Hurts to Lose:*

"By death, or divorce, it hurts to lose. Twenty-two years and three days after Bob was killed, my second marriage was legally terminated. The end didn't come as suddenly as it had the first time.

Few divorces, however, do come as a complete surprise. Nor, is it possible to put your finger on the exact day and hour when the problem was born. For me, it took this marriage eight long months to die. It was almost as if a 'marriage doctor' had announced, 'The disease is terminal. It could go at any time.'

"If you don't want the marriage to die, you pray right up to the very end that somehow — someway — things will work out. Even after the judge says, 'Divorce granted,' there is still hope. This is one way that losing your mate by divorce differs from death."[1]

One of the reasons why divorced people suffer intense pain is that they were not aware of the emotional strain that divorce would place upon them, and were not prepared to face it.

There are six overlapping stages which a person goes through in the course of a divorce:
1. Emotional Divorce
2. Legal Divorce
3. Economic Divorce
4. Co-Parental Divorce
5. Community Divorce
6. Psychic Divorce

Although the stages are not always undergone in the same order and with the same intensity, most divorced persons experience them.

Advance knowledge of these steps will be helpful to the person whose divorce proceedings have just begun. One who has already been divorced will find an understanding of this process helpful in reflecting upon his own experience and in evaluating his responses and adjustment. One who has not faced the problem of divorce will find knowledge of it helpful in knowing what divorced friends are experiencing and in learning how to offer them support.

The first visible stage of divorce has been called *Emotional Divorce*. It occurs when one or both spouses begin to withhold emotion from their relationship. Their attraction to and trust for each other has diminished and they have ceased to reinforce love feelings for each other. Many married couples in our society experience this stage, and although they remain together and never initiate legal separation or divorce proceedings, they remain emotionally detached from each other and fail to improve their relationship.

When a person first marries he feels good because he feels that out of all others in the world he has been chosen by his partner to be that person's spouse. When a person divorces, he feels pain for now he feels that to his spouse he is no different than all those others. In emotional divorce, the reality of no longer being "number one" impresses itself more and more upon a person. Feelings now are concentrated upon the weak areas of the other's personality rather than upon the positive areas of the two lives.

The second stage is *Legal Divorce*. One or both spouses may retain a competent lawyer or decide to plan their own divorce and complete the multitude of forms. The legal process involves fees which can be expensive and court action which can be lengthy. The laws have been written to make dissolution of a marriage a relatively simple procedure, although the division of accumulated property may require extensive litigation. One of the reasons why divorce is a trying emotional experience is that the legal process, although providing for the dissolution of a marriage, does not provide for the release of emotions which are created during both emotional divorce and the legal process.

The third stage, *Economic Divorce*, may alter the couple's life style. A nonemployed mother may find herself seeking a job out of economic necessity. She may seek employment as an exercise of newly found freedom. Perhaps this is the first time she has had an opportunity to work. Decisions concerning who gets the car, the house, the stereo, the pets, and so on, may be made during this stage. Alimony or spousal support, child support, and community property (or other property rights depending upon the state of residence) are issues to be discussed with a lawyer and decided upon by the parties or the court.

Yet another stage of divorce is *Co-Parental Divorce*. The most enduring hurt can be experienced at this stage. The word "co-parental" indicates that a child's parents are divorced from each other and not from their child. Yet many children do feel that they have been divorced from one of the parents. The court grants physical custody to one parent. He has the right to have the child live with him; the other parent may be granted visitation privileges.

The divorce process can be as easy or as hard upon a child as his parents wish to make it.

A fifth stage, *Community Divorce*, is characterized by loneliness. Loneliness may be caused by a change in social status. If before a divorced person was in a social club for couples or an adult Sunday school class, he may now feel out of place and ill at ease. Some of the other couples may feel that way too. They may not know what to say and what not to say to a divorced person. Some married persons are threatened by the presence of a single person. Their reactions are more a reflection of their own insecurity than rejection of the divorcee.

From his own experience with divorcees, one minister estimated that 80 to 90 percent of a divorced couple's friends either ostracized both from their social group or else favored the husband. With a change in social groups and community activities comes a change in friendships.

However, this phase of a divorced person's life is one of the best handled in our society.

The last stage is *Psychic Divorce*. During this stage a divorced person becomes autonomous — separate from the influence, presence, and perhaps even the thoughts of the former spouse. Achieving autonomy is the process of creating distance between one person and another. This is one of the most difficult stages, but it can be a time of learning to become a whole, independent, and creative person. It can be a time of reflection upon one's own responsibilities and actions and a time to begin making positive changes.

The divorced person must be aware of the emotional adjustment and even mourning which continues during this stage. Divorce can bring with it separation shock. The longer and more involved the marriage was, the greater the possibility is of these symptoms of separation shock occurring.

It is not uncommon for persons who have been divorced to say that they could have handled the break more easily if their partner had died. This reaction identifies their experience as one of grief. Some Christians have said that the loss of their spouse, had it been through death, would have been less painful because they would have been free to remarry and would not have had to bear the stigma of a divorcee.

Who has the most difficult time adjusting to divorce — men or women? Dr. Mel Krantzler suggested that the recovery rates for men are different than for women.[2] Women appear to have a greater part of their total identity destroyed during a divorce and often hit rock bottom during the first months of separation. They must come to grips with their emotions and discover a workable new way of life as a means of survival. Men in our society, on the other hand, tend to run away from their feelings. They seem to have roles other than that of a husband and father to sustain them, and they may be able to suppress feelings of no longer being a complete person.

During this state of becoming autonomous, mistakes will be made and a person will suffer attacks of loneliness. Even after a person feels that he has himself well under control, he will have occasional attacks of loneliness. Holidays or birthdays can remind him of either happy or painful times spent together with his ex-spouse.

Seeing a former spouse because of financial arrangements or visiting the children may raise doubts in his mind about the divorce. "I wonder if we could have worked it out."

There are twelve very common reactions of friends of a divorced person:[3]

1. A friend may experience some *anxiety or fear* upon hearing of the divorce. Perhaps if he has looked up to the person and the marriage relationship as a model, part of his security now begins to crumble. Maybe he will begin to reflect upon his own marital relationship and question its direction.

2. A second reaction is *shame.* Other friends may be experiencing the very same difficulties and yet have not done anything to deal with their problems. They have not chosen to divorce nor have they chosen to take any constructive steps. When they are now confronted with someone who has taken a step they could feel uncomfortable for ignoring their own relationship.

3. Sometimes a friend is overly *preoccupied* with the subject of divorce. It is upon his mind constantly, He talks about it at every occasion and seeks out additional information. He may feel as though he has been let in upon a secret, especially if the divorce came as a surprise. He could show little tact and sensitivity by asking too many personal questions.

4. It often happens when a separation or divorce occurs that friends have *fantasies and desires* for a sexual relationship with one of the partners. Fantasies that occurred before the divorce may become intensified, and even be expressed openly after the divorce. A divorced woman could suddenly be given an inordinate amount of attention from married male friends.

Such attention is given in the guise of interested help and support.

5. Strange as it may seem, there are some who experience *pleasure* from the suffering and failure of another. If the couple occupies a place of prominence or they have wealth, social status, or an abundance of talents, the failure of the marital relationship might be looked upon with pleasure by those of less importance or those who are envious.

6. Friends have been known to *feel superior* to the divorcees. They are proud of enduring their own marriage relationship. They look upon divorcees as weak, inferior people, quitters, second-class citizens who have sinned.

7. *Surprise* is another very common reaction. Some friends cannot imagine that this couple would have any difficulties. Sometimes the surprise takes the form of a protest: "It can't be, not you! You don't mean it! Go for some help! Think of the children!" If the surprised person is a close friend or business associate, he may be afraid that the other's divorce will reflect upon him.

8. Friends of the divorcing couple may experience some degree of emotional *loss and grief.* The stability of the divorcing couple's marriage may have been an emotional support in their own life and now that support has been removed. If the relationship between the couples is close, feelings of empathy are natural.

9. If there is bitterness between the divorcing parties, a friend may experience *conflict* over allegiances. These allegiances may mean a loss of an emotionally significant friend. This loss can intensify the emotional turmoil and grief of the friend, and if feelings of rivalry, envy, and preferences are aroused, the loss could incite guilt and shame in the friend.

10. Another reaction, especially of vulnerable people, is feelings of *disillusionment* about the untrustworthiness of friends and the impermanence of relationships. Depression in a friend is not uncommon, especially if his self-esteem is built partially upon this relationship. Often people are not aware of the intensity of the friendship and when the divorce occurs, they become disillusioned.

11. A personal *identity crisis* may also occur. Friends who were involved in the mutuality of the marriage and in the lives of the individual spouses may need to assess who they really are and what is important about their own life.

12. Finally, some friends are *curious about the settlement.* Some become preoccupied with it. They want to know how much money was

involved, who received what, whether a good lawyer was retained, who had the advantage, and what was decided about support for the children. If the inquisitive friend strongly identifies with one spouse more than the other, his curiosity may be more intense.

PANEL DISCUSSION
Time: 30-50 minutes.

Ask the three or four divorced individuals, who you invited prior to this session, to share some of their experiences with the group. Ask them to emphasize what they felt as they went through the experiences, what some of their greatest adjustments were, and what other people did for them that helped them the most during their time of adjustment. Ask them to share what kind of counseling would help them the most. Let the class ask questions.

CONCLUSION
Time: 10 minutes.

If there is time, you may want to read to the group "Letter to a Couple on the Brink of Divorce." Be sure that these have been duplicated prior to the session and give a copy to each person. They may be able to use this letter with those who are not yet divorced but are considering this action. Also distribute to each one a copy of *The Divorce Decision* and ask them to read this as a reinforcement of what has been presented.

Conclude with prayer.

REFERENCES
1. Amy Ross Young, *By Death or Divorce — It Hurts to Lose* (Denver: Accent Books, 1976), p. 39.
2. Mel Krantzler, *Creative Divorce* (new York: Evans & Co., 1973).
3. Adapted from Paul Bohannan, ed., *Divorce and After* (Garden City, N.Y.: Doubleday & Co., 1968).

THE SIX STAGES OF DIVORCE

1. Emotional
2. Legal
3. Economic
4. Co-Parental
5. Community
6. Psychic

REACTIONS FROM FRIENDS

1. Anxiety or fear
2. Shame
3. Preoccupation
4. Fantasies and desires
5. Pleasure
6. Feeling superior
7. Surprise
8. Loss and grief
9. Conflict
10. Disillusionment
11. Identity crisis
12. Curiosity about
    the settlement

LETTER TO A COUPLE ON THE BRINK OF DIVORCE

This was a radio message given by Hank Vigavino several years ago. Many pastors have reprinted this and given it to couples to read as a means of having them reconsider their pursuit of a divorce.

Dear Betty and Bill,

It was good to be able to talk with you when you came to see me the other day, but I wanted to follow up with a letter since I didn't have a chance to answer some of your questions. In sharing your conflicts with me, you made a concrete attempt to avoid a divorce, and in spite of the seriousness of your situation that was an important step. Would you agree that most couples entertain the possibility of divorce at some time during their marriage?

Of course it's not difficult to obtain a divorce. Lawyers know the technical language, and it doesn't take much to turn your back on a troublesome relationship. One lawyer has a sign on his door which reads: "Satisfaction guaranteed or your honey back." The real trick in life is to find satisfaction without going to court and losing your honey. But that's why you came to talk, wasn't it? Your objective was to discover some way through your conflicts.

As happens quite frequently with couples, you repeated the phrase: "But we don't seem to love each other any more." Yes, if falling in love is as heady as the songs and movies tell it, it is a cinch to fall *out of love,* too. But love is more than something you fall into and out of. Love isn't just receiving a good feeling. Love is something you give to marriage, and you keep on giving continually, willingly, without grudging.

I'm sure you both believe that. What you were exploring was the problem how this love could remain a reality within a relationship that is presently marked by hostility and resentment. I'll try to deal with that question before the end of this letter.

"We don't seem to be compatible," you said. Who is? I have never found perfect compatibility in human relationships. A couple of sardines in a can are compatible, but you want more individuality than that! Someone has called mental incompatibility "nothing more than a case of carefully nurtured, garden-variety selfishness." That sounds a bit different, doesn't it? Incompatibility is so much kinder a word than selfishness.

Betty, do you remember how you said: "I can't stand being criticized by my husband"? Bill, you need to be more aware of your tendency to judge. It's a mark of self-centeredness also. An overly critical attitude will drive the other person away from you. It's true that with that measure we give, it will be measured to us again.

But why are you so upset about this criticism, Betty? Do you remember that you also added: "I can't stand being criticized because I don't want him to have the last word"? Why can't you stand for him to have the last word? Because you must have it? Isn't that selfishness, too?

In our conversation you raised the question on what the Bible teaches about divorce, and we did not take time to discuss this. I'm going to outline it for you, briefly. Because you were both brought up in the Christian faith and have always been taught that divorce is wrong, you have come face to face with an increasingly frustrating marital situation, and you don't know which way to turn.

You are certainly aware of the fact that all churches do not interpret the biblical teaching on divorce in the same manner. If they did it would be so easy. One church teaches no divorce, ever. Another may allow divorce, but no remarriage. Still other denominations allow divorce and remarriage for what they call "the innocent party." And there are Christians who permit divorce with remarriage for all who repent. So it goes. But it all must sound very puzzling. Who is right?

Jesus taught that marriage is a holy, beautiful, enduring relationship. He came into the world where men generally acted as they pleased without being ashamed or having a bad conscience. Rabbi Hillel had taught that a man could put away his wife for most any cause. And that was the accepted practice.

On one occasion the relgious leaders approached Jesus with a question: "Is it lawful for man to put away his wife for every cause?" (Matt. 19:3).

If Jesus had replied that it was not lawful, the majority opinion would have been against him. The leaders knew that Jesus could not agree with loose divorce laws either. In answer Jesus turned to the opening chapters of Genesis. He pointed out that the two were one, "whom therefore God has joined together, let no man put asunder" (Matt. 19:6).

Since they couldn't argue that, they returned with: "Then, why did Moses command to give a writing of divorce and put away the wife?" (Matt. 19:7). Such was the Mosaic law. If Moses permitted it, is this not reason enough for divorce?

Jesus answered: "Moses because of the hardness of your hearts suffered you to put away your wives: But from the beginning it was not so. And I say unto you, whosoever shall put away his wife, except it be for fornication, and shall marry another commits adultery" (Matt. 19:8-9).

The ideal is no divorce. The plan of God from the beginning was for union throughout a lifetime. True enough the Scriptures allow two causes for divorce. Jesus speaks of fornication as one — a violation of trust, a breaking of this oneness, a betrayal of that relationship which God has established. Does this mean something physical only? Can there also be mental adultery? Spiritual unfaithfulness? Is it possible to be unfaithful in marriage through hostility and rebellion, resentment and critical judgments?

Of course I must add that adultery does not mean that divorce should follow automatically. Every sin can be forgiven, and in many a marriage such forgiveness of sin has led to a deeper love.

The other cause is willful desertion (see I Cor. 7:15). Suppose a husband deserts his wife and children. He runs off with another woman, lives with her and has more children. He does not return to his former wife. What should this Christian woman do? Legally she is still married. Should she obtain a divorce? Should she be penalized never to remarry?

Marriage is for life, but for the hardness of your hearts Jesus makes allowances. Do you not recognize this principle in the ministry of Jesus, in His merciful attitude toward the children of men? We must not see Jesus as a greater Pharisee than the Pharisees. They adhered strictly to the law. They were upset by Jesus as He kept breaking their regulations of cleanliness, separationism and the sabbath. I see His life characterized by compassion, kindness, love, a deep understanding of human nature, the forgiveness of sins and an acceptance of failure.

For Jesus, divorce was against the will of God, but He never rejected the divorcee. Nor did He keep anyone from the love of God. One of His longest conversations recorded in the New Testament took place with a woman who had been married five times and was then living with number six.

I would summarize Jesus' position this way: The law of God is strict, but the love of God is all-embracing. I take my clues from the life and teaching of Jesus, from all that He embodied, all that He did, and all that He presented as God in human flesh. I think that we must move beyond laws to the incarnation, the living out of the Father's love in mercy and compassion.

How, then, can you avoid a divorce? What can you do about your situation? That's the big question. Well, you will have to open up channels of communication to remove those hostilities and resentments. As the wife said to her husband hiding behind the newspaper at the breakfast table: "Pretend I'm a barber. Talk to me." The magazines and marriage columns are full of this type of advice.

Norman Vincent Peale suggests something more. A half hour experiment which he wants a couple to try for a week. During that half hour you project yourselves into the future as you consider what divorce will involve, what it will mean financially, emotionally, and to the children. You also recall the past and bring to remembrance happy memories. You consciously stop judging the other person during this half hour and turn critical eyes on yourself. "Unless you face up to the immaturities in yourself, unless you learn more about self-discipline and unselfishness than you have shown so far, you will probably find eventually (in case you divorce and marry someone else) that you have simply exchanged one set of emotional problems for another." (Taken from Guideposts magazine, September 1964)

He also includes in his little experiment a time for meditation and prayer: "Be still and know that I am God" (Psalms 46:1). Betty, you said that Bill won't spend time with you for family devotions. And you asked how important it is for husbands and wives to pray together. Well, how important is it to do anything together? Isn't it of the utmost importance *now*? Would you therefore be willing to read and then meditate on that great chapter on love (I Cor. 13) every night for a week? I have asked couples to do this before, and in some cases it has become the turning point for a better marriage.

That takes us back to the one question I have not answered yet. "We don't love each other any more." What is love? Is it something which you feel for someone who is good and worthy of love? But anyone can love another who is lovable. That is not yet Christian love. Christian love finds its pattern and origin in God. God loves us even though we are unlovable. God loves us in spite of the fact that we are undeserving. We haven't earned His love. We are unworthy. This love, expressed at the cross of Jesus, is agape-love, unmerited and free.

God's love proceeds spontaneously because it cannot help itself. It is not motivated by man's worthiness. It is entirely free and flows from itself. This is what we mean when we affirm that God is love.

As we open ourselves to this divine love, as we receive the love of God into our lives, we can become channels of that love to one another. And this means that we do not love another because of what we see in him or her. Rather, it is the very nature of love to love. You cannot rationalize this. You cannot explain it. If it is real, it must be both spontaneous and unmotivated.

Of course all this is easier said than done.

How do you suppose Jesus gained the power (as a man) to love those unlovable nobodies in Galilee and Jerusalem? And He loved them even to the point of death: "Christ died for the ungodly" (Romans 5:6). From where did Jesus receive the love to love us as we are, when He knows everything about us? He loves us because He looks through our crust of sin, our degeneration, our unloveliness.

When we become aware to love in this light, Jesus Himself will give us new eyes, new eyes to see one another as He sees us. Unworthy, yet worth dying for. Unlovely, yet loved to the point of death. Unacceptable, yet accepted. And this is how we love one another. I don't suppose it sounds quite right to point out for married people that we are to love even our enemies (although at times you may think of each other as enemies!). But how else can you love your enemies, unless you wake up to the realization that love is not extended to the worthy but to those who are totally undeserving? And "when we were enemies, we were reconciled . . ." (Romans 5:10). That's how much Jesus loved us.

No, you are not Christ, but you are to be a Christian — little Christs, followers of Jesus. And what else would it entail to live the Christian life?

Bill and Betty, don't give up your marriage yet! You won't really gain anything by calling it quits. But if you are willing to persevere and live in this new love, you will discover that just as when you're driving in a tunnel, the way out is the way through.

Prayerfully and sincerely,

MINISTERING TO THE DYING AND BEREAVED PERSON, PART I

OBJECTIVES
— To clarify attitudes and beliefs concerning death.
— To demonstrate an ability of how to minister to a terminally ill person.
— To describe and identify the stages a person experiences when he knows that he is terminally ill.

ADVANCE PREPARATION
1. Prepare transparency.
2. Duplicate the list of questions.
3. Order *Recovering from the Losses of Life* by Norman Wright.

INTRODUCTION
Time: 10 minutes.

(Begin this session by reading to or sharing with your class the following.)

Death was walking toward a city, and a man stopped Death and asked, "What are you going to do?" Death said, "I'm going to kill 10,000 people." The man said, "That's horrible." Death said, "That's the way it is. That's what I do." So the day passed. The man met Death coming back, and he said, "You said you were going to kill 10,000 people but 70,000 were killed." Death said, "I only killed 10,000. Worry and fear killed the others."

Robert Burton said, "The fear of death is worse than death." The scriptures have much to say about death. (Read the following passages to the class: Psalms 17:15; 23; 116:15; Heb. 9:27; Rev. 21:4.)

What is death? It is the permanent, irreversible cessation of vital functions of the body. Not all functions stop at the same time. It used to be that the lack of heartbeat was considered final evidence of death but now the attention has shifted from the heart to the brain for a reliable indication of when death has occurred. Joe Bayly has said that death is a wound to the living.

Why is it that we fear death so much? Modern man denies death and we shrink from even discussing it. We criticize the Victorians because of their attitude toward sex, but they were very aware of and dealt openly with death. Our society is very open about sex, but closed about death.

People live much longer today than they used to live and there is a striving for not only the good life but the long life. In 1900 the infant mortality rate was much different than it is today. At that time, for every 1,000 live births 100 of the infants died. In 1940 for every 1,000 live births 47 died. In 1967 for every 1,000 live births there were 22.4 infant deaths. There has also been a significant decline in the death rate of mothers at birth as well.

We fear physical pain and suffering. We fear the unknown and fear what we don't understand. We also fear leaving loved ones and friends. It has been estimated that the average person can go through a twenty-year period of time without being exposed to death of a relative or friend. Today 80 percent of individuals in our society die away from home or familiar surroundings. This in itself creates a fear response as we do not want to be alone when we die. Cyris L. Sulzberger said in his book, *My Brother Death*, "Men fear death because they refuse to understand it." In order to understand death we must deal with our fears of death. Joyce Landorf said in her book, *Mourning Song*, "Here, then, is part of the answer as to why death frightens us so much. While, as a Christian, I know Christ has removed the sting of death and death can never kill me for eternity — death still exists. It is still fearfully ugly and repulsive. I probably will never be able to regard, imagine, or fantasize death as a being a loving friend.

"Whenever and wherever death and dying connects with us — no matter how strong we are

133

in our Christianity or how well we are prepared for it — it still slides and slithers into our lives and freezes us with fear. Such is the nature of death."[1]

DISCUSSION GROUPS

Time: 1 hour.

Distribute the list of questions found in the resource section for this session to each person and ask them to take 15 minutes to read them over and write their own answers. Then divide the class into discussion groups of 4 or 5 and ask them to share and formulate their answers for 45 minutes.

Following this activity take a brief break.

MINISTRY TO THE TERMINALLY ILL PERSON

Time: 20-30 minutes.

Begin by reading Samuel 12: 19-23.

What does a person experience when he knows he is going to die? (Use the transparency.) It is important for us to know what a person experiences at this point for two reasons: some of us may be aware prior to our death that we are going to die, and in order to minister to another person who is in this state we need to know the stages. Dying means change. Even when we think we are prepared, we also live with the fear that we will not be able to cope. We are afraid of what kinds of changes will occur in us and what this change will do to others as well.

When a person knows he is going to die, he usually experiences five different stages of emotional response. We also find that his loved ones go through these same emotional reactions as well.

Stage 1: Denial and Isolation. The first reactions are those of, "It can't be. They're wrong. It's not me that they are talking about." Some people make statements such as, "They'll find that someone in the lab made a mistake and then they'll come and tell me that I'll be all right." Or this person may go to doctor after doctor seeking another diagnosis and seeking a ray of hope. Not only does the person himself not want to hear that he will die, but the relatives and loved ones do not want to hear it either. The disciples didn't want to hear Jesus speak about His dying. Again and again He told them about His betrayal and crucifixion but they did not want to hear it.

Often a person experiences a shock reaction upon hearing the news. One way in which shock manifests itself is through denial. Denial has been called the human shock-absorber to tragedy. Through denial our emotions are temporarily desensitized. Our sense of time is somewhat suspended because of our attempt to delay the consequences. Not only can the denial aspect of shock manifest itself in a reaction such as "Not me! No, I won't believe it," but in some cases denial can take the form of displaced concern. Some relatives who are shocked with the news about the loved one may try to act as though they are emotionally detached. But denial freezes the emotions and they must be thawed out eventually.

Joyce Landorf said, "We need denial — but we must not linger in it. We must recognize it as one of God's most unique tools and use it. Denial is our special oxygen mask to use when the breathtaking news of death has sucked every ounce of air out of us. It facilitates our bursting lungs by giving them their first gulps of sorrow-free air. We breathe in the breath of denial and it seems to maintain life. We do not need to feel guilty or judge our level of Christianity for clutching the mask to our mouth. However, after breathing has been restored and the initial danger has passed, we need not be dependent on it.

"I think God longs for us to lay down the oxygen mask of denial, and with His help begin breathing into our lungs the fresh, free air of acceptance on our own."[2]

What do we do to help a person at this time as we visit him at home or in a hospital? Don't judge him for what he is saying at this time. No matter how difficult he seems or what he says, do not judge him. If the person is in the hospital, do not expect too much response on the first, second, or even third visit. He may not feel like talking. Don't become discouraged and quit coming. Eventually he will respond because he needs someone with whom to share his loneliness. Perhaps the example we find in Job can be a pattern for our response to the person (read Job 2:13).

Stage 2: Anger. A person experiences anger, rage, envy, and resentment. "Why me, God? Why me? Why not someone else?" The person is angry at those around him who are well — friends, relatives, doctors. He is angry at the doctors who cannot make him well. He is angry at God for allowing this to happen and for not immediately healing him. In Job 7:11 we read, "Let me be free to speak out of bitterness of my soul." Perhaps this is what the person is experiencing at this point in his life. We should not take the anger personally. We may become the object of his anger simply because we are there. Nor should we become judgmental and say he should feel this anger. This is part of the normal process any person will experience. The person could be demanding attention. Honest and open communication can help him feel understood.

Stage 3: Bargaining. "Spare me Lord and let me recover and be filled with happiness again before my death" (Ps. 39:13) is the prayer of so many people at this time. The person makes promises: "If I can get well then I will serve the Lord more than ever" or "If only I can live until June to see my son get married . . ." Then, if they live that long, they say, "If only I can live to see my grandchildren," and the bargaining goes on and on. This stage usually lasts only a brief period of time but it can be intense while it lasts. Hezekiah, a man noted in the Old Testament, was told by the Lord, "Set your affairs in order, for you are going to die; you will not recover from this illness" (Isa. 38:1). When he received the news he turned his face to the wall and bargained with God. He reminded God of how he had served and obeyed Him and then broke down with great sobs (Isa. 38:3). Hezekiah's prayer was heard by God and he was given fifteen more years to live.

His response to this experience was recorded in Isaiah 38:1-20: "Yes, now I see it all — it was good for me to undergo this bitterness, for you have lovingly delivered me from death; you have forgiven all my sins. For dead men cannot praise you. They cannot be filled with hope and joy. The living, only the living, can praise you as I do today . . . Think of it! The Lord healed me!"

The question arises, Should we pray for complete healing? Perhaps the question should be, What is God's will at this time? Perhaps the person has completed his task and God is calling him home. Healing does occur but it is not common. Family members can bargain just as much as the terminally ill person. Perhaps our prayer ought to be for more pain-free moments for the person, for his complete knowledge of God's purpose and will, for the person's relationship to Christ to become stronger, and for the person's witness with the doctors, nurses, friends, and relatives.

Part of the bargaining process could reflect our reaction to death and to God. We feel that God doesn't know what he is doing, in some cases, and we need to straighten Him out. Others could be allowed to die, but in this case He is wrong. Joe Bayly wrote in *The View from the Hearse*, "Death for the Christian should be a shout of triumph, through sorrow and tears, bringing glory to God — not a confused misunderstanding of the will of God to heal."

Joyce Landorf shared the story of a lady and her experience with bargaining. "She had lost her first husband after thirty years of marriage. Two years later she had married again and had seven years with a second husband. Then he got cancer.

"She told me they had been so very happy and the seven years had been so short that she pleaded and bargained with God to heal her husband. He was very close to dying and she knelt by his bed and begged the Lord to heal him so he wouldn't die. She said the Lord's voice spoke so clearly that she was quite startled by it. She heard Him say very distinctly in her mind, Your husband has prepared himself to accept death and to die right now. Tell Me, do you want him to prepare himself for death again — later on? She opened her eyes and looked at her husband — he was at peace — he had reached acceptance. She said, 'Oh, Joyce, I knew right then I'd have to release him. I didn't want to make him go through that again — later on — so I released him. At that moment a great peace settled over me. He died a few hours later. *Both* of us were at peace.' If she had hung on, begged God to let her husband live, she would have missed what God wanted to do in their lives."[3]

Our ministry at this time is to be a listener. James 1:19 in the Amplified states that we are to be "a ready listener." This is a time to listen and not to give the dying person false hope. False reassurances do not help him. Simple reflection and a touch and listening will minister to him. (To amplify this section, use pages 64-68 of Joe Bayly's book, *The View from a Hearse*.)

Stage 4: Depression. Denial has not worked, anger has not worked, bargaining has not worked; thus the individual facing death concludes that nothing works, and now the depression sets in. This depression has two parts. One is what is called reactive depression — thinking about past memories — and the other is called preparatory — thinking about impending losses. This is a time when the person needs to express sorrow and to pour it out. We can minister best at this point by sitting silently with the person or holding his hand and letting him know that it is all right to express his feelings. Don't argue or debate with him, for the consequences can only be negative.

Step 5: Acceptance. The person now rests in the knowledge of what will happen. This is somewhat of a peaceful acceptance of the inevitable death. There is nothing else to do except accept the inevitable. The person may lose all interest at this point and even become less talkative. We need to be honest with him and be truthful. He might ask how long he has to live and we should never give a time limit.

The family members need as much or more help and support as the person himself. They may not want the person to be told that he is terminally ill, but it is better for all concerned that he be told. The family members should be encouraged to face this crisis of life with the patient and not isolate him.

One of the problems that can occur is the Abandonment Syndrome. Dying people express the fear that their condition will make them so unacceptable to others around them that they will be abandoned, and in many cases studies have confirmed their fears. Some of the ways that this occurs are as follows:

1. *A brief and formal monologue.* A relative or even a doctor may come in and ask a few rhetorical questions and then leave without letting the person express his inner fears and hurts. People breeze in but seem to respond only on a superficial level. Some come in and inform the person how he ought to be feeling and promise to come back, but never return.

2. Treating the person as though disease or accident has turned him into a *nonperson.* He feels badly when others talk in front of him as though he were not there any longer. But even some unconscious persons can hear what is being said. Many who have survived a coma have said that the faithful, verbal prayers of others were heard and meant so much to them. We should pray with the person whether we know he can hear or not.

3. *Ignoring or rejecting the cues* that the person attempts to give. He may want to talk about what is happening. What would you say to the person who says, "I think I am going to die soon"? Many respond with nonsense: "You're going to live on for many years." That is not what he needs to hear. His feelings and interpretation are important to him.

4. *Literal abandonment.* Sometimes people in nursing homes as well as terminally ill patients are actually abandoned. People say they want to remember the person as he used to be or he receives better care at the home than they could give. Often this is a reaction to the fears that the person has of his own death. Because of the implications of the loved one's death, we have to try to separate ourselves from him in some way. It has also been observed that some loved ones initially have close contact with the terminally ill person such as kissing him on the lips. Then they begin to kiss him on the forehead, then the hand, and finally they simply blow a kiss from across the room. The patient can sense this form of rejection.

Should the person return to his home to die? For some this may be best if they so desire but others would feel more comfortable staying at the hospital. It is where they can feel the most secure in an honest atmosphere and receive the best care.

ROLE-PLAY

Time: 20-25 minutes.

Divide the class into groups of two. Each person should have the opportunity to practice counseling a person who is terminally ill. Each person should select which stage he is in as he role-plays the patient.

CONCLUSION

Time: 5-10 minutes.

Ask each class member to write his response to this question. If you had only three months to live, what would you do? Please be specific. After they have had sufficient time ask them to go back over their list and decide which of these things they should do now whether they die or not. Put a check mark by these items. Then ask what is keeping them from doing these things now and if they will do them. Give them time to think about this and then conclude the class with prayer.

HOMEWORK ASSIGNMENT

Ask the class to study the following death scenes in the scriptures and discover how these men felt about death and what they were able to accomplish during their last days: Jacob (Gen. 47-50:14), Joseph (Gen. 50:15-26), David (1 Kings 1:1-2:11), Elisha (2 Kings 13:14-21), Hezekiah (2 Kings 20), Stephen (Acts 6:8-7:60). As you begin the next session, take 5 to 10 minutes to share your response to these examples from the scriptures.

Distribute copies of *Recovering from the Losses of Life.*

REFERENCES
1. Joyce Landorf, *Mourning Song* (Old Tappan, N.J.: Fleming H. Revell Co., 1974), p. 26.
2. Landorf, p. 53.
3. Landorf, pp. 83-84.

STAGES OF EMOTIONAL RESPONSE IN THE TERMINALLY ILL PERSON

1. Denial and isolation
2. Anger
3. Bargaining
4. Depression
5. Acceptance

THE ABANDONMENT SYNDROME

1. Brief formal monologue
2. Nonperson reaction
3. Ignoring or rejecting cues
4. Literal abandonment

QUESTIONS ABOUT MINISTERING
TO THE TERMINALLY ILL

1. How do you think you could help a dying person cope with the reality of his ensuing death?
2. If you had a terminal disease, would you want to know it? State your reasons. If you would want to know, who would you want to tell you and how should he express it to you?
3. If a Christian is terminally ill and expresses bitterness toward God, how do you think you would react? What would you say?
4. You have been called to the hospital to visit a Christian who knows he is going to die but believes it is really God's will to heal him. How would you pray for this person?
5. What is the best environment to provide for a person who knows he is going to die?
6. Do you talk about death in your own family? Why or why not?
7. If you have experienced the death of a loved one, what was your greatest need? What was the best manner in which others met your needs at that time?
8. What passages from the scriptures would be most comforting to you if you knew that you were going to die?
9. Should a child be told that he is going to die if he is terminally ill?
10. Should a terminally ill child be told that he is "going to be with Jesus"? How do you think he would respond? Who does he want to be with?
11. How would you describe the normal process of grief?
12. How long does the grief process last?
13. Did Jesus ever experience grief? If so, how was it expressed? (See Matt. 26:36-37, Amplified.)
14. How do you feel about a terminally ill Christian bargaining with God about prolonging his life?
15. Should a terminally ill person have the right to decide whether the physicians should attempt to prolong his life or allow him to die? What about the choice of hastening his death?
16. What do you fear most about dying?
17. How would you like to die? What are your reasons for this choice?
18. What does death mean to you?

MINISTERING TO THE DYING AND BEREAVED PERSON, PART II

OBJECTIVES
— To identify the normal and abnormal stages of grief.
— To demonstrate an ability to minister to the bereaved person.

ADVANCE PREPARATION
1. Prepare transparencies.
2. Order the films *Though I Walk through the Valley* and *Until I die.*
3. Duplicate copies of the "Bibliography on Death and Dying."
4. You may want to invite a guest speaker. See the alternate suggestion for this session.

DISCUSSION OF HOMEWORK
Time: 5-10 minutes.

Begin by asking several to share what they discovered in their scripture homework study during the past week.

FILM PRESENTATION
Time: 60 minutes.

You may want to begin by showing the *Until I Die*, which illustrates the five stages of emotional response in the terminally ill, which were presented in the last session. (You may want to show the film prior to the presentation in Session 15.)

Both films are suggested because of the contrast of the secular presentation with the film carrying the Christian message.

Until I Die is a half-hour film with Dr. Elisabeth Kubler-Ross. The five stages of dying are illustrated as she interviews dying patients. The film rents for $25 from the American Journal of Nursing Co., Educational Services Division, c/o Association-Sterling Films, 600 Grand Ave., Ridgefield, N.J. 07657.

Though I Walk through the Valley, by Gospel Films, details the actual final months of a Christian professor and the reactions of his family. Check with your local Christian film distributor. This is a very moving presentation; do not be surprised if many in your group express their responses through tears. You might want to use this film at the close of your session.

PRINCIPLES OF HELPING THE BEREAVED
Time: 25-35 minutes.

What is grief? (Ask each person to spend one minute talking with another member of the group in defining grief. Have them describe the feelings and how a person might act. Ask for several responses after one minute.) Grief is tears, an overwhelming sense of loss, a desire to be alone or to have social contacts severed or restricted. During this time some might even question God's wisdom or love. Feelings of guilt are not that uncommon. Reactions such as "Why didn't I ———" begin to be raised. "If I had treated him better or if I had sought help earlier, or if I had found a better doctor or hospital this might not have happened."

The first response is a shattering, devastating shock that comes with the news of the death. This shock is followed a month or so later by intense suffering and extreme loneliness. Sometime during the first or second year there is a slow, gradual strengthening and healing of the mind and emotions. For most people the grief process can take up to two years.

How do most of us respond to the bereaved? We continue to pray for them for two or three weeks and we may continue to show them concern in tangible ways such as cards, phone calls, taking an occasional meal to them for two or three months. But at the time when they need our support the most, most people discontinue their ministry. It might be better if the church would develop a program of ministry wherein twelve families would commit themselves for a period of two months each to minister to the bereaved over the two-year period of time and thus help them through the hurt process. Cards, phone calls, inclusion within the family activities, helping them to feel useful and productive, etc., would be a part of sharing their concern.

The stages of grief that people pass through are normal and can be immediate or postponed. *People should be encouraged to do their grief work.* (This is explained in detail later.)

(From your own experience and reading you may want to expand each of these stages. Use the transparency pattern.)

Stage 1: Shock and Crying. We should not deny them this outlet for it is normal. Some uninformed and mistaken Christians have made comments such as, "Stop your crying. After all your husband is with the Lord now." Such comments are not helpful and are quite insensitive. Psalm 42:3 states, "My tears have been my food day and night." Let the person cry. Read also Psalm 38:17 and 2 Samuel 18:33.

Stage 2: Guilt. This is almost a universal phenomenon. Statements or reactions such as, "If only ———". "Why didn't I spend more time with him?" and "Why didn't we call in another doctor?" are often made.

Stage 3: Hostility: Anger at the doctors for not doing more, anger at the hospital staff for not being more attentive, anger at the person who died. A husband might react by saying, "Why did she die and leave me with three children to care for?" Then guilt and remorse sink in because of this spontaneous feeling. People are helped by knowing that these reactions are normal.

Stage 4: Restless Activity. The bereaved begin a lot of activities but lose interest and switch to another project. It is hard for them to return to their regular routines.

Stage 5: Usual life activities lose their importance, and this brings on further depression and loneliness. Their usual activities were important only because they were done in relationship with the deceased.

Stage 6: Identification with the Deceased. The bereaved person may continue the projects or work of the deceased. A wife may carry on the person's unfinished hobby. A husband may continue to add to the house which had really been his wife's project. They begin to do what the other person did and they do it according to the former person's style. In some cases people begin having pains where the deceased experienced symptoms. If their husband's back hurt extensively, they find that their own back starts to ache. But all of this is just part of the identification process.

Granger Westberg suggested, in his book *Good Grief*, that there are ten stages of grief which the normal person must pass through:

1. *Shock.* This is our temporary anesthesia, our temporary escape from reality. How do we help at this point? Be near the person and available to help. But do not take away from the person what he can do for himself. The sooner he has to make some decisions and deal with the immediate problem the better off he will be.

2. *Emotional release.* Encourage the person to cry or talk it out.

3. *Depression and loneliness.* Be available to the person and let him know that whether he can believe it or not this stage will pass too.

4. There may be some symptoms of *distress.* Some of these could be due to repressed emotions.

5. *Panic* about ourselves or the future may set in. This can come because of the death being ever present in our mind.

6. We have a sense of *guilt* about the loss. The person needs to be able to talk through these feelings with another person.

7. *Hostility and resentment.*

8. *Inability to return to usual activities.* Unfortunately, people tend not to talk about the deceased. They may remember an important time in the person's life or a humorous incident, but refrain from talking about it in the presence of the remaining partner. And yet if he were to do so he would probably find a positive response. In fact, the person may express gratitude that the other talked about his loved one in this way. He is aware that those around him are very cautious about what they say but fond remembrances talked about are healthy.

9. Gradually *hope* begins to return. Rabbi Joshua Liebman, in his book *Peace of Mind*, wrote an excellent chapter on "Grief's Slow Wisdom," which speaks most effectively to this temptation not to return to usual activities. Liebman said, "The melody that the loved one played upon the piano of your life will never be played quite that way again, but we must not close the keyboard and allow the instrument to gather dust. We must seek out other artists of the spirit, new friends who gradually will help us to find the road to life again, who will walk that road with us."[1]

10. The final stage is the *struggle to affirm reality.* This does not mean that the person

becomes his old self again. When one goes through any grief experience he comes out of it as a different person. Depending upon how one responds, he can come out as a stronger or weaker individual.

(At this point you may want some class members to share with the others their experience with grief when they lost a loved one. Ask them to remember what was helpful to them and what was not.)

Earlier the topic of grief work was mentioned. It was said that a person needs to complete his grief work. What does this mean? (Use the transparency.) Grief work means (1) emancipating oneself from the deceased (read 2 Sam. 12:33), (2) adjusting to life without the deceased, and (3) making new relationships and attachments.

Grief work is the reviewing by the bereaved of his life together with the deceased. This involves thinking about the person, remembering dates, events, happy occasions, special occasions, looking at photos, and fondling trophies or items important to that person. In a sense, all of these activities are involved in the process of psychologically burying the dead.

Our tendency many times is to deny the person his opportunity for grief work. We may come into the widow's home and find her looking at pictures in her husband's workshop and crying. How do we usually react? Perhaps we say, "Let's go do something else and get your mind off of this." But it would be better if we could enter her world of grief and feel with her and perhaps cry with her. Romans 12:13 states that we are to "weep with those who weep."

Tears are all right. Joyce Landorf said, "We must not be ashamed of our tears. Jesus wept on hearing of his friend Lazarus' Death (even though He knew He was about to give Lazarus a remission from death!). To weep is not to be guilty of a lack of faith, nor is it a sign of hopelessness. Crying is a natural part of the grieving process."[2]

When grief is not expressed, there is a higher degree of what we call psychosomatic reactions such as ulcerated colitus, hypertension, etc. During the time of grief work, you may notice irritability and some strained interpersonal relationships. This is normal. (Use the overhead transparency to illustrate the healthy process of grief as contrasted with the unhealthy manifestation of grief which is also presented on the same transparency.)

What can we say or do at this time of grief?

1. Begin where the bereaved person is and not where you think he should be at this point in his life. Do not place your expectations for behavior upon him. He may be more upset or more depressed than you feel he should be, but that is his choice.

2. Clarify his expressed feelings with him. This can be done by restating his words in your own words. Help him surface his emotions. You might say, "You know, I haven't seen you cry for a week. If I were in your situation, I would probably feel like crying." If the person is depressed, be near him and assure him that it will pass in time. He probably will not believe you and could even ask you to leave. Do not be offended by this.

3. Empathize — feel with him.

4. Be sensitive to his feelings and don't say too much. Joe Bayly gave this suggestion: "Sensitivity in the presence of grief should usually make us more silent, more listening. 'I'm sorry' is honest; 'I know how you feel' is usually not — even though you may have experienced the death of a person who had the same familial relationship to you as the deceased person had to the grieving one. If the person feels that you can understand, he'll tell you. Then you may want to share your own honest, not prettied-up feelings in your personal aftermath with death. Don't try to 'prove' anything to a survivor. An arm about the shoulder, a firm grip of the hand, a kiss: these are the proofs grief needs, not logical reasoning. I was sitting, torn by grief. Someone came and talked to me of God's dealings, of why it happened, of hope beyond the grave. He talked constantly, he said things I knew were true. I was unmoved, except to wish he'd go away. He finally did. Another came and sat beside me. He didn't ask leading questions. He just sat beside me for an hour and more, listened when I said something, answered briefly, prayed simply, left. I was moved. I was comforted. I hated to see him go."[3]

5. Don't use faulty reassurances with the person such as, "You'll feel better in a few days," or "It won't hurt so much after a while." How do we know that?

Remember not to give up helping the person too soon. The grief has been described in this way: "It seems when the initial paralyzing shock begins to wear off, the bereaved slowly returns to consciousness like a person coming out of a deep coma. Senses and feelings return gradually, but mingled in with the good vibrations of being alive and alert again is the frightening pain of reality. It is precisely at this time when friends, assuming the bereaved is doing just fine, stop praying, stop calling, and stop doing all those little kind things that help so much. We need to reverse this trend. In fact we must hold the bereaved person up to the

Lord more during the first two years of grief than in the first two weeks."[4]

A bereaved person needs:

1. Safe places. He needs his own home. Some people prefer to withdraw because their home reminds them of loss, but giving up the home and moving creates more of a loss. A brief change may be all right but familiar surroundings are helpful.

2. Safe people. Friends, relatives, and minister are necessary to give him the emotional support he needs. It is better to visit the person four times a week for ten minutes than to come once a week for an hour. This is more of a continual support without becoming exhaustive.

3. Safe situations. Any kind of safe situation that provides the bereaved person with worthwhile roles to perform benefits him. They should be uncomplicated and simple, and should not be likely to create anxiety. One pastor called upon a home in which the woman had just lost her husband. He could tell that people had been coming in and out all day long and she was tired of receiving them and their concern. As he came in he said, "You know, I've had a tiring day. Would it be too much to ask you to make me a cup of tea or coffee?" She responded and fixed the coffee. When he was leaving she said, "Thank you for asking me to make you the coffee. I started to feel worthwhile and useful again."

Perhaps what we need in order to be able to minister to others is a clear understanding of what death is. For the Christian death is a transition, a tunnel leading from this world into the next. Perhaps the journey is a bit frightening because of leaving what security we can feel here for the unknown, but the final destination will be well worth the present uncertainty.

Close your session by reading the following dedication written by John Powell in *The Secret of Staying in Love.* "This book is gratefully dedicated to Bernice. She has been a source of support in many of my previous attempts to write. She has generously contributed an excellent critical eye, a cultivated literary sense and especially a confident kind of encouragement. She did not help with the preparation of this book. On July 11 she received a better offer. She was called by the Creator and Lord of the Universe to join the celebration at the banquet of eternal life."[5]

Conclude with prayer.

ALTERNATE SUGGESTIONS

You may want to ask a nurse, medical doctor, or hospital chaplain to come and speak to the class and share his experiences about death as he has worked with patients. Some classes have gone to a funeral home and interviewed a director of the mortuary concerning his views on the meaning of the funeral service. You may want to spend a few moments discussing which of the eighteen questions the group answered in the first session still need to be clarified. You may want to ask if any changed their answers since the first session.

REFERENCES

1. Joshua Liebman, *Peace of Mind* (New York: Simon & Schuster, 1946).

2. Landorf.

3. Joe Bayly, *The View from a Hearse*, pp. 40-41.

4. Landorf.

5. John Powell, *The Secret of Staying in Love*, Dedication.

UNHEALTHY, DESTRUCTIVE GRIEF REACTIONS

1. Suppressed Emotions: holding it all in

2. Indecision: can't get started at anything

3. Behavior Detrimental to Self: selling possessions, giving things away

4. Self-Punishment: often related to guilt in reference to deceased

5. Apparent Insensitivity to Loss

6. Hyperactivity: avoidance of mourning by keeping very busy

7. Avoidance of Memories: sealing off room of deceased or possessions of deceased

8. Altered Relationships (Long-Term): becoming a recluse or an alcoholic (especially after sudden deaths)

NORMAL PATTERNS OF GRIEF

1. Shock and Crying
2. Guilt
3. Hostility
4. Restless Activity
5. Usual Life Activities Lose Their Importance
6. Identification with the Deceased

GRIEF WORK

1. Emancipating Oneself from the Deceased

2. Adjusting to Life without the Deceased

3. Making New Relationships and Attachments

HOW TO MINISTER
TO THE BEREAVED

1. Begin where they are

2. Clarify feelings

3. Empathize

4. Be sensitive and don't say too much

5. Don't use faulty reassurances

THE BEREAVED PERSON NEEDS

1. Safe Places

2. Safe People

3. Safe Situations

A BIBLIOGRAPHY ON DEATH AND DYING

BOOKS

GENERAL

Green, Betty, and Don Irish, eds. *Death Education: Preparation.* Shenckman, 1971.

Grollman, Earl, ed. *Concerning Death — A Practical Guide for Living.* Beacon, 1974.

Kubler-Ross, Elisabeth. *Death: The Final Stage of Growth.* Prentice-Hall, 1975.

Kubler-Ross, Elisabeth. *On Death and Dying.* Macmillan, 1970.

Kubler-Ross, Elisabeth. *Questions and Answers on Death and Dying.* Macmillan, 1974.

Mannes, Marya. *Last Rights.* Morrow, 1974.

Mills, Liston. *Perspectives on Death.* Abingdon, 1969.

Neale, Robert E. *The Art of Dying.* Harper & Row, 1973.

Pearson, Leonard. *Death and Dying.* Case Western Reserve, 1969.

Rheingold, Joseph. *The Mother, Anxiety, and Death.* Little, Brown, 1967.

Ruitenbeek, Hendrik M. *The Interpretation of Death.* Jason Aronson, 1973.

CHRISTIAN

Anderson, J. N.D. *Evidence for the Resurrection.* InterVarsity, 1966.

Bayly, Joseph. *Psalms of My Life.* Tyndale, 1969.

Bayly, Joseph. *The View from a Hearse.* Cook, 1969.

Carlozzi, Carl G. *Death and Contemporary Man.* Eerdmans, 1968.

Carlson, Paul. *Before I Wake.* Cook, 1976.

Hunt, Gladys. *The Christian Way of Death.* Zondervan, 1971.

Johnson, Margaret Woods. *We Lived with Death.* Word, 1975.

Kollar, Nathan. *Death and Other Living Things.* Pflaum-Standard, 1974.

Landorf, Joyce. *Mourning Song.* Revell, 1974.

Rudolph, Erwin P. *Goodbye, My Son.* Zondervan, 1971.

Stephens, Overton. *Today Is All You Have.* Zondervan, 1971.

Thielicke, Helmut. *Death and Life.* Fortress, 1970.

Vetter, Robert J. *Beyond the Exit Door.* Cook, 1974.

Westberg, Granger E. *Good Grief.* Fortress, 1962.

PROBLEM OF SUFFERING

Carlson, Dwight and Wood, Susan. *When Life Isn't Fair.* Harvest House Publishers, 1989.

Howard, David M. *How Come, God?* Holman, 1972.

Lewis, C. S. *A Grief Observed.* Seabury, 1963.

Lewis, C. S. *The Problem of Pain.* Macmillan, 1943.

DEATH AND CHILDREN

Cook, Sarah S. *Children and Dying.* Health Sciences, 1973.

Easson, William M., M.D. *The Dying Child.* Thomas, 1972.

Grollman, Earl, ed. *Explaining Death to Children.* Beacon, 1969.

Harris, Audrey. *Why Did He Die?* Lerner, 1965.

Wolf, Anna W. *Helping Your Child Understand Death.* Child Study, 1972.

TAPES

Joseph Bayly, Gordon L. Addington, M.D., Balfour M. Mount, M.D., and Merville O. Vincent, M.D. *Ministering to the Terminally Ill* (3 cassettes with study guide). Cook, 1975.

FILMS

Occurence at Owl Creek Bridge
The Great American Funeral
Weekend

All three are available from Mass Media Ministries, 2116 N. Charles St., Baltimore, Md. 21218 — or possibly from your local public library.

MINISTERING TO THE SICK: HOSPITAL CALLING

OBJECTIVES

The content of this session may be included in your overall program of developing lay ministers or you may find it more useful in training deacons or elders if their ministry is that of helping those who are sick.

ADVANCE PREPARATION

1. Duplicate the true/false test.
2. Select, invite, and confirm the guest speaker for this session — either a medical doctor or hospital nurse.

TRUE/FALSE TEST

Administer the true/false test which is in the resource section for this session. Give each person a copy and ask them to answer the questions. You may then want to spend time answering and discussing each question or you may want to have the group select the questions they had trouble answering or the ones about which there appears to be disagreement among the group. The time for this will vary. You will be the one to determine the time allotment for each section in this session.

LECTURE PRESENTATION

Present the following guidelines in a lecture. You may want to use some of your own examples or even ask the group for some of their examples. You may have a class member who has been hospitalized share what was helpful and what was not helpful to him regarding visitors calling upon him.

GUIDELINES FOR VISITATION AND COUNSELING WITHIN A HOSPITAL

1. Do not enter a room with a closed door without first asking a nurse.
2. The physician is in charge of the sickroom. What you do, do in conjunction with the physician's requests and requirements.
3. Be aware of hospital administrative requirements, visiting hours, fire regulations, etc.
4. Note "no visiting" and "isolation" signs. Be aware of and respect them. Ask a nurse if it is all right to enter.
5. Get what information you can about the patient and his condition before you make the call. Get the information from the proper sources — the doctor, the nurse, the family. Do not ask the nurse for information she is not permitted to give.
6. Take note of the light above the door — the patient's needs are first. Sometimes a light knock before entering is permissable.
7. Prepare yourself in mind and spirit before entering the room. Recall any previous contacts with the patient.
8. Do not touch the patient's bed, crank, or cords attached to it.
9. Size up the room at a glance — flowers, position of patient in the bed, special equipment, tubes, etc. There is a difference between a patient in bed and one sitting in a chair.
10. Let the patient take the lead in shaking hands. Respond with like pressure.
11. Recognize the importance of such mechanical things as where you sit or stand. Do not jar or sit on the bed. Never stand or sit with a bright light (sun, a lamp) behind you. Never sit where the patient has to lean on one elbow or strain to see you.
12. This is not a time for a pathological conference or a sharing of our own problems.
13. Excuse yourself when the doctor is present unless he asks you to stay. Excuse yourself when a meal is being served. Food and rest are important in convalescence. Food is not good when it is cold. Excuse yourself when

other visitors are present. A hospital room is no place for a crowd. There are exceptions when these rules do not apply, but in the main they should be observed.

14. Help the patient relax. Put the patient at ease. Your words have power — let them bring a "deep seated peace" to the patient. Your relaxed attitude sets the pace.

15. Avoid carrying "emotional germs" from one room to another (for example, after a sordid confession). Time is well spent in the coffee shop or in prayer in the chapel before moving on to the next visit.

16. Do not reveal negative emotional reactions through your tone of voice, facial expressions, or mannerisms. Burn patients are accompanied with a disagreeable odor. Dying patients often are aware of the odor, and are humiliated by their condition. If the patient is a heart patient, do not sit and stare at any machine that is measuring heart beat or rate.

17. Maintain an attitude of quiet, peace, and confidence. Attitudes are contagious.

18. Do not visit if you are sick. If the visit is a must, secure a gauze mask to cover your nose and mouth.

19. Make visits short.

20. Do not whisper or speak in low tones. Patients may interpret wrongly or lose courage. Coma patients have heard and understood, even when they were unable to respond. Avoid the "holy whine." If you are relaxed, quiet, and calm, the patient will be helped to be relaxed and quiet.

21. Leave when meals come. Though a patient says stay and visit, he may later, eating cold meat, wish you had gone earlier. "Well, your meal has arrived. May I join you in a blessing for the food before I go?"

22. In a small ward, speak to every patient present so none will feel slighted.

23. Don't give medical advice or use medical terms. This is the doctor's field. Don't discuss other people's illnesses or your own. Don't get maneuvered into discussing one doctor against another. Don't discuss the medical fees, except as you may discuss the patient's concern about them. The fairness of a fee is between the patient and the doctor.

Some patients may resent you or seem suspicious. Some patients may feel you are checking on behavior, church attendance, etc. Some patients look at the chaplain or pastor as Santa Claus. Some patients feel he is a holy, other worldly person who doesn't experience fears about death or illness, or interpret his visit as a sign of sure death. Others see him as someone who can help work out an emotional or spiritual problem.

(Adapted from *The Pastor's Hospital Ministry* by Richard K. Young, 1954)

GUEST SPEAKER

Ask a medical doctor on the staff of a hospital or a hospital-based nurse to share with the group some of the procedures followed in a hospital to ensure the welfare of patients. Ask him to share what hospitals expect from visitors and pastors when they call. He may also want to explain some of the tests, operations, etc., which are conducted within a hospital. Ask him to share his viewpoints on illness, sickness, and death, and some of his own struggles with illness in the life of patients he works with. Ask this person to share guidelines and hospital calling procedures with the group.

Conclude with prayer.

TRUE/FALSE TEST ON THE THEOLOGY OF SUFFERING

   The following true/false statements are but a very few that should be carefully considered and prayed about before visiting the sick and the dying.
 1. A good bedside salutation is, "How are you?"
 2. After the patient has been greeted the visitor should introduce himself.
 4. Another good opener is "We come to cheer you — get your mind off your troubles."
 5. The visitor should try to show that everyone has troubles and many are worse than the patient's.
 6. The patient should be encouraged to report any complaint he can think of.
 7. The visitor should explain that suffering is the will of God and is not to be resisted.
 8. The patient should be advised about his problems so he will have all the right answers.
 9. Most of the visitor's time should be spent in earnest, friendly listening.
10. The visitor should try to hear what the patient feels.
11. All questions should be answered with scripture.
12. Prayer can be used with the patient.
13. The visitor should carry a large Bible so all will know he is a Christian worker.
14. A patient should never be left without scripture reading and prayer.
15. Good Christians should not be sick because Christ died for our sickness.
16. It should be emphasized to the patient that in EVERY GRIEF "thou art with me."
17. The visitor should suggest that God is probably chastening for some good reason.
18. The biblical statement "We are saved by hope" refers to the salvation of one's soul from sin.
19. All suffering should be opposed by every means.
20. Suffering always mellows and matures people.
21. Mrs. Job's "curse God and die" is irrational.
22. Job settled on one decision — understand Him or not — he would trust God.
23. Nietzsche was mistaken when he said, "A man who has a 'why' for his life can win with any 'how'."
24. Ultimate glory beyond all human imagination infinitely justifies the vast mystery of human suffering.
25. Christians do not suffer in the flesh as do the unsaved.
26. Christians should bear their own burdens but dedicate all good things to God.
27. "Fully turning one's eyes upon Jesus" dissolves all vexing questions.
28. The statement "Eat, drink and be merry for tomorrow we die" is comforting to sufferers.
29. Those who live by the "Eat, drink and be merry" philosophy have only despair and escapism in suffering.
30. Sympathy and not theology is best for those who minister to the sick.
31. Sufferers must be stoical because all suffering is God's will.
32. God has a plan, so wonderful beyond all human ken, as to make any suffering seem like a very short, unpleasant dream.
33. The key words in suffering are "Thou art with me" and "Through ALL grief (even 'the valley of the shadow of death')."
34. The "hope" that saves is not wishful thinking but rather our immutably promised prospect.

Duplicating Pattern
Alternate Session

35. To glory in tribulation is unreasonable for anyone.
36. Jesus Christ is the answer in regard to the innocent suffering.
37. Those who have faith and pray will not be sick.
38. Accidents do not happen to obedient Christians.
39. Mental breakdown is a disgrace to a good Christian.
40. Mental breakdown proves aberration from faith and obedience.
41. Nothing that can hurt God's child is incapable of being used for his good.
42. The visitor should explain that any tragedy is good for the patient.
43. "I will fear no evil" is really just brave poetry.
44. The visitor should be sure to guide the conversation so he can advise the patient.
45. Patients often waste the time of a visitor with their talk.
46. All cases are sufficiently similar to enable the visitor to learn the right answers.
47. If a patient is wrong in his beliefs, he should be put straight.
48. The love and grace of God's eternal purposes should be dwelt upon.
49. Bitter, hostile people need not be visited.
50. The agnostic and the abusive should be put in their place because such are beyond redemption.

(Adapted, source unknown)

THEOLOGICAL TEACHING IN COUNSELING

by Betty Chase

This paper by Betty Chase is an example of how theological teaching can be used in counseling. The writer suggested relating one of the attributes of God to a counselee's life.

An awareness of the attributes of God is not only important in one's personal growth as a Christian, but it also can have a great impact on how we counsel and on those we counsel. This paper will focus upon God's omnipresence and its meaning in the counseling situation. Omnipresence means present or existent everywhere at once.

Having a concept of God's omnipresence helps Christian counselors. They have God, their Heavenly Father, "present" (close to, next to, here) with them as they counsel. There are times when a counselor does not know the answer to a problem, or how to further direct a person, or how to answer a question; these times he has God's presence to guide and help him.

God's omnipresence has meaning for the client in the counseling situation, also. As the client is guided and directed to discover and define the problem, God is present, working in the client's life. As he is making value judgments and decisions, God is there working. When the client leaves, the counselor has the assurance that God is with the client not only during the counseling session, but also between counseling sessions.

If the client really understood and comprehended God's omnipresence, there would be far reaching effects in his life. All of life becomes easier to accept when one understands that God is present in all of it — the unexpected, the tragedies, the unexplainable, the insurmountable difficulties, and the inner struggles. When we couple that with God's attributes of love and compassion, His presence is of great comfort. God's omnipresence assures a client that He is always there; he is not alone in any experience. God's presence also helps the client to realize that nothing is hidden from God and all of his life becomes open before God.

A client discovers God's omnipresence not by envisioning that God is everywhere, but by recognizing that He IS there already. This can be dealt with through two means — through the counseling session and through assignments between sessions. The Scriptures dealing with this concept are Psalms 16:11; 23:4; 73:28; 121:1-8; 139:7-12; Joshua 1:9; Hebrews 13:5; and Matthew 28:20.

The list that follows contains specific ways to help a client understand the meaning of God's omnipresence to his life. The Scriptures can be interchanged in some of the methods and they can be completed verbally during the counseling session or in written form in between counseling sessions. Some of these assignments accomlish the same aim only in a different way, so the counselor needs to select the way of dealing with the concept according to whichever way the client will be most comfortable.

1. Memorize the last part of Joshua 1:9: ". . . for the Lord your God is with you wherever you go." Then concentrate on being more conscious about God's presence by selecting one piece of jewelry that you always wear and changing its position for a day (turn your watch around, etc.). Then each time that day that you are conscious of that jewelry, say the verse and consider God to be there with you.

2a. Read Psalms 73:28; 16:11; 23:4; 121:1-8; Matthew 28:20; Joshua 1:9; and Hebrews 13:5, and identify the characteristic of God that these verses describe.

b. Select one passage and memorize it.

c. Write a paragraph describing what your life would be like during the next week if you were to be more aware of this attribute of God.

3a. Same as 2 above.

b. Same as 2 above.

c. Write one of these verses on a card and post it in a prominent place where you spend a lot of time (by the kitchen sink, on your bulletin board, on your desk, on the refrigerator, etc.).

4a. Read Psalm 139:7-12 and paraphrase it.

b. List at least 15 different places where you will be this week and write a paragraph explaining how this passage could relate to this list.

5. Describe a time in your life when you felt closest to God. Describe a time in your life when you felt farthest away from God. Then read Psalm 139:7-12 and explain how this passage relates to those two times. What do those two times in your life have in common? How does this passage relate to the present situation in your life which we are working on in counseling?

6. Describe your life tomorrow if you were to be consciously aware of God's presence every hour of the day.

7. List five happy times in your life and five unhappy or difficult times in your life. Then read Psalm 139:7-12 and write a paragraph explaining how this passage relates to those 10 areas and how it relates to tomorrow.

8. Compare the lives of two Bible characters — one who was aware of God's presence and one who was not aware of God's presence. (For example, David and Saul — during the latter part of his reign.) What are the benefits of being aware of God's presence in our daily lives?

For both the counselor and client, God's omnipresence is an important concept to recognize and practically apply to their lives.

BIBLE STUDY IN COUNSELING

Here is an example of a Bible study which could be used in counseling a person experiencing difficulty.

HOPE IN AFFLICTION

Read 2 Corinthians 4:7-18 from two or three different translations or paraphrases. Recommended are the *New International Version, The Living Bible,* the *New American Standard Bible,* and *The Amplified Bible.* After you have read the passage, complete the following questions.

1. What is the "treasure" (v. 7) _____

_____

2. What did Paul mean by "jars of clay"? (v. 7) _____

_____

_____

3. Why was this "treasure" in "jars of clay"? (v. 7) _____

_____

_____

4. In verses 8 and 9 Paul listed several feelings of affliction that he had experienced or was experiencing. List these experiences. _____

_____

_____

5. Are any of Paul's experiences similar to the experiences you are having or have had? Which ones? _____

_____

_____

_____

6. Paul compared his experience of affliction with what most people would consider the end result of each affliction. Four phrases show that Paul was greatly afflicted but that he still had hope. List these four phrases below. (vv. 8-9)

a. _____ but not _____

b. _____ but not _____

c. _____ but not _____

d. _____ but not _____

7. Paul said that we always carry around in our body the _____ of Jesus so that the _____ of Jesus may also be revealed in our _____ (v. 10).

8. Verse 11 says basically the same thing as verse 10. Read these two verses and relate them to 2 Corinthians 12:8-10. Is there a similar message? _____ What would you say this message is to you? _____

_____

_____

_____

9. What was Paul's hope in the midst of his affliction? (vv. 13-14)

_____

_____

_____

10. In verse 16 Paul pointed out that our outer body is _____ away but that we are bing renewed _____ day by day.

11. Paul compared our affliction with our hope in verse 17. Write this comparison in your own words. _____

_____

_____

_____

12. Paul's conclusion was that we should not _____

_____ but we should _____ .

Because what is seen is _____, but

what is unseen is _____ (v. 18).

13. Rewrite Paul's conclusion in your own words.

_____

_____

_____

14. Upon what do you choose to focus your attention? Are you going to focus on the

seen or the unseen? _____

_____

_____

15. Write a prayer to God expressing what *your* hope is, in light of your affliction, and

telling Him of your commitment to focus upon the internal and eternal working in your life.

_____

_____

_____

_____

From Waylon O. Ward, *The Bible in Counseling* (Chicago: Moody Press, 1977), pp. 40-41.

BIBLIOGRAPHY FOR COUNSELING

The books and articles listed here have been the most beneficial of any that have been read. From this compiler's perspective, these are the best available.

BOOKS

Ables, Billie, *Therapy For Couples* (San Francisco, CA: Jossex-Bass), 1977.

Ard, Ben and Constance. *Handbook of Marriage Counseling.* Palo Alto, Calif.: Science & Behavior Books, 1969.
A good overview of the entire field of marriage and family counseling.

Beck, Aaron. *Cognitive Therapy and The Emotional Disorders.* International Universities Press, 1976. A must!

Deutsch, Ronald M. *The Key to Feminine Response in Marriage.* New York: Ballantine Books, 1968.
Excellent help for the nonorgasmic woman.

Egan, Gerard. *The Skilled Helper.* Belmont, Calif. Wadsworth Publishing Co., 1975.
Exceptional book with accompanying workbook.

Glasser, William. *Reality Therapy.* New York: Harper & Row, 1965.
Excellent basic approach.

Gurman, Alan S. and David G. Rice, eds. *Couples in Conflict.* Jason Aronson, 1975.
The following chapters are very helpful: "Status and Sex-Role Issues in Co-Therapy," by Joy K. Rice and David G. Rice, p. 145; "A Family Therapist Looks at Marital Therapy," by Carl A. Whitaker, p. 165; "Desensitization of Sexual Dysfunction: The Present Status," by Thomas P. Laughren and David J. Kass, p. 281; "Group Facilitative Training with Conflicted Marital Couples," by Richard A. Wells, Jeanne A. Figurel, and Patrick McNamee, p. 383; "Some Therapeutic Implications of Marital Therapy Research," by Alan S. Gurman, p. 407.

Haas, Harold. Pastoral Counseling *with People in Distress.* St. Louis, Mo.: Concordia, 1970.

Haley, Jay. *Strategies of Psychotherapy.* New York: Grune & Stratton, 1963.
Very helpful with some fresh thinking.

Hyder, Quentin O., M.D. *The Christian's Handbook of Psychiatry.* Old Tappan, N.J.: Fleming H. Revell Co.
A good basic abnormal psychology text from a Christian perspective.

Knox, David. *Marriage Happiness — A Behavioral Approach to Counseling.* Champaign, Ill.: Research Press Co., 1971.
Behavioral modification techniques and how to set up contracts in counseling.

Lazarus, Arnold. *Behavior Therapy and Beyond.* New York: McGraw-Hill Book Co., 1971.
A good basic text on behavior modification techniques.

Lum, Dorman. *Responding to Suicidal Crisis: For Church and Community.* Grand Rapids: William B. Eerdmans Publishing Co., 1969.
The best book available.

Luthman, Shirley G. with Martin Kirschenbaum. *The Dynamic Family.* Palo Alto, Calif: Science & Behavior Books, 1974.

Olson, David H. L. *Treating Relationships.* Graphic Publishing Co., 1976.
The following chapters should be read: "An Operant Interpersonal Program for Couples," by Richard B. Stuart, p. 119; "Research Findings on the Outcomes of Marital Counseling," by Dorothy Fahs Beck, p. 431; "Evaluating Different Approaches to Marriage Counseling," by J. Richard Cookerly, p. 475.

Satir, Virginia. *Conjoint Family Therapy.* Palo Alto, Calif.: Science & Behavior Books, 1969.
One of the best in the field.

If you do any counseling with homosexuals, the following books should be read:

Aaron, William. *Straight.* Garden City, N.Y.: Doubleday & Co., 1972.

Davidson, Alex. *The Returns of Love.* Downers Grove, Ill.: InterVarsity Press, 1970.

Drakeford, John. *Forbidden Love.* Waco, Texas: Word Books, 1971.

Hatterer, Lawrence J. *Changing Homosexuality in the Male.* New York: McGraw-Hill Book Co., 1970.
This is the only book that gives you the

specific techniques to use in helping a person overcome this condition.

ARTICLES

Blue, Jack. "The Present Status of Family Therapy," *The Journal of the Family Therapy Institute of Marin*, Vol. 1, No. 1 (Summer 1972).

Address: Libra Publishers, 391 Willets Road, Roslyn Heights, N.Y. 11577.

Luthmañ, Shirley. "The Growth Model in Marital Therapy," *The Journal of the Family Therapy Institute of Marin*, Vol. 1, No. 1 (Summer 1972).

McAllister, Edward W. C. "Assertive Training and the Christian Therapist," *Journal of Psychology and Theology*, (Winter 1975), pp. 19-24.

Tweedie, Donald. "Contract Therapy and the Christian Covenant," *Journal of Psychology and Theology*, Vol. 1, No. 2 (April 1973), pp. 73-76.

Tweedie, Donald. "Contract Therapy: The Renogation of Marriage and the Family," *Journal of Psychology and Theology*, Vol. 1, No. 1 (January 1973), pp. 76-81.

Wagner, Maurice E. "Hazards to Effective Pastoral Counseling: Part I," *Journal of Psychology and Theology*, Vol. 1, No. 3 (July 1973), pp. 35-41.

Wagner, Maurice E. "Hazards to Effective Pastoral Counseling: Part II," *Journal of Psychology and Theology*, Vol. 1, No. 4 (October 1973), pp. 40-47.

Witkin, M. H. "Sex Therapy and Mastectomy," *Journal of Sex and Marital Therapy*, Vol. 1, No. 4 (Summer 1975), pp. 290-304.

TAPES

Carlson, Dwight. "Jesus' Style of Relating: A Search for a Biblical View of Counseling." Atlanta: The Religious Consultation and Research Society (P.O. Box 54271, Zip 30308), 1976. RPC-11.

This tape is very helpful.

Neiger, Steven. "Overcoming Sexual Inadequacy." Chicago: Human Development Institute (166 E. Superior St., Zip 60611), 1973.

The set of 12 tapes is very detailed and explicit. For those involved in extensive secular marriage counseling, these could be quite helpful to some couples. Listen to all the tapes first. You may agree with everything you hear and you may not.

Wheat, Ed. "Sex Problems and Sex Techniques in Marriage." Denver: Christian Marriage Enrichment (8000 E. Girard, Suite 602, Zip 80231), 1975.

One of the most detailed and best presentations available in three hours of cassette listening.

Wright, H. Norman. *Premarital Counseling*, Moody Press, Chicago. *Marital Counseling*, A Biblically based bahavioral, cognitive approach. Christian Marriage Enrichment, Santa Ana, California.

RESOURCES TO USE
WITH THE COUNSELEE

Since this listing was originally compiled in 1977, there have been many new resources published and substitutions for books which have gone out-of-print. Please write to the author for an updated listing.

Please read the books or listen to the tapes before giving any to a counselee.

RESOURCES FOR NERVOUSNESS, WORRY, TENSION

Gockel, Herman W. *Answer to Anxiety.* St. Louis, Mo.: Concordia, 1965.

Hauck, Paul A. *Overcoming Worry and Fear.* Philadelphia: Westminster Press, 1975.

Lee, Earl. *Recycled for Living.* Glendale, Calif.: G/L Publications, Regal Books Division, 1974.

Lloyd-Jones, D. Martyn. *Spiritual Depression: Its Causes and Cure.* Grand Rapids: William B. Eerdmans Publishing Co., 1965.

Read chapters 8, 10, and 11.

Seamands, David. "How Jesus Handled His Emotions" and "God's Prescription for Life's Greatest Fears"; "Damaged Emotions." Pasadena, Calif.: Tape Ministries, 1975.

Order these tape series from Tape Ministries, P.O. Box 3389, Pasadena, Calif. 91103.

Wright, H. Norman. *Uncovering Your Hidden Fears.* Wheaton, Ill.: Tyndale Publishers, 1989.

Wright, H. Norman. "Handling Worry and Anxiety" (tapes). Denver: Christian Marriage Enrichment, 1975.

Scripture References:

Psalm 131:2	Philippians 4:6-7
Isaiah 26:3	Hebrews 13:6
Matthew 6:34; 11:28	1 Peter 5:7
John 16:33	1 John 4:18
Romans 5:1; 15:13	

RESOURCES FOR DEPRESSION

Cammer, Leonard. *Up from Depression.* New York: Pocket Books, 1969.

Flach, Frederic. *The Secret Strength of Depression*. New York: J. B. Lippincott, 1974.

Hauck, Paul A. *Overcoming Depression*. Philadelphia: Westminster Press, 1973.

Kraines, Samuel and Eloise Thetford. *Help for the Depressed*. Springfield, Ill.: C. C. Thomas, 1972.

Lloyd-Jones, D. Martyn. *Spiritual Depression: Its Causes and Cure*. Grand Rapids: William B. Eerdmans Publishing Co., 1965.

Seamands, David. "How Jesus Handled His Emotions" and "God's Prescription for Life's Greatest Fears"; "Damaged Emotions"; "The Spirit of a Person" and "The Hidden Tormentors." Pasadena, Calif.: Tape Ministries, ND.

    "Damaged Emotions" is an introduction to a series of sermons based on biblical psychology. Excellent!

Wright, H. Norman. *Beating the Blues*. Ventura, Calif.: Regal Books, 1988.

Scripture References:

Scripture References:
  Job 4:6
  Psalms 3:5-6; 40:1-2; 42:5,11; 43:5; 147:3
  Proverbs 14:30
  Isaiah 41:10
  Matthew 12:20
  Luke 4:18

RESOURCES FOR THOSE WHO ARE NOT INVOLVED WITH PEOPLE AND THOSE WHO DO NOT SHARE THEIR FEELINGS

Augsburger, David. *Caring Enough to Confront*. Scottsdale, Pa.: Herald Press, 1973; Glendale, Calif.: G/L Publications, Regal Books Division, 1973.

Druck, Ken & Simmons, James C. *The Secrets Men Keep*. New York: Ballantine Books, 1987.

Powell, John. *Why Am I Afraid to Love?* Niles, Ill.: Argus Communications Co., 1967; rev. 1972.

Powell, John. *Why Am I Afraid to Tell You Who I Am?* Niles, Ill.: Argus Communications Co., 1969.

Seamands, David. "Wishing, Wanting and Willing" and "Is Everyday Halloween for You?" Pasadena, Calif.: Tape Ministries, 1975.

Wright, H. Norman. *Communication: Key to Your Marriage*. Glendale, Calif.: G/L Publications, Regal Books Division, 1974.

Wright, H. Norman. "Communication: Key to Your Marriage" (tapes). Denver: Christian Marriage Enrichment, 1974.

Wright, H. Norman. *How to Speak Your Spouse's Language*. Old Tappan, N.J.: Fleming H. Revell Co., 1988.

Scripture References:
  2 Timothy 1:7
  James 5:6

RESOURCES FOR HELPING THE COUNSELEE CARE FOR AND LOVE OTHERS MORE

Becker, Wilhard. *Love in Action*. Grand Rapids: Zondervan Publishing House, 1969.

Bisagno, John. *Love Is Something You Do*. New York: Harper & Row, 1975.

Powell, John. *The Secret of Staying in Love*. Niles, Ill.: Argus Communications Co., 1974.

Powell, John. *Why Am I Afraid to Love?* Niles, Ill.: Argus Communications Co., 1967; rev. 1972.

Scripture References:
  1 Samuel 12:23; 23:21
  Romans 12:10,15; 14:19; 15:1
  I Corinthians 13
  Galatians 6:2
  Ephesians 4:31-32
  Hebrews 2:18; 4:15-16
  1 John 4:7

RESOURCES FOR HELPING THE SUBJECTIVE PERSON

Backus, William & Chapian, Marie. *Telling Yourself the Truth*. Minneapolis, Minn.: Bethany, 1980.

Burns, David D., *Feeling Good, The New Mood Therapy*. New York: Morrow, 1980.

Seamands, David. "Is Your God Fit to Love?" and "The Hidden Child in Us All"; "The Healing of the Memories" and "My Grace Is Sufficient for You." Pasadena, Calif.: Tape Ministries, 1974.

Wright, H. Norman, *Making Peace with Your Past*, Old Tappan, N.J.: Fleming H. Revell Co., 1984.

Scripture References:
  Psalm 119:66
  1 Corinthians 9:27
  2 Corinthians 13:5
  Philippians 1:27; 2:5; 4:8-9
  Colossians 1:10
  1 Peter 1:14

RESOURCES FOR THE OVERLY DOMINANT OR SUBMISSIVE PERSON

Augsburger, David. *Caring Enough to Confront.* Herald Press, 1973; Glendale, Calif.: G/L Publications, Regal Books Division, 1973.

Jabay, Earl. *The God-Players.* Grand Rapids: Zondervan Publishing House, 1969.
  For the dominant person.

Lembo, John. *Help Yourself.* Niles, Ill.: Argus Communications Co., 1974. Chapter 3.

Smith, Manuel. *When I say No I feel Guilty.* Bantam Books, 1975.

Scripture References:
  Psalm 32:9
  Ephesians 5:21
  James 4:17
  1 Peter 2:13

RESOURCES FOR HOSTILITY OR ANGER

Carlson, Dwight. *Overcoming Hurts and Anger.* Eugene, Ore.: Harvest House, 1981.

Wright, H. Norman. "Handling Anger and Depression" (tapes). Denver: Christian Marriage Enrichment, 1974.

Scripture References:
  Psalm 4:4
  Proverbs 14:29; 15:1,18; 16:32; 29:11
  Ecclesiastes 7:7-9
  Matthew 5:22
  Romans 12:1,19; 14:13
  Ephesians 4:26, 31-32
  Colossians 3:8,10
  Titus 1:7

RESOURCES FOR THOSE WHO ARE IMPULSIVE OR TOO SELF-DISCIPLINED

Carlson, Dwight. *Run and Not Be Weary — The Christian and Fatigue.* Old Tappan, N.J.: Fleming H. Revell Co., 1975.

Hauck, Paul A. *How to Do What You Want to Do: The Art of Self-Discipline.* Philadelphia: Westminster Press, 1976.

Lembo, John M. *Help Yourself.* Niles, Ill.: Argus Communications Co., 1974.

Smidt, Jerry. *Help Yourself — A Guide to Self Change.* Champaign, Ill.: Research Press, 1976.

Oates, Wayne. *Confessions of a Workaholic.* Nashville: Abingdon Press, 1972.

Swindoll, Charles. "Lessons Learned from Failure" (tape). Fullerton, Calif.: First Evangelical Free Church (643 Malvern, Zip 92732), 1976.
  Useful for those who are too self-disciplined and must strive for perfection.

  Use the Self-Discipline Worksheet.

Wright, H. Norman. *Making Peace with Your Past.* Old Tappan, N.J.: Fleming H. Revell Co., 1984.

Scripture References:
  Proverbs 3:5-6; 14:17; 25:28
  Romans 12:11
  1 Corinthians 14:40; 15:58
  Galatians 5:22-24
  Philippians 3:14; 4:13
  Titus 2:2
  Hebrews 10:36
  James 1:4; 5:7
  1 Peter 1:13-15

RESOURCES FOR COUNSELEES WITH SELF-IMAGE DIFFICULTIES

Ahlem, Lloyd H. *Do I Have to Be Me?* Glendale, Calif.: G/L Publications, Regal Books Division, 1973.

Hoekema, Anthony. *The Christian Looks at Himself.* Grand Rapids: William B. Eerdmans Publishing Co., 1975.

Maltz, Maxwell. *The Magic Power of Self-Image Psychology.* Englewood Cliffs, N.J.: Prentice-Hall, 1964.

Narramore, Bruce and Bill Counts. *Guilt and Freedom.* Santa Ana, Calif.: Vision House, 1964.

Narramore, Bruce. "Guilt and Self-Image." Forest Falls, Calif.: Forest Home, 1975. Tape No. 4 from Family Camp No. 1, 1975.

Packer, J. I. *Knowing God.* Downers Grove, Ill.: InterVarsity Press, 1973.

Tozer, A. W. *The Knowledge of the Holy.* New York: Harper & Row, 1961.

Wagner, Maurice. *Put It All Together.* Grand Rapids: Zondervan Publishing House, 1974.

Wagner, Maurise. *The Sensation of Being Somebody.* Grand Rapids: Zondervan Publishing House, 1975.

Wright, H. Norman. *The Christian Use of Emotional Power.* Old Tappan, N.J.: Fleming H. Revell Co., 1974.

Wright, H. Norman. *Improving Your Self-Image.* Harvest House, 1977.

Zunin, Leonard. *Contact — The First Four Minutes.* New York: Ballantine Books, 1972. Chapters 13 and 14.

RESOURCES FOR COUNSELEES EXPE-
RIENCING GUILT

Narramore, Bruce and Bill Counts. *Guilt and Freedom.* Santa Ana, Calif.: Vision House, 1964.

Seamands, David. "Damaged Emotions"; "The Spirit of a Person" and "The Hidden Tormentors"; "Is Your God Fit to Love?" and "The Hidden Child in Us All"; "The Healing of the Memories" and "My Grace Is Sufficient for You"; "Wishing, Wanting and Willing" and "Is Everyday Halloween for You?" Pasadena, Calif.: Tape Ministries, N.D.

RESOURCES TO HELP A COUNSELEE
WITH FORGIVENESS

Linn, Dennis and Matthew Linn, *Healing of Memories.* New York: Paulist-Newman Press, 1974.

Seamands, David. "Love, Honor and Forgiveness." Pasadena, Calif.: Tape Ministries, 1974.

Smedes, Lewis B. *Forgive and Forget.* New York: Harper and Row, 1986.

RESOURCES ON SEXUALITY

Penner, Cliff & Joyce. *The Gift of Sex.* Waco, Tex.: Word Books, 1981.

Wheat, Ed & Gaye. *Intended for Pleasure.* Old Tappan, N.J.: Fleming H. Revell Co., 1981.

Wheat, Ed. "Sex Problems and Sex Techniques in Marriage." Tustin, Calif.: Christian Marriage Enrichment.

Most of the resources listed here can be ordered from:

Christian Marriage Enrichment
1913 E. 17th Street, Suite 118
Santa Ana, CA 92701

PART II

ARTICLES ON COUNSELING

The articles contained in this section of the manual have been selected because of their practicality, content, and helpfulness in the ministry of counseling. They reflect both Christian and secular thought. Many of the principles and approaches suggested have been used in individual counseling and with groups and have proven beneficial. A few of these articles will be incorporated into some of the teaching sessions on training laymen how to counsel. The others are for your own reading and hopefully for the enrichment of your counseling ministry. You may agree with all of the material or just part of what is presented, but hopefully the articles will encourage you to consider and think about your own counseling ministry and how some of the thoughts presented here could be used in your own approach.

HAZARDS TO EFFECTIVE PASTORAL COUNSELING: PART ONE[1]

MAURICE E. WAGNER
Private Practice

The contemporary pastor is doing more and more counseling. There is a very realistic need in our society for someone who understands how life should be put together for fulfillment in living. The pastor has answers from the Bible and insights derived from the doctrines of Scripture, and is constantly learning more about how God intended man to think and live. But the pastoral counselor is confronted with certain hazards which interfere with his effectiveness. Ten hazards are discussed and suggestions are offered which are intended to help the pastor avoid these dangers and counsel more effectively.

Generally speaking, all persons who attend church feel some personal relationship with the pastor. Even though he may scarcely know who they are, they have identified with him and read the lines of his soul as he has poured out his heart in delivering the messages he believes are God's message for the hour.

The people listen, but often they have questions. Usually they cannot ask questions in a public meeting, and sometimes their questions are not even completely articulated in their minds. This calls for personal involvement with the pastor. The pastor who fellowships with his people personally answers their questions, counsels them with their problems, becomes sensitive to their anxieties and knows their immaturities. He has a more accurate concept of the needs he is addressing from the pulpit and a little better gauge of how his messages are reaching those needs. Often there is a discouraging gap between what the preacher thinks is important to the people and what the congregation is actually wanting to hear.

When people with questions can get to their pastor, and he has a ready answer and a sincere interest in them and their welfare, they are set free to continue relating to him and to his messages. He becomes a vital agent of God in their emotional and spiritual growth. This is a traditional aspect of pastoral counseling that has high value.

But today's pastor is expected to do a level of counseling that goes beyond the vital ministry of answering questions, giving comfort, and praying with those in a crisis. People are coming to their pastor with serious emotional disturbances. They want him to be competent in handling all sorts of psychological problems. Christians, especially, want their pastor to give them help that is Bible-centered and godly. They do not want to expose themselves to counseling with non-Christian professionals who are ungodly and minimize their faith in God. They believe God has answers to their problems, and they want their pastor to lead them to those answers.

This paper is addressed to the sincere pastor who wishes to improve his counseling ministry. Every counselor, regardless of how little or much specialized training he has, must face several hazards that lurk in the shadows of every counseling office. If these hazards are not properly understood they will minimize and neutralize the effectiveness of counseling endeavors.

Visiting Instead of Counseling

One of the first hazards in pastoral counseling is the tendency to visit. Visiting is fine and sometimes it is a therapeutic agent, but the counselor must be aware of the difference between these two forms of conversation. Whatever the counselor does in the counseling room, he should do with deliberation. He should have some sense of *why* he is approaching the problem as he is.

Visiting is a mutual sharing. Counseling is not a mutual, but a limited sharing. It is important for the counselee to share intimately whatever is on his mind. The counselor, on the other hand, controls what he shares of himself and whatever he does share is done with a specific therapeutic purpose.

This may, at first thought, seem like counseling introduces a superficial element into the conversation. It may, but it should not. Counseling ought to be viewed as a goal-centered conversation. The goal justifies the one-sidedness of the communication. This, of course, is no excuse for phoniness. No real therapy can take place in the presence of empty pretense.

In conversation, each person usually speaks about some interesting situation; feelings are in the background. In counseling just the opposite is true. Personal feelings and reactions, memories and relationships are the major focus. The effective counselor trains himself to listen to the emotions and attitudes of the counselee and gives them a priority over the substance of the thoughts related.

The counselee usually turns for help because he is in some difficulty he can't handle alone. The problem is usually caused by some improper emotional reaction or method of coping. For instance, he may be having difficulty controlling his temper. He explains the matter without much awareness of his weak impulse control, or just why he became angry. The counselor listens to *what* he says, but pays more attention to the emotional reactions of the counselee than to the specifics of the situation. He also listens to the emotions still resident but unnoticed by the counselee. There are important observations in a counseling situation that seldom take place in ordinary conversation.

If the counselor introjects some similar problem he once had or some friend had explained to him, as he would if he were visiting, he will block the counselee from discovering the insight needed to work his way out of his own problem.

Furthermore, it is important for the counselor to listen to his own emphatic reactions to what the counselee is saying. His own reactions are important intuitive guidelines to helping the counselee toward a solution to his emotional problem. Without this identification, he would be handicapped in summarizing the problem, making appropriate interpretations, and pointing out how the counselee is practicing certain self-defeating modes of thinking.

In brief, the counselor practices a sort of one-sided conversation because he is directing his attention to the inner needs of the counselee. He is listening to the motivating emotions and giving them more importance than the complexity of the situation itself. After all, it is the counselee's emotions that are the problem, not his external environment.

Visiting begins when the counselor loses this objective attitude, gets emotionally caught up in the external situation and tries to find an immediate solution for his counselee. There are occasions, of course, when he may choose to give some suggestions to the counselee about his complex situation, but this should only be done so that the counselee will be free to consider his style of coping with life that contributed to the problem occurring.

Being Hasty Instead of Deliberate

The pastor is a busy man. He is usually dividing minutes carefully trying to get to what he didn't have time for yesterday, patiently accepting unexpected interruptions today, and ever trying to catch a few minutes to meditate on the message he must deliver tomorrow! The pressure to work 170 hours in a 168 hour week and still find time to get needed rest, time with his family, and nourish himself spiritually naturally biases his mind to be hurried in his personal counseling.

The professional counselor usually does not have this problem. He is committed to just one center of attention—counseling. He has little or no administrative details to attend to, seldom if ever speaks in public, and regulates his counseling by appointment. If he has outside interests, he compartmentalizes his thinking so that when he is counseling his mind is free to listen to the person in distress.

Both the professional counselor and the pastoral counselor must give attention to this subtle hazard to effective counseling—hastiness. Much of any counselor's success rests upon his own quiet, thoughtful attention to what the counselee is saying. His poise is often a resource of strength for the troubled person. His optimism about the possible solution to the problem then has a feeling of realism to the person in distress. If the counselor is hurried, or divided in his attention, his remarks of encouragement are likely to be taken with suspicion that he is only saying something the counselee wants to hear so he can get to something else.

A relaxed and deliberate pace also makes the counselee feel the undivided attention and serious interest of his counselor. This is vital to feeling understood, and feeling understood builds faith in everything the counselor discusses about the problem.

When the counselor is hasty and hurried, he is inclined to formulate judgments based upon immature impressions. In his diagnosis, he is likely to leap to a conclusion and then try to find evidence to support that conclusion. He will not be allowing the evidence presented to evolve into a diagnosis in a natural way. In his haste, he reads into what his counselee is saying various elements that may not be there. Sometimes he will misjudge the counselee's sincere motives. This can do serious damage. He may give incorrect advice which he will have to retract later or leave the counselee feeling that he is to blame for the lack of success.

It is important for the counselor to be deliberate. His procedures for dealing with problems need to be chosen carefully and with some cognitive reason. This deliberation cannot be accomplished if one is in a hurry to get finished with the problem. One's mind needs to be at ease to think in a relaxed mode in order to find objectivity in choosing counseling strategies.

But being relaxed and taking time to be deliberate does not excuse wasting time in counseling. This also is easily done. Counselors can be timid and lack positiveness in their convictions about the problem. They may be afraid of formulating an incorrect diagnosis. This can be avoided by estimation. Estimate what the problem is, where the real difficulty lies. Hold the estimate carefully and be ready to dismiss one estimate for another if new evidence appears. Being courageous to estimate with a willingness to change brings the counselor more rapidly to a conclusion about the problem, its diagnosis and possible solution.

Being Disrespectful Instead of Sympathetic

Few counselors would own up to being disrespectful of the people who seek their help. Naturally, they want to be helpful to the distressed, and they know that effectiveness is based upon a fundamental rapport of mutual respect.

One counselee was seriously handicapped in his ability to speak fluently. The counselor's authoritative position frightened him so that he could not formulate his sentences. He was an intelligent young man with college degrees and a responsible position, but a misfit socially. The counselor admitted failure with him as he referred him to me. "He drives me up the wall," the counselor explained, "He won't say anything. After 10 or 15 minutes trying to get him to talk, I give up. I've got better things to do. I just tell him that I'm ready to listen whenever he is ready to talk, then I pick up the paper and read or I write some letters until the session is over. But he never talks!"

I found the young man to be a sensitive person who felt seriously rejected by his former counselor. I discovered he owned a cassette tape recorder, so I suggested he talk to me on tape in the privacy of his home, then play the tape in our session and we would discuss what he said. This got him started talking, and after a few sessions he could talk to me without the recorder. Our counseling proceeded with a fair measure of success.

The minister who is very busy may unconsciously be rude by hastily dismissing a person in distress with some quick, conclusive advice. It is as though the pastor only has time for serious problems, and this one was not very important. Such an implication can do serious damage and interfere with developing rapport. The person will be inclined to reject both the preaching and the counseling of his minister.

Another way in which a pastor may seem rude to his people is in his attitude toward them. He may unconsciously think of people as projects instead of sensitive persons like himself. He may assume a sort of mass production attitude instead of imparting a sense of individual interest. When this happens people begin to feel like statistics instead of feeling loved.

This can also happen when people are not followed up after a crisis is past. Some people have felt loved until they accepted Christ, then they were dropped. The person who nurtured them into the kingdom was too busy working with someone else to give them continuing attention. Similarly, some people have felt very close to their pastor during a crisis, perhaps an operation or a death, but as soon as the crisis was over, they felt no further personal concern from their pastor. They got the feeling of being just another raisin in the box.

Pastors must also beware of categorizing people. This is natural for one must organize his thoughts and compartmentalize in order to get things done. But people do not like to be categorized, especially as deficient or mediocre. They can feel trapped by a categorical label; they want to outgrow being a "carnal Christian," a "divorcee," and "irresponsible person," or an "alcoholic."

The sinning person needs his counselor to identify with him in his struggles with guilt and temptations. Because of his guilt, he is inclined to feel the minister is rejecting him and condemning him personally when they discuss sins of which he is already aware. As he feels the caring, non-judgmental attitude of his counselor, he can identify with his counselor's strength and begin to straighten out his life. Jesus did not come to condemn the world, "but that the world through Him might be saved (John 3:17)." We, His counselors, represent Christ in identifying with the sinner and helping him find a way out of his condition. We are not called to condemn, but to love.

Being Judgmental Instead of Unbiased

The preacher renounces sin from the pulpit. This is one way he represents God to the people. This automatically leads his counselee to expect him to be judgmental in the counseling office as well.

It is important for all counselors to be non-judgmental, but it is especially important for the pastor to listen non-judgmentally. Every person must be granted the full *right* to be himself. If he must hide his true feelings to avoid being judged by his pastor only a limited benefit will result from the counseling experience. This means counselees must be free to express anger with their usual profanity. They must not feel they have to be different from their usual self in order to please the pastor.

It may be surprising to some pastors to believe they can be justified in allowing profanity or vulgarities in their presence without openly disapproving of the language. He should remember, however, that God already knows the counselees' heart and styling of living. While God doesn't approve of evil, He doesn't interfere with the person being what he is. He waits for the person to decide to clean up his language, and the minister is not above His Lord; he can also wait knowing that his own lack of profanity or vulgarity abides as a positive example of how to talk more discretely.

Perhaps it would be helpful to define more specifically what is meant by being judgmental and explain why being judgmental depreciates the effectiveness of counseling. There is a difference between making an objective evaluation and being judgmental. Being judgmental subtly attacks a person's sense of worth. It deals with what a person *is*, not what a person *does*. In contrast to this, objective evaluation concerns itself with what has been done and why it was done. A judgmental attitude says the person himself is good or bad instead of evaluating the impact of the deeds.

This is why the judgmental attitude is so devastating to counseling success. When a person is judged he begins to defend himself against his counselor's attitude. He either tries to please him as though he were a parent, or he starts to hide his deepest problems. When a counselee does not feel defensive, he can identify with his counselor's acceptance of him as a person and find an island of security from which he can attack his own problem more objectively. When he feels criticized, he tends to be more concerned with persuading his counselor that he has overcome his problem than he is with actually working on his problem. On the other hand, he may give up trying, and take the attitude, "It's no use, I can never do anything about my problem. Even my counselor condemns me."

When a person is used to preaching, of discovering philosophical truth and biblical insights, he tends to carry this interest over into counseling. This makes the pastor susceptible to preaching instead of listening in the counseling office. He usually does this without realizing how much he dogmatizes. He comes *at* a person instead of being *with* him. He tends to be caught up in the details of the problem instead of waiting to evaluate the situation and discover how he might help the counselee improve his method of coping. Thus he finds himself in a fatherly role preaching at the counselee, telling him what to do and why he should do it, and not realizing how he is handicapping the person from developing his own abilities to discern and to reason.

On other occasions ministers are threatened by certain kinds of problems. They may be embarrassed by discussion of intimate sexual experiences. They may feel overwhelmed when strong profanity is used. If a person bursts out with a blast of violent hostility, they tend to hold it down and mute the expression as very evil. They project their own anxiety to the counselee in a defensive manner and this makes them appear judgmental. An illustration might be a pastor saying, "Please don't use the Lord's name in vain in my presence. You are insulting the person I love." A little practice at being casual in the presence of most anything will help one become less judgmental. Allowing the person to be what he is and express himself without inhibition is another necessary frame of mind for the effective counselor.

We are called as Christian counselors to represent Christ, the mighty Counselor who is "touched with the feelings of our infirmities." He is leading us in our counseling just as He is leading us in our preaching. He brings people to us one by one for counseling help just as he brings people into the congregation family by family. We have to guard against over-reacting in any situation.

Overloading the Session Instead of Pacing the Counseling

Another subtle hazard to effective counseling is attempting to do too much in one session. Forty-five to sixty-minute sessions are usually long enough to cover all the counselee can possibly assimilate. It is easy for the busy minister to try to accomplish too much at one setting. This is unwise. By observing a consistent schedule of counseling and regulating the length of counseling sessions, the pastoral counselor can be more effective.

A person cannot usually assimilate more than one or two major insights at a time. It takes time for the mind to assimilate insights and to rest or rearrange itself before it is ready for more.

Overloading any one session with insights can be discouraging for the counselee. He may feel that he cannot possibly live up to all he sees. For these reasons it is better to terminate a counseling session before the counselee reaches the saturation point.

The counselor also needs to keep in mind the difference between intellectual and emotional insights. Intellectual insights are merely rational understandings of new truths. These are not the major insights to which the counselor is aiming. Insights of an emotional nature have to do with patterns of behavior, ways of coping, and styles of thinking and feeling. These kinds of insights are much more likely to produce lasting personality change and character improvement.

In communicating emotional insights the counselor should beware of trying to impress his counselee with how much he knows or how much insight he has into the problem. This can easily happen when the counselor suddenly gains new insight into the counselee's problem and immediately wants to share the information. This is desirable in most forms of communication. But we must remember the counselor-counselee relationship is somewhat like a doctor-patient interview. It is important for the counselor to understand the needs of his counselee and have in mind the insights he wishes to lead him to discover, but it is important to parcel out the information at the appropriate time so the counselee can use it to his best advantage.

The pastoral counselor may be more in danger of this hazard than other counselors, since he is used to giving out insights into the doctrines of the Bible. Usually, these insights are intellectual in nature. While they may be impressive and accurate and add an authoritative impact to the counseling session, they can easily overload the counselee and become more discouraging than helpful.

The pastoral counselor also needs to be sensitive in how he communicates spiritual concepts. The pastor usually senses a reality to God and spiritual truth, but the counselee may not have this sense of the reality of spiritual things at all. To him, God may seem to be only a name and biblical truth, only a dogma. It has no vitality and personal significance.

The pastoral counselor must take this sense of spiritual reality into awareness in his counseling. If his counselee is feeling deficient, spiritually inferior, or guilty at some point, these obstacles need to be reckoned with before he is showered with biblical insights. The counselor may do well to occasionally ask himself, "If I were he with his background and present feelings about God, would I appreciate hearing this?

How can I lead him into the sense of reality in Christ that I know and enjoy?"

Since the feelings of unreality about God are directly related to feelings of unreality in relationships with people, the counselor can help bridge this gap. By initiating an empathic relationship with his counselee, the counselee may gradually come to join him in the sense of spiritual realities. When this happens he may announce with delight, "God seems real again."

Used by permission. Reprinted from THE JOURNAL OF PSYCHOLOGY AND THEOLOGY - July 1973, Volume 1, Number 3 - Pages 35-41.

HAZARDS TO EFFECTIVE PASTORAL COUNSELING: PART TWO

MAURICE E. WAGNER

Being Directive Instead of Interpretive

Many people automatically view their pastor as a father figure. Emotionally disturbed people, especially, attach themselves to their pastor to satisfy some unmet need for a relationship with their own father. When this happens, they may relate to their pastor with seemingly unpredictable behavior. At one time they idolize him and may even be sexually attracted to him. On other occasions they are obsessive with angry feelings toward him. In some forms of therapy, these transference feelings are allowed to develop, so this can be explored in depth. In pastoral counseling, however, this is not advisable. The pastor has neither the time nor training to work through this complex "transference neurosis."

Unfortunately, the pastor who is not alert to these transference dynamics may unwittingly get caught up by them. The pastor who is habitually directive or who assumes a parental role over his people can feed into this unhappy situation. Anyone who has a neurotic need for a father figure will be inclined to attach himself to that kind of pastor. While this dependent adoration may do the pastor's ego some good at first, it will soon become annoying to the pastor, for it will hinder the counselee's emotional maturation. A pastor who is habitually directive tends to attract people to himself who are afraid of feeling rejected or guilty if they don't follow the pastor's guidance. This confuses the pastor's opinion with the will of God and promotes neurotic dependency and irresponsibility. It also handicaps people from discerning the will of God for themselves and overcoming their immaturity (See I John 2:27).

If, instead of displaying a superior, parental attitude toward his people, the pastor assumes a peer attitude and identifies with their personal needs in a friendly manner, he can avoid much of this problem. To do this, the pastor should concentrate on being in touch with his parishioners' particular level of maturation and need. He should be non-judgmental and loving, yet react to people's style of thinking to make them aware of both how they are defeating themselves and what they might do about it. He should try to open their understanding of how they are responsible for perpetuating their own distresses, and how they are responsible for working their way out of their predicament, even though someone else may have caused the problem!

When a pastor takes these attitudes, he discourages neurotic attachments to himself, for he is emphasizing each person's own responsibilities. While all pastors occasionally find themselves trailed by someone who is trying to find some "special" relationship, the likelihood of this happening is decreased when the pastor is less directive in his counseling and style of life. When this does happen, the pastor should not encourage it, but frankly tell the person of his need for professional counseling and make an appropriate referral. If the person persists and refuses to go to the professional counselor, as some do, then the pastor may be justified in firmly but lovingly telling the person he will be unable to talk with him further.

Being directive is a role of the preaching ministry. Being more or less non-directive is a role for the counseling ministry. While there are clearly times to be directive in counseling, it should be with the deliberate intention of helping the counselee through some immediate crisis. Care should be taken not to deprive the counselee of the opportunity to develop good judgment and ability to formulate reliable decisions. He can do this much better if someone is helping him think through his situation than he can if someone is telling him what to do. Each person, in order to mature emotionally, needs to develop his own powers of good judgment and ability to formulate reliable decisions. He cannot do this if his pastor is continually telling him what to do.

Being Emotionally Involved Instead of Remaining Objective

All counselors are called upon to deal with people who have had extraordinarily dramatic or emotionally charged experiences. It is not easy for the counselor to leave this situation without becoming emotionally involved. The pastor is aware of the love of God and feels compassion for people in distress. The right kind of involvement and rumination is very beneficial. Through it the counselor may be able to develop a better perspective in coping with the person's immediate needs. But excessive emotional involvement can cause a counselor to lose his objectivity. When this happens his involvement has ceased to be an asset and becomes a liability.

This loss of objectivity is very subtle. Every counselor must consider it an imminent danger. There is an exceedingly fine line between caring and being too emotionally involved to be helpful. On the other hand, there is a fine line between being indifferent and being objective. The effective counselor will be aware f these possiblities and guard himself accordingly. Most counselors become overinvolved when a client's problem is strange or bizarre, or when the counselee's problem somewhere touches the counselor's own emotional needs.

A common example of emotional involvement that can destroy effectiveness in counseling may be helpful. All ministers have busy schedules and many demands. A pastor or counselor who does not retain his right to time alone with his family, free time for meditation and recreation, or time for rest and relaxation is overly involved. Some counselors allow counselees to interrupt their family time, including meals, with phone calls or personal visits and they break into their night's rest with phone calls when there is no particular life and death crisis. One pastor received a call at 2 a.m. from his counselee who explained, "I couldn't get to sleep, Pastor, so I thought I'd call you and visit awhile."

Frankly speaking, pastors tend to be so busy meeting the demands of their church work that they often fail to meet their own needs in constructive ways. Some pastors allow themselves to become so busy they would feel guilty taking time for their own personal pleasure. This is most unfortunate. Pastors and their wives become emotionally starved for each other. Children also grow up to resent the demands of what they understand to be Christian commitment. Romance can grow cold in a pastor's home just as readily as in any other home, and when it does their love deteriorates into a Christian duty. They miss the delights of the God-given privilege of a happy romantic oneness which would please and glorify God and be a blessing to the children. A potluck dinner at the church is no substitute for a romantic evening with your wife, and working with the young people of the church is no excuse for not finding time with your own children for fun and personal pleasures.

Pastors who are so committed to the Lord's work in the church that they neglect their romantic relationship at home are easily motivated to lose their objectivity and become too involved with some younger woman who comes to them for help. One hazard which confronts the average pastor is the disturbed female whose marriage is a disappointment. She finds the pastor's gentle, loving, considerate attitude just what she has been looking for in a male. She will often track him to the counseling room to discuss her marriage problem. Usually she means no evil, but if the pastor is not in touch with his own emotions enough to hold his objectivity, he may fall prey to her "innocent" seductive mannerisms.

Statistics list a large number of pastors who could still be productive in the Lord's work today if it had not been for this human factor in the equation of their own lives. Unfortunately, it might have been avoided if they had followed God's order of priorities more carefully in the Pastoral Epistles — first the home, then the church. If a man is not what he should be at home, he is not qualified to lead the church. Counseling both husband and wife in these marriage situations is another safeguard. Not only will the counseling usually be more effective, but the pastor can also keep his objectivity.

Being Defensive Instead of Empathic

Empathy is the ability to feel another person's feelings. It is a natural talent, similar to intelligence and is perhaps the single most important ingredient of effective counseling. Small children, even before they are able to understand the language of their parents, have a cognizance of their parents' feelings. We lose empathy when its ability to function is blocked by various forms of anxiety. When we remove the block, the ability to empathize returns. Every counselor needs to be sensitive to the experiences, feelings and situations that hinder his capacity to empathize with others.

Anxiety is the basic hindrance to the functioning of empathy. Anxiety is the mind in a self-centered, self-protective attitude. Empathy is the mind in an other-centered, non-defensive attitude. Anxiety positions the mind to be concerned about oneself while empathy occurs when the mind is at peace with itself and interested in others.

Anxiety manifests itself in physical ways, but also in three reactionary emotions: hostility, guilt and fear. Hostility projects the blame for our uneasiness or irritation to some object outside ourself, usually another person. This attitude depreciates the intrinsic value of that person in the eyes of the anxious and hostile one. Thus when a counselor is angry he cannot relate to others empathically; his anxiety has blocked his wholesome use of empathy.

Guilt functions oppositely to hostility. Instead of projecting blame to someone else, the blame is accepted by oneself. The thought is, "I am anxious, and it is my own fault." In the case of guilt, anxiety is often related to the fear of painful consequences of being wrong. Instead of the other person's being depreciated in worth as with hostility, the person himself feels depreciated because of guilt. He thinks, "I am no good, and I'm afraid you will discover it." Needless to say, this blocks a counselor's empathic ability.

Fear is anxiety with a definite object. "I am afraid of being hurt, afraid of high places, afraid of being punished, etc." Anxiety is to fear as a bud is to a blossom. Fear is a development of anxiety around a specific object which, as a result, has become phobic. Fear, therefore, is a preoccupation with one's own insecurity; this inhibits the wholesome use of empathy in relationships.

The biggest problem comes when a counselor is not aware that he is being influenced by his own anxieties. His hostilities or fears are repressed. He is not angry and he is not anxious. Because these feelings do not show themselves overtly, the counselor fails to recognize their presence. But unfortunately, they have established biases in his thinking and attitudes in his mind which interfere with effective counseling.

For instance, a counselor who was reared by a mother who was threatened by his normal male aggressive competitiveness may have an opinion of women which is not realistic. He may view them as trying to control him. In the counseling room, this bias will seriously thwart a woman's need to express all of her feelings. He will not be empathic, but defensive, and she will soon discover it.

Unresolved hostilities of the past tend to make a person feel he has to be right regardless of what opinion he expresses. He will be unusually reticent to accept blame or applogize. These hostilities condition the mind to view others as inferior to himself, to enjoy being excessively helpful, to be thankful he is not as other men are, to be argumentative and to reject anyone who disagrees with him. They also make a person feel unduly suspicious of others and their motives. Seen in this light, repressed hostilities interfere with the counselor's maintaining a receptive frame of mind to listen empathically to what the counselee is trying to communicate to him and with his ability to sense the subtle, valuable innuendoes the counselee is not aware of communicating.

Repressed guilt feelings interfere with empathic communication in a different manner. Repressed guilt may make a counselor overly gracious, too accommodating, or too easily discouraged with his results. There are ways that guilt and hostility manifest similar symptoms from the repressed, but generally speaking, guilt makes a person preoccupied with how poorly he is doing. Repressed hostilities may sponsor unrealistic optimism while repressed guilt usually sponsors pessimism. Repressed hostility conditions the mind to be suspicious or paranoid, while repressed guilt causes dark clouds of depression to hover over the counselor's mind so that he cannot feel able to meet others, even in a peer relationship.

Repressed fears are difficult to explain in a short paragraph, even as hostility and guilt. Fears employ distortion and displacement to conceal their reality. A person, for instance, may be afraid of destroying himself by carrying out some wish for no limits in enjoying sexual liberty. The original idea may be so unthinkable that it is distorted so that the mind will not recognize it and then displace the idea to another object. The fear remains, but it is obviously without realistic, conscious meaning. For instance, the fear of heights may be related to a fear of the uninhibited feeling of floating in space which is related to the desire to feel uninhibited in sexual expression. Since falling leads to sudden pain, the fear of heights may also be a fear of sudden punishment for being out of control. The person believes that if he stays away from heights, he will feel safe from feeling total freedom.

One factor which complicates understanding the influences of repressed emotions is that fear, guilt and hostility are all reactive emotions to an underlying anxiety and they can substitute for each other. They are like three men in a tub: If one cannot row another will row for him, and the one who rows will be the one who causes the least anxiety in the present situation.

Professional counselors often undergo a serious didactic counseling experience to work through their own repressed emotions, so they will be more able to relate to their counselees empathically. The pastor who counsels very seldom has the opportunity for such a self-purifying experience, and so he is much more vulnerable to his own inner world of repressed emotions. He is likely to find himself uncontrollably losing his objectivity when his counselee confronts him with outbursts of hostility, or of unreasonable guilt, depression, sexual promiscuity, various phobias or psychopathic behavior. He may wish to be as empathic as the Lord who is "touched with the feelings of our infirmities (Hebrews 4:15)," but when the counseling crisis occurs he will lose his empathic contact with his counselee. He may not be aware immediately of his loss of empathy, but he may wonder why he seems to be losing rapport with his counselee.

The purpose of discussing this hazard is not to discourage pastors with limited training in counseling, but to suggest their need for lifting their own world of repressed emotions so as to increase their ability to empathize. Whenever anyone catches himself being influenced by some repressed emotion, he is on his way to discovering an insight which will help lift the repressed and find a release from its control. The repressed only functions effectively because it is not recognized. It is often a handy tool in the hands of Satan, the deceiver, to manipulate the Christian's mind to neutralize his ambitions to serve Christ effectively. As we become aware of these hidden feelings, we become more effective in our counseling roles, not to mention our total lives.

A complete discussion of the nature of repression and how the repressed is lifted is beyond the scope of this paper. It is helpful to keep in mind, however, a few guiding principles when dealing with one's own repressed feelings. Each repression is related to some experience in the past where the person has been afraid to handle the emotion. Repressed emotions are usually related to authority figures who had the power to reject, humiliate and punish. The fear of this rejection, humiliation or punishment caused the person to disown his own emotion and to act as though it never happened.

To lift repressed emotion means to recall situations of the past and dare to allow yourself to feel as you once were afraid to feel. If the emotion was a hostile one, admit the grudge and before the Lord honestly forgive that person as though it all happened today. Forgiveness is basically dying to the desired pleasure of vengeance. If the emotion was guilty, a simple confession of the wrong to God lays the foundation for accepting His forgiveness. If fear is the basic repressed emotion, reaffirm to yourself the caring presence of God with you in the feared situation. Some repressions can be relieved by the person alone, but others call for careful sharing with someone else, sometimes a professional counselor.

Being Divulging Instead of Strictly Confidential

This is a constant hazard to the effectiveness of the pastoral counselor. As a preacher, he needs to be in touch with his people and be sensitive to their needs. He also needs life-situation illustrations that are interesting. Counseling provides a ready resource of stories to tell which are both gripping and expose people to the fact that he does counseling.

Unfortunately, dipping into counseling experiences for illustrations deteriorates both the effectiveness of the preacher and the counselor. His illustrations may be interesting and be remembered, but his overall effectiveness will seriously wane. Why? Because he may be telling everyone that he can't be trusted with confidential information. He disregards the confidence that people have placed in him. He does not hold their secrets as a sacred trust before the Lord. Even though he may not be divulging the identity of the person "who came to see me last week for counseling with a difficult problem," he may be causing many in his congregation to think, "If I told him my secrets, he would be telling them next Sunday from the pulpit."

Leakage from the pulpit is a serious hazard to pastoral counseling and its effectiveness. Leakage in friendly and social conversations is also unadvisable. Telling family secrets, stories about certain members of his immediate family which obviously embarrass them is also a way of short-circuiting counseling effectiveness. The congregation will reason, "If he will tell that on his own family, what will he do with what I want to tell him?"

Most any life-situation revealed in the counseling room can also be found in some literature and other resources if the pastor is willing to dig for them. If he makes it a rule not to divulge publicly what he is told in secret, he will find himself increasing his effectiveness in both his preaching and his counseling ministries.

Trying to Help the Emotionally Ill Instead of Making Prompt Referral

There is a tendency among ministers to assume that they should be able to call upon the power of God to deliver everyone from distress. Certain passages of Scripture seem to indicate that we should do this and exercise faith that God will heal. If healing does not come, we are to exercise more faith or expect the person to forsake some sin. But the Bible also indicates that there are certain cases which are especially difficult and require unusual procedures.

When preaching, instruction or pastoral counseling does not bring results as a direct answer to our prayer, it is wise to pray for new insight and exercise patience. God may have a more detailed procedure in mind for the healing than we anticipate, and we know that whatever He does is good!

There are agencies established and authorized by the government for caring for the emotionally ill. Since all government is ordained of God, we need not avoid these agencies just because we want to see God glorified by a miracle in answer to our faith.

For instance, there are certain emergency situations which call for an immediate referral for psychiatric attention. Any person who is a serious threat to his own life or to the lives of others must be considered critical and referred to someone authorized to handle the problem. If the person will not go to a psychiatrist voluntarily, then the nearest relative or the police should be advised to take care of the situation. The minister should avoid becoming a party of the first part in initiating any involuntary commitments or arrests.

Another problem which should be referred immediately to a psychiatrist is psychotic behavior in a person. A minister should not try to counsel a person who is out of contact with reality. Usually some medication is advised, and only a psychiatrist or a medical doctor can prescribe the needed medicine.

Another emotional problem the minister usually should not try to counsel is aberrant sexual behavior (e.g., homosexuality). This type of character disorder involves long-standing maladjustments and requires the skills of a psychologist or a psychiatrist.

A good rule for any pastor to follow is to make friends of certain psychiatrists, medical doctors and psychologists in the area and confer with them occasionally about certain counseling situations. A pastor can learn much from a few minutes of friendly exchange about a problem, and he is at the same time acquainting professional help with his counseling ministry so that when he needs to make a referral, he has an available referral source. Knowing when and to whom to make a referral is a very important discernment for any pastoral counselor.

Referring the seriously emotionally ill person for proper medication and expert help may be the wisest move a pastor can make. It can free his time for being productive with others, and it will assure him that the right thing has been done for the benefit of the person in question.

When we speak of hazards to effective counseling, we recognize that vigilance is required for any type of effective witness for Christ (I Peter 5:8). It is not only important to prevent making mistakes, but it is also important to recognize and correct a mistake when it happens. We glorify the Lord by doing a good job, and we also glorify Him by recognizing our failings and correcting them. It is a commendable skill in counseling to be able to use our mistakes as stepping stones to improvement for both ourselves and our counselees.

Apologize if that is the proper thing to do. It takes a big person to admit when he is wrong, and if the apology is sincere, it will win the respectful admiration of the counselee. Often a frank acknowledgement to the counselee of our error will recapture the situation. A good way to compensate for an error might be to admit: "I was too emotionally involved for your good. I should have said or done this or that. Let us see how we can use this experience for our mutual benefit."

In conclusion, knowing where some of the hazards are in the counseling situation is a good safeguard against making serious mistakes. Most mistakes are not irreversible tragedies but can be remedied; many of them can be overcome before the counselee is aware anything is amiss.

Perhaps the most important concept to keep in mind is that Christ is really the Counselor; we are His agents doing His work, representing Him. His Holy Spirit is our Comforter and Guide and will lead us to deliver those He has brought to us for help. In this regard Paul wrote:

And the servant of the lord must not strive; but be gentle unto all men, apt to teach, patient, in meekness instructing those that oppose themselves; if God peradventure will give them repentance to the acknowledging of the truth; and that they may recover themselves out of the snare of the devil, who are taken captive by him at his will (II Timothy 2:24-26).

AUTHOR

WAGNER, MAURICE E. *Address:* 969 Ade Lante Avenue, Los Angeles, California 90042. *Title:* Licensed Marriage, Family and Child Counselor. *Degrees:* B.S. Lewis and Clark College, Th.B. Western Conservative Baptist Theological Seminary, B.D., Th. M. Northern Baptist Theological Seminary, Ph.D. Southern California Institute of Psychology. *Specializations:* Counseling psychology; pastoral psychology.

Used by Permission. Reprinted from THE JOURNAL OF PSYCHOLOGY AND THEOLOGY, October 1973, Volume 1, Number 4, Pages 40-47.

JESUS' STYLE OF RELATING:
THE SEARCH FOR A BIBLICAL VIEW OF COUNSELING

DAVID E. CARLSON

Trinity College

Presented at a conference on Research in Mental Health and Religious Behavior, Atlanta, Georgia, January 24-26, 1976. Used by permission of the author.

As professionals in the mental health field, we have been separated from each other because of our differing academic preparations and theoretical orientations. But that is only part of a sad story. More importantly, we have been separated from a large part of the body of Christ who fear psychology.

This paper is directed toward the task of bridging the gap between varying helping professions and dedicated to communicating with those in the church who are threatened by us. The major task facing us is integration between mental health professions and between Christian therapists and the Christian church. It is within this context — the need for integration — that I offer these thoughts regarding Jesus' style of relating.

Harry Blamires (1953) argues that there is no Christian Mind. That is, there is no collective viewpoint from which Christians can begin talking with each other about the Christian view of the major issues of our day. I believe conferences and articles are a start in establishing a collective Christian Mind. But we have several hurdles to overcome if we are to bridge the gap between the two cultures — one theological, the other scientific.

Culture Conflict

The first hurdle we must face is the problem of cultural conflict. Christianity has historically been confronted by challenges to faith. Often these challenges have come from within Christianity. Christians who are uncomfortable with the ambivalent position of being "in" the world but not "of" the world have historically presented much of the challenge. As evangelical Christians we are still struggling with an uneasy relationship to culture. Richard Niebuhr (1951) describes this as the Christ against culture position. If we are to accomplish integration, we must find ways to bridge this anticulture position. Some of us have ignored this issue by separating our counseling profession from our Christian faith. I don't believe this is an adequate response to the challenge. But ignoring the Christ and Culture controversy is no more satisfactory than the segregationist posture. We need

to affirm and demonstrate that Christ is not necessarily against mental health perspectives, psychology, social work, sociology. We need to find ways for the church to cope with perspectives that appear threatening and challenging to its view of the world. I am convinced that if integration is to be accomplished, we need to rethink the question of the relationship of Christ to culture. It will mean that we do not confuse Christ with Christianity or cultural evangelicalism with Christian culture (Dolby, 1972).

At the heart of the problem of integrating Christianity with mental health, then, is the need for a reintegration of our two cultures — one theological and the other scientific. Some have abandoned the quest altogether as impossible, nonsensical, or anti-Christian. But the problem still faces us, how are we going to relate revelation with research? It seems to me we need to try something that Constantine, Calvin, and a host of others attempted and succeeded to do with questionable results — to go beyond theology and psychology. We need to develop a Christian mental health perspective.

If we are to develop an integrated model, we can only do so by assuming a posture quite different from the Christ against Culture perspective. While we need to maintain a commitment to the authority and inspiration of Scripture and a belief in the corrupting, distorting, and destructive influence of sin in human thinking, we cannot long maintain a vital culture or community by renouncing everything which has its source in extra-biblical thinking or research. I assume that most of us submitted to the old evangelical culture of denial only to find out that as we acted out most of those ritualistic denials of knowledge and pleasure, they no longer contributed to our spiritual or mental health (Rieff, 1968, p. 254). It seems to me our efforts may be understood as an individual and communal attempt to stabilize our own ambivalent relation to our faith. We must be aware of a break in the continuity of evangelical culture and Christian community in order to take steps toward restoration and healing.

Cultural Lag

A second problem facing those of us who are interested in integration is cultural lag. Our techniques and tools for assisting hurting people are advanced beyond our theology. It seems to me we have a 19th century theology and a 20th century methodology of helping people. I hasten to point out that I view theology as a changing interpretation of scriptural truth. That is, theology is not a static view of Scripture. I am committed to propositional unchanging truth, but I believe our conceptions of truth change. What we need is a contemporary interpretation of Scripture which can relate to the developments and insights of contemporary mental health viewpoints.

To add to this difficulty, no systematic theologian as far as I know has addressed the problem of integrating the helping professions and biblical truth. There are literally hundreds of psychologists, psychiatrists, social workers, and others who have attempted to relate their discipline with Christianity. But where are the theologians' attempts at integration? I suppose one would recognize Tillich and the Niebuhrs as approaching integration from the theological left. And within the evangelical camp Carnell, Buswell, and Henry could be recognized for some attempt at integration. But, most theologians seem to have little interest or preparation to discuss integration with those of us in the mental health professions. This has left most of us with having to develop our own scriptural and theological foundation to our counseling practice through informal or formal seminary education. We are in a curious position as Christian professionals; seemingly, we are either professionals in the helping professions and amateurs in theology or professionals in theology and amateurs in helping theory. In this age of specialization, we need to engage in dialogue, to study and learn from each other. The job of integration is certainly too big for one person to develop competency in both fields.

Those of us who are attempting to integrate Christian theology and therapeutic theory must face our theological and psychological limitations squarely. We must be willing to reexamine our integration model. We must reject the temptation to defend our position through the use of overworked biblical texts proclaiming these as the only important words God has spoken. I'll let you supply your own illustrations of this problem to avoid the criticism of taking potshots at anyone. Yet, my point is that we must be willing to welcome controversy and debate because it is through these processes that our theory and practice are enriched, modified, and corrected.

Authority

A key problem confronting those interested in integration is the issue of scriptural authority and relevance. This question can be described in several ways. At one level the controversy is between a conception of Scripture as the *only* source of truth and ultimate source of truth. At a second level the controversy is over the relationship of special revelation to natural revelation. Often persons who hold this view tend to confuse scriptural data with theological interpretation. That is, they ignore the need to discover, study, and research the meaning of special and natural revelation. More specifically, the controversy can be expressed by asking three questions:

(1) What are the permissive limitations of man's creativity in counseling theory and technique beyond the biblical record? That is, is it permissible for man to create theory and technique beyond that which Scripture describes?

(2) Is Scripture our only legitimate source of information about counseling?

(3) What is the interrelationship between revelation and research? How should (can) these inform and enrich each other?

Within the evangelical community many are defensive about learning from extra-biblical sources and non-Christian persons. This posture often leads to a distorted and exaggerated set of claims for what the Bible says.

These persons attempt to discover a biblical basis or approach for counseling to the exclusion of clinical and experimental data. Others have bought a view of counseling to the exclusion of any biblical or theological input. I am concerned about both groups of people. Those who have enthusiastically bought counseling as a legitimate methodology of ministry but continue to renunciate the sources of counseling theory as necessarily anti-Christian. And I am concerned about those who buy counseling theory and practice yet remain uncritical of its theological presuppositions or implications.

Hermeneutics

There are at least two other major integration problems both of which I will address more specifically later in the paper. One hindrance to integration is the issue of selective hermeneutics — that is, choosing only those portions of Scripture which support your particular view of counseling. The other hindrance to integration is the personality needs of the counselor which encourage the counselor to proclaim Jesus as the answer to all problems in an immediate sense. At the heart of the issue is this question: In what sense is Jesus the answer to problems immediately and/or ultimately?

Integration: The Basic Issue

I sense we are in a curious position — caught between those Christians who attempt to escape culture and the helpers who attempt to escape Christ. I see us Christian professionals caught between those who would transform psychology into theology and those who would transform theology into psychology. To me the process and problem of integration is quite different. I conceive of integration to be the conscious bringing together of the component aspects of psychology and theology without violating their individual autonomy or identity and without ignoring conflict, paradox, and mystery. In this view, integration is more than baptizing psychology with scriptural texts or lining up psychology and theology to see their points of correlation and convergence.

As I suggested earlier, integration is only a concern for the Christian who is willing to consider the relationship between special and natural revelation as informative, corrective, expanding, and interrelated holistically. I expressed this as going beyond theology and psychology.

The basic question, as I see it, for developing a model of integration is, what is the relationship between biblical and nonbiblical data? We must ask more than how Scripture and academic disciplines are related, compatible, or contradictory. We need to go beyond correlation and convergence to confluence and congruence. Integration is more than a harmonizing of Scripture and human research. Integration is built on the foundational belief that all truth is God's truth wherever it is discovered. If one assumes the relationship between Christianity and culture to be necessarily antithetical, then integration is defined as impossible. Taking this Christ against Culture position prevents one from asking an essential question, Is there a larger reality or whole of which these disciplines, theology, psychology, psychiatry, and social work are merely the parts?

I would like to suggest a model which has the possibility of integrating doctrinal and theoretical counterpoints without rejecting them as dogmatic contradictions. If I have any unstated assumptions, I suppose they are: (a) that Christ is the living, functioning resolution of the differences between the disciplines, that Christ embodies this greater reality (Colossians 2:4), that Christ, rather than one's theology, is the organizing principle because theology has led us all too often to our anticulture posture; (b) that theology and science are compatible as long as they both direct their search toward what is, and as long as they both continue to assume that some consistent theory and system of description, explanation, and prediction is possible.

The Search for Jesus' Style of Counseling

The search for Jesus' style of counseling is, I suppose, an inevitability for evangelicals. With our high view of Scripture, we are rightly cautious about accepting a view or approach toward helping which is not first checked out with our absolute rule and guide for faith and practice. There is something authoritative, if not romantic, to claim that your style of counseling is biblical and follows our Lord's approach to people. Yet the search for a biblical style of counseling has its pitfalls. For example, to claim an approach is biblical may lead to a wholesale uncritical acceptance of the position. Also, it may be overly optimistic to think one can define Jesus' style of counseling with any more preciseness than defining the New Testament Church. And third, one must remember that Jesus was more than a man. Whatever his techniques of counseling, he possessed something quite unique, God-power and God-perspective and God-understanding.

Did Jesus Have a Style of Counseling?

Did Jesus have a style of counseling? Originally, I titled my paper, "Jesus' style of counseling." I've reconsidered that idea from both the biblical and current use of the word "counseling." I now believe it is more correct to talk about Jesus' style of relating. Biblically, the word counseling is never used. When the word counsel is used, it is limited to giving or taking advice. The word counselor is used in both the Old and New Testaments. Of the three times used in the New Testament (Boulutees, Mark 15:43, Luke 23:50; Sumboulos, Romans 11:34), it is descriptive of a person's employment as advisor. The same meaning is in the Old Testament (see Proverbs 11:14, 15:22, 2 Chronicles 25:16, Isaiah 1:26, 9:6).

Strictly speaking, the 20th century concept of counseling was foreign to the writers of the New Testament. Counseling as defined currently in the mental health field goes beyond advice giving and broadly describes a variety of interventive strategies. In this paper I choose not to get into the debate over the differences between counseling and psychotherapy. Rather, I prefer to use the concept counseling in its generic sense. That is, counseling is descriptive of a wide range of interventive, interpersonal relationships intended to bring about change in another person. Therefore, I conclude that given the current broad use of the word counseling and the narrow biblical use of the word counselor, it would be more precise to describe Jesus' style of relating than limit him to only advice giving or taking.

However, in the current debate among evangelicals, frequently it is claimed that Jesus had a style of counseling. Adams (1967, 1973, 1974) and Solomon (1975) are among those who specifically claim Jesus' style of counseling was directive, confrontive, and one of preaching. One of these authors describes his style of counseling supposedly patterned after Jesus' model as, "I simply attempt to speak the truth and face the facts" (Jabay, p. 44). I have come to describe this position as "prophetic counseling."

On the other side are those authors (Hulme, 1956; May, Lake & Clinebell, 1966; Hiltner, 1945, 1949) who claim their counseling is Christian and implicitly suggest they are modeling Jesus. I describe this counseling approach as "priestly counseling." For the sake of clarity I have outlined what I see to be the major differences between these two approaches:

Christian Counseling Approaches

Prophetic	Priestly
convicting	comforting
confronting	confessional
preaching	interviewing
lecturing	listening
thinking for	thinking with
talking to	talking with
proclaiming truth	affirming truth
disturbing the comfortable	comforting the disturbed

Broadly speaking, these two basic approaches could be described as directive and nondirective counseling regardless of their claims to be distinctively Christian. While I independently arrived at this conceptualization of Christian counseling approaches in the two categories "prophetic" and "priestly," they appear to be similar to Frank's (1963, pp. 147-148) two classes of therapeutic methods, directive, and evocative. Also, they largely parallel Wolberg's (1967) reeducative and reconstructive categories. This distinction in counseling positions, of course, has its historical roots in the '40s long before evangelical Christians accepted counseling as a legitimate ministry.

Christian therapists have generally recognized this distinction in their writing. However — and this is the *crux* of the issue — few counselors, Christian or non-Christian, view these divergent counseling approaches as a integrated continuum. For example, Christian counselors generally argue either for an eclectic or dichotomistic approach. On the one hand, the *similarities* of counseling approaches are emphasized, and, on the other hand, the *differences* between counseling approaches are also emphasized. The eclectic view often is an attempt to marry Christian and secular thought with the result that Christian thought often takes second place. The dichotomous view often is an attempt to preserve the authority of Scripture over secular thought with the result that the secular thought is described in almost demonic terms.

A Biblical View of Counseling

The Prophetic and Priestly approaches appear contradictory and are often claimed to be antithetical to one another. However, I would like to suggest that Jesus' style of counseling incorporated both of these divergent approaches. To assist in presenting my argument, I have utilized the sociological concept of role. For those of you unfamiliar with this concept, "role" can be defined as expected behavior of a person holding a specific social status (position).

I began my exploration of the question, What is Jesus' style of counseling by searching the Gospels to observe what approaches Jesus made to people. What I found is this: Jesus' style of relating to people was varied, not monistic. While it is true that Jesus used confrontation, it is equally accurate to describe Jesus' technique of relating as comforting. Jesus' approach was multivaried; that is, he taught from Scripture, listened, drew pictures, asked questions, told stories from which he asked his listeners to draw their own conclusions. As we take the whole counsel of God into consideration we begin to see that Jesus was not limited to one style of relating.

Reviewing Jesus' dealings with people, there appears an interesting relationship between the role Jesus chose to play and his style of relating. For example, when Jesus took the role of "prophet," he preached, taught, confronted, and called for repentance. When he took the role of "priest," he listened, forgave, mediated, and called for confession. When he assumed the role of "king," he paraded, ruled, and called for the establishment of the kingdom. When he chose the role of "lamb," he sacrificed, accepted ridicule and rejection, and called sinners to be healed by his stripes and bruises. When he submitted to the role of "servant," he washed feet, served food, gave of himself, and called for humility. When he played the role of "shepherd," he fed his flock, nurtured, protected, and called the lost to be found.

Table 1
Jesus' Role Repertoire

Status	Role
Prophet	Preaching, teaching, confronting, calls for repentance
Priest	Listening, forgiving, mediating, calls for confession
King	Parades, rules, calls for establishment of kingdom
Lamb	Sacrificing, accepts ridicule, rejection, calls sinners to be healed
Servant	Serves food, nurtures, washes feet, cares for, gives self, calls for humility
Shepherd	Nurtures, protects, calls lost to be found

If we attempt to model our counseling or relating after Jesus' example, then, like Jesus, we should play a variety of interventive roles as we relate redemptively to hurting people. I submit that the biblical view of counseling is a multivaried one. It seems to me that if my analysis of Scripture is correct, then it is a mistake to claim one style of relating as distinctively Christian or biblical. It is a mistake in at least two ways: first, because it is based on selective reading and interpretation of Scripture, and second, because it limits the mobility of responses essential for helping. "One of the measures of competence for the change agent is his ability to shift to another model when this is called for" (Seifert & Clinebell, 1969, p. 54).

A dichotomous view of Christian counseling then is unacceptable. But so is an eclectic view which tends to ignore paradox and conflict. I would like to suggest a biblical view of counseling which is continuous rather than dichotomous, integrative rather than eclectic. The model of counseling which I believe is more accurately descriptive of Jesus' style of relating than either the dichotomous or eclectic views can be conceptualized on a status-role continuum. Notice that the roles and technique are intimately related but technique is not exclusively limited to one role. Also notice that I have added a third descriptive term which I believe is a necessary conclusion from the biblical data.

Table 2
Jesus' Style of Relating

Counseling: A continuous View*

Statuses	Prophetic	Pastoral	Priestly
R O L E S	Critic, preacher, teacher, interpreter, mediator, confronter, convictor, corrector, confessor, admonisher, advocate, sustainer, supporter, lecturer, advisor, burden bearer, listener, reprover, warner, helper, consoler, pardoner.		

* Illustrative not exhaustive

By this model I am suggesting that our interventive roles can be the result of professional training and commitment or they can be personal characteristics and capabilities. Ideally, the range of therapeutic responses represents an integration of a person's professional role and personality so that the counselor does not merely act out a particular helping role but actually possesses the attitudes and feelings of that role. As you can see from this continuum of statuses and roles, therapists have many interventive role possibilities. Whatever our primary counseling role, whether it be prophetic, pastoral, or priestly, I see the need for us to expand our repertoire of interventive roles and therapeutic responses to include all three role models if it is to be correctly a biblical style of counseling.

I am arguing that the prophetic, pastoral, and priestly roles in counseling are different but they are not antagonistic. In Scripture each role is related to another role and is an integral part of the larger role network identified as the body of Christ (see Romans 12, 1 Corinthians 12). There is an organismic and functional relationship between these roles (see Ephesians 4:11-16). The New Testament documents described these roles as gifts necessary for the development of each person in the Christian community. I conclude that Jesus' style of relating utilized the repertoire of roles now found in the church.

Whoever named the journal of the National Association of Christians in Social Work, *"Paraclete,"* understands my argument. The cognate verb of this Greek word is often translated "to exhort," but as John Carter (1975) observes, "the concept is broad enough to support a variety of therapeutic techniques from crisis intervention to depth therapy, and it is a gift given to the church which is clearly different than the gift of the prophet or teacher." Another student (Ulrich, 1976) has observed, "this gift of the Spirit describes many forms of relating, ranging from the paregoric (consolatory) and encouraging, to the hortatory and paraenetic (admonitory)."

What Can We Learn from Jesus' Multirole Ministry?

What can we learn from Jesus' multirole ministry? First, therapeutic role integration is possible when one takes into consideration the whole counsel of God. Specific roles can be differentiated and distinguished from each other, but they cannot be logically or biblically segregated from each other. There are many interventive roles from which the Christian counselor can choose. Jesus' roles were not mutually exclusive, but they did have relative importance based on both who and why he was relating to a person. Jesus demonstrated role flexibility and variability. The implications of this for our Christian counseling is rooted in the observation that Jesus related to people where they were. Jesus was never in a dichotomous bind, having to choose between prophetic, pastoral, or priestly roles. The Christian counselor, for example, can be both directive and nondirective. He does not need to choose a directive approach which is dogmatic, that is, to the point of not being able to listen to where and why people hurt. He can be a listener without excluding teaching. The Christian counselor may be prophetic but not at the expense of the needs of the hurting person for a priest. He may reprove, correct, and instruct, but like prophets in Scripture, he must at times be the bringer of a message of consolation and pardon.

Granted that the Scriptures describe role variability in redemptive relationships, some counselors will have difficulty in achieving role flexibility largely for two reasons. First, the counselor may be inadequately socialized into other therapeutic intervention models. Second, the counselor may be unable to achieve role flexibility due to the rigidness of his personality. The first problem can be overcome through additional education and training, but the second problem poses more difficulties in bringing about change. If one's identity, self-concept, and ego-ideal are exclusively invested in one of the role models, then there will be a tendency to maintain the one particular role at all cost. I am suggesting that role integration is possible only if the personality of the counselor is integrated. In other words, integration between Christ and culture in the therapeutic encounter can be achieved only if the counselor can become an integrated personality.

Second, we can learn from Jesus' style of relating that one can "know" what the problems and solutions are and yet be willing to listen and understand. Because one has knowledge does not preclude a willingness to listen and understand. Nor does it suggest that a counselor must ignore his preconceived ideas of what the client needs. However, it does mean that one can be explorative without excessive explaining, and, he can be confrontive without unnecessarily challenging or raising the person's defenses. Prophets bring a message as God's representative to man. The message relates to where the people are and what they are doing. Unlike the biblical prophets, the "prophetic counselor" gathers his data from the person he is serving rather than receiving privileged information about his client from God. Priests also bring a message from God to man, but this message of forgiveness follows man's confession to God, i.e., the priests' message to God. Like the biblical priests, "priestly counselors" must remember that listening only is never enough. Forgiveness and pardon must follow confession. And many times directives for restitution will also be part of the priestly counselor's role.

Third, Jesus' style of relating suggests that a counselor can be authoritative without being authoritarian. A danger of prophetic counseling is not the style of counseling as much as the personality needs of the counselor. The prophetic approach lends itself to be used by persons who need their counseling to be evidence of their authority. On the other hand, counselors may be attracted to a priestly style out of needs to avoid using their authority therapeutically. The implication is that authority is an intrinsic quality in each of the counselor roles and need not be avoided for effective counseling to take place.

Fourth, Jesus' style of relating indicates that one can be right without having to demand that the counselee accept and recognize the counselor's rightness. For example, most of the prophets were not heard, but that is not evidence that their message was incorrect. Often the issue for the counselor is not rightness as much as affirmation of one's worth and dignity. I might add this is often the issue for our clients also. Truth is truth regardless of another's acceptance of it. Most people can be led to the truth more easily than given the truth. While as counselors we may know the truth, our truth for another person cannot change his behavior until it becomes "his truth." That is, the client must hear the truth and understand it for himself before it will effectively change his behavior.

Fifth, Jesus' style of counseling raises the issue of the counselor timing his confrontations and interpretations. Jesus shared ideas, advice, and solutions without demanding his audience hear these before they were ready. The prophetic style counselor is often a person who expects he can change people by saying the right words regardless of their preparation and readiness. As one minister confessed, "When I entered the ministry, I held the rather firm conviction that the Bible possessed all the answers to every human need and problem. I was under the impression that all a counselor had to do was come up with the right Bible verse for the problem, and presto, the problem would be solved. I soon learned in the crucible of everyday ministry that problems are not solved that easily, nor feelings changed that simply." He goes on to claim, "This does not imply that I lost confidence in the authority of the Scriptures to deal with human needs. It does imply that I lost a great deal of confidence in the approach and method I was using. I saw that it was ineffective and too simplistic" (McDill, 1975).

Jesus teaches us also that sin and guilt are concerns equally important to all counseling roles. One can believe in sin and the importance of the consciousness of sin without necessarily playing the role prophet. Many times clients are painfully aware of their sinfulness and wrongdoing. They are looking for one who can help them deal with their guilt and the negative consequences of their behavior. They come to the counselor craving for the intervention of someone whom they can trust to help them out of seemingly impossible feelings and circumstances. These clients come not because they need to be confronted with their sin but because they need to confront their sin through confession and repentance. This is the very fundamental difference between the prophetic counselor proclaiming truth previously unheard or rejected and the priestly counselor affirming truth the hurting person finds difficult to face. Yet, whenever confrontation is necessary, it is more than speaking the truth. To the Christian counselor confronting is speaking the truth in love (Ephesians 4:15). "Always with grace, seasoned with salt" (Colossians 4:6).

In addition, prophetic counseling will be convicting rather than condemning. The "paraclete," whether Jesus, the Holy Spirit, or a fellow Christian, plays the role of convictor. Therefore, the client will experience acceptance yet reproof and correction. Particularly for our Christian counselees we can proclaim, "There is therefore now no condemnation for those who are in Christ Jesus" (Romans 8:1). It is imperative to remember, however, that while the truth is freeing (John 8:32) at first it often creates considerable discomfort. Also, I have found that when the client experiences condemnation, its source is often self-inflicted, or the work of Satan, or the result of family and friends who are helping the Holy Spirit with his role. The Spirit convicts; people and Satan condemn (see John 16:8). When a person is hurting, whether feeling convicted or condemned, it is at these times the counselor must be able to be a priest more than a prophet.

And last, we learn from Jesus' style of relating that the role of counselor-priest is to mediate between the divine and the human. He is man's representative to God. In counseling this priestly mediatorial function takes on the added dimension of assisting the Christian client to be his own priest, to develop his own priesthood abilities. We do want the client to be decreasingly dependent on the therapist and increasingly dependent on God to work out his own salvation. Hulme argues that the counselor "never violates the priestly prerogatives" of his clients to be their own priest (Hulme, p. 120-121). While the counselor may mediate for his client, this is not to be the end of the therapeutic exchange. The counseling relationship should be a means to an end, the means to help clients do their own mediating, to develop their own confessional-prayerful relationship with God. "As the priestly function of the counselee becomes blocked, the (counselor's) task is not to jump in and mediate for him, but to (help him) remove the block so that he may resume his own mediatorship" (Hulme, p. 130).

Conclusion: Advantages and Affirmations

I have argued for the integration of therapeutic roles. I believe there are several advantages to expanding our repertoire of interventive roles. We will avoid two important pitfalls. The pitfall for the nondirective priest-counselor is the temptation never to speak the words of comfort, forgiveness, and healing. The pitfall for the directive prophet-counselor is the temptation never to listen, to jump to conclusions, to speak the words of God before the person is ready to hear them. Bonhoffer makes an important suggestion to both the prophetic and priestly counselor: "We should listen with the ears of God that we may speak the words of God" (p. 99).

Another advantage to adopting this model of counseling is the dialogue it can facilitate between those of us who are at polar extremes on the status-role continuum. We do need to talk *with* each other. We need to end the debate regarding the biblical view of counseling by recognizing there are many approaches illustrated in Scripture. But we must go beyond an exclusivistic hermeneutic which limits man's creativi-

ty in developing counseling approaches. We need to affirm that Christ's creative work is to be legitimately continued by his creation, man. Let us affirm that human creativity and culture are good when they are produced to the honor and glory of God (Colossians 3:16-17).

The third advantage of this integrated model is its potential to direct research. A key issue for research is: When are the various interventive roles most effectively utilized in the therapeutic process? We need to learn when to confront, comfort, speak, listen. Paul writes: "In all its complexity, the question toward which all outcome research should ultimately be directed is the following: *What* treatment, by *whom*, is most effective for *this* individual with *that* specific problem, and *under* which set of circumstances" (Patterson, 1973, p. 539). I am strongly suggesting that we end the argument whether there is a biblical view of counseling. We need to move on to research what specific interventions produce what specific changes in what specific clients by what kind of therapists.

A second research issue is the development of an integrated counseling model which is tested clinically and empirically. I have attempted to show that an integrated model is possible. Like Rogers, I believe, the divergences in counseling only "seem irreconcilable because we have not yet developed the larger frame of reference that would contain the polar extremes." Allport said it well, "the trouble with our current theories is not so much that they are wrong, but that they are partial" (Patterson, 1973, p. 532).

Jesus' style of relating suggests a wide range of redemptive approaches to helping people. What I have tried to suggest in this model of counseling is a repertoire and range of counseling roles which can legitimately be labeled biblical. The focus of this paper has been more on the various roles which can be played by Christian counselors and on their presuppositional view of Christ, culture, and Scripture than on counseling technique per se. I have argued for the recognition of a repertoire of counselor roles which can be described on a status-role continuum as prophetic to priestly. Counseling from a Christian perspective assumes an overall gestalt, a holistic view which recognizes, accepts, and uses various role relationships in the helping process. It assumes that Christ and culture are distinguishable (separate) but not necessarily divorced (contradictory). It recognizes that love, wisdom, kindness, listening are virtues of Christian relating and are common denominators between the prophetic and priestly counseling approaches. This is, Jesus' style of relating suggests that the principles of counseling are more importantly executed in spirit than method. This model of counseling assumes that one of the measures of competence for the counselor is his ability to shift to another counseling role when the client's readiness and needs indicate.

As we sort from the treatment maze which is called "Christian Counseling," let us recognize that the differences between the many counseling approaches are often more complementary than conflicting. Let us recognize that there are "differences" among counseling methods: different theoretical tenets, different words to express concepts and terms, and different mechanics to implement the various strategies. However, when considered in a broad perspective, these differences are almost inconsequential. Perhaps the real difference lies in the counselor — he understands some methods better than others, and because of his personal style and emotional comfort level, he can apply some methods better than others" (Peoples, 1975, p. 372). Perls reached the same conclusion, "by and large the various theories are not logically incompatible . . . (they) often nearly supplement and indirectly prove one another" (Patterson, 1973, p. 523).

In addition, as we take into consideration the divergences and convergences of counseling theory and technique, it is important from a Christian perspective to keep in mind that his spiritual gifts also dictate what style of relating the counselor may choose to utilize. I assume that all counselors will not possess the full range of "paraclete" gifts. When a counselor's spiritual gifts are limited, it is imperative that he utilize others in the body of Christ as cotherapists.

Let us affirm today that methodology is not supreme or sufficient in Christian counseling. What is important? You and I as the helper. What are we like? How well do we relate? Truax and Carkhuff (1967) taught us eight years ago that approach is not the most important ingredient in counseling. What is? The personal characteristics of the counselor, such as accurate empathy, non-possessive warmth, genuineness, congruence.

While the importance of relationship may not be equally recognized in directive (prophetic) and nondirective (priestly) techniques, it seems relationship is a common denominator in these divergent counseling approaches. Patterson, summarizing divergent counseling theories, concludes the counseling relationship is "characterized not so much by what techniques the therapist uses as by what he is, not so much by what he does as by the way he does it" (Patterson, 1973, p. 536).

Therefore, Jesus' style of relating is based more on *who* Jesus is than on *what* Jesus says or does. Whatever role Jesus plays — prophet, priest, pastor, king, savior — he is Christ. Whatever Jesus' approach to hurting, sinful people, he is Christ. Whatever role or approach we use in counseling, let us above all imitate Jesus' Christlikeness more than his techniques. Moreover, let us depend on "Christ in us" (Colossians 1:27) as we counsel.

Jesus' style of relating provides a model for us today, but it does not necessarily provide a norm. There are no commands in Scripture to imitate Jesus' style of counseling. But there are commands to be like Jesus. "So if there is any encouragement in Christ, any incentive of love, any participation in the spirit, any affection and sympathy . . . Have this mind among yourselves, which you have in Christ Jesus" (Philippians 2:1-5).

REFERENCES

Adams, J. *Competent to counsel.* Nutley, N.J.: Presbyterian & Reformed, 1974.

Adams, J. *Christian counselors manual.* Grand Rapids: Baker, 1973.

Blamires, H. *The Christian mind.* New York: Seabury, 1963.

Bonhoffer. *Life together.* New York: Harper, 1954.

Carter, J. Adams theory of nouthetic counseling. *Journal of Psychology and Theology,* 1975, 3(3), 143-155.

Clinebell, J. H. *Basic types of pastoral counseling.* Nashville: Abingdon, 1966.

Dolby, J. R. Cultural evangelicalism: The background for personal despair. *Journal of the American Scientific Affiliation,* 1972, 24(2), 91-101.

Frank, J. D. *Persuasion and healing.* New York: Schoken, 1963.

Hiltner, S. *Clinical pastoral training.* New York: Abington, 1949.

Hulme, W. E. *Counseling and theology.* Philadelphia: Muhlenberg, 1956.

Jabay, E. *Search for identity.* Grand Rapids: Zondervan, 1967.

Lake, F. *Clinical theology.* London: Darton, Longman, Todd, 1966.

May, R. *The art of counseling.* New York: Abington, 1939.

McDill, T. *Peer counseling in the local church.* Unpublished doctoral dissertation, Bethel Seminary, 1975.

Niebuhr, H. R. *Christ and culture.* New York: Harper & Row, 1951.

Patterson, C. H. *Theories of counseling and psychotherapy.* New York: Harper & Row, 1973.

Peoples, E. *Readings in correctional casework and counseling.* Pacific Palisades, Calif.: Goodyear, 1975.

Reiff, D. *Triumph of the therapeutic.* New York: Harper, 1968.

Rogers, C. *Counseling and psychotherapy.* New York: Houghton Mifflin, 1942.

Seifert, H., & Clinebell, H. J. *Personal growth and change.* Philadelphia: Westminster, 1969.

Truax, C. B., & Carkhuff, R. P. *Toward effective counseling and psychotherapy: Training and practice.* Chicago: Aldine, 1967.

Ulrich, J. *The practice of the gift of exhortation according to the New Testament.* Unpublished masters thesis, Wheaton College, 1976.

Wolberg, L. *The technique of psychotherapy.* New York: Grune & Stratton, 1967.

AUTHOR

CARLSON, DAVID E. Trinity College, Deerfield, Illinois. Assistant Professor of Sociology. *Degrees:* MA Northern Illinois University, BD Trinity Evangelical Divinity School, MSW University of Chicago.

EFFECTIVE COUNSELING AND PSYCHOTHERAPY:
AN INTEGRATIVE REVIEW OF RESEARCH

KEITH J. EDWARDS

Rosemead Graduate School of Psychology

A review of research relevant to the practice of psychotherapy is presented. Research on the central role of cognition in emotional behavior is reviewed as the basis for the therapeutic approach known as cognitive behavior modification. The three stages of the therapeutic approach offer the potential of a unified explanation for the effectiveness of a variety of therapeutic schools as well as a basis for integrating psychology and theology in therapeutic practice. The potential for a theology of the thought life informing therapeutic practice is explored. Finally, the cognitive behavior modification model is embedded in an interpersonal view of therapy to account for the overwhelming evidence of the importance of the therapeutic relationship in effective therapy. The influence of client-therapist value similarity and therapist's characteristics on the quality of the therapeutic relationship are explored. The biblical and psychological data reviewed suggest a fruitful approach to formulating effective and integrated intervention techniques.

The field of counseling and psychotherapy has experienced a growing tradition of rigorous research directed at answering the problem. Is psychotherapy worthwhile? Does it work? In the face of a rising empiricism in psychology in general and direct challenges of the efficacy of therapy by critics such as Eysenck (1962), the therapist could no longer justify his efficacy with ambiguous case studies and personal testimonies. Early research efforts were directed at proving that therapy in fact was effective or that certain orientations were superior to others. These initial defensive reactions eventually gave way to the realization that psychotherapy was a complex enterprise, the process and outcome of which was contingent on a variety of interdependent factors (Kiesler, 1966). Research studies became either complex or focused as researchers began to search for answers to the complex question of what treatment by whom is most effective for this individual with that specific problem under what circumstances and how does it come about (Paul, 1969). The resulting research literature is voluminous and diverse, and it is not my intent to try to give any systematic treatment of it. Several other writers have devoted themselves to this task, and I would simply refer the interested reader to their work. (See for example Meltzoff and Kornreich, 1971; Strupp and Bergin 1969; Luborsky, et al., 1971; Bergin and Garfield, 1971). Rather, I would like to concentrate my attention on a few promising areas of research in psychotherapy which in my view have implications for the integration of psychology and theology in psychotherapeutic research and practice. I approach this task primarily as a researcher with limited formal experience in therapeutic practice.

The areas I would like to discuss are the cognitive determinants of emotional or affective states and the treatment of neurotic anxieties via cognitive behavior modification; the role of value similarity and difference in the therapist-patient dyad; and therapist characteristics related to therapy outcome. While these three areas may appear diverse, they are related in that the first deals primarily with the client and the core aspect of the problem he or she brings to the therapeutic setting, the second with the patient-therapist dyad, and the third with characteristics of the therapist. Taken together these three emphases constitute major aspects of the therapeutic milieu. For each of these three areas relevant research is reviewed and then implications for integration are explored. The first area on cognition serves as a basis for understanding and interpreting the research in the other fields.

Cognition, Emotion, and Behavior:
As A Man Thinks So Is He

In psychology today in a variety of settings there is a revolution going on. Dember (1974) has referred to it as the cognitive revolution. From clinicians to experimentalists, from Freudians to behaviorists, the role of thought and cognition in controlling behavior and emotion has become a central concern. In the words of Dember "psychology has gone cognitive" (1974, p. 161). Psychodynamic theorists have for a long time emphasized the role of cognition and symbolic processes as determinants of emotion and behavior. Social learning theorists such as Dollard and Miller (1950) and Bandura (1969) have also placed great emphasis on the importance of cognition for understanding emotion and behavior but have rejected the highly inferential and nonverifiable constructs of psychodynamic theories. Psychologists of all theoretical stripes recognize the uniqueness of humans in our capacity to think symbolically and mediate our physiological states and behavior via covert verbalizations. Some consider man qualitatively different from other species in this respect, others consider him on the same continuum as other species but quantitatively superior. Whatever the orientation there is agreement that man's symbolic processing ability is the key to understanding the complexity of human behavior. Charles Eriksen characterizes this uniqueness of man well when he says:

"The laboratory rat can be conditioned to show fear or anxiety in response to a buzzer or other external stimulation but only man has the extensive capacity to carry within himself numerous anxiety-provoking cues in the forms of thoughts, memories, and other mediational processes. Due to his time-binding characteristics he can relive in the present, anxiety experienced in the past or anticipate disasters and dangers in the future. With plenty to eat, good health, lack of pain, and an opportunity for enjoyment of a variety of pursuits, man still can be miserably ill with anxiety through preoccupation with memories of an event that occurred weeks ago or with anticipation of a stressful situation weeks in the future (1966, p. 327).

Cognition or symbolic processing plays a central role in mediating humans' behavior and physiological arousal. It is important to emphasize at this point that the meaning of cognition as used in the present context is not limited to verbal statements or propositional logic. As Eriksen states above, human beings are capable of symbolic processing of both verbal and nonverbal symbols. Language acquisition in humans certainly facilitates symbolic processing but cognition is not limited to linguistic content. This point is illustrated in the skiing example in the following section.

Cognition and Behavior

All of us at one time or another have had the experience of learning a new skill, say tennis, golf, skiing, or whatever. Typically, in the initial phases of learning, we get instructions from a coach on proper technique. We then repeat the coaches instructions, usually out loud, to ourselves as we attempt the task (e.g., knees flexed-weight on the down hill ski-weight forward, etc.). As we practice and interact with our coach further instructions including a variety of statements, encouragements, corrections, wisecracks, *and even nonverbal images* become cognitions which we internalize and use to instruct and cajole ourselves down the slopes. This process of first overt then covert symbolic self-instruction appears to be universal in human learning. Two Russian psychologists, Luria (1961) and Vygotsky (1962), have made extensive study of the role of language in the development of behavior

control both normal and abnormal. After experimentation with children Luria (1961) concluded that "the speech system, which is formed in the process of the child's social interaction with adults, is a powerful means of systemic organization of our mental processes, and the precise study of this will help us to solve the important task of modifying and perfecting the higher nervous activities of man" (p. 144). It is important to emphasize that cognitions and especially language play their most significant role in early developmental stages of the learning sequence as in our skiing example. Once the behavior is mastered, the thinking processes used for mediational control become automatic and seemingly involuntary, like most overlearned sets. In the case of adaptive learning, such as for athletes, the phasing out of conscious verbal mediation is efficient and necessary. When the learning has been maladaptive, such as is neurotic anxieties and behaviors, the lack of awareness or "insight" the individual experiences is a major roadblock in helping him change.

Donald Meichenbaum and his colleagues at the University of Waterloo in Canada have successfully employed the cognitive-mediational view of behavior in the treatment of impulsive children (Meichenbaum & Goodman, 1971). Requiring impulsive children to talk to themselves using task-relevant statements modeled by the clinician, first overtly and then covertly, led to significant decreases in errors on a motor task compared to control children. The improved performance was evident in a one-month follow-up assessment. Similar self-instructional training was effectively used by Michenbaum with schizophrenic patients. The training emphasized practice in monitoring intra- and inter-personal behaviors with a view to providing the patient with cues for emitting task-relevant self-statements. The treated group improved significantly over controls on a variety of tasks including the amount of "healthy talk" emitted in a structured interview. The improvement was still evident in a three-week follow-up assessment (Meichenbaum, 1969; Meichenbaum & Cameron, 1973). Similar treatment approaches have been used effectively in reducing smoking (Stiffy, Meichenbaum, & Best, 1970) and in enhancing the creativity (Meichenbaum, 1975) and academic performance of college students (Meichenbaum & Smart, 1971). This research clearly establishes the clinical importance of changing cognition in facilitating behavior change. In fact, Loveless and Brody (1974) argue that the success of behavior therapies using operant or classical conditioning (e.g., systematic desensitization) is due as much or more to the precise insight gained by the client as to the conditioning paradigm employed. Given that cognition is central in behavioral acquisition and change, the question arises as to the role cognition plays in emotional behavior.

Cognition and Emotion

Men are disturbed not by things, but by the views they take of them.

Epictetus, 1st Century A.D.

There are several sources of evidence concerning the important role of cognition in emotion. Lazarus and Averill (1972), in their analysis of stress reactions, postulate that the human being is an evaluating organism who searches the environment for cues about what is needed or desired and evaluates the relevance of each input. The cognitive process of apprehending and interpreting that mediates between the environment and the emotional reaction is termed *appraisal*. Appraisal involves judgment of the situation, judgments of available coping skills, and evaluations of feedback after one responds.

Research relevant to the appraisal process and emotion has identified particular aspects of the cognitive process which are key. One aspect is perception of control. Aversive situations are viewed as less threatening and arouse less anxiety when one believes he has some control over the aversive stimulus (Glass & Singer, 1972). Whereas, lack of control and unpredictability of the aversive stimulus leads to "learned helplessness" (Thornton & Jacobs, 1971).

Another important aspect of cognitive mediation of emotional response is the labeling of emotions. Schachter (1966) has demonstrated that a state of induced physiological arousal (via adrenaline shots) gives rise to "evaluative needs" in the individual to search for a cognitive label for the arousal and thereby "understand" it. In a series of fascinating experiments, Schachter and his colleagues have demonstrated that emotion involves the interaction of two components: cognition and physiological arousal. Further, Schachter argues that it is the cognition, arising from the immediate situation as interpreted by past experience, which determines whether the state of arousal will be labeled "joy" or "anger" or whatever (1966, p. 194). He further notes that while autonomic arousal greatly facilitates the acquisition of emotional behavior, such arousal is not necessary for the maintenance of the behaviors. Such a process of behavior acquisition may be involved in certain neurotic behavior patterns, especially of the obsessive-compulsive variety.

The labeling process can also lead to or *cause* physiological arousal. Velten (1968), in an experiment where subjects read self-referring statements, found that mood varied as a function of the type of statement read (elation vs. depression). Albert Ellis' (1962) system of rational, emotive psychotherapy is based on the central proposition that irrational beliefs held by an individual mediate neurotic anxiety. A recent study by Goldfried and Sobocinski (1975) lend experimental

support for Ellis' position. Persons with a tendency to endorse irrational beliefs about need for approval, personal blame, perfectionism, etc. reported more anxiety in interpersonal and achievement settings and were more prone to anxiety in an imagined situation of social rejection than people low in the endorsement of the so called irrational beliefs.

Clinical views of the link between cognition and emotions vary according to the therapist's theoretical orientation. Specifically, cognition may be viewed as behaviors, automatic images and self-statements, irrational thinking styles and belief systems, or defense mechanisms to mention a few. Most of the research and treatment of various anxieties via cognitions has been based on the view of cognition as automatic images and self-statements or as irrational thinking styles and belief systems. Client use of facilitative "self-talk" in therapy has been successfully applied to reducing avoidance behavior of snake phobics (Meichenbaum, 1971), test anxiety (Meichenbaum, 1972), speech anxiety (Meichenbaum, Gilmore, & Fedoravicius, 1971), social inhibition (Ludwig & Lazarus, 1972), and homosexuality (Shealy, 1972). Even in studies where behavioral treatments have not explicitly included a cognitive intervention component, the importance of cognitions has emerged. Wolpe (1971) reports the use of systematic desensitization in the treatment of frigidity in which the woman's beliefs about her husband's attitude toward her had to be clarified in order to facilitate deconditioning. Loveless & Brody (1974) note that the detailed analysis of anxiety producing situations involved in establishing anxiety hierarchies for systematic desensitization gives the client the cognitive information needed to formulate helpful restructuring of attitudes, values, and verbal mediations of emotional responses.

My colleague, Dave Cabush, and I have reported a study in which clients trained in facilitative self-responding improved significantly more than clients receiving individual empathy-based counseling (Cabush & Edwards, 1976). Following the suggestion of Carkhuff (1971) that the preferred mode of treatment is to train clients directly, Dave designed a self-instructional program using the empathy model of Truax and Carkhuff (1967). We interpret the efficacy of the treatment in terms of its changing the client's self-talk in ways known to facilitate self-exploration and change.

A promising treatment strategy which explicitly address the client's self-talk and includes direct change of such talk as an explicit part of treatment has been formulated by Donald Meichenbaum (1973, 1974, 1975). Meichenbaum presents a three-stage process which is said to be the basis for therapeutic change. In the first stage the client must become an observer of his thoughts, feelings, and behaviors by means of heightened awareness and expanded cognitions (insight). The client comes to view his problem and develops insight in interaction with the therapist. The process of self-observation acts as the stimulus for stage two in which the client begins exercising more control by emitting cognitions and behaviors incompatible with the original emotion. Stage three is a feedback loop where the client interprets the effects of the newly acquired behaviors in terms of the new cognitions. Success at this stage determines whether or not behavioral change will persist and generalize.

Stage two of the model is where the client actually begins to acquire new thought patterns and coping styles based upon the insight gained in stage one. Meichenbaum has found the use of extensive modeling with a coping rather than mastery model as well as behavioral rehearsal by the client are essential for change to occur.

A coping model is defined as a person who demonstrates a process of coping with an anxiety producing situation. Particular emphasis is placed on the "internal dialogue" the model carries on with himself to cope with anxiety. The emphasis is on the internal process and the cognitive and physiological aspects of the anxiety. Research on coping models with an emphasis on process has resulted in more generalized improvement. Mastery models which focus only on external behavior tend to produce situation-specific improvement.

The therapy model presented has the potential of explaining the effectiveness of a variety of therapy styles from analytic to behavioral. Also, it suggests a means by which psychology and theology may be theoretically, empirically, and practically integrated into therapy. It is to the latter issue that I would now like to turn. In doing so I would like to emphasize these aspects of Meichenbaum's three stage model: 1) client conceptualization of his problem; 2) use of self-instruction via coping models and behavioral rehearsal to facilitate change; 3) client's evaluation of new behaviors based upon the feedback of others in terms of the new self-talk acquired in steps 1 and 2.

Cognition and Theology

At the beginning of this section on cognition I presented a paraphrase of Proverbs 23:7 "For as a man thinketh in his heart so he is . . ." This basic truth about man can be found throughout all of Scripture and is perfectly consistent with the research literature reviewed above. The master teacher Jesus Himself taught his disciples the centrality of man's thought life when he said "that which comes out of man is what defiles him . . . All these evil things come from within and defile a man" (Mark 7:20, 23). The writings of the Apostle Paul similarly reflect this theme. I would like to propose for the present discussion that the book of Philippians, and particularly Philippians 4:4-9, 11, 13, 19, is the foundation passage for relating the previously reviewed psychology of cognition to a theology of the thought life. In Philippians 4 Paul writes:

Rejoice in the Lord always; again I say, rejoice! Let your forbearing spirit be known to all men. The Lord is near. *Be anxious for nothing, but* in everything *by prayer and supplication* with thanksgiving let your requests be made known to God. And the peace of God, which surpasses all understanding, shall guard your *hearts* and your *minds* in Christ Jesus.

Finally, brethren, whatever is true, whatever is honorable, whatever is right, whatever is pure, whatever is lovely, whatever is of good repute, if there is any excellence and if anything worthy of praise, *let your mind dwell on these things.*

The things you have learned and received and heard and *seen in me, practice* these things; and the God of peace shall be with you.

. . . for I have learned to be content in whatever circumstances I am . . . I have learned the secret . . . I can do all things through Christ who strengthens me (*New American Standard Bible*).

Paul, under inspired wisdom, recognizes the connection between thoughts and feelings and provides God's antidote for anxiety. Imbedded in this passage and the entire Epistle are the three stages of behavior change as proposed by Meichenbaum. Paul points out that it is the positive, Christ-centered thought-life that counteracts anxiety and leads to the peace of God. From a variety of theoretical orientations using clinical sensitivity to our client's specific needs, the first goal of a Christian therapist should be to help the client recognize this central truth and help him come to see how his present patterns of thought deviate from it. I hasten to add that his is a very general goal, and I have no preconceived notions as to how this initial goal looks as an operationalized process. The maturing of psychotherapy research required the banishment of simplistic myths in favor of a more complex and realistic view of the therapeutic process (Kiesler, 1966). In like manner, integrative approaches to helping clients conceptualize their problems in terms of the central truth of Philippians 4 must respect this complexity. But one thing is clear, both psychologically and theologically, the types of thoughts we think determine whether autonomic arousal will be debilitating or facilitating.

It is important to further emphasize that the truth of Philippians 4 is written for Christians. The therapeutic power of the passage is made possible through a personal relationship with Jesus Christ. As Paul states, "I can do all things through Christ who strengthens me." To experience the reality of peace of mind and heart one must first be "in Christ Jesus."

Another aspect of Philippians 4 is Paul's reference to himself as a model. And what I find especially fascinating is that Paul uses modeling in precisely the way that has been empirically shown to be most effective — the coping model (Meichenbaum, 1971). Paul says in chapter 3 verses 12-13,

Not that I have already attained it (conformity to Christ) or have become perfect, but I press on . . . I do not regard myself as having laid hold of it yet; but one thing I do; forgetting what lies behind and reaching forward to what lies ahead, I press on toward the goal for the prize of the upward call of God in Christ Jesus.

Paul was very much in the process of maturing as a believer and he conveys this in his writings.

It is also interesting to note that Jesus is pictured as a coping model. Both in the temptation in the desert (Matthew 4:1-11) and the agony in the garden (Matthew 26:36-46), Jesus struggled with personal conflict. The relevance of the incarnation to the psychological principle of modeling is summed up well in Hebrews 4:15:

For we do not have a high priest who cannot sympathize with our weakness, but one who has been tempted in all things as we are, yet without sin.

In light of these last three words "yet without sin," it is important to note that the benefits of a coping model are derived from the process of coping modeled and not the mastery level attained. No one can expect to achieve the level of mastery Jesus did here on earth. But is the process of coping with temptations and limitations of human existence that Jesus went through with which clients can identify and counteract anxiety (see also 2 Timothy 4:7, 8).

The process of Jesus coping with temptation in the desert emphasizes two aspects. The first is knowledge of truth, "Man shall not live by bread alone but by every word that proceeds out of the mouth of the Lord" (vs. 4). The second is His relationship to God, "You shall worship the Lord your God, and serve Him only" (vs. 10). In the agony in the garden He models an honest, open struggling between human self-will and God's divine will with a submission to the latter. "My Father, if it is possible, let this cup pass from me; yet not as I will, but as Thou wilt" (Matthew 26:39).

Throughout the whole of Paul's writings he self-discloses his struggles and relates how personal relationship with Christ and a Christ-centered thought life had been key in his coping. I'm sure all of us have found personal encouragement at one time or another as we have identified with Paul's struggles such as the inner conflict of good and evil described in Romans 7. Having drawn the reader to emotional identification with the anxiety generated by the conflict, Paul expounds the great truth of Romans 8:1 which has banished guilt-ridden anxiety for ages "There is therefore now no condemnation to those who are in Christ Jesus." From time to time we have also encouraged clients, through a personal identification with Paul, that there is hope — we *can* cope. But now and then is not enough, providing clients with coping models is central to integrative therapy.

Also included in Paul's prescription for coping with anxiety is behavioral rehearsal. In Philippains 4:9 he not only says to view him as model but goes on to prescribe: "practice these things." Meichenbaum has found that the client's new thoughts must initiate a new behavior chain, one which is incompatible with his maladaptive behavior, if change is to be maintained and generalized. Self-instruction becomes a "psychological litany," a "rote-repetition of emotionless banter" unless task demands of increasing generality are part of treatment (Meichenbaum, 1975, p. 22). How many of us have seen clients' insight into spiritual truth rendered useless because they refuse to act and experience the reality of it. Behavioral practice via imagery, role playing, and therapeutic homework following the instructions of a coping model are specific techniques which should be a part of any integrative therapy. Jesus' brother James recognized the important connection between beliefs and behavior when he wrote "Faith if it has not works, is dead being by itself. I will show you my faith by my works" (James 2:17, 18).

Any professional who seeks to integrate mental health and religous behavior must consider the clients' total belief system — their faith. The analytic Greek Lexicon defines the most commonly used meaning of faith in the New Testament as a "firm mental conviction or persuasion." One's faith is thus intimately involved via cognition with one's emotions and behaviors. It is common in integrative discussions of faith and mental health to draw heavily on social psychological theory concerning attitudes, values, and beliefs to explain religious faith (e.g., Lewis, 1974). However, a look at a common definition of attitude suggests that they fit the two component model of emotional behavior of Schachter (1966) discussed above. Consider the following definition given by Johnson and Matross (1976, p. 52): "Attitudes may be defined as a combination of feeling and beliefs which result in a predisposition to respond favorably or unfavorably to a group, person, idea, event, or object." They further note that attitudes are relatively enduring predispositions which give continuity to behavior. I would argue that the cognitive behavior modification model of Meichenbaum subsumes the social psychological concepts of attitudes and provides a more clinically efficacious model for integrating the theological concept of faith.

Cognition and Scripture

The development of one's faith is an emotional process with a strong cognitive component for "faith comes from hearing and hearing from the word of Christ" (Romans 10:17). One of the goals of integrative therapy is to effectively use Scripture to help clients come to view their problems and formulate change producing thought patterns. The central role of scriptural truth in the change process is the thrust of two key New Testament passages.

All Scripture is given by inspiration of God and is profitable for reproof, for correction, for instruction in righteousness: that the man of God may be perfect, thoroughly furnished unto all good works (2 Timothy 3:16, 17).

The Word of God is living and active and sharper than a two edged sword, piercing as far as the diversions of soul and spirit, of both joints of marrow and able to judge the thoughts and intents of the heart (Hebrews 4:12).

In the Old Testament as well we find the power of Scripture extolled by the Psalmist:

Wherewithall shall a young man direct his way? By taking heed thereto according to thy word: Thy word have I hid in my heart that I might not sin against thee (Psalm 119:8,9).

Given that Scripture is essential to integrative therapy and its power lies in its influence on the thought life of the client, the question arises as to how should it be used? Any answer will be a function of the creativity, sensitivity, and theoretical orientation of the clinician as well as of the client's presenting problem, developmental history and belief system. Some of you may be concerned that many Christian clients are already characterized by a self-preoccupation and a belief system well integrated into the maintenance of their neuroses as in the case of the obsessive. The role of the therapist in stage one of the change process is to help the client come to see how this is so. But in any event what the client attends to and how he uses spiritual truth prior to therapy should be qualitatively and quantitatively different than his perspective following therapy. We need systematic research on the distinctions between the spiritual development and belief systems of various pathological groups and normals. Books such as Shapiro's *Neurotic Styles* would provide a basis for theorizing about such distinctions. We need a systematic theology of the thought life which attends to significant conflicts of human existence and which provides sound exegetical treatment of the texts. Whatever one's approach, we should eschew simplistic answers. We need to find out "which Scripture, by whom, is most effective for a given individual with a specific problem under what circumstances, and how does it come about? In developing scientifically based guidelines for the clinical application of spiritual truth we need to avoid uniformity myths and overgeneralizations.

Cognition and Prayer

Much of religious cognition occurs in the process of praying. Again the potential of this process as portrayed in Scripture has mental health implications. In Mark 11:24 Jesus says to the disciples, "Therefore I say to you, all things for which you pray and ask believe that you have received them, and they shall be granted you." Note the past tense in regard to the type of belief enjoined. This type of attitude appears to me to be similar to the mental set induced in experimental studies of expectancy or self-fulfilling prophecy effects (e.g., Meichenbaum & Smart, 1971).

An extensive study by Parker and St. John (1957) of the prayer lives of 15 individuals in distress who prayed "random personal prayers" as compared to 15 individuals in distress in a "prayer therapy" group suggested some interesting differences. The "random personal" group tended to employ negative prayer "as they reiterated their unhappy symptoms holding them directly in the focus of their minds, reaffirming them, they held them firmly in place and did not let them go. What they believed they got" (p. 44). In contrast, one of the major guidelines followed in the prayer therapy group was to hold positive, healthful, wholesome thoughts and images in the minds and believe and act as though the specific help requested had been received (p. 204).

A clinical colleague of mine, Nancy Duvall, reports on a case where a client who was making unusually rapid progress in therapy revealed a practice of pretherapy prayer for openness to change and a petition for insight on the part of both parties involved. Clearly, the potential of prayer as an adjunct to therapy when clinically directed in facilitative ways needs to be systematically formulated and investigated. In saying this I don't intend to limit our concept of prayer to a psychological bootstrapping technique. But Scripture is clear that our mental attitude, our faith inherent in our prayers makes a difference.

In all the areas mentioned above — theology, Scripture, and prayer — there are striking parallels to the clinically effective treatment mode of cognitive behavior modification; parallels which have great potential for integrative theory and practice of psychotherapy.

Client Therapist Value Similarity and Therapy Outcome

Having discussed at length the centrality of changing a client's thoughts as common to all therapy and the basis for formulating an integrative view of therapy, I would like to turn now to the issue of patient-therapist value similarity. There are some who have maintained that therapy is and should be a value free enterprise where the therapist avoids imposing his values on the client (Rogers, 1951). However, the consensus of theory and research to date is that psychotherapy is a moral enterprise in which the values of the therapist and those of the culture he represents permeate the therapeutic relationship (Beutler, 1972; Ehrlich & Weiner, 1961; Kessel & McBrearty, 1967; Krasner, 1966; London, 1964;

Pattison, 1968, 1969; Pruyser, 1971; Strupp, 1973). In discussing values and therapy Shostrom (1966) addresses the issue directly when he states: "Whether we like it or not . . . many therapies do teach values and the only question is whether we are going to make such values explicit or implicit."

The research evidence indicates that clients change in the direction of the therapist's values (Welkowitz, Ortmeyer, & Cohen, 1967) and therapist ratings of client improvement are related to the degree of client value change in the direction of the therapist's values (Rosenthal, 1955). Patient-therapist value similarity is also important for the establishment of a therapeutic relationship in the early phases of therapy. There is some evidence that deeply religious, fundamentalist clients tend to terminate or do not benefit from therapy with a counselor who doesn't share the client's religious belief system (Rosenbaum, Freidlander, & Kaplan, 1956; Rogers & Dymond, 1954). How value similarity facilitates therapy can be understood in terms of the first stage of Meichenbaum's model presented earlier. Recall that the first stage is the conceptualization phase where the client comes to formulate a cognitive view of his problem which serves as a basis for change. Meichenbaum points out that it is important for the therapist and client to have a common conceptual system in stage one. This is in part developed through initial therapeutic interaction. It is undoubtedly facilitated by initial similarity in belief systems (Frank, 1972).

While the evidence indicates that value similarity is facilitative of the therapeutic process, Pattison (1969) maintains that too specific a value consensus between client and therapist can limit therapeutic progress. Cook (1966) found a curvilinear relationship between value similarity and client improvement. A medium degree of value similarity resulted in the most positive change in self-concept. I would hypothesize that the influence of value similarity in therapy is a function of which phase the therapy is in. The concept of relationship complementarity of interpersonal psychology is helpful in theorizing about this functional relationship. The basic principle is that people will maintain and value relationships with persons whose interpersonal styles complement and thus reinforce their own. In healthy relationships both persons in a dyad are able to express a variety of needs and emotions and engage in a variety of behaviors to fulfill expressed needs and understand expressed emotions. Healthy individuals engage in a variety of give and take encounters with others which contribute to mutual growth. Clients seeking help because of problematic anxiety, on the other hand, are limited in their repertoire of interpersonal skills and are typically extreme in the behaviors they do employ (Leary, 1957; Carson, 1969). Within this conceptual system, a successful therapist is one who can engage in a controlled level of complementarity over the course of therapy. Initially, the therapist engages in high levels of complementarity to establish the relationship. However, such interactions contribute to the maintenance of existing behavior patterns and thus cannot be maintained if change is to occur. Dietzel and Abeles (1975) have found that therapists effective in helping people change are initially high in complementarity but reduce their interpersonal complementarity with the client during the middle phase of therapy. Effective valueladened therapeutic interactions most likely follow this same pattern. As Christian therapists working with Christian clients we are acutely aware of how the client's belief system is intimately involved with his neurotic anxieties and behaviors. Indeed the research on cognition suggests beliefs are the essential element in maintaining the maladaptive patterns. We recognize the need for the client's theological reeducation and may begin by avoiding behaviors which complement or reinforce the client's belief system. Such a strategy early in therapy may be less than optimal. Explicit maneuvers early in therapy which exploit the value similarity as an ally may be more facilitative. The question then becomes, what is the role of such things as therapist self-disclosure of beliefs, prayer, confession. Bible study, Christian community, etc. during these initial stages and throughout therapy? Admittedly, the use of such techniques with certain types of pathologies in religious clients is full of potential pitfalls. But neither is avoiding them a uniformly best solution. A recently reported case study by Vande Kemp (1975) is an example of one Christian therapist's struggle with the interaction of her value framework with that of the client's. We need more therapists addressing this issue.

Therapist Variables and Therapeutic Outcome

One of the shortcomings of Meichenbaum's model for therapy as outlined previously is that he doesn't account for the therapist's role in the change process explicitly. It is my view that any integrative model of therapy must include the therapist as part of the conceptual system. There is wide spread agreement among psychotherapists that a curative factor common to all modes of therapy is the quality of relationship offered to the client by the therapist (Strupp, 1973; Rogers, 1957). In this last section I would propose two biblical concepts which help define an effective therapist and which are supported by current research.

In order to relate to the client in a therapeutic manner the therapist must be mature, relatively free of personal conflict, and possess a high degree of personal self-awareness. In Galations 6:1 Paul writes, "Brethren, even if a man be caught in a trespass, you

186

who are spiritual restore such a one in a spirit of gentleness; looking to yourself lest you be tempted." I take the phrase "you who are spiritual" to imply maturity rather than to set up a dichotomy between Christians and non-Christians as Adams (1973, p. 34) does. Therapists who are more anxious, conflicted, defensive, or "unhealthy" are least likely to promote change in their clients. In fact, Bergin (1966) notes a disturbing deterioration effect for clients of such therapists — their clients get worse and would have been better off without therapy. Bandura, Lipher, and Miller (1960) found that therapist anxiety about hostility was directly associated with avoidance responses to client's expressions of hostility toward them. The client's self-explorations diminished in this area and the conflicts remained unresolved or deepened. Winler, Ahmad, Bandura, and Rau (1962) found the same relationship between therapist anxiety about dependency and client resolution of such conflicts with the therapist. Finally, Bergin and Soloman (1963) found that measures of therapists' degree of personal disturbance correlated negatively with their level of empathy as rated from actual therapy tapes. This finding brings us to the second major characteristic of effective counselors, their ability to be warm or empathic.

A therapist's inability to be empathic is one of the major causes of the "deterioration" effect (Truax & Carkhuff, 1964). In Romans 2:4 we see that the basic element in God's plan for our change is His love: "Or do you think lightly of the riches of His kindness and forbearance and patience, not knowing that the kindness of God leads you to repentance." Psychologically and theologically, empirically and theoretically, love is the basic force for human change. The ability to love others is a central characteristic of spiritual maturity (I Corinthians 13; Galatians 5:22). The ability of the therapist to exhibit warmth, empathy, or love toward the client determines whether the therapy will be for better or for worse.

We can incorporate the therapist as a variable in the model for change via cognitive behavior modification by viewing the emphathic relationship the therapist offers as the primary source of reinforcement for the client to adopt a new view of his problem and change patterns of thought and behavior. An extensive discussion of this view of therapist empathy is given by Martin (1972) under the rubric of learning-based client centered therapy.

God and Therapeutic Change

A significant omission to this point has been a consideration of God's influence in the change process. In general I believe the major influence of God is through the cognition of both the client and the therapist. As previously noted, Scripture is one of the key sources of such divine influence. Through scriptural truth the client and counselor develop a specific understanding of the problem. Through biblical revelation of the person and work of Christ, the client comes to understand and is motivated by God's love (Romans 2:4). Using scriptural truth as guide, the client and counselor by faith invoke God's appointed means of grace. The latter may include a variety of actions such as prayer, Bible study, fellowship, confession, forgiveness, encouragement, confrontation, etc. These may appear to be rather naturalistic explanations of how "God works" but they are a part of His will and not to be minimized.

I would go a step further and postulate that most of God's supernatural influence on His people is through cognitions inspired by the Holy Spirit. It is in the thought life that the spiritual, psychological, and physical interface. The question arises then as to whether Christians are qualitatively and quantitatively different from non-Christians in the thought life. Scripture does seem to support that there is a difference which should result in psychological and behavioral differences (cf. 2 Corinthians 5:17). We need theologians to help us understand the biblical distinctions between the thought lives of believers and nonbelievers. Then we as psychologists can explore the implications of such distinctions for emotion and behavior.

One specific difference between Christians and non-Christians relevant to our present discussion is acceptance of the message of salvation through Christ's death on the cross. In 1 Corinthians 1:18 Paul writes, "For the word of the cross is to those who are perishing foolishness, but to us who are being saved it is the power of God." Further on in verse 21 he says, "For since in the wisdom of God the world through its wisdom did not come to know God, God was well pleased through the foolishness of the message preached to save those who believe." Thus it appears that the watershed of integrative therapy is salvation. The efficacy of the doctrines of grace in dispelling anxiety-producing thoughts is dependent upon the faith of the client. The truth of the Philippians 4 passage cited earlier is applicable to individuals who have a personal relationship with God through the Savior, Jesus Christ. The emphasis upon relationship permeates the passage, "Rejoice in the Lord . . . the Lord is near . . . guard your hearts and minds in Christ Jesus . . . the God of peace shall be with you . . . I can do all things through Christ who strengthens me" (Philippians 4:4-9). Without faith in Christ as Savior the individual is left with the conflict of conscience described by Paul in Romans 7 because he is under the judgment of the law written on his heart (Romans 2:4-16). The Romans 8 message of no condemnation in Christ is without power for the nonbeliever. Alternative belief systems may be employed to counteract the conflict conscience. Albert Ellis' (1962) rational-emotive psychotherapy is the most explicit of secular therapies in addressing the issue of belief systems and conscience. But R-T, as the therapy is called, is effective in so far as the therapist can convince the client that there are no absolutes of right and wrong and there is no ultimate or absolute level of personal responsibility. In reality, R-T clients must become, at some level, psychopathic to relieve their anxiety. They must become insensitive to the conflict of conscience by defining it as stemming from irrational beliefs. The Apostle Paul teaches that the conflict of conscience is a universal human experience stemming from an instinctive response to God's absolute moral law (Romans 2:14). At the point of ultimate accountability, man's cognition, his internal disposition toward God, and not his behavior, will be the central focus. Paul says of nonbelievers:

... their conscience bearing witness, and their *thoughts* alternately accusing or else defending them on the day when according to my Gospel, God will judge the *secrets* of men through Christ Jesus.

In the face of this ultimate conflict of conscience only the truth of Romans 8:1 will suffice: "There is now therefore no condemnation to those who are in Christ Jesus." The integrative therapist uses this basic truth as a foundation to help Christian clients develop healthy thought patterns. Thus it is in the God-centered relationship begun with the client's salvation experience that God's influence on therapeutic change is most profound. It provides the belief framework, client receptivity, and spiritual power to respond to spiritual truth. This truth is the basis for restructuring thought patterns which in turn mediate emotional and behavioral change.

From Journal of Psychology and Theology. Volume , Number pages 94, 107.

REFERENCES

Adams, J. *The Christian counselor's manual*. Nutley, N.J.: Presbyterian and Reformed, 1973.

Bandura, A., Lipher, D. H., & Miller, P. E. Psychotherapy approach avoidance reactions to patients expression of hostility. *Journal of Consulting Psychology*, 1960, 24, 1-18.

Bergin, A. Some implications of psychotherapy research for therapeutic practice. *Journal of Abnormal Psychology*, 1966, 71, 235-246.

Bergin, A., & Garfield, S. (Eds.). *Handbook of psychotherapy and behavior change*. New York: Wiley, 1971.

Bergin, A., & Solomon, S. Personality and performance correlates of empathic understanding in psychotherapy. *American Psychologist*, 1963, 18, 393. (Abstract)

Beutler, L. E. Value and attitude change in psychotherapy: A case for diadic assessment. *Psychotherapy: Theory, Research, and Practice*, 1972, 9, 362-367.

Cabush, D. W., & Edwards, K. J. Training clients to help themselves: Outcome effects of training college student clients in facilitative self-responding. *Journal of Counseling Psychology*, 1976, 23, 34-39.

Carkhuff, R. R. Training as a preferred mode of treatment. *Journal of Counseling Psychology*, 1971, 18, 123-131.

Carson, R. C. *Interaction concepts of personality*. Chicago: Aldine, 1969.

Cook, T. E. The influence of client-counselor similarity of values on change in meaning during brief psychotherapy. *Journal of Counseling Psychology*, 1966, 13, 77-81.

Dember, W. Motivation and the cognitive revolution. *American Psychologist*, 1974, 29, 161-168.

Dietzel, C.S., & Abeles, N. Client-therapist complimentarity and therapeutic outcome. *Journal of Counseling Psychology*, 1975, 22, 264-272.

Dollard, J., & Miller, N. P. *Personality and psychotherapy*. New York: McGraw-Hill, 1950.

Ehrlich, B., & Wiener, D. N. The measurement of values in psychotherapeutic settings. *Journal of General Psychology*, 1961, 64, 359-372.

Ellis, A. *Reason and emotion in psychotherapy*. New York: Lyle-Stuart, 1962.

Eriksen, C. W. Cognitive responses to internally cued anxiety. In C. Spielberger (Ed.), *Anxiety and behavior*. New York: Academic Press, 1966.

Frank, J. D. *Persuasion and healing* (Rev. ed.). Baltimore, Md.: Johns Hopkins, 1972.

Glass, D.C., & Singer, J. E. *Stress and adaptation: Experimental studies of behavioral effects of exposure to aversive events*. New York: Academic Press, 1972.

Goldfried, M. R., & Sobocinski, D. Effect of irrational beliefs on emotional arousal. *Journal of Consulting and Clinical Psychology*, 1975, 43, 504-510.

Johnson, D. W., & Matross, R. Interpersonal influence in psychotherapy: A social psychology view. In A. Gurman & A. M. Razin (Eds.), *Therapist contribution to effective psychotherapy: An empirical assessment*. Elmsford, N.Y.: Perjamon, 1976.

Kessel, P., & McBrearty, J. F. Values and psychotherapy: A review of the literature. *Perceptual and Motor Skills*, 1967, 25, 669-690.

Kiesler, D. J. Some myths of psychotherapy research and the search for a paradigm. *Psychological Bulletin*, 1966, 65, 110-136.

Lazarus, R., & Averill, J. Emotion and cognition: With special reference to anxiety. In C. Spielberger (Ed.), *Anxiety: Current trends in theory and research* (Vol. 2). New York: Academic Press, 1972.

Leary, T. *Interpersonal diagnosis of personality. A functional theory and methodology for personality evaluation*. New York: The Ronald Press, 1957.

London, P. *The modes and morals of psychotherapy*. New York: Holt, 1964.

Loveless, E. J., & Brody, H. M. The cognitive base of psychotherapy. *Psychotherapy: Theory, Research and Practice*, 1974, 11, 133-137.

Ludwig, L. D. & Lazarus, A. A. A cognitive and behavioral approach to the treatment of social inhibition. *Psychotherapy: Theory, Research, and Practice*, 9, 1972, 204-206.

Luria, A. R. *The role of speech in the regulations of normal and abnormal behavior*. London: Liverright, 1961.

Martin, D. G. *Learning-based client-centered therapy*. Monterey, Ca.: Brooks-Cole, 1972.

Meichenbaum, D. H. Cognitive factors in behavior modification: Modifying what clients say to themselves. In Rubin, Brady, & Henderson (Eds.), *Advances in behavior therapy* (Vol. 4). New York: Academic Press, 1973.

Meichenbaum, D. H. *Cognitive behavior modification*. Morristown, N.J.: General Learning Press, 1974.

Meichenbaum, D. H. Cognitive modification of test anxious college students. *Journal of Consulting and Clinical Psychology*, 1972, 39(3), 370-380.

Meichenbaum, D. H. Enhancing creativity by modifying what s's say to themselves. *American Educational Research Journal*, 1975, 12, 129-146.

Meichenbaum, D. H. Examination of model characteristics in reducing avoidance behavior. *Journal of Personality and Social Psychology*, 1971, 17, 295-307.

Meichenbaum, D. H. The effects of instructions and reinforcement on thinking and language behaviors of schizophrenics. *Behavior Research and Therapy*, 1969, 7, 101-114.

Meichenbaum, D. H. Toward a cognitive theory of self-control. *Paper presented at the Annual Convention of the American Psychological Association*, 1975.

Meichenbaum, D., & Cameron, R. Training schizophrenics to talk to themselves: A means of developing attentional controls. *Behavior Therapy*, 1973, 4, 515-534.

Meichenbaum, D., Gilmore, J. B., & Fedoravicius, A. Group insight versus group desensitization in treating speech anxiety. *Journal of Counseling and Clinical Psychology*, 1971, 36, 410-421.

Meichenbaum, D., & Goodman, J. Training impulsive children to talk to themselves: A means of developing self-control. *Journal of Abnormal Psychology*, 1971, 77, 115-126.

Meichenbaum, D., & Smart, I. Use of direct expectancy to modify academic performance and attitudes of college students. *Journal of Counseling Psychology*, 1971, 18, 531-535.

Parker, W. R., & St. Johns, E. *Prayer can change your life: Experiments and techniques in prayer therapy*. Englewood Cliffs, N.J.: Prentice Hall, 1957.

Pattison, E. M. Ego morality: An emerging psychotherapeutic concept. *Psychoanalytic Review*, 1968, 187-222.

Pattison, E. M. Morality, guilt and forgiveness in psychotherapy. In E. Mansell Pattison (Ed.), *Clinical psychiatry and religion*. Boston: Little, Brown, & Co., 1969.

Paul, G. L. Behavior modification research: Design and tactics: In C. Franks (Ed.), *Behavior therapy: Appraisal and status*. New York: McGraw-Hill, 1969.

Pruyser, P. W. Assessment of the patient's religious attitudes in psychiatric case study. *Bulletin of the Menninger Clinic*, 1971, 35(4), 272-291.

Rogers, C. R. The necessary and sufficient conditions of therapeutic personality change. *Journal of Consulting Psychology*, 1957, 21, 95-108.

Rogers, C. R., & Dymond, R. F. *Psychotherapy and personality change*. Chicago: University of Chicago Press, 1954.

Rosenbaum, M., Friedlander, J., & Kaplan, S. M. Evaluation of results of psychotherapy. *Psychosomatic Medicine*, 1956, 18, 113-132.

Rosenthal, D. Changes in some moral values following psychotherapy. *Journal of Consulting Psychology*, 1955, 19, 431-436.

Schachter, S. The interaction of cognitive and physiological determinants of emotional state. In C. Spielberger (Ed.), *Anxiety and behavior*. New York: Academic Press, 1966.

Shapiro, D. *Neurotic styles*. New York: Basic Books, 1965.

Shealy, A. E. Combining behavior therapy and cognitive therapy in treating homosexuality. *Psychotherapy: Theory, Research, and Practice*, 1972, 9, 221-222.

Shostrom, E. L., & Knapp, R. R. The relationship of a measure of self-actualization (POI) to a measure of pathology (MMPI) and to therapeutic growth. *American Journal of Psychotherapy*, 1966, 20, 193-202.

Steffy, R. A., Meichenbaum, D., & Best, J. A. Aversive and cognitive factors in the modification of smoking behavior. *Behavioral Research and Therapy*, 1970, 3, 115-125.

Strupp, H. H. On the basic ingredients of psychotherapy. *Journal of Consulting and Clinical Psychology*, 1973, 41, 1-8.

Thornton, J. W., & Jacobs, P.D. Learned helplessness in human subjects. *Journal of Educational Psychology*, 1971, 87, 367-372.

Truax, C. B., & Carkhuff, R. R. For better or for worse: The process of psychotherapeutic change. In *Recent Advances in behavioral change*. Montreal: McGill University Press, 1964.

Vande Kemp, H. From pathological systems to differentiated individual, interpersonal and religious issues. *A paper presented at American Psychological Association Convention*, 1975.

Velten, E. J. A laboratory task for induction of mood states. *Behavior Research and Therapy*, 1968, 6, 473-482.

Vygotsky, L. *Thought and language*. Cambridge: MIT Press. 1962.

Welkowitz, J., Ortmeyer, D., & Cohen, J. Interactional effects of value system convergence: Investigation of patient-therapist dyads. *Journal of Consulting Psychology*, 1967, 31, 48-55.

Winder, C. L. Ahmad, F. Z., Bandura, A., & Rau, L. Dependency of patients, psychotherapy responses, and aspects of psychotherapy. *Journal of Consulting Psychology*, 1962, 26, 129-134.

Wolpe, J. Correcting misconceptions in a case of frigidity: A transcript. *Behavior Therapy and Journal of Experimental Psychiatry*, 1971, 2, 251-258.

RAPID TREATMENT
FOR A TROUBLED MARRIAGE

ANDRE BUSTANOBY

Andre Bustanoby is a marrage and family counselor in Bowie, Maryland, and a member of the American Association of Marriage and Family Counselors. He is an ordained Baptist Minister and has pastored churches in Arlington, Virginia, and in southern California. He also conducts communication workshops and family life conferences. Mr. Bustanoby and his wife Fay have four sons.

The treatment of troubled marriages is not a complex, mystical procedure. Aside from specialized problems such as sexual dysfunction or difficulties arising from the rest of the family system, most dilemmas that couples face may be approached with the same therapeutic methodology.

I should say parenthetically, however, that no one should get the idea that counseling is a bag of tricks. It is a therapeutic relationship. If you have not read Charles B. Truax and Robert R. Carkhuff's book *Toward Effective Counseling and Psychotherapy: Training and Practice*,[1] do so. They point out that there are many approaches to counseling, but three characteristics are common to every successful counselor: accurate empathy, nonpossessive warmth, and genuineness. For the Christian counselor and pastor an integration of biblical truth in this therapeutic triad is also important.

I will describe a methodology that I have found very workable in bringing about rapid change in a troubled marriage. By rapid change I mean enabling a couple to function on their own after eight to ten counseling sessions. If a couple is not making it on their own by then, one of them—or perhaps both—is resisting the process of change. The counselor's task becomes, then, not the marital problem but the resistance. In such a case further work on the resistance is needed.

I should say one further word before describing the procedure. I am assuming that the couple is *committed* to making the marriage work and that each is willing to *accept responsibility* for making it work. I will not work with a couple without this basic foundation. I do attempt to help them make such a commitment and accept responsibility, but we can go no further until this is done. With a cooperative, highly motivated couple the method I follow gets quick results. It involves four steps: (1) communication, (2) diagnosis, (3) negotiation for change, and (4) follow-up.

Communication. Almost without exception the couple with the troubled marriage is having a communication problem. If they knew how to talk to each other constructively, they would be solving their own problems. Their communication is probably following the pattern of attack, defense, and withdrawal.

I use two primary means of bridging the communication gap. The first is the Marital Communication Inventory.[2] This document is composed of 46 multiple-choice questions. The overall score for the average successful marriage is 105 out of a possible 138. A score below 95 indicates that communication is quite poor. In using this test, I tell the couple how each scored the communication in the marriage, and then I focus on the responses that reveal problem areas and have them talk about their communication style. Here we get down to specifics. For example, the first question is, Do you and your husband (or wife) discuss the manner in which the family income should be spent? If the answer is never, I want to know why. As I listen to the couple, I am able to pick up patterns in their communication style that keep them from conversing constructively. The pattern will often be an attack on the spouse and defense of self. By being very directive and not permitting attack or defense, I attempt to break up the couple's dysfunctional communication.

Sometimes a couple needs a more structured approach. The relationship may be so tense that they can't even talk in the counselor's office without fighting. I use a second device called the Revolving Discussion Sequence (RDS). This exercise slows down the process and keeps each from attacking the other. It is also designed to put each in touch with the other's feelings without judging whether or not those feelings are valid.

I start out by giving some basic rules. The couple must communicate in a way that does not sound attacking. This has to do with the content of what they say as well as the tone of the voice and body language (gesture, expression on the face, etc.).

Also, when they are spoken to, they must not defend themselves. When you try to tell a person how you feel and that person defends, explains, or justifies himself in any way, you will feel it's useless to tell him how you feel. The important thing is not to judge the rightness or wrongness of the feelings but to get in touch with what is there.

Finally, the emphasis must be on how each feels. This is conveyed with an "I" message rather than a "You" message. Instead of saying, "You are insensitive," it is better to say, "When my feelings are ignored, I feel like a nobody." Instead of saying, "You are a nag," say, "When I keep hearing what a poor husband I am, I feel beaten down, and I get angry."

The Revolving Discussion Sequence (RDS) attempts to teach these concepts by doing. I first ask one of the spouses to make a feeling statement to the other and to give the reasons for the feeling. The statement should be short and to the point. For example the wife may say to the husband, "I feel like a worthless person when you seem to have time and energy for everyone but me."

I then have the husband repeat the statement. This is to see if the husband heard exactly what she said and to slow down the exchange of words between them when tempers are hot.

She will then tell him if he correctly repeated what she said. If he doesn't, we repeat this step until it's right. He must be accurate.

The next step is for him to agree. He can agree with both the factuality of the statement and the feeling, or he may agree only that she feels that way. Many times the man will say something like, "But I don't give my time and energy to everyone but you." He wants to defend himself and argue the facts. I answer, "The facts are unimportant. The important thing is that your wife *feels* that way. Do you agree that she feels that way?"

The reasonable man will usually agree. Sometimes he will say, "No, she doesn't feel that way." My response is; "How do you know how she feels? Can you get inside her skin and feel her feelings? Are you saying that you don't want her to feel that way or that she has no right to feel that way? The fact of the matter is that she *does*, and only a change in your behavior will make her feel different."

Then I ask him to go through the same steps and make a feeling statement to her on the same theme. He may say, "I feel annoyed because you want more of my time than I'm willing to give you." She repeats the statement to check for hearing accuracy, and he corrects her where necessary. Then I tell her that she must agree with him. Sometimes a woman will say, "Well, shouldn't a husband be willing to give his wife his time before he gives it to total strangers?" My answer is, "The important thing is not to beat on him with shoulds and oughts but to listen to his feelings. When you understand his feelings, you're in a position to change what is causing problems in the relationship."

Couples spend a lot of time arguing about facts and shoulds and oughts, but they get nowhere. The primary thing in communication is to get in touch with feelings and the reason for them. You don't need to agree with the facts, but you must agree that the person feels as he says he does.

Sometimes couples have a hard time getting a feeling statement together; so I ask them to huddle with me. I help them put together a functional statement.

Sometimes one or both of the spouses will sabotage the process by *crazymaking*, a communication device we all use from time to time whenever the conversation begins to make us feel uncomfortable or trapped.[3] Crazymakers may derail you—get you off the subject—or they may overload with volume or content. The victim of crazymaking leaves the scene with his mind in confusion, actually feeling that he's going crazy. One couple went through a fifty-minute session of RDS and gave me just two functional statements. She was the crazymaker and spent the rest of the time derailing me, overloading me, and using every device she could to keep me from getting her to make a clear functional statement of her feelings.

Diagnosis—How to Identify What's Happening. My emphasis in diagnosis is interpersonal rather than intrapsychic. Intrapsychic has to do with behavior that is produced by internal condition of body and mind. Interpersonal has to do with behavior that is produced by our interaction with people. My diagnosis and therapy has to do largely with helping people understand their problem in terms of their relations with and reactions to other people.

Now I don't eliminate the intrapsychic entirely. Any client who tends to be depressive I refer to a doctor for a complete checkup before he begins counseling. There could be a physical cause for his problem. A common problem I run into is menopausal syndrome. One of my clients has hypoglycemia, a physical disorder marked by an inability to maintain a proper blood sugar level. Deep depression and irrational anger mark this disorder.

Once I determine that the client is not suffering physical disorder, I diagnose and treat him with a view of interpersonal problems—how does he relate to significant other people in his life? If it is a family problem, I want to see how the entire family operates together. If it is a problem between husband and wife, I want to see them together and work with them together. It is extremely difficult to get anywhere with a marital problem by seeing just one spouse. You need the input that both offer.

The first step in diagnosis is to identify the fight issue. Psychologist George Bach suggests that there are eight basic problem areas in troubled marriages. He calls them "fair fight" issues—basic stimuli that cause the spouse to feel anger, threat, or any other negative emotion which in turn jeopardizes the relationship. The presenting issue may appear trivial, but the fact that it arouses heavy emotional involvement is a clue that it represents a more basic issue that threatens the well-being of either or both spouses.

For example, heated arguments often arise over tardiness, household disorganization, or the extravagance of one of the spouses. These are surface issues that hook into a more basic issue—the issue to which they ought to be giving attention. Perhaps tardiness really hooks into the basic issue of centricity—am I important? When the husband is habitually indifferent about punctuality in dealing with his wife, she may feel, "I am unimportant to him. He seems to be on time for everyone but me." They may argue whether or not it's important to be on time for supper, with numerous side issues like the price of meat, but neither will win because each can assemble the facts to support his own view. Nevertheless, one thing cannot be argued: the wife *feels unimportant* and taken for granted by her husband. His protesting that she shouldn't feel that way is entirely out of order. The fact is that she *does* feel that way, and her husband's behavior causes the feeling. It is far easier for the husband to change his behavior than for the wife to change how she feels about that behavior. And, indeed, when he does change his behavior with respect to tardiness, he gives his wife the unmistakable message that he is listening to her, that he values her feelings, and that she is significant enough for him to change his ways.

Space does not permit my going into the fair fight issues in detail. My tapes on rapid treatment give fuller treatment as does my booklet, "How to Fight with Your Spouse." I will simply list the fight issues and identify what they are:

a. *Distance.* Every person has a psychological distance that is comfortable. Couples have problems establishing a proximity that is comfortable for both.
b. *Power struggle.* Who defines the relationship—one spouse or both? Do they struggle over who calls the shots?
c. *Trust.* Can feelings be exposed without fear of attack?
d. *Defense of self-identity.* Does each feel natural in his or her role as husband or wife?
e. *Sex.* Do they agree on what kind of sex, how often, when, and under what circumstances?
f. *Centricity.* Do both have the capacity to make the other feel important?
g. *Unrealistic illusions and expectations.* Do they expect things of each other that are unrealistic?
h. *Territorial aggression.* Every husband and wife has his or her own "turf." Is this turf violated by the other spouse?

Usually when a couple is taken through the Revolving Discussion Sequence and the Communica-

tion Inventory, the fight issue surfaces. When it does not become apparent through the use of these exercises, I employ yet another tool—the Caring Relationship Inventory.[4] The test measures five elements of love: affection, friendship, eros, empathy, and self-love. It also measures the concepts of being loved and deficiency love.

By comparing the test response to the real spouse and the ideal spouse, the counselor is able to find in what particular area love is being inhibited. In the average successful marriage the real and ideal spouses are found to have on an average only eleven differences. In a troubled marriage the differences can go as high as fifty. By discussing the differences the fair fight issue becomes clearer.

Negotiation for Change. Once I identify the fair fight issue or issues—there may be more than one—I'm ready for the change step. The first thing I want each spouse to do is to express feelings about the issue. At this point they will have become accustomed to the idea of expressing feelings through the use of RDS. Now I want them to express their feelings about the specific issue that is bothering them. For example, a woman's husband and children may be thoughtless about continually tracking mud into the house or not picking up their clothes or putting things away in the bathroom. The natural response of the wife is to attack them. She may tell them they're thoughtless. She may tell her husband that he must have been raised in a pigpen. This is bound to escalate into a free-for-all.

The fair fight issue is probably that of self-identity and centricity. What will her friends think of her when they see this messy house (self-identity)? What is more, she feels that when the family behaves like this they are taking her for granted; they're treating her like a slave (centricity).

When she identifies the issues, she must get in touch with her feelings about the issues. She can argue with her husband all she wants about the rightness of his picking up after himself, but he may argue that point, declaring that he doesn't have time or that he does pick up after himself or that's what he married her for. But when she gets in touch with her feelings and shares those feelings with her family, they can't argue with that. They may say that she shouldn't feel that way, but the fact is she *does*, and they are doing something to make her feel that way.

She may say, "When I see clothes lying around the house and dirty dishes stacked in the sink after I've cleaned up, I feel abused and put down. I feel responsible for keeping the house nice, but when this happens, I feel like a slave who is expected to go around picking up after the family." Centricity is the issue—"Am I important or am I a slave?" She may go on to say, "I can't leave the house a mess because I feel that the opinion my friends have of me is conditioned by how the house looks." Self-identity is also an issue—"What kind of a person will others think I am?"

A proper response to feelings like that is not, "You shouldn't feel that way." She does feel that way, and as a matter of fact, she has a right to feel that way because her basic human dignity is being destroyed—centricity and self-identity.

I must add that these feelings must be communicated without attack or defense. Attack and defense throw up barriers to good communication. When you verbally attack, you force your spouse to defend himself. He does so by rationalizing or justifying his behavior, and you invite counterattack from your spouse which is met by your own defense.

When you refuse to attack, you need not justify your feelings. Attack demands justification, but your feelings need no justification when there is no attack or accusation.

An example of both attacking and nonattacking communication may help. A husband is repeatedly late for supper. He seems indifferent about punctuality and permits any little thing to delay him. When he arrives late for the third time in so many days, his wife says in an accusatory tone and with agitated gestures, "You're late again. Look at the supper. It's cold. I went to a lot of hard work, and you spoiled it all."

She has attacked her husband! His response will be to justify his lateness and to attack her for not being understanding or placing too much importance on supper.

Let's see how this might be handled in a nonattacking way. First, she should make sure the timing is right. Don't hit him with it when he comes home. If she is agitated, he'll know she wants to talk. She should wait until later when the kids are in bed and she and her husband are settled in for the evening. Then the wife may say, "Honey, I have a problem." Note that *she* has a problem. She starts with herself and her own feelings and avoids attacking him.

She continues, "When I prepare a nice supper and it's left to get cold, I feel unappreciated." Note that there are no "yous," no attack. Her husband may get defensive and justify his repeated tardiness. She can avoid putting any pressure on him to defend by saying, "Honey, I'm sure that you have good reasons for being late. I just want to tell you how I feel."

By telling her husband that she feels unappreciated, she has introduced the fair fight issue of centricity—Am I important to you? She has also shared a feeling about it—I don't feel appreciated. And she has shared in a nonattacking manner.

Of course, the husband must be concerned about making his wife feel appreciated or important. Here is where commitment and responsibility are essential. If this is a concern to him, he will get the message that punctuality will make her feel appreciated and important. But he also may be tempted to brush this aside as an unimportant matter. If he does, his wife has another opportunity to make her point because this is the same fair fight issue. She may say, "Honey, I tried to tell you that your being late for supper makes me feel unappreciated and unimportant. And then when my feelings about that are brushed aside as unimportant, it makes me feel even more unimportant."

At this point he will see all his justifications and rationalizations as futile. He will see that a change in his behavior, not an excuse, is the only thing that will make her feel better.

This certainly is an oversimplification of the matter because sometimes it is compounded by a game on the part of the husband. It may be that he *knows* being late for supper bugs his wife and that it's a sneaky, covert way to make her angry without having to take the blame or responsibility for hurting her. This is called passive-aggressive behavior, the hardest type of behavior to deal with. It can also be classified as crazymaking.

Once the feelings about the fight issue are identified and communicated, the counselor is ready for the second step, negotiating contracts for change. There are two kinds of contracts: (1) a learning contract and (2) an action contract.

A learning contract is an agreement between a couple whereby one is told immediately when his behavior is making trouble for the other. It may seem strange that such a contract is needed, but it is.

I think, for example, of a husband who was continually putting down his wife without knowing it. She'd say something, and he'd reply, "Oh, what do you know?" He also called her "the moose" (she had a rather large nose) and "dummy" and "idiot." He put her down nonverbally with facial expressions and gestures of disgust. It came as a complete surprise that his wife felt continually put down by him; so I got them into a learning contact. Whenever he did anything to make her feel put down, she was to say, "Honey, whenever you do (or say) that, I feel put down." And he could only answer her with, "Thank you for telling me."

That last part is important—"Thank you for telling me." The tendency is to excuse or justify behavior that hurts someone else, which leads to a fight or alienation. A learning contract is a controlled way of getting a person to change behavior that is hurting someone else.

Now those words *behavior change* are the key to the rapid treatment process. If you change behavior, you'll change feelings.

The traditional approach to counseling is to change the feelings of people, but there's a better way. Change behavior that is creating bad feeling in others and you will change their feelings. When their feelings are changed, they will be disposed to change their behavior too. Consider the following diagram of the effect of behavior and feeling change:

```
HUSBAND        WIFE
Behavior ——     Behavior
Feelings    ——→ Feelings ⌐
Behavior        Behavior ⌐
Feelings ←——    Feelings
```

Either spouse may initiate the behavior change, or they may both initiate it. When I change my behavior and make my spouse feel pleased, she is most likely to change her behavior to please me.

The second kind of contract is an action contract—a method of getting a couple to *do* something to change their behavior. Once we have determined what behaviors are producing a bad effect, we must do something about them.

Take for example a couple who have been guilty of territorial aggression. She keeps leaving junk on his workbench in the garage. He is incensed because that workbench is his turf, and she keeps intruding. It might be a small issue, but this one action represents many encroachments on his turf, which put together are making him furious. Leaving junk on his workbench is at the head of the aggression list.

The action contract I want from her for one week—and it is specific—is to leave nothing on his workbench. This follows the two rules of an action contract. It should be *time limited* and *specific*. It is time limited so we can revise it the next week if necessary. It is specific so there is no doubt what is to be done to relieve the the irritation. A third element ought to be included if possible. It is a penalty for breach of contract. This may take the form of an added obligation.

One of my clients complained that her husband never did a thing to improve the appearance of the house or yard. She wanted to rearrange the bedroom, and he wouldn't even help move the bed. He agreed that it was reasonable to help her move the bed; so he gave a date at which time it would be done. Then I said, "Suppose you don't do it? What penalty should I attach?" She cheerfully supplied the information that the backyard was high with weeds that needed to be cut. So he agreed that his penalty for not moving the bed by the deadline would incur having to cut the weeds. The bed was moved according to agreement, and a new pattern began to emerge in which he accepted at least one household chore a week.

Some counselors maintain that the only workable contract is *quid pro quo* contract—this for that. In this kind of contract the husband will agree to do certain things in exchange for the wife's doing something for him. If one fails to deliver on the contract, the other is not obligated. They use a written, signed form in this kind of agreement.

The problem I have in using this kind of contract is that the man in the aforementioned case may be getting everything he wants from his wife and may not be able to think of something of equal value he wants from her that he is not getting. There may be nothing to exchange.

If the reasonableness of the request is agreed on, I find little trouble in getting a delinquent spouse to deliver the goods without a *quid pro quo* contract.

Now I make negotiation for change sound very easy, but it isn't always. Often a spouse may agree that a request is reasonable, but when it comes right down to negotiation, he may resist and say that it is unreasonable. When we begin to talk about the unreasonableness of it, he may come up with many more feelings about their relationship that he had not voiced before. We then start the process all over to get to the root of his feelings. I may find that he not only suffers from territorial aggression, but he also suffers from centricity—he doesn't feel that he's important to his wife. Perhaps she is always running off to this meeting or that activity and never has time for him. Then I can get her into an action contract that may curtail her outside activities and get her to spend more time with him.

Negotiation for change is an important step in rapid treatment for a troubled marriage because it gives the couple something *specific to do* to remedy their situation. Unless we show them exactly how to change their behavior, it will be just so much talk. Sometimes just insight into what they are doing to each other will bring change on their own initiative, but don't count on it.

Follow-up. The final step is follow-up. Once a couple is doing well on their own, a checkup approximately four weeks after the last session should be scheduled. This is important because they may permit the situation to deteriorate and not seek help until it becomes desperate, or they may be too embarrassed to come back and admit failure. The results of that checkup will help the counselor determine if further checkups are in order.

It is also helpful to put a couple like this in a marriage enrichment or communication workshop or other therapeutic group. A number of couples whose marriages are on the mend can form a therapeutic group.

Now I have mentioned nothing of the spiritual dimension of treating the troubled marriage. With believers I integrate spiritual truth as I work with them. I use the format I have described, but it is permeated with what the Bible says about their situation. Sometimes it has to do with confession and a guilty conscience, other times with assurance.

Some Christian husbands have blown the scriptural concept of the submissive wife all out of proportion and need to be taught 1 Peter 3:7—he must share equally with his wife the good things of life because she is a co-heir in grace. And if he doesn't, his prayers will be hindered.

With unbelievers I take a different approach. I begin with the common ground of their human dilemma and my ability to intervene therapeutically. When they begin to benefit from my counseling, they are more disposed to hear what I have to say about eternal things. Before I release them from counseling, I tell them that the things I have given them will be of use only in this life, but I want to give them something of eternal value. I then present to them the claims of eternal life through Christ.

Sometimes an unsaved client will bring up the question of his spiritual condition early in counseling. This gives me an opportunity there and then to deal with his soul.

This is actually only the application of apologetics to counseling. I have gained the confidence of this person by making his marriage better. Why shouldn't he listen to the good news of eternal life in Christ? I look at it as the Nicodemus dialogue in reverse: "If I have told you of earthly things and you have believed, certainly you'll believe if I tell you of heavenly things."

NOTES

1. Charles B. Truax and Robert R. Carkhuff, *Toward Effective Counseling and Psychotherapy: Training and Practice* (Chicago: Aldine-Atherton, 1967).

2. Order from Family Life Publications, Inc., Box 427, Saluda, N.C. 28773.

3. For more information on *crazymaking*, see George Bach and Yetta M. Bernhard, *Aggression Lab: The Fair-Fight Training Manual* (Dubuque, Ia.: Kendall-Hunt, 1971), and "Crazymaking: Why You Can't Communicate with Some People," Andre Bustanoby, 13211 Overbrook Ln., Bowie, Md. 20715.

4. Order from Educational and Industrial Testing Service, P. O. Box 7234, San Diego, California 92107.

From *Make More of Your Marriage.* Edited by Gary Collins. Article by Andre Bustanoby 1976. Used by permission of Word Books, Publisher, Waco, Texas, Pages 108-121.

MARRIAGE THERAPY

by

JAY HALEY

The typical marriage therapist brings a couple together and tells them he wants them to talk and correct the misunderstandings which have arisen, to express their feelings, and to gain some insight into their difficulties. However, merely because this procedure for change is outlined to the married couple does not necessarily mean that therapeutic change is brought about by self-expression, correcting misunderstandings, or gaining insight into difficulties. The explanation to a patient of what will bring about change need not be confused with what actually brings about a change.

The argument that insight and self-understanding is the primary factor in producing change cannot be sufficiently supported. Some couples will undergo a change from following directives without insight. Other couples will evidence considerable understanding, particularly of their unconscious motivations and the effects of the past on their present behavior, and yet they will continue to behave in distressing ways. More important, understanding and self-expression cannot be separated from the effects of the therapeutic context in which they occur. Shifts in relationships with the therapist can effect a change which appears as a shift in understanding. For example, a wife can "discover" that she is unwilling to let her husband be the authority in the home because of the inadequacies of her father in the past. However, when she makes this discovery in the therapeutic context, she will be presenting the idea to the therapist and so accepting him as the authority on the point she is making. What change occurs may not be brought about by her self-understanding but by her acceptance of the therapist as an authority when she has never allowed anyone to be in that position with her.

The Effect of The Third Person

When a couple come to a marriage therapist, changes can occur in their relationship because of the mere existence of the therapeutic triangle. The marital partners may have various motivations for entering therapy, including a determination to prove that the other is the villain in the marriage. The ways spouses attempt to use third parties are often what needs to be changed about their relationship. Most couples have managed to use in-laws, intimate friends,

or children against each other. A marriage therapist, by dealing fairly with each spouse, deals differently with them than others have. By not letting himself be provoked into condemning either marital partner, the therapist disarms a couple and prevents many of their usual maneuvers. (Actually on the basis of his fee alone the therapist is involved in a different way with a couple than family members can be.)

The mere presence of the therapist, as a fair participant, requires the spouses to deal with each other differently. Each spouse must respond to both therapist and mate instead of merely to mate. For example, a husband who handles his wife by withdrawing into silence will find that he cannot easily continue with this maneuver in the therapy setting. Instead of being incapacitated by his silence, the wife can discuss it with the therapist and use it to prove her point. The husband must change his tactics to deal with both people. Many maneuvers a spouse habitually uses to provoke a response in his partner can lose their effectiveness when used against two people at once, particularly if the third party is not easily provoked.

Although it is not possible for a marriage therapist to be "objective" with a couple since he rapidly becomes a participant in the interaction, it is possible for him to side with one spouse and then with another and so be fair. It is convenient for some therapists to argue that they do not take sides in a marital struggle but merely "reflect" back to the couple what they are expressing. Such an argument requires considerable naiveté. If a therapist listens to a wife's complaints and then turns to her husband and says, "How do you feel about that?" he cannot make his classic statement without his inquiry being in some sense directive. A therapist cannot make a neutral comment; his voice, his expression, the context, or the mere act of choosing a particular statement to inquire about introduces directiveness into the situation. When the therapist is being directive, coalition patterns are being defined and redefined, and a crucial aspect of this type of therapy is continually changing coalition patterns between therapist and each spouse. The wife who drags her husband into marriage therapy soon finds that the therapist does not join her in condemnation of the fellow, and the dragged-in husband discovers with some relief that the focus also shifts to how difficult his wife can be.

A further effect of the presence of the therapist is the change brought about by each spouse when he has the opportunity to observe the other dealing with the therapist. For example, a man who had paid little attention to his wife's protests must sit and observe an authority figure treat her in a symmetrical way by paying careful attention to what she says and encouraging her to say more. Not only do questions of coalition arise in such circumstances, but a model is being set for the spouse. Similarly, a therapist can prevent a wife or husband from dealing with him the way he or she has habitually provoked the marriage partner. For example, by commenting on how he is being handled the therapist can set a model for dealing with such provocations.

The difficulty a couple have in accepting a complementary relationship with each other is profoundly affected by the fact that they place themselves individually and collectively in a complementary relationship with a marriage therapist by asking for his services. When the therapist cooperates in such a relationship by taking charge, as most marriage therapists tend to do, he is accepting this type of relationship. Although such a therapist is not necessarily overtly authoritarian, in fact that may not be wise or possible except in special circumstances, he is willing to listen and explore the problems and offer directives like the expert he is expected to be. If a couple is to pay attention to him, he must be an authority figure, although not so omnipotent that it is necessary for the couple to topple him. Their acceptance of an authority figure, and therefore the acceptance of a complementary relationship, becomes a part of the process of working out types of relationships with each other.

Defining the Rules

Besides intervening in a marriage merely by being present, a marriage therapist will actively intervene by relabeling or redefining, the activity of the two people with each other. In the early stages of treatment his comments and directives tend to be permissive as he encourages the couple to express themselves in a context where each will have a fair hearing. Accusations and protests are nurtured so that as much as possible is made explicit. One way of encouraging a more free discussion is to define the consultation room as a special place, a "no man's land," where the rules are different from ordinary situations. In this special place it is appropriate to bring up matters which they have on their minds but have avoided discussing. Although this framing of the therapy situation appears a mild directive, couples will often accept the idea that they can protect each other less

in that room. Sometimes a therapist may forbid the couple to discuss certain topics between sessions so that only in that special place are they discussed.

As a couple express themselves, the therapist comments upon what they say. His comments tend to be the following: Those comments which emphasize the positive side of their interaction together, and those comments which redefine the situation as different from, if not opposite to, the way they are defining it.

An emphasis upon the positive typically occurs when the therapist redefines the couple's motives or goals. For example, if a husband is protesting his wife's constant nagging, the therapist might comment that the wife seems to be trying to reach her husband and achieve more closeness with him. If the wife protests that her husband constantly withdraws from her, the husband might be defined as one who wants to avoid discord and seeks an amiable relationship. Particularly savage maneuvers will not be minimized but may be labeled as responses to disappointment (rather than the behavior of a cad). In general, whenever it can be done, the therapist defines the couple as attempting to bring about an amiable closeness but going about it wrongly, being misunderstood, or being driven by forces beyond their control. The way the couple characterize each other may also be redefined in a positive way. If a husband is objecting to his wife as an irresponsible and disorganized person, the therapist might define these characteristics as feminine. If the husband is passive and inactive, he can be defined as stable and enduring. When the therapist relabels a spouse in a positive way, he is not only providing support, but he is making it difficult for the couple to continue their usual classification. In addition, when the therapist redefines a spouse, he is labeling himself as the one who classifies the couple. By emphasizing the positive, he does his classifying in such a way that they cannot easily oppose him.

The other type of comments by the therapist emphasize the opposite of what the couple is emphasizing. If both husband and wife are protesting that they remain married only because they must, for religious reasons or for the children's sake, the therapist focuses upon the voluntary aspects of their relationship. Emphasizing how they chose each other and have remained together for many years, he minimizes the compulsion in the relationship. When husband and wife are protesting that their relationship is strictly voluntary and they can separate at any time, the therapist indicates that they have remained together so long despite their difficulties and they obviously have a deep unwillingness to end their association.

The therapist also relabels the type of relationship of a couple. If a wife protests that she is the responsible one in the family and must supervise her husband, the therapist not only commiserates with her for depriving herself by cooperating in this arrangement, but he also points out the husband's supervision and responsible acts. In addition, he might suggest to the wife that the husband is arranging that she be the responsible one, thereby raising the question who is supervising whom. Similarly, if a husband labels his wife as the helpless one, the therapist points them in the direction of discovering who gets her own way. By subtly focusing upon the opposite, or a different, aspect of a relationship, the therapist undermines the couple's typical ways of labeling the relationship and they must define it in a different way and so undergo a change.

A further product of encouraging a couple to talk about each other is to make explicit many of the implicit or covert, marital rules. When they are explicit, they are more difficult to follow. For example, if an implicit agreement between a couple is that they will visit his in-laws but not hers, the therapist might inquire whether they both prefer this arrangement. If they have not discussed the matter explicitly, an issue is then raised where a decision can be made. Similarly, there may be an implicit agreement that the wife never lets her husband speak. When the therapist points out that the wife seems to be interrupting her husband before he has a chance to say what is on his mind, the wife will be less able to do so, even though the therapist is not suggesting a change but "merely" commenting on what is happening. A comment can also make mutual protection less effective. By suggesting to a husband that his wife seems to be treating him like a sensitive plant, the therapist can provoke a more straightforward discussion. Conflicts about what rules to follow can be resolved by encouraging a couple to discuss their lives together and to work out compromises with a therapist emphasizing the positive. However, conflicts about who is to set the rules require more active direction from a therapist.

Resolving Problems of Who Is To Set The Rules

Although the major conflicts in a marriage center in the problem of who is to tell whom what to do under what circumstances, the therapist might never discuss this conflict explicitly with the couple. If a husband says that he gets angry because his wife always gets her own way and is constantly supervising him, the therapist will not emphasize the struggle for control but will emphasize the strong feelings in the situation. Explicitly talking about the control problem can solidify it. However, specific directives given by the therapist are most effective when they are designed to resolve the struggle over who is to set the rules for the relationship.

Any comment by a therapist has directive aspects, if only to indicate "pay attention to this," but the marriage therapist often specifically directs a marital couple to behave in certain ways. These directives can be classed for convenience into two types: the suggestions that the couple behave differently, and the suggestions that they continue to behave as they have been.

A marriage therapist will direct a spouse to behave differently only in those cases where the conflict is minor or where it is likely that the spouse will behave that way anyhow and is only looking for an excuse. That is, a husband who never takes his wife out may be advised to take her out to dinner, but usually only if the husband is moving in that direction. Such a suggestion permits a couple an evening out without either spouse having to admit they wish it. Mere advice to a couple to treat each other in more reasonable ways is rarely followed or goes badly if it is followed. A couple, like an individual patient, can only be diverted into more productive directions and cannot be forced to reverse themselves. To tell a husband and wife that they should treat each other more amiably does not provide them with new information or give them an opportunity to follow the directive. More important, if a therapist directs a couple to behave differently, he has often been led into this directive by the couple and so is responding to their directive. A couple in distress have provoked many people to advise them to behave more sensibly; such advice proves only to the couple that the other person does not understand them and they continue in their distress. In general, when a therapist is provoked into giving advice the advice will be on the terms of the person doing the provoking and therefore will perpetuate the distress. For example, if a wife says to the therapist, "Don't you think my husband should stay home nights instead of going out every night of the week," if the therapist agrees he is being led down the garden path. If instead of agreeing and so offering such advice the therapist says, "I think it's important to understand what this is about," the therapist is not only encouraging understanding but making it clear that he offers advice on his own terms only, not when provoked into it. However, this does not mean that the therapist should not offer advice or directives on his own terms. The psychoanalytic approach to couples is to merely listen and such a procedure avoids being led into directives by the couple. Although there may be theoretical rationales for remaining silent, such as developing deeper layers of the intrapsychic conflicts, the main function of silence is to avoid behaving on the patient's terms. However, a therapist who remains silent also avoids taking those actions which would move a couple in the direction of a more satisfactory relationship. To be silent when provoked by the couple may be necessary; to remain silent when directives which would produce change could be given on the therapist's terms is wasting time.

A couple can be instructed to behave differently if the request is small enough so that the implications of it are not immediately apparent. For example, if a husband says he always gives in and lets his wife have her own way, he may be asked to say "no" to his wife on some issue once during the week. When this is said in the wife's presence, the groundwork is laid for the suggestion to be more easily followed. Further, the suggestion is more likely followed if a rationale is provided, such as saying that any wife should feel free to do what she pleases with confidence that her husband will say "no" to her if she goes too far. Given such a directive, the couple may at first treat the "no" lightly. However, if it is on a major issue, or if the instruction is followed for several weeks, there will be repercussions in their relationship. The more rigid the previous "agreement" that the wife will always have her own way, the greater the response in both of them if he says "no" and thereby defines the relationship differently. The fact that he is doing so under direction, and so still accepting a complementary relationship, will ease the situation. But since the message comes from him, the wife will react. Similarly, an overly responsible wife may be asked to do some small irresponsible act during the week, perhaps buy something she does not need that costs a dollar or two. If the previous agreement was that she was the responsible one and her husband the irresponsible one, a small request of this kind undermines this definition of the relationship. Even though the wife is being irresponsible under therapeutic direction, and so doing her duty by doing what the therapist says, she is still spending money for something she does not need and so behaving irresponsibly. However, in general whenever a directive is given for a husband or wife to behave differently, and so break the marital rules they have established, the request must be so small that it appears trivial.

Actually it is extremely difficult to devise a directive which is a request for marital partners to behave differently from their usual ways when their usual ways of behaving are conflictual. That is, a wife who insists she is the responsible one in the marriage is usually irresponsible at another level. For example, she may be so responsible about the budget that she is irresponsible because she is overemphasizing money at a cost to her husband and children. To ask her to do something irresponsible is not necessarily to ask something new of her. Similarly, a husband who never says "no" to his wife directly, is usually a man who is constantly saying "no" by passive resistance. To tell him to say "no" is only partly asking for different behavior. Even if one should suggest that a husband who is treating his wife coldly be more considerate of his wife, this may not be a request for a change in behavior because treating her coldly may be considerate of this type of woman. In fact, if her husband treated her more amiably she might feel great demands were being placed upon her or become so overwhelmed with guilt that sudden amiable behavior on his part would actually be inconsiderate.

Often a directive can appear to be a request for different behavior when actually it is not. For example, a husband had spent some years crusading to have his wife enjoy a sexual orgasm. He had made such an issue of the matter, and become so angry and exasperated with her, that the issue had become a grim one between husband and wife. The wife was told, in the husband's presence, that one of these days she might enjoy some sexual pleasure and when she did she was to tell her husband that she did not enjoy it. If her husband insisted on her saying whether she had really not enjoyed it or was just following this directive, she should say she had really not enjoyed it. This directive had various purposes, including the purpose of introducing uncertainty into the situation and freeing the man from his overconcern about his wife's pleasure (he suffered from ejaculatio praecox). However, from what had been said, there was some indication that the wife was enjoying sex while denying it and so the directive actually was an encouragement of her usual behavior.

Encouraging a couple to behave in their usual way is paradoxically one of the most rapid ways to bring about a change. Such a directive can be calculated or it can occur as a natural result of encouraging a couple to express themselves. A wife can say that her husband should stop being so ineffectual, and the therapist might respond that perhaps he needs to behave in that way at times and they should try to understand his reasons for it. When the therapist makes such a statement, he is permitting—if not encouraging—the husband to continue to be ineffectual. Most procedures which ostensibly emphasize bringing about understanding can be seen as subtle encouragement of usual behavior. Note that this procedure is quite different from the way the spouse typically handles the problem: a spouse usually tells the other to stop certain behavior and the result is a continuation of it. When the therapist permits and encourages usual behavior, the person tends to discontinue it.

When a therapist "accepts" the way a couple is behaving he begins to gain some control of that behavior. He is placed immediately in the center of their problem: Who is to lay down the rules for the relationship? Although a couple cannot easily oppose the kind of relationship the therapist is prescribing if they are already interacting that way, they can still respond to the idea of someone else defining their relationship for them and this response will produce a shift. For example, if a wife is managing her husband by being self-sacrificing and labeling all her behavior as for the good of others, the husband cannot easily oppose her, even though he may not wish to be in a secondary position in a complementary relationship with her. Such a woman will tend to handle the therapist in a similar way. However, if the therapist encourages her to be self-sacrificing, the woman is placed in a difficult position. She cannot manage him by this method when it is at his request. If she continues to behave that way, she is conceding that she is managed by the therapist. If she does not, then she must shift to a different type of relationship. If the therapist goes further and encourages the wife to be self-sacrificing and the husband to attempt to oppose her and fail, then the couple must shift their relationship with each other to deal with being managed by the therapist.

As an example of a typical problem, a couple can be continually fighting, and if the therapist directs them to go home and keep the peace this will doubtfully happen. However, if he directs the couple to go home and have a fight, the fight will be a different kind when it happens. This difference may reside only in the face that they are now fighting at the direction of someone else, or the therapist may have relabeled their fighting in such a way that it is a different kind. For example, a husband might say that they fight continually because his wife constantly nags. The wife might say they fight because the husband does not understand her and never does what she asks. The therapist can relabel or redefine their fighting in a variety of ways: he might suggest that they are not fighting effectively because they are not expressing what is really on their minds, he can suggest that their fighting is a way of gaining an emotional response from each other and they both need that response, he might say that when they begin to feel closer to each other they panic and have a fight, or he can suggest they fight because inside themselves is the feeling that they do not deserve a happy marriage. With a new label upon their fighting, and directed to go home and have a fight, the couple will find their conflict redefined in such a way that it is difficult for them to continue in their usual pattern. They are particularly tempted toward more peace at home if the therapist says they *must* fight and that they must for certain reasons which they do not like. The couple can only disprove him by fighting less.

As a marriage therapist encourages a couple to behave in their usual ways he gains some control of their behavior because what occurs is being defined as occurring under his direction. At this point he can shift his direction to bring about a change. The change he brings about may be an expansion of the limits of the type of relationship of a couple, or a shift to a different type of relationship.

An example of extending the limits of a type of relationship is a classic case reported by Milton Erickson. A woman came to him and said that she and her husband were finally going to purchase a home, as they had hoped to all their married life. However, her husband was a tyrant and would not permit her any part in the choice of home or in the choice of furnishings for it. Her husband insisted that everything connected with the new house would be entirely his choice and she would have no voice in the matter. The woman was quite unhappy because of this extreme version of a complementary relationship. Erickson told the woman that he wished to see her husband. When the old gentleman came in, Erickson emphasized the fact that a husband should be absolute boss in the home. The husband fully agreed with him. Both of them also enjoyed a full agreement that the man of the house should have complete say in the choice of a house to buy and the choice of furnishings for it. After a period of discussion, Erickson shifted to talking about the type of man who was *really* the boss in the house. When the old gentleman expressed a curiosity about what type of man was really the boss, Erickson indicated that the real boss was the type of man who was so fully in charge that he could allow his underlings a say in minor matters. Such a boss kept full control of everything, but he could *permit* certain decisions to be made by those beneath him. Using this line of approach, Erickson persuaded the tyrannical old gentleman to lay out 20 plans of houses and 20 plans of house furnishings. Then the husband permitted his wife to choose among *his* plans. She chose a house she liked and the furnishings she liked. In this way the husband was still fully in charge of all aspects of the house purchase, but the wife could choose what she wanted. The limits of a complementary relationship were extended to satisfy both partners' needs.

Accepting what a couple offers, or encouraging them to behave in their usual ways and later suggesting a change can also provoke a shift in the type of relationship. For example, a wife was protesting that her husband avoided her, and that he would leave the dinner table when the family was eating to sit in the living room alone and later make himself some dinner. Although the husband at first indicated he did not know why he behaved this way, he also indicated that his wife spent the time at the dinner table nagging the kids and nagging at him. At the first suggestion that she was behaving in this way at the table, the wife said that she had to correct the children at the table because he never did. The husband said that when he attempted to, she interrupted, and it was not worth a battle.

The wife was instructed to correct the children at the table during the coming week, and to observe the effect of this upon her husband. Her husband was instructed to observe the way his wife dealt with the children, and if he strongly disagreed with it he was to get up and leave the table. Actually the instruction was merely to continue to behave as they had been.

However, when they were instructed to do so, the couple found it difficult to behave in their usual ways because the behavior became both deliberate and occurred under duress. After a week of this procedure, the couple was instructed to shift their behavior: for a week the wife was to be relieved of all responsibility for discipline at the table and could just enjoy her meal, and the husband was to fully take charge at the dinner table. The wife was not even to point at one of the children to indicate that her husband should take some action. Since their behavior was defined as occurring at the instigation of the therapist, rather than originating within each other, the couple could tolerate this shift in their relationship at the table with a consequent carryover into other aspects of their lives together.

Similar encouragement of typical behavior occurs if the therapist instructs a distant couple to maintain a certain distance from each other and not risk becoming too close for a period of time, if he instructs a non-fighting couple to avoid a fight but to rehearse in their minds what they would like to say to each other, if he instructs a spouse who always gives in to give in for a period of time, and so on. This procedure not only gives the therapist some control of what the couple is doing and lays the ground work for a later shift, but it also utilizes whatever rebellious forces are latent within the couple.

Often an instruction to one spouse in the presence of the other has its effects on them both. For example, a couple who are constantly fighting and the wife is flaunting her extramarital affairs before her husband will see their struggle from a particular point of view. They will usually see what they do to each other in terms of revenge. If the therapist, from his vantage point of an expert, advises the wife that she is protecting her husband by her dalliances with other men because he is uneasy about sex, the wife is faced with a different point of view. To label her behavior as protective, when she sees it as vengeful, makes it more difficult for her to continue it, particularly if the therapist suggests that it may be necessary for her to continue to help her husband in this way. When such a comment is made in the husband's presence, he is almost obligated to prove that he does not need such protection by attempting a closer relationship with his wife. Naturally the couple will disagree with such a comment, but the idea will continue to work upon them. If there is sufficient disagreement, the therapist may suggest they should experiment; if they manage a closer relationship, they will find that they panic. To disprove this, they must manage a closer relationship. If they become upset as they become closer, they are accepting the therapist's interpretation of the situation and so accepting him as someone who can arrange a change. If they do not become upset, they have a closer relationship which is the therapist's goal.

When a therapist provides a framework which is to bring about a change, and within that framework he encourages a couple to continue in their usual ways, the couple is faced with a situation which is difficult to deal with without undergoing change. If, in addition, the therapist makes it an ordeal for them to continue in their usual ways, the problem is compounded for the couple. Relabeling what they do in a different way often makes it more of an ordeal for the couple to continue their usual patterns. This "different way" might be a relabeling of negative behavior as something positive; it can also be the reverse. The therapist can suggest that certain behavior by one of the spouses, which they consider positive is is really negative. For example, the therapist might define protectiveness as really selfishness because of the protecting person's needs being satisfied. Another procedure is to raise the question with the marital partners how they usually punish each other. Typically they say they do not, but when the punishment is defined as that behavior which the other spouse feels as punishment then they become more loquacious. Couples will then discuss such behavior as withdrawing, complaining, arguing, refusing to do what the other asks, and so on. Such a discussion makes explicit many of the maneuvers a couple use against each other, and also leads to a relabeling of those maneuvers. It is possible to lead up to the idea of symptomatic behavior as punishing. Since symptoms in one spouse are always hard on the other, one can suggest that a symptom is a way of punishing the other. A spouse with an obesity problem, headaches, hysterical symptoms, or compulsions usually prefers to define the symptom as something occurring independent of the spouse. To call such a symptom a way of punishing makes it more difficult to exist. At times a spouse can be asked to inquire of the other, "Why are you punishing me," when the other complains of a symptom. Such an inquiry provokes a denial but also provokes an inhibition of the symptomatic experience. This procedure is similar to other relabeling of symptoms so that they are characterized differently and thus a change is induced. For example, one can ask a spouse, in the presence of the other spouse, to choose a time when the symptom is better that week and announce that it is worse. Such an instruction increases the uncertainty of the severity of the symptom and lays the groundwork for change.

The idea of a therapist encouraging a couple to behave in their usual ways can be varied by a therapist directing a spouse to encourage the other spouse to exhibit symptomatic behavior. Typically the mate of a spouse with symptoms oppose the symptomatic behavior but also encourages it. If a marriage therapist directs a mate only to encourage symptomatic behavior in the spouse, there is often a rather drastic response. For example, a wife became anxious whenever she tried to leave the house alone. When she attempted to go out, she suffered anxiety feelings and a terrible pain in the eyes. She had suffered this problem for years and her husband was constantly assuring her that she should go out alone and that it was perfectly safe. However, he was also fully cooperating in her staying at home by doing all the shopping, escorting her where she needed to go, and indicating some uneasiness whenever she started to go out alone. After several sessions of marriage therapy, the husband was asked, in the presence of the wife, to do something he might think was silly. He was asked to tell the wife each day as he left for work that she was to stay home that day and not go out alone. He could say this seriously, or as a joke, or as he pleased. The husband agreed to follow this procedure. On the third day that he told her to stay at home the wife went out to the store alone for the first time in 8 years. However, the next interview was devoted to the husband's expressions of concern about what his wife might do if she went out alone, where she might go, whom she might meet, and would she even get a job and become so independent that she would leave him.

This directive to the husband to tell his wife to stay at home was actually a double encouragement of usual behavior: the husband was directed to encourage his wife to stay at home, as he had been covertly doing, and the wife was being encouraged by the husband to stay at home, as she had been doing. The product of such a directive is a shift in type of relationship. Although the wife had been behaving like the helpless one, *she was in charge* of being the helpless one by insisting on staying at home. When her husband directed her to stay at home, the question of *who* was laying down the rules for their relationship was called in question. The wife responded by a symmetrical move, leaving the house, which was her only way of taking charge of this situation. Although it seems a mild directive when a therapist directs a spouse to encourage the other spouse to behave as usual, there is inevitably a marital upheaval because such a directive centers on the crucial problem in a marriage; who is to define what kind of relationship the two people will have.

Changing the Stability of a System—Summary

A marital couple in difficulty tend to perpetuate their distress by attempting to resolve conflict in such a way that it continues. The goal of a marriage therapist is not only to shift, or to expand, the types of relationships of a couple, but also to provoke a change in the ways the couple keep the marital system stable. Such a change requires influencing the corrective variables in the system so the system itself can undergo a change.

The appearance at the door of a marriage therapist is essentially an attempt by a couple to find a more satisfying means of perpetuating their relationship. The therapist provides an opportunity for change in a variety of ways: he encourages discussion to resolve conflict rather than previous methods, such as withdrawal and silence; he provides a reasonably impartial advisor and judge; he encourages a couple to examine motivations which they might have outside awareness; he makes many maneuvers explicit and therefore more difficult to follow; and he engenders habits of dealing with sensitive topics. Granting that discussion, encouragement of understanding, and new points of view are offered in the marriage therapy context, there is another source of change which has been emphasized here—the paradoxical position a couple is placed in if they continue distressing behavior when undergoing marriage therapy. The paradoxical strategies of a marriage therapist are formally similar to those used by therapists of individuals.

From *Strategies of Psychotherapy* by Jay Haley. Reprinted by permission of Grune and Stratton, Inc. and the author, 1973, Pages 136-149.

THE MARRIAGE CONFERENCE

By

RAYMOND J. CORSINI

It does not require much in the way of knowledge of human nature to accept the idea that practically all marriages must be happy. To prove this statement, consider only the following propositions:

1. All people desire happiness

2. It is common knowledge that if you mistreat another person that the person will be unhappy.

3. If the person you mistreat is your mate, you will make that person unhappy, and he/she, in turn, will make you unhappy.

4. If we live with a person in close intimacy for extended periods of time (as occurs in marriage) we soon learn what the other person considers good treatment and what is poor treatment.

5. The longer we live with a person, the better we get to know that person, the more we accommodate to that person, and the more we get to like that person.

6. Apart from all these considerations, there are many other reasons why married people should treat their partners properly and therefore be happy: the effects of the marital relationship on others, friends, family and of course children.

Pure logic based on these propositions, most of which will be accepted by reasonable people as true, leads to the inescapable conclusion that most, if not all marriages are happy. Stubborn facts indicate another story: approximately one-fifth of all marriages contracted end in divorce; another fifth end in other kinds of separation; and of the remaining three-fifths at least half of the marriages appear to be pure hell. How can this be in view of the six propositions and in view of the fact that in this country marriages are viewed as a very serious step to be well throught out, and are contracted usually after extended and intimate acquaintanceship?

This is a problem that has troubled many people. We know from various research studies that on a statistical basis, that data indicate that homogamy is related to happiness in marriage (Terman, 1938; Burgess and Wallin, 1953; Corsini, 1956). However, clinical investigations show that many couples who seem to be ideally mated do not succeed in finding happiness in marriage. We have some nomothetic generalizations such as couples should have similar interests, but we have no explanation for the many cases that should be happy in terms of statistical facts, but who are quite unhappy. Is there a single important underlying factor that explains many unhappy marriages?

Some time ago I became puzzled by my own reactions while doing marriage counseling. If I listened to the husband first, I could see his point of view, it made excellent sense, and I was sympathetic to him. But then when I listened to the wife, I understood and agreed with her, and I became sympathetic to her. To be understanding and sympathetic to both parties, each of whom is in conflict with the other imposes a great strain on the middle party. I tried to take the position that I was the doctor to the marriage and not to the individuals, but a marriage is an abstraction. It is the real individuals that one has to deal with. When I tried to bridge the gaps between the two, they often turned and attacked me for trying to be a peacemaker, and for trying to bring some order and rationality into the relationship—for trying to do what they hired me for!

One day I got an idea. The idea come from a common word so often used in marital problems: *misunderstanding.* "We had a misunderstanding," was the statement, and suddenly I thought I understood everything. My hypothesis, as weird and as paradoxical as the statement that many marriages are unhappy, was that in many marriages, the couples really did not communicate! Now, how foolish a proposition that is, is evident on the face of it: two people who live in close intimacy, even sharing sleeping accommodations, not communicating! And yet, the idea made sense, especially in terms of observations of couples in my office who heard but didn't listen to one another. I had listened to each intently and I had understood each, but it was evident that something had happened in the marriage in many cases in which regardless of how loud and clear the other spoke, there was no real listening. The trick in repairing such marriages, it seemed to me, was to help couples learn effective communication.

Towards A Solution

Some twenty years before I had developed a technique in group psychotherapy that appeared to be dramatically effective in handling some problems. A patient would be given a block of uninterrupted time, say twenty minutes, to "tell all about yourself" and then when he had finished, he would turn his back to the group while they would talk about him. I had found that this uninterrupted talking about oneself tended to make the individual feel free, and he could open up with unusual frankness, and that turning his back had the effect of freeing others to talk about the "absent" person, and, most important, made the person who was being talked about extremely alert to what was being said. (Corsini, 1953). I wondered whether something of the sort might not be effective in helping people in trouble in their marriage to communicate better.

It so happened that at the time of this thinking a new couple came to consult with me. It was a classic case. The husband was cold and distant. The wife was angry and wild. They had ceased any normal marital relationships, except for quarreling. They had four children, ranging from six to sixteen. They were contemplating divorce. When one would speak, the other would assume an attitude of indifference or anger. They shouted one another down. And yet, when I saw them individually, as usual, they seemed very nice, quite reasonable, quite persuasive, and it seemed, as it often does, a tragedy that the family should be broken up. We met for a number of sessions and it seemed as though there were no hope that relationships could be improved. Out of desperation, I suggested the technique, which I have labeled, *The Marriage Conference*, which will be soon described. The results were dramatic. Between the time I suggested this technique and the time I saw them again, this couple had had four sessions of the Marriage Conference. When they returned they were smiling and evidently happy with each other, and the three of us had a very good session. I continued seeing this couple for several more weeks and then kept in touch with them for over a year. They both insisted that it was the technique that had made the difference, that it was this that had brought them together, and that they would make the Marriage Conference a permanent part of their marriage.

Being rather cynical and suspicious of miracles, I probed this couple intently about the change, but they kept insisting they had finally broken through to each other, finally understood each other, and thanked me extravagently for bringing them together. Naturally, at the first opportunity I prescribed the Marriage Conference again. To my surprise both individuals rejected the idea out of hand, saying things such as, "We didn't come here to play games," "we are not interested in gimmicks," "we want to get to the root of the problem," and "we communicate all right — perhaps too much," and "no, thank you, we are not interested in this Marriage Conference." This couple dissolved their marriage eventually.

Intrigued by the first success, and the second adamant refusal, I began explaining and prescribing the technique to couples that came to see me, and soon a very clear pattern appeared. Almost every case that employed the method exactly as prescribed succeeded in the sense that the marriage continued and in the sense that they both were happy with their conferences with me. In almost every case where the couple did not accept the notion, or where they started the Marriage Conference but didn't keep it up for the prescribed four sessions, or where they made variations of any kind, the marriage failed!

Now, the writer is not so naive as to think for one moment that the high rate of success of those who employ the Marriage Conference is due exclusively to the use of this technique, but it is still possible that some of the success is due to this method. In the two years since the method was discovered, I have employed it on approximately forty couples, and have made some minor changes in it. Since there may be something worth exploring in this technique, I would like to make it available to other marriage counselors. I shall give below two sets of instructions, one for the marriage conselor, and the other for couples.

Instructions for the Marriage Counselor

1. In using this technique, regardless of your orientation, you must take a strong and positive stand in the manner of a physician giving a prescription. If you can take this position: "You have consulted with me. I want you to use this method in your own home, and to use it precisely as prescribed, and if you (a) don't want to use it, or (b) don't use it after you agree to, then please find yourself another marriage counselor, so much the better. That is, you have to be convinced this technique is likely to work for the couple and you must insist that it be used exactly as prescribed.

2. In explaining the method, add this argument: "I want you both to cooperate with me, and I want you to feel that you have done everything possible to improve matters. The marriage conference is done by you two alone—and it costs you nothing." This economic argument is often impressive.

3. It is most important that the counselor insist that the instructions be followed to the letter. Emphasize to the couple that you will make a point-by-point check to make certain that both did precisely what was called for in the instructions. Absolute rigidity and insistence is needed here.

4. To emphasize this point the counselor may say something to this effect: "If you make any variations at all, it means you are not really serious. I want you to use this method just as it is given to you."

204

5. If after the couple has been instructed what to do, and when they return, inform the counselor that for some reason or other they did not do what they were told to do, I would suggest that the counselor inform them that they must start again, and this time follow instructions. I would suggest telling the couple that you will not counsel them unless they do what you tell them to do. The counselor must be adamant that this technique be used exactly as prescribed.

Instructions in Using the Marriage Conference

1. These instructions are to be agreed to by both the husband and the wife in every respect otherwise this technique should not be used. There must be no variations at all. Any violations of the procedures must be reported to the counselor. The counselor may then require you to begin all over again.

2. At the soonest possible time, go to a calendar and set up four one-hour appointments with each other. Agree on the place, the day and the hour. Select, if possible, a place where there will be no visual or sound distractions; and a time that is mutually convenient, where you will be reasonably alert, unfatigued and in as good mental and physical condition as possible. Have no more than one conference a day. Try not to have conferences on adjacent days. Ideally, a conference every two or three days is best.

3. Each person is to go to the agreed-on place at the time appointed without notifying the other. Just go to your appointed place at the appointed time. Be exact with respect to time. This conference appointment should have precedence over every other event, except dire emergencies. Treat it precisely as if you had an appointment to have X-ray treatment for suspected cancer. You have no responsibility for reminding the other to be present. His/her absence will be an indication that the other is not serious about improving the marriage.

4. If the other person does not appear, act as though he or she were there. You are to stay in the appointed place for the agreed upon hour and you will act precisely as if the other were present. If your mate does show up late make no acknowledgement. Keep on doing whatever you were in the process of doing.

5. The wife always starts first in the first session by doing whatever she wants. Usually she will talk, she may want to be silent. She has the floor for precisely thirty minutes.

6. Now, comes the first hard part. The husband during the first thirty minutes of the first session does nothing, except perhaps look at a clock that should be in the line of sight of both parties. He is not to say anything, of course, but also, he must not make any noises or exclamations or gestures, or grimaces. He is to be absolutely silent and motionless.

7. If the husband does anything at all to distract the wife, she is to get up and leave the room in silence. Likewise, when it is the husband's turn, and the wife makes any remark of any sort, or if she should make faces, etc., the husband is to get up and leave the room in silence.

8. Should this happen, it should be reported to the marriage counselor who will suggest probably that you start over again and may suggest some means to prevent distraction by one of the couple or the other.

9. If everything goes well, and if the husband listens in absolute silence without any distraction, at the half hour, the wife stops talking (if she has been talking) and the husband begins.

10. Now, the wife listens in absolute silence, and the husband talks, or does whatever he wants. Even if he should talk for only five minutes, both remain in the room, and the wife keeps absolute silence, for thirty minutes. They cannot agree to end the session, but must remain there, perhaps just looking at each other in silence until the exact minute of the end of the hour.

11. Now comes what is the most important part of the instructions. The husband and wife are not to discuss anything between sessions that was taken up during the session. To repeat and to emphasize this simple point: there must be no discussion whatever—not a word—between them in the interval between the appointed sessions about anything taken up during the session. It would be best between sessions to avoid any argumentative topics, but anything taken up between sessions that was mentioned during the session is cause for canceling the whole set of conferences. Should either bring up any element of any topic discussed, the other should leave the scene immediately and refuse to discuss the topic. Please keep in mind this is the most important element of the Marriage Conference.

12. At the next session, as usual, the husband and wife meet at the appointed place at the appointed time, and this time it is the husband who starts first. The same instructions apply. The husband says or does whatever he wants, for the first thirty minutes, and the wife looks and listens. If either one feels that the one who is looking and listening is disturbing, he can ask at any time for the other to turn his/her back. At the end of the thirty minutes the husband shuts up, and now the wife has thirty minutes for herself.

13. The next two sessions continue as before, with the wife starting off on the third session, and the husband having the second thirty minutes; and the husband beginning with the first thirty minutes at the fourth session, so that after four sessions, each has had four opportunities to speak without any interruption or distraction for thirty minutes.

Discussion

I shall ask myself some questions and give myself some answers about this technique, hoping that in this way I may be able to respond to questions that may be in the mind of the reader.

What is the theoretical rational of the Marriage Conference?

'I have already stated that I believe that in many marriages things come to such a pass that real communication no longer exists. Each knows the other's arguments and does not really listen to them. Often, one or both are so hurt, that they don't want to listen to the other, and are waiting for the other to stop talking so that he/she can get in with counter-arguments. Complete silence is seen as a sign of acceptance. Following the orders strictly is seen as a sign of acquiescence, evidence of good will, and indication of love.

The person who is gagged (and some people may actually gag themselves if they feel they are unable to keep quiet otherwise) and who is unable to do anything else, such as knit, or read, is forced to listen. This forced listening under these restricting conditions may actually lead the person to understand the other, to finally get empathy, and feel with the other. We are trying to do two things: (a) get the couple to submit to the discipline of the counselor, so that both become his children as it were, and (b) force each to listen intently to the other.

Why not permit some interaction by the passive partner, such as saying "Uh-hu" or nodding or smiling, etc.?

In cases where the Marriage Conference is used, any reaction, no matter how apparently innocuous, may be seen by the other party as hostile and offensive. Any stimulus emitted by the passive party, auditory or visual, can be interpreted by the active one as a hostile gesture or sound. In one of my unsuccessful cases, a sneeze was interpreted by the wife as evidence of lack of interest. Both theory and experience indicate the notion of complete silence and passivity is best. In some cases, even rolling of the eyes, or looking in a glazed manner, etc., can be disturbing. The important thing then is for the passive partner to be as inconspicuous and as neutral as possible.

Do you really believe that lack of communication is the real problem in most problem marriages?

Not really. Often, there is too much communication, but it is the quality of communication that is important. We hear things like this often, "I told him a thousand times . . ." or "he keeps telling me . . ." So, there is communication in the intellectual sense. What is missing is empathic communication, or real understanding in the emotional sense, a lack of comprehension of the person himself.

Why all the rigidity of rules? Why all the insistence that things be done just so?

I have found that it is best that the counselor be exceedingly firm, so that both parties feel that they are in competent hands. If the counselor gives evidence that he knows what he is doing, and if he is insistent that things go just as he prescribes, then both will feel confidence in him and will surrender themselves to his demands. This in turn means they will tend to do exactly what is involved in the instructions, which cooperation with each other (and with the counselor) can be the turning point in the marriage. We are looking for a breakthrough.

Why the insistence that there be no discussion of disputed or argumentative matters between sessions?

There are several good reasons. First, and perhaps foremost, this leads to a respite from the bickering and arguments that are so frequently found in couples that come to a marriage counselor. It is like letting a wound heal. Second, during this respite period both tend to be very active internally, doing a great deal of self-arguing and thinking, planning on rebuttals, considering the other's argument, and otherwise ruminating and meditating. Third, the very fact that each is aware that the other is following orders tends to make each one sympathetic to the other, in that this compliance is evidence of good will. So each is doing a lot of thinking and self-communicating in a peaceful state of relationships.

Suppose a couple reports it is unable to find time to meet for the marriage conference?

One can do a number of things. First, you can offer them your office, charging them your usual rates, while you are outside of the room. Second, you can regard this as evidence that they don't mean business, and discharge them as patients. Third, you can help them try to find time.

Won't you lose patients by such an intransigent attitude?

No. What brings clients and patients to any professional person is his success. If he takes the reasonable attitude that those who come to him have to follow his advice or leave him, patients are much more likely to stay with him than if he takes a weak attitude. I have found that when I try to discharge patients for this reason, they are incredulous, and usually decide to follow my orders.

Can a non-directive therapist employ such a technique?

I don't see why not. He can say to them that he believes that each should be the other's therapist, as it were, and that this rather simple and restrictive technique may help them help themselves, and if they will not employ the method in the spirit of a working hypothesis, that he feels that he cannot handle them.

What about your rule that a person should stay in the room alone by himself/herself if the other doesn't show up?

Several good reasons for this. First, if the other does not show up, the solitary one will spend time thinking about the marriage. So, the time is well spent. Second, if the other comes in late and sees that his/her mate is waiting patiently, this will affect that person favorably in terms of attitude. Say a husband comes in ten minutes late and sees and hears his wife talking to herself. This can affect him deeply, and may be the crisis point in changing his attitude.

What are the philosophical implications of the marriage conference?

The basic one is that couples ought to learn how to settle their problems by themselves, and that before neither one really listened to the other. The alert and responsible marriage counselor may find that by using this method the couple can experience a breakthrough which he then can exploit and lead them to more useful patterns of living.

Is the conference to be only four sessions?

No. I have found that some couples use the conferences as a regular part of their marriage, meeting routinely in this manner once a week. Others employ it from time to time. I may prescribe it for two, four, six more times if it seems indicated.

Summary and Conclusions

The Marriage Conference is a technique that depends on the autochthonous creativity of the couple.

It is highly structured and rigidly controlled to permit one person unlimited freedom of communication while the other is forced to listen. It seems to be quite useful in some situations. When and with whom to apply it is up to the discretion of a marriage counselor. Whether it is in its final stage of perfection is unknown. The writer suggests that whoever uses it, tries it first in its present form, and that variations should be attendant upon experience with in it this orthodox manner.

As stated earlier, when couples "buy" the concept and use it, the rate of success is high, whatever be the reason. I suspect this rate of success is dependent on the degree of confidence expressed by the counselor in the probable efficiency of the method.

I do not wish to give case histories, but I have found this method successful with some cases that I had thought would be unsuccessful. Since we cannot replicate individual cases, we can only come to probably conclusions on the basis of judgment. My judgment is that this method should be in the ammamentarium of marriage counselors for those cases where it may appear to apply as either the method of choice or as an auxiliary technique.

Perhaps the strongest argument that I have for its employment is my belief that any real improvement in any marriage must be attributable by the couple themselves to themself. In this procedure, the couple feels they succeeded on their own. This is an illusion, but isn't all of life an illusion?

References

Burgess, E. W. & Wallin, P. *Predicting Success and Failure in Marriage.* New York: Prentice-Hall, 1939.

Corsini, R.J. The Behind-the-Back Technique in Group Psychotherapy. *Group Psychotherapy*, 1953, 6, 102-109.

Corsini, R.J. Understanding and Similarity in Marriage. *Journal of Abnormal and Social Psychology*, 1956, 52, 327-332.

Terman, L.M. *Psychological Factors in Marital Happiness.* New York: McGraw-Hill, 1938.

Used by permission of the author, Raymond J. Corsini, Ph.D., Senior Counselor. Family Education Center of Hawaii, Honolulu, Hawaii.

THE GROWTH MODEL IN MARITAL THERAPY

SHIRLEY LUTHMAN, LCSW

Growth Model

In practice, most family therapists have, consciously or unconsciously, focused either on the "salvation" of the marriage and the family unit, or the development of the individual. This often meant that either the individual sacrificed himself in some way to maintain the family or the individual chose to grow and sacrifice the family.

In contrast, the author's therapeutic focus is threefold: 1) maximize the family's potential to fulfill its nurturing function and stimulate growth of its individual members; 2) assist individuals within the family unit to take responsibility for the total expression of their own desires and limitations necessary to the realization of their own growth potential; 3) assist in the development of processes for handling change and experimentation without cutting into either the family's basic functions or the individual's growth.*

Underlying this approach is the concept that the individual needs constant growth in two major areas throughout life: That of understanding and expressing his individual uniqueness, and that of making connections with others which, momentarily at least, supercede his aloneness by putting his "insides" in touch with the uniqueness and the similarities of the "insides" of others. For that reason, the therapist must work for the development of each patient's awareness of his wholeness and his totality as a complete entity, and assist in the development of processes that make it possible for him to touch and share with other his dependence and need, without a loss to himself.

In this framework, marriage ideally becomes a relationship between two whole individuals who do not need each other for survival, but for fulfillment, creation and mutual enhancement. They develop processes for sharing their deepest feelings and experiences, giving when they can, touching even when they cannot. They are *in touch* with one another no matter where they are emotionally — giving or non-giving, angry or loving, happy or sad, sick or well. The therapist's major task, then, is not changing how they are, but helping them stay in touch, no matter how or where they are.

The theoretical basis for the development of such a marital relationship is the concept of the *growth model.*

Structurally, the growth model is a framework internalized by the individual as his basis for psychological survival.

Existentially, the growth model is based on the individual's acceptance of his aloneness. He alone is responsible for his insides. It is he who is the architect of his dreams, fantasies, and memories. Everything that comes from him is an expression of some part of himself.

Were he to dream, for example, of a monster chasing a small child to mutilate him, but thwarted by a hero on a white charger, total acceptance would require taking responsibility within himself for all the parts expressed — the monster, the mutilator, the frightened child, the hero, the white charger, the setting in which the dream occurs, and so on. Every facet of the dream is in some way an expression of who he is.

He also takes responsibility for his speech and behavior. He accepts that no one can "take him over," that he can survive emotionally without environmental support, and that he is unable to "take over" anyone else. He takes the risk for the determination, expression, and evolution of what is fitting for himself, and uses that as his *modus operandi.*

The behavioral component of the growth model is the outer, clear, congruent assertion of the individual's internal processes (thoughts, feelings, sensations, perceptions, cognitions, assumptions and conclusion). Such assertion is characterized by authenticity, spontaneity, integrity, courage and commitment to total honesty. The price involved in such commitment is the very real risk of not connecting with others and consequent loneliness and isolation.** Growth, therefore, is tightly bound to the ability to differentiate aloneness from death. Internalization of the growth model makes possible maximum development of the individual's creativity, and the consistent experience of one's self as totally alive.

---

*Of course, it is not always possible to achieve all three goals together, but we are finding families are capable of much more change and adaptability than has been thought.

**Most people live with the illusory risk that "If I lose you, there is a death in part of me."

Pathological Alternatives To The Growth Model

By comparison, the dysfunctional or symptom-bearing individual is operating on the basis of a structure which may be quite foreign to who he really is, but which his experience has led him to believe is necessary to maintain connections to others and receive the approval he deems vital to his survival.

For example:

A. *The "should" structure* — Parents who construct their manifestation of themselves around a *should structure* communicate to their child that he can maintain a relationship with them only by adhering to a rigid code which determines how he should behave and, more damaging, how he should *feel*. If the child adheres to this code, he is "responsible, mature, reliable, good and acceptable;" if he does not, he is "bad, sick, stupid or crazy."

By the time he reaches adulthood, the *should structure* may be oppressive, but at least it is comfortable, familiar and safe. As long as he sticks to that structure, he feels above criticism and certain that society will, if not smile upon him, at least not attack him.

In point of fact, there may be little that is undesirable in the qualities he is exhibiting. They may or may not fit what is really inside him, and often he honestly does not know. Neither may he know who he really is and how he feels about the virtues he manifests. He may even believe that the structure from which he operates is his own, rather than one superimposed upon him by the parent he still carries around inside. Should he realize that the structure does not fit, he may nonetheless choose to keep it because, unaware of his own insides, he assumes there is nothing else there. Without his *should structure*, he feels as if lost in space.

B. *The paranoid structure* — The basis of the *paranoid structure* is emotional deprivation. The child reared in an atmosphere of emotional deprivation perceives early in his development that his external world is unresponsive to his needs and perhaps even hurtful should he reveal vulnerability. Therefore, he comes to believe that his survival is dependent on his being able to disguise his real feelings and manipulate the environment around him in such a way that his needs are met without his having to take responsibility for those needs. As he sees it, almost any kind of manipulation is permissible in a hostile and dangerous world. His repertoire of manipulative methods can be endless, depending on his intelligence and sensitivity, and can include helplessness, blame, martyrdom, "niceness," seduction, intimidation, "reasonableness," or deliberate lying, stealing and physical attack. The mere thought of relinquishing this structure is terrifying because he believes he will be destroyed without it. Should he begin to consider the world as less hostile, he becomes overwhelmed with guilt and loss of self-esteem.

C. *The fragmented or compartmentalized structure* — Precursor to the child's development of the *fragmented or compartmentalized structure* is his parents perception of the outside world as unreliable and unpredictable. They communicate this to him along with a conviction that survival is dependent upon his ability to please, to accurately anticipate and adjust to any shifts in the expectations of the survival parent or parents.

As an adult, this structure remains a means of survival, based on the individual's continuing perception of himself as a weak, ineffective, helpless victim. His boss, wife and anyone else important to him become parent surrogates. His personality, totally plastic, may change completely, depending on who he is with, where he is, and whether or not he deems the place or people crucial to his survival. Without this structure, the individual sees himself as helpless and abandoned.

D. *The messianic structure* — In the development of the *messianic structure*, the child comes to perceive his external world as caring and reliable, but ineffective. He comes to believe that he must fill the gaps in his survival figures or hold them together, or in some way support the parental framework so that his needs can be met and he will survive. He sees his survival as dependent on his being in charge, in control and strong.

This is usually the easiest structure for the therapist to help modify because the individual is usually aware of who he is and is in touch with his feelings. He is certain, however, that no one could respond favorably to his "weak" feelings and he does not express them. As he grows older, secondary gains are often so great that he continues his "great white father" approach to others for the purpose of self-aggrandizement. The price of retaining this structure is isolation, however, and once the individual recognizes his dilemma, he is often eager to give it up.

Therapeutic Techniques

The major task of the therapist is that of shifting the individual from one of the above described structures to the growth model. This is the basis of real change.

Clinical Examples:

In attempting to help families effect this shift, the therapist is likely to encounter, and must deal with, certain problems best described through clinical illustration.

1) Problems of Intimacy (the Pooles — fifth session)

This is a couple with five children. They came to therapy because of a delinquent son with whom the father had engaged in physical violence.

209

In working with the family, it became evident that the delinquent behavior of the child was connected to the parents' vague awareness of each not getting what they needed from the other. They were not even considering this as a problem, however, as they were geared to "the children come first." When the therapist brought this into the open and focused on the possibility that they might be able to get what they needed without leaving the marriage if they would but risk growth, it opened up a previously undreamed of dimension in their relationship.

Therapist: "Have there been any changes in the bedroom?"

Wife: "Well, yes — I was a tiger last night. I have never done that before. I always let him take the lead."

Husband: (smiling, looking pleased) "I liked that — it surprised me, but it was nice,"

Therapist: "Did you have any mixed feelings? Usually people do when they make a change, even if it is a change they want and like."

Wife: "Well, I felt like I was manipulating him, like if I am nice to him he will do anything I want."

Therapist: "Where did you get the idea he was such a patsy? Is it a familiar feeling to you to manipulate others?"

Wife: "Yes, I manipulated both my parents. I was a good girl with my mother, always doing the right thing and then doing what I really wanted behind her back, constantly playing tricks on her to keep her from finding out. I think she pretended not to know — as long as I played the game on the surface, it was o.k. My father I could wheedle, smile, tease him, and he gave me what I wanted. If I came out with what I really felt, we would "turn me off.' "

Husband: "I feel like you are phony sometimes, telling me what you think I want to hear."

Therapist to wife: "You don't want to manipulate any more. I can see that it is depreciating to you. You did it to survive as a child and it worked, but it is defeating you now. However, it is very hard to shift that."

Therapist to husband: "If your wife starts coming out straight, that means you won't always like what you hear, but when you do connect, it will be stronger and more exciting. Can you accept that kind of change?"

Husband: "I could not have before. If she did not give me something I really wanted, I would have thought she did not love me. Now I realize that only means she is at a different place, and if I want the best of her, I have to take the parts I don't like so well also."

Therapist to Wife: "What do you want to do?"

Wife: (soft, loving look on face) "I want to touch him." (They hold hands and look into each other's eyes.)

Therapist: "Now tell each other what you feel inside."

Wife: "There are times when I feel very angry with you and I don't say anything."

Husband: "I want you to tell me how you feel, I want to know."

Therapist to both: "You have been living with a myth, that the expression of anger or the assertion of yourself in some way the other does not like is destructive. The reality is that anger or differences can be the route to some of the most beautiful experiences in marriage, if you can learn to express it in ways that keep the connections open between you."

2) Problems in handling feelings (the Merritts — third session)

In this instance, husband and wife experience the need and the willingness to shift from stereotyped roles of what a male and female should be like, to an exploration of what each is really like, apart from any externally imposed structure. Note that the intervention of the therapist is aimed not at changing feelings but at enabling each spouse to express himself fully and accept the other's expression of feeling in a nonjudgmental way.

The therapist's interventions thus enable each of them to see the other's expression of feeling as a gift — human contact.

Husband: "Things have been pretty hectic this week; a lot has been going on."

Therapist: "You seem low to me."

Husband: "Low?"

Therapist: "Sad, somehow. Your posture is slouched, your expression is somewhat sad, your tone is low."

Husabnd: "Well, I am tired, I've been busy . . ."

Wife: "Well, Tom died Wednesday, it was sudden. You have not said much, but I'm sure it upset you."

Husband: "Oh, yes. (Aside to therapist) Tom was a good friend my age I have known for 20 years. Also, our daughter went to camp this week and . . ."

Therapist: (Interrupting) "You shifted very quickly from Tom. You must have had lots of feelings about that. Could you respond to your wife's offer to hear your feelings?"

Husband: (glances at wife, then down) "Well, it did hit me pretty hard, it was so sudden, made me think of my own death."

Therapist: "I notice you are talking to your wife, but not looking at her."

Husband: (looks up with tears in eyes) "I don't know why I am doing this. I never cry."

Therapist to wife: "Your husband is giving you a gift of his feelings and you seem very far away — what are you feeling?"

Wife: "I have never seen him like this. It frightens me . . ."

Therapist: "Could you share that with him? Would you look at each other and share that?" (They look at each other.)

Wife to Husband: "I have never seen you cry before. It frightens me like something bad is happening."

Husband: "I don't feel bad, it feels good, like a relief — like I have been holding it in a long time."

Therapist (to wife): "Could you explore further with your husband what his tears mean to you?" (To husband): "Could *you* listen and hear her words as an effort on her part to understand herself and you and not as a criticism of you?"

Husband: "I think so."

Wife: "I always want you to be strong. I guess tears mean weakness to me. Yet, I don't *really* feel that way. People should cry if they feel like it. My father could cry, but I did not respect him very much — I never felt I could depend on him."

Therapist to wife: "Maybe you made a connection there where there really isn't one."

Wife to husband: "I never thought of that. You are dependable, you have never really let me down; I am sorry if I have kept you from expressing what you really feel to me."

Husband: "I guessed I thought it was weak to cry, too — my father was a stoic, a good man but the strong, silent type."

Therapist to both: "So we have a discovery, that the expression of feeling, no matter what the feeling, is a strength rather than a weakness. It is the road to understanding and profound contact between husband and wife."

3) Problems of closing off

The growth model separates judgment from feelings. Feelings are not right or wrong, good or bad. They are simply feelings, and need to be understood as such. The therapist must provide a safe arena to get them out in the open so that they can be understood in terms of the individual and his relationships. There is an element of risk in this, for as marital partners get in touch with what they really feel, they may find themselves quite different from the facade they had previously adopted. Getting in touch with feelings, therefore, means, in effect, establishing a new and very different basis for their relationship, which they may or may not be able to do. As individual growth becomes more important, people seem more willing to take that risk, so that, in a sense, regardless of what course their marriage takes, they use the current structure of the relationship to make it possible for each to take the risks necessary for his or her individual growth — a tremendous gift, no matter what the outcome of the marriage itself.

(The Ellis' — first session)

Therapist: "What brought you to us?"

Husband: "Well, I am a weakling. I drink periodically. I don't come home when I say I'm going to. I don't always keep my word."

Wife: "Oh, he is not as bad as he says. He is always over-doing things. The truth is . . ."

Therapist: "You are speaking for him."

Husband: "She usually speaks for me. She is more articulate."

Therapist: "I don't have any trouble understanding you."

Husband: "Well, it is easier to let her talk for me."

Therapist: "You don't look happy about it."

Wife: "Well, really doctor, we are here because of our daughter who is taking drugs and we can't seem to control her."

Therapist: "I appreciate your concern about your daughter, but I do not understand your changing the subject."

Husband: "She often changes the subject in the middle of a conversation."

Therapist: "Could you say that to her and let her know how you feel about that?"

Husband to Wife: "It makes me angry when you change the subject in the middle of a conversation."

Wife: "Well, darling, I . . ."

Therapist: "You are interrupting. (To husband): You are letting her interrupt."

Husband: "Let me finish. I can never keep my train of thought. You are always off somewhere else. Why don't you stick to one thing?"

Wife: "Well, I was concerned about our daughter because . . ."

Therapist: "There you go again."

Wife: "What do you mean?"

Therapist: "Changing the subject. Could you respond to what your husband said to you?"

Wife: "What did you say, dear?"

Husband: "I said, why don't you stick to one thing?"

Wife: "Well, you know I always have so many things hanging over me, right?"

Husband: "Right."

Wife: "Well, you never seem to be around when I need you, right?"

Therapist: "You just did it again."

Wife: "What?"

Therapist: "You set him up. Do you notice what is happening? You constantly cut your husband off from expressing himself by talking for him, by presenting him with conclusions — 'that is the way it is, isn't it, dear?' — by interrupting him, by telling him he does not mean what he says, by defending yourself, and presenting your case instead of exploring his feelings. You (husband) cooperate beautifully in this by withdrawing, agreeing, keeping your feelings to yourself. It is as though the two of you are operating like you have an agreement not to make any real contact. What are you afraid of?"

Husband: (after long pause) "I am afraid I could kill her."

Therapist: "You are sitting on a lot of anger."

Husband: "Yes, all my life."

Therapist: "Then part of your anger that has never come out is connected to your wife, and part, perhaps, to your family before her?"

Husband: "Yes, I used to have temper tantrums when I was a young child . . ." (discusses family's difficulty in expressing or accepting anger during his childhood).

Wife: "I have felt this and I am very frightened of it — more that he would leave me if he got angry enough at me."

Therapist: "I feel that both of you have many strong feelings that have never come out and that you are frightened of them. That is understandable. If you have never experienced expressing strong feeling in a constructive way, it seems overwhelming and catastrophic. However, the route to being in charge of your feeling is to let it out and find out it is not as overwhelming as you thought. So, I would like to recommend that you come into a married couples group. The group makes it possible for you to begin to learn how to express your feelings with others who are not connected so deeply to you and such expression serves as a bridge to beginning to express to each other. Also, if the expression does get out of hand, which it sometimes does in the beginning because it has been building up for so long, there are enough people in the group so that we can exert controls from outside so you don't have to worry about hurting yourself or someone else.

(The Haywards — seventh session)

Husband: "I am really pissed off at you. You treat me like a little boy. I try to tell you what I feel, and you, in effect, pat me on the head like I have not got good sense. I am sick and tired of it."

(Wife sits with hands folded primly and smiles benignly.)

Therapist: "You mean like she is doing right now?"

Husband: "Exactly. What's the matter with you?"

Therapist to wife: "Your husband is coming out with some real feeling, but I don't get any message from you about what you are feeling inside."

Wife: "Well, he is probably right."

Therapist: "Well, that wraps that up!"

Wife: "Well, there is no point in both of us getting mad."

Therapist: "What would happen?"

Wife: "No one would be in control."

Therapist: "What is the worst that would happen?"

Wife: "He would hit me."

Husband: "I did hit you, but that was three years ago — I can change."

Therapist to wife: "Do you believe that?"

Wife: "Maybe, but I am still afraid . . ."

Therapist: "What is the fear — what is your worst fantasy — let's pretend . . ."

Wife: (begins to cry) "I will be alone and no one can hear me."

Therapist: "Your husband is listening. Hold his hand and tell him about the loneliness."

Wife to Husband: "It is like when I was little and I would hide in my room and hear my mother and father fighting. He would beat her up and she would be screaming. Then he would leave the house and stay away for days. One day he did not come back." (She begins to sob deeply, husband takes her in his arms).

Therapist to both: "Maybe you can't promise each other that you will be there always, or even that you will love each other always. However, you can make a commitment to each other that you will stay with each other until feelings are resolved."

"It isn't the leaving or even the hitting that is the most destructive thing. It is that both these acts may cut off contact and leave people hanging with their feelings, so that the expression of feeling becomes synonymous with abandonment or violence. The reality is: If people can learn to handle their own and the feelings of others in a fitting way, there may be separation, but there is never abandonment or violence."

In these examples, there is not much talk about sex, money, religion, children, and the other "problems" people usually fight about, not because these issues do not come up or have ceased to be important, but because we see them merely as vehicles around which people express their feelings and attempt to make contact. Thus, as therapists, we do not focus on the content — on the problems, *per se*. People can resolve these easily enough if they are in touch with how they really feel about them, and if they are able to express their differences to each other in a way that separates these differences from the issue of whether or not they love each other.

Our focus then, is on the growth processes people use for making contact. We see therapy as changing old, defeating, lethal processes, and teaching new ones rather than resolving problems, softening conflicts, or even changing people, although people do change, often drastically, as a result of letting go of destructive processes and adopting those which enhance the uniqueness of each in his own eyes and those of the other.

4) The task of getting marital partners in touch with their feelings may be complicated by each being in different stages of growth.

(The Jones — 20th session)

Husband to wife: "I am suddenly aware that I am not really happy with what I am doing at work, but I don't know what I really want to do either — I feel depressed and immobilized much of the time.

(To therapist): I am even impotent with my wife. I know this is frustrating to her and I feel guilty about that."

Wife: "I feel as though you leave me hanging. I really do not want sex with you if you are going to get me aroused and then just not follow through."

Husband: "You sound as though I do it deliberately; I just can't help it!"

Therapist to husband (burlesquing): "Poor baby!"

Husband to therapist: "I do feel helpless . . ."

Therapist to husband: "Look at your wife and say to her, 'I am helpless like a little baby.'"

Husband (looking at wife): "I am helpless — God damn it, I am not helpless! I am just sick and tired of your control and your demands and your endless bitching about what I don't do right. I feel like my mother ran my life until I married you, and you have run it ever since."

Therapist to husband: "Whose responsibility is that?"

Husband: "Mine. I am responsible for my life."

Therapist to husband: "Could you look at your wife and say that to her?"

Husband: (Looking at wife) "I am responsible for my life, for what I do. (Looks intently at wife) You know it really does not have to do with you that I feel controlled and helpless. I invite you to step in and you do it."

Wife: "I really do not want to control you anymore."

Therapist to husband: "Do you believe that?"

Husband: "Yes, I think I really do. But I am afraid to take responsibility for myself. What happens if I begin to do what I feel and to take risks to act on my feelings — what if I make an ass of myself?"

Therapist: "Yes, what would be so bad about that?"

Husband: "I don't know, nothing I guess . . ."

Therapist: "What is the worst that could happen?"

Husband: "No one would like me and I would be alone."

Therapist: "What does being alone feel like to you? Could you lean back, close your eyes and try to get in touch with that feeling of aloneness?"

Husband: (does this for several seconds, then puts head down to lap, assumes a "fetal" position) "It feels like I am dying — I felt that way when I was five years old — my parents used me to get at each other."

Therapist: "What is coming out then is that you have powerful feelings connected to your experience of being abandoned and used as a child that are getting in the way of your feeling in charge of yourself now as a man with your wife. We need to understand that connection so that you can resolve it."

Therapist to both husband and wife: "You are at very different places right now. That is not bad in terms of your relationship, but it is frustrating. (To wife) You are beginning to come out very directly to your husband and with how you feel without blaming or attacking him. (To husband) You are more concerned at this point with what is going on inside of you connected to your past. The feelings you are experiencing now are connected more to that past rather than to the current situation. We have to get past that barrier in order for you to get in touch with and respond with your feelings in the here and now. Then we can again focus on the relationship between you."

5) The therapist must neutralize a judgmental framework whenever it appears.

(The Carters — tenth session)

Wife: "I can't say how I feel because then you will tell me what a bitch I am and how bad I am . . ."

Therapist: "He is in charge of whether or not you are o.k.?"

Wife: "Well, actually, that is so — it's very important to me what he thinks."

Husband: "I feel the same way. It is painful to me when you tell me I am not a man and you don't respect me. I try to please you all the time, and nothing seems to be good enough."

Therapist: "Her response determines how you come out with your feelings?"

Husband: "What's wrong with that? I am sure this is the case in 75% of the American marriages; most husbands try to please their wives and American women are becoming very demanding . . ."

Therapist: "Let's bring in the troops!"

Husband to therapist: "Well, you can make fun of me, but just ask . . ."

Therapist: "It is not my intent to make fun of you. I am trying to get you to see what is happening. You are trying to make contact with each other, and it is coming out like each of you is helpless, the other is in charge of you, and you can bring in the legal briefs, the statistics, and the jury to prove it. All your evidence may prove you are absolutely right, so where does that leave you? If you pursue this way of getting in touch, one of you always has to lose, to be one down. When that happens, both of you lose."

6) It is not unusual for a therapist to see pseudo-family structures in which there are several adults who are having sexual relationships with more than one other adult member. It is then important for the therapist to focus on what such a structure has to do with each individual's desire for intimacy, i.e. the total sharing of inside feelings, and the barriers in the way to such contact. Our task is understanding the processes connected to meeting people's desires for intimacy, not imposing frameworks upon which this might be achieved.

(The Bakers — eighth session)

Wife to husband: "I wish you would do your own thing and let me do mine."

213

Husband: "What does that mean?"

Wife: "Like the other night when Steve came over. He and I were on our private trip and you had to butt in — it did not concern you!"

Husband: "Well, when he started playing around with you, I felt left out, partly angry and partly aroused."

Therapist to both: "Our last session both of you really began to connect with each other. I notice that every time you get close, you (to wife) begin to run. You invite other people in to stay with you, you get involved with other guys, you go on LSD trips. You (husband) cooperate beautifully in the games even though you are very angry about the game maneuver. Neither of you seems to want to pin yourself or the other down. What are you both afraid of?"

7) This next couple was seen by male and female co-therapists together so as to provide "parental" affirmation and support as a bridge from their early experience of deprivation to beginning to learn how to give freely to each other

(The Tracys — fifth session)

Husband to wife: "You are always taking care of things in the family, always in control, never trusting me. . ."

Wife: "I would like to be able to trust you, but you always let me down."

Husband: "It is true I have let you down often in the past, but I am trying to change that (looks down and slouches)."

Therapist: "I notice that when you start to come out with how you feel to your wife, she responds and then you sort of fold up."

Husband: "I start to feel guilty. I really don't want to hurt her."

Wife: "It doesn't throw me as much for you to tell me how you feel as it does for you to 'fold up'."

Therapist to husband: "Do you believe that?"

Husband: "Yes, I guess so . . ."

Therapist: "O.K., let's go back — how come you fold up?"

Husband (talks softly, head hanging): "I guess I am afraid she'll stop giving to me."

Therapist: "She's a good mama."

Wife: "I don't want to be his mother."

Therapist: "So how come you keep taking over?"

Wife: "I guess I have always been the one who was there when the chips were down. I always took care of everybody else's feelings; taking over is all I know."

Therapist: "In different ways, both of you felt very lonely as children, no one really heard or took care of your feelings. (To husband): Your mother, from what you said last week, took good care of you physically as long as you didn't cross her. So being given to is connected with not asserting yourself."

Husband: "That's true. She was a good cook. She was always there when I was sick. She kept my clothes clean and ironed, but she would not let me have a thought of my own."

Therapist to wife: "No one took care of you physically or emotionally. If you begin to let your husband take care of some of your feelings now, you have to give up being the 'Big Mama' always in control — that's scary." (Wife starts to cry.)

The Growth Model and Survival

Working with a marital pair is, in some respects, like working with six people — the two patients and their four parental 'ghosts.' Couples often have a difficult time staying in the present with each other because they are still not separated completely from their parents, and are projecting on to their spouses, perceptions and expectations connected more with early experiences, rather than with the present relationship. Though the treatment focus is always on the current relationship, we move in and out between past and present as the process of growth in therapy demands. Treatment is a flowing process, just as any relationship is a flowing process.

The individual internal shift to the growth model is the goal in all therapy regardless of the method used to get to that core. The methods of family therapy, group therapy and marital therapy, when successful, get to the deepest level of intimacy between people, a level not possible without a shift to the growth model by the individual involved. The focus of therapy may move back and forth from individual to marital or family relationships so as to develop new processes for relating that fit the new internal structures. The interactional processes among family members, between the marital pair, or between the individual and the therapist are the media through which the therapist can assess the nature of the individual internal structure. Once that assessment is made, the therapist can, through a variety of techniques, make known to the individual his unproductive manner of manipulating the environment and how that defeats his hopes of achieving growth and other treatment goals. When the pain involved in the patient's current situation outweighs the fear, and he sees his way of operating as basically defeating him, or, when he glimpses the potential for much greater satisfaction than he has ever known through his current structure, he may opt for change, now that the choices are clear to him.

Should he choose to move toward the growth model, he must incorporate the therapist as his survival figure, a bridge between his old structure now relinquished and what has yet to take its place. This interim experience is often perceived, on an existential level, as death, which may be manifested as intense depression, internal chaos, lack of control, perhaps even psychosis. But he has to experience it and to know he can survive it in order to develop an understanding of aloneness as wholeness, rather than as death. The bridge which makes this possible is his experience of a clear, consistent congruent message from the therapist that, "If you make room for all parts of you, together they will be better than anything you could manufacture or superimpose on yourself from the outside." Once the experience of the death of the old structure is complete and the individual finds he has not been destroyed, the process of building the new structure based on the growth model begins.

He first learns to distinguish aggression, selfishness, immorality and rule-breaking from forthright assertion of who he really is and what he really wants. This distinction is made through enabling the individual to get in touch with the "growth intent" in his feeling (i.e., desire for contact), and express it in ways that fit who he is. He must understand that in the process of learning what fits him, he may make many mistakes and appear quite different from what he really is. He then has to learn to assess his assertive attempts on the basis of whether or not they fit, rather than whether they were right or wrong or successful.

The therapist then helps him to integrate the *feeling* and *knowing* aspects of an assertive experience, so that both are integrated into a whole, and then incorporated into his internal structure. When the individual has developed his own processes for asserting his feelings, receiving feedback from others about his assertions, evaluating that feedback, fitting the feelings and feedback to what he knows intellectually, and using the resulting knowledge from this total experience to facilitate his growth, then he begins for the first time to experience on his own the intense excitement and power of this new structure. At that point, his survival shifts to himself, and the therapist becomes a friend and an equal.

From Family Therapy, The Growth Model in Martial Therapy, by Shirley Luthman, LCSW. Volume I, Number 1, Summer 1972, pages 63-83. Reprinted by permission of Libra Publishers

GROUP PROCEDURES FOR INCREASING POSITIVE FEEDBACK BETWEEN MARRIED PARTNERS

by
CARL CLARKE, PH.D.
Assistant Professor of Psychology, University of Florida
From The Family Coordinator, October 1970.
Used by permission of the magazine and the author.

A great deal has been said about an increase in leisure time with opportunities for enriching one's life. However, very little has been said about how husbands and wives may enrich their marital experience. These group procedures were developed with that goal in mind. They were designed to help married people express to each other very specifically certain feelings they had for each other; feelings such as love, respect, acceptance, and appreciation.

Three groups of five to six couples were formed, who were not in therapy at the time, and who were not participating in these groups for therapeutic reasons. These couples were more representative of the typical couple today, the majority of whom will never seek marriage counseling. The group process focused on the positive aspects of the relationship and how recognizing and sharing these aspects with each other creates an emotional experience which is highly satisfying to both partners. This is not to say that some of the couples did not receive help with problems, but simply that their problems were seven basic elements in the procedures which the couples followed:

1. They talked about the positive features of their relationship.
2. They went through some warming up exercises, such as talking to someone other than their own partner.
3. They told their marriage partner the positive things they had said about their marriage to someone else.
4. They described the feelings they experienced listening to each other.
5. Most of the sharing with each other and reporting of feelings took place in the presence of the other group members so that there were opportunities for emphathizing and identifying with the experiences of many other couples.
6. From session to session each participant kept a log book in which he recorded his feelings and thoughts about certain aspects of his marriage and marriage partner, which were related to what was to be discussed in the next session.
7. Discussion assignments were given to the couples to carry out during the week, assignments that were related to what had been introduced in the previous session.

Rationale

One grows accustomed to a person's good qualities and is far too eager to find and report the faults of another. One usually fails to recognize and appreciate the creative power he possesses to make others feel good with praise. The society seems much more adept at citing ulterior motives than in giving praise where it is appropriate. The groups were formed for the sole purpose of helping couples become more aware of all that is positive in a relationship, to be able to receive as well as give love, and to be able to share with one another.

Procedures

The following are some illustrations of what the couples discussed:

1. What is it about your marriage that most pleases you?
2. Describe an experience in which you felt especially close, felt you were understood, or valued.
3. What is it that your wife does which causes you to feel she loves you, values, and respects you? (Wives, of course, were asked the same thing regarding their husbands.)
4. What do you do that expresses your love, shows that you love your husband — your wife?
5. What are the positive traits, qualities, attributes you see in your wife or your husband?
6. What specific needs does your wife — husband meet?

Sometimes husbands and wives were paired as unrelated couples. At times husbands talked in one group, while wives talked in a separate group. Or at other times, they were grouped in two concentric circles, husbands and wives alternately in the inner circle, while the other group sat in an outer circle and listened. All of these arrangements were used to facilitate communication between husbands and wives at the time when they would be brought together. The group met for six two and a half hour sessions.

216

Session I

In the first session, husbands were asked to describe what it was about their marriage that satisfied them. The wives listened and then discussed how they felt about what their husbands had described. This procedure was repeated with the wives talking and the husbands listening.

The group then separated into unrelated couples, and spent fifteen minutes discussing with the other what each would like his marriage to be three to five years hence. After the discussion, each person wrote on a large poster his hopes for his marriage. When the group was reformed, the expectations were compared. In some instances, they were similar, but often they were not, ranging from the more personal and spiritual to the materialistic and pragmatic.

At the end of this session, two assignments were given to be carried out at home. Each participant was asked to record in his log book the things his partner did which made him feel loved, valued, appreciated, etc. Further discussion of their goals was the discussion assignment given to the couples.

Session II

At the beginning of the second session, couples talked about their reactions to the discussion of goals during the previous week. Following this, the wives took turns describing experiences in which they felt very close to their husbands, felt that they were understood and respected. The husbands then talked about how they felt, listening to their wives. This procedure was repeated for the husbands. Very often the husband and wife reported the same experience.

One wife talked about a pretty young girl who lived next door and who was quite flirtatious. The girl made this wife very much aware of her age and the fact that she was not as attractive; her husband was obviously attracted to this young woman. However, she felt that her husband understood this threat and therefore did not encourage the younger woman in her flirtation. The wife therefore felt understood and less threatened. Another wife talked about having her husband with her in the labor room at the birth of their first child, which made her feel valued and loved by him. A husband described how when things at his office became intolerable for him he would telephone his wife and just talk to her. He felt very loved and understood by this simple act, and thought at that moment he may not have been very important at the office, he was most important to her.

The husbands and wives were separated into role groups. Each group discussed what it was that the partner did that made him feel loved. In this instance, the two groups talked as long as they liked so that every person had an opportunity to talk.

One large group was formed again. At one place in the circle of chairs, two chairs were arranged facing each other. These were called "sharing seats," and were designated as a place where two people could talk directly to each other as though there were no one else present. Yet they were a part of the circle, and therefore what was said while sitting in these two chairs was shared with the group.

Each couple had a turn in the sharing seat. The structure was that of a personal dialogue. They were instructed to speak in the first person to each other — "I — You," "You — Me". They were to speak about their loving behavior in the present tense, that is, "These are the things you do which make me feel that you love me, want me, value me." The husband was to describe to his wife how it was she communicated this to him. The wife was then asked to share how she felt just now, listening to what her husband said. The roles were then reversed.

After a couple finished, the other participants described what they felt listening to that couple. This "sharing seats" procedure and the sharing of feelings within the group, most of which were very positive, generated closeness, togetherness and involvement. The group began to be.

For a discussion assignment couples were instructed to try the "sharing seats" procedure, reporting to each other what had happened during the week which communicated loving, valuing, understanding, etc.

Session III

During the first ten minutes of the third session, group members talked about what had happened during the week when they tried the "sharing seats" procedure at home. The couples were then instructed to find a place to sit together at a distance from other couples. They were given fifteen minutes to talk to each other about the specific ways in which each communicated his love and appreciation to the other, and to find out if his behavior was understood by the other.

Husbands said they showed their love by:
1. Helping around the house, sharing duties, protecting the wife from doing too much.
2. Showing affection, tenderness, not forcing sexual relations, expressing love, and offering comfort.
3. Making it plain that the wife came first, even before the children.
4. Urging the wife to take part in activities outside the home.
5. Taking an interest in the children.
6. Being the provider.

Wives said they showed their love by:
1. Cooking for him, cleaning the house, mending his clothes.
2. Trying not to bother him with petty details.

3. Encouraging him in his work.
4. Greeting him enthusiastically when he comes home.
5. Expressing tenderness and love with words.

They reassembled as a group to describe the feelings they experienced while sharing as a couple.

Two assignments were given for the following week. The couples were to list in their log books all the positive traits that their partners possessed; they were also to make a similar list about themselves. They were asked to try the "sharing seats" procedure again and to discuss with each other what they had done during the week to show their love.

Session IV

At the beginning of the fourth session, the couples again talked about their "sharing seats" experiences. The circle was then arranged with the two "sharing seats." Husbands and wives took turns in describing the positive traits of the other. Each reported what he felt as the other talked; these feelings were, on the whole, positive rather than negative.

The group was asked what it thought about this procedure. Some felt that it was too contrived and would make them feel uncomfortable. They were surprised, however, at the depth of the feelings that were experienced and expressed in the "sharing seats."

For assignments the couples were to try the "sharing seats" procedure at home, and to write about the needs of each that were fulfilled by the partner.

Session V

In the fifth session two concentric circles were formed with the husbands in the inner circle. The wives were to listen without comment as the husbands discussed among themselves the various needs which were met by their wives, using their log books for reference. The wives then were asked to describe what they felt while listening to their own husband and the other husbands. This entire procedure was reversed with wives in the inner circle.

Each couple then sat at a distance from the other couples. After a period of silent consideration each partner described to the other two loving behaviors he was willing to begin doing more frequently and two loving behaviors he wished his partner would do more frequently. They discussed the similarities and differences between each others' commitments and wishes. Finally, they returned to the group and each partner described the feelings he experienced while sharing in this way. Many couples experienced a greater degree of openness in communication and sense of togetherness.

The two assignments for the week were to note in the log books any changes that had occurred as a result of the group experience, and try the "sharing seats" procedure discussing the needs they met in each other.

Session VI

At the beginning of the final session, there was described in detail what the couples were to do. The group was to separate into couples and to find places where they could sit close together. They were to do four different things and would be told when to start and when to stop.

1. For eight minutes, they were to tell each other what had happened to them and to their relationship during the six weeks.
2. At a given signal, they were to stop talking and spend the next four minutes silently recalling rewarding experiences they had had during the previous five sessions. They were to try to remember what they had said, what had been said to them.
3. Again, at a signal, they were to stop thinking of the past, and instead, concentrate on one particular feeling they had for the other. This was to be the feeling they most wanted the other to feel. They had only two minutes to experience this feeling.
4. At a signal, they were to try to communicate this feeling without speech.

When they regrouped, they were asked to tell each other what the feeling was they had been thinking about and how they had tried to communicate it. Sometimes they both knew what it was, other times they had to explain it in words what it was.

The non-verbal communication ranged from looking very intently into each other's eyes with occasional smiles and tears, to reaching out to each other, squeezing hands, thighs, or arms, embracing and kissing. Each person described what he felt while trying to communicate this way. Several couples were very surprised at the discrepancy between what they thought was going to happen and what actually did happen. For most of them this had been a very intense and satisfying emotional experience.

They talked about the changes in themselves and in their ability to talk to each other. It was emphasized that there could be value in continuing the "sharing seats" procedure on a weekly basis as a means of maintaining the ability to give positive feedback to each other.

Conclusion

Some examples of the typical emotional experiences that were reported or observed during the group sessions were as follows:

1. A husband described the frustration he experienced because his wife so seldom let him know the ways in which he could help her, and thereby enable him to express to her how important she was to him.

2. A wife crying with joy said, "I wish everyone might feel as loved as I do by my husband."

3. A wife, who was a very self-sufficient person and seen by her husband as both strong and independent, wanted her husband to know how much she needed him.

4. A husband wanted his wife to understand that he was so pleased with the fact that it was she who was his wife.

5. A wife whose husband almost never shared any of his feelings with her, and who wanted him to do so more than anything else in the world said, "I looked into his eyes and, for the first time, saw his soul."

Most couples experienced an increased awareness of the other's feelings, and a better understanding of the needs of the other. They felt a greater desire to please. There was a sense of the marriage having gained more confidence and enthusiasm. One couple put it, "The group sessions made each of us more aware of the marriage, more aware of what we had earlier in the marriage. Since the children came and, also, being in graduate school, we have just taken each other for granted and had really forgotten just how we felt during the beginning months and years of our marriage."

Three months later, most of the couples reported that the changes had continued, though some said the changes were temporary.

These procedures emphasized recognizing and communicating what was liked and appreciated in the marital relationship and yet many couples openly expressed negative feelings about aspects of themselves or their relationship, but in such a manner that usually resulted in goal-setting behavior. There was no exploring of the dynamics of any presented problems, but rather, a group structure was provided within which positive aspects of the relationship would be expressed.

These sessions provided opportunities for the couples to communicate in a type of dialogue that is often a forgotten interpersonal art.

COUNSELING THE HOMOSEXUAL

by

David Antisdale, Jerry Hamilton, Roger Johnson, Robert Krauss,
and William Reeves — Graduate Students at Talbot Theological Seminary,
La Mirada, California

Agree/Disagree Questionnaire

Agree Disagree

――	――	1. A homosexual can be a Christian.
――	――	2. A homosexual should be asked to leave the church.
――	――	3. A person chooses to be a homosexual.
――	――	4. The Bible condemns homosexual lust but not homosexual love.
――	――	5. The Bible condemns homosexual perversion but not homosexuality.
――	――	6. You can identify a homosexual by his or her physical appearance.
――	――	7. Homosexuality is a form of mental illness.
――	――	8. Homosexuality can be biological in origin.
――	――	9. When a homosexual is born again, his homosexuality is gone.
――	――	10. It is possible to be a homosexual and yet be happily married to the opposite sex.
――	――	11. Once a homosexual, always a homosexual.
――	――	12. Homosexuals are a menace to society.
――	――	13. Homosexuals commit more criminal acts than heterosexuals.
――	――	14. Some professions contain a greater percentage of homosexuals.

Counseling The Homosexual: Part I

A wide spectrum of opinions exists concerning the homosexual in our society. In 1969 a poll taken for CBS television revealed that two out of three Americans looked on homosexuals with disgust, discomfort, or fear, and one out of ten regarded them with outright hatred. A Louis Harris poll in October 1969 reported that 60 percent of the nation considered homosexuals harmful to American life.[1]

That opinion is rapidly changing. In the past, a homosexual had basically two choices in which to live. He could hide in a closet and live in loneliness and in fear of rejection and discovery, or he could come out of the closet and enter into the gay ghetto. Today, with the liberal attitudes of the late 60s and early 70s and with the popularity of minority groups fighting for rights, the homosexual has come out into the public. With the increasing power of gay activist groups has come increasing acceptance and rights in our society. Homosexuality is no longer considered by the American Psychological Association and American Psychiatric Association as mental illness,[2] and in some religious circles, the Metropolitan Community Church being a primary proponent, it is no longer considered to be a moral disease either.

An important aspect of counseling a homosexual is to understand the view he has of himself. Until recently the homosexual viewed himself as abnormal, different, or less of a human being in comparison to heterosexuals. Today, the trend is toward self-acceptance. The slogan "self-acceptance is the first step to happiness" appeared in a homophile publication a few years ago.[3] The slogan captures the current attempt of not only the acceptance of oneself, but his acceptance in the community. No longer do homosexuals want to remain feeling inferior.

How does a person who is a born-again Christian and who has a homosexual orientation view himself? A Christian's view will depend greatly on what he believes to be the cause of his homosexuality and on how he interprets Scripture. A person who believes that his homosexuality is genetically caused, who believes that God made him that way, is left with the only option of accepting himself the way he is. He can remove guilt by rationalizing that he does not need to change and, in fact, cannot change. A Christian who accurately understands Scripture and believes that his homosexuality is not God-given but learned (the stance that most research holds) is left with the conscious feelings of guilt, but he also has the strong motivation to change. Change, however, is not easy. A paragraph of a letter written in the book *The Returns of Love* illustrates the frustrations and turmoils of such a person.[4]

Dear Peter,

Can you understand it? This is the impossibility of the situation — what I may have, I don't want, and what I do want, I may not have. I want a friend, but more than a friend, I want a wife. But I don't want a woman . . .

The writer strongly desires to live a godly life but finds himself physically attracted to Peter. With God's help, he is able to overcome temptation and not act out his homosexual orientation or inclinations.

A Christian homosexual often goes through periods of despair, loneliness, idleness, and self-pity. At these times the mind is free to wander, frustrated at not being able to act out his sexual tendencies, realizing that they are wrong. Scriptures do not deal harsher though with the homosexual than with the adulterer.[5] The temptation in both cases can lead to sin or to obedience. A person who views his homosexuality as wrong and desires to change, can change — not only in behavior but in orientation as well. Many Christian men, by condition homosexual, who seek means of understanding themselves and their obligations before God undergo a positive change in their sexual orientation. Others find a sense of grace and resolution regarding their condition but without a change in sexual orientation.[6]

The following are some practical suggestions from a Christian who formerly was gay on dealing with a person who is gay.[7]

1. Recognize that homosexuality is sin. Make clear that it is not merely your position, but the Word of God.

2. Do not overreact when one tells you he is gay.

3. Condemn the act, not the person.

4. Honor the trust that the person has placed in you.

5. Help him understand the cost of discipleship — what it means to take up the cross daily, what it means to be a son of God.

6. Do not touch the person in the beginning of your relationship. Show sincere love without physical contact.

7. Pray for the Holy Spirit to change his life.

8. Do not allow a person to isolate himself, but encourage participation in mixed group activities.

9. Have him memorize Scriptures that deal with temptation.

The Biblical Perspective of Homosexuality

In supporting their own views and feelings, the leaders of the Universal Fellowship of Metropolitan Community Churches (UFMCC) have been guilty of inaccurate exegesis of those portions of the Bible which classify homosexuality as sin. A thorough analysis of their interpretation of Scripture passages are presented in order to give the Christian counselor the biblical basis for maintaining that homosexual acts are sin.

Genesis 19 (cf. Judges 19:22)

The UFMCC[8] attack this passage by observing that the Hebrew verb "to know" in Genesis 19:5 does not usually refer to sexual relations in the Old Testament. The NASB translation, however, uses "have relations" or "have intercourse." The *Midrash* indicates that this verb means to know for sexual purposes just as Adam knew his wife and she conceived.[9] Clement of Alexandria, a church father from the second century, condemned sodomy and taught that it was the reason God destroyed Sodom.[10] For a more complete refutation of the UFMCC position, see Derek Kidner's commentary on Genesis.[11]

The UFMCC also argue that the sin of Sodom was homosexual rape. But this does not explain why Lot offered his virgin daughters to the men (Gen. 19:8). Also this view cannot be reconciled with Jude 7.

Leviticus 18:22; 20:13

The UFMCC claim that these regulations are not for today, since believers in Christ are no longer under the Mosaic Law. They compare these prohibitions to the eating of rabbit, lobster, clams, shrimp, oysters, and rare steak in Leviticus 11 and 17.

It is clear that "by the works of the Law no flesh will be justified in His sight; for through the Law comes the knowledge of sin" (Rom. 3:20). UFMCC have the first part of this verse correct, but they neglect the second part, that the Law reveals the sinfulness of men. In Romans 7:7 Paul made a clear statement of how the Law reveals sin: ". . . I would not have come to know sin except through the Law; for I would not have known about coveting if the Law had not said, 'You shall not covet.' " The immediate contexts of Leviticus 18:22 and 20:13 contain listings of acts which even the UFMCC label as sin.

I Samuel 18

The UFMCC use the love between Jonathan and David to argue that God blessed a practicing homosexual. However, there is no statement that any homosexual act took place between them. The Hebrew word for love in I Samuel 18 is used for the love between man and woman, but it is also used of the love between a slave and his master and love between neighbors and friends.[12] In discussing the meaning of the word "love" in this passage, Dr. J. A. Thompson attaches political overtones to the word. He writes: "Sensing the certainties of the future, Jonathan was ready even then to acknowledge David's sovereignty over himself and over the nations."[13]

Romans 1:26-27

The UFMCC believe that Paul was stating that people should not change their sexual orientation. Someone who is born heterosexual should not try to become homosexual, and likewise, someone who is homosexual should not try to become heterosexual. They also teach that this passage condemns lust which is sinful regardless of sexual orientation while homosexual love is just as desirable as heterosexual love.

There is no biblical or biological basis for the concept of a person's being a homosexual by birth. God made a man, and when it was apparent that no creature was suitable for meeting his needs, God made a woman rather than another man (Gen. 2:18-25). The concept of the family consisting of husband and wife and children is found throughout the Bible (Prov. 18:22; 31:10-31; I Cor. 7; Eph. 5:22-6:4; Col. 3:18-21; I Pet. 3:1-7). The natural sexual function is carried out through the male-female relationship. Romans 1:27 clearly describes the sin as males leaving the natural use of the female and then desiring other males. The change of sexual orientation is from heterosexual to homosexual.

The UFMCC confuse the issue by stating that homosexual love is desirable. Love, in the Bible, is not only desirable but is in fact commanded by Christ. However, the Bible does condemn homosexual lust or physical desires which are consumated. The Greek participle "committing" always expresses the bringing to pass or the accomplishment.[14] Homosexual lust (cf. Matt. 5:28) and its consumation are sin.

I Corinthians 6:9 and
I Timothy 1:10

The UFMCC teach that these verses do not condemn homosexuality, but they do condemn homosexual perversion. They quote the *Good News for Modern Man* which uses the term "homosexual perverts." Homosexual perversion is just as wrong as heterosexual perversion. When this argument fails, they say that you cannot take this part of the Bible literally.

The Greek word *malakoi* (I Cor. 6:9) translated "effeminate" in the NASB refers to "men and boys who allow themselves to be misused homosexuality."[15] The second Greek word is *arsenokoitai* which is a compound word meaning a "male" and a "bed." According to Thayer it refers to "one who lies with a male as with a female."[16]

The correct meaning from the Greek is that homosexuality in any form is a perversion. Even a homosexual act done in love is sinful.

The UFMCC are inconsistent in their hermeneutical principles. They do not understand the literal, historical, grammatical system of biblical interpretation. This can be seen in their confusion concerning the meaning of such passages as Mark 10:11-12; I Corinthians 6:1-7; 7:10-11; 14:34-35; I Timothy 2:9-10; and, II Timothy 2:11-12 which they call discrepancies resulting from fallible human authors, e.g., Paul.

What is Homosexuality?

In December 1973 the American Psychiatric Association decided to eliminate homosexuality as a mental disorder. A new category was instituted titled "Sexual Orientation Disturbance."[17] This new category is for "individuals whose sexual interests are directed primarily toward people of the same sex and who are either disturbed by, in conflict with, or wish to change their sexual orientation."[18] In making this change, the psychiatrists have advocated the opinion that homosexuality is merely one form of sexual behavior. However, many psychiatrists are not in agreement with this new definition and they are trying to reclassify homosexuality as a mental disorder.[19]

Dr. John Powell, a professor of psychology at Michigan State University, has defined homosexuality as "overt or psychic psychosexual attraction to or relationships between members of the same sex."[20] Dr. Charles Wahl, associate professor of psychiatry at UCLA, defines homosexuality as a "persistent conscious sexual attraction to members of the same sex."[21]

According to the controversial Kinsey report, 37 percent of the total male population has at least some overt homosexual experience to the point of orgasm between adolescence and old age; 10 percent of the males are more or less exclusively homosexual for at least three years between the ages of 16 and 55; and 4 percent of the white males are exclusively homosexual throughout their lives, after the onset of adolescence.[22]

It is important to note that a homosexual cannot be identified by appearance. Both heterosexual and homosexual include the super masculine and the feminine. Even big, tough football players may be gay.[23]

Other Important Terms

Gay — being free from shame, guilt, misgivings, or regret over being homosexual.[24]

Bisexuals — individuals who choose to have sexual relations with both males and females.[25]

Transvestites — those who prefer to dress in clothes of the opposite sex.[26]

Transsexuals — people who claim to be members of the sex opposite to that of their own bodies and who seek out sex transformation procedures to transform their bodies hormonally and surgically into apparent congruence with their gender role.[27]

The Cause of Homosexuality

One of the most controversial questions of the day centers around the origin of homosexuality. Theories of its cause can be divided into two categories. The genetic theory maintains that "an individual inherits a predisposition for homosexuality." The psychogenic theory espouses the view that "family constellation and other environmental factors determine a person's sexual identity."[28]

In 1952 F. J. Kallman found that there was a much higher incidence of homosexuality among identical twins than among fraternal twins. His studies were later discredited as proof of a genetic basis for homosexuality. Most modern geneticists do not teach that the basis of character traits or behavior patterns is found in the genes.[29] According to Dr. Charles Wahl, the vast preponderance of evidence clearly indicates that homosexuality is a learned disorder and is not genetically inherited.[30]

Some researchers have indicated that a hormonal imbalance in a pregnant mother could affect the brain, endocrine system, or sexual development of the fetus.[31] However, there is no proof that homosexuality is caused by a hormonal imbalance. Dr. Evelyn Hooker, who is famous for her research on homosexuality, states: "There is no evidence that homosexuals have faulty hormone levels, or that their sexual orientation can be changed with hormone injections."[32]

Psychogenic or psychological theories point to common factors among the families of homosexuals. Dr. Irving Bieber studied the family backgrounds of 106 male homosexuals. A sampling of his statistics demonstrated that 81 mothers were dominating, 67 were overprotective, 66 made the patient their favorite, 87 of the fathers spent very little or no time with their sons, and 79 of the fathers maintained a detached attitude toward their sons.[33]

According to Dr. Armand Nicholi, professor of psychiatry at Harvard Medical School, "current research indicates that the family most likely to produce a homosexual boy comprises an overly intimate, possessive, and dominating mother and a detached, hostile father." He also writes that "many mothers of lesbians tend to be hostile and competitive with their daughters. They interfere with establishing a close relationship with the father, as well as with boyfriends. The fathers of female homosexuals seldom appear to play a dominant role in the family and have considerable difficulty being openly affectionate with their daughters."[34]

In discussing the etiology of homosexuality Dr. John Powell lists the factors of fear of the opposite sex, failure to achieve proper sex role identification, and for male homosexuals, overidentification with the mother figure and underidentification with the father figure.[35]

While many years of research have contributed to our understanding of homosexuality, its cause or causes remain controversial. However, it can be maintained that there is no justification for a homosexual to claim that he was born a homosexual or that he cannot change his attitudes and behavior.

Counseling The Homosexual: Part II

Therapeutic Attitudes

One of the most important factors in a counseling situation is the attitude of the therapist. The attitude of the therapist is especially important when counseling a homosexual. The following list is to help the counselor to develop the right attitude.

1. Wherever appropriate, the therapist should *verbally* express *positive* belief that some form of help or change is possible. The counselee comes with an attitude of hopelessness and it is up to the therapist to give him hope for his problem.

2. From the outset the therapist must inform the patient that his problem is not solely a sexual one. The counselee will most often come feeling guilty and that he is just a sex pervert. The counselor must inform the counselee that his problem involves other aspects besides sex; for example, his relationship with parents and siblings. This information will help relieve some of the patient's guilt.

3. From the outset the therapist should show verbal and nonverbal support of all efforts the patient has made in the past to change. Also, any efforts made by the patient which coincide with what the therapist believes will lead to change should be reinforced at the very time they are made or expressed.

4. Early in treatment, the patient should be advised that all homosexual imagery will not disappear and that he should not be discouraged by reappearances of homosexual attractions during therapy and later in life. This will help the counselee to deal with fantasies and attractions when they come and he won't get discouraged as easily.

5. The therapist must treat the patient as a unique human being. The therapist must not force change. The therapist will also be tempted to stereotype change. Don't expect the patient to become "typical man." The homosexual will most likely not become aggressively involved with women or actively involved in sports.

6. The therapist should treat the patient on a man-to-man basis. The therapist must interpret and discourage the patient's attempts at transference. The therapist must also be vigilant against subtle attempts to shift responsibility to the therapist.

7. The therapist should, whenever possible, express belief in the patient's capacities for independent, assertive activity. The counselee will need this

encouragement to help him change his effeminate behavior patterns.

8. The therapist should not be afraid to express genuine, warm feelings for the patient when he has made an effort to or actually mastered a difficulty. Any non-erotic exchange of warmth can be helpful.

9. The therapist should support all the patient's efforts, past or present, to establish appropriate female contact. Any episodes of physical excitation in kissing, petting, or physical contact with a woman should be supported.

10. The therapist should support all attempts the patient has made, past or present, at avoiding homosexual activity.

Overcoming Resistance

How do we as therapists help a patient overcome his resistance to change?

1. The therapist must support from the outset the patient's desire to change.

2. It is important for the patient to understand how he relates to people as he related to his father and mother. The homosexual seeks these people and this just perpetuates his homosexuality.

3. The patient needs to learn and understand why he withdraws from people who see him as an intact male.

4. People are capable of altering their homosexuality consciously, and the therapist must reassure the patient that he has the freedom to make this change.

5. The therapist must explore the patient's sexual values to better understand how resistant he will be to change.

6. The patient's passivity must also be understood and talked about. The more passive, the more resistant to change. The more passive, the more encouragement is needed.

7. It is also very important for the therapist to understand thoroughly any past or present homosexual affairs of the patient. These must be discussed so they can be dealt with and understood by the patient to better understand how he reacts homosexually.

8. Any ambivalent feelings of the patient must be dealt with. Homosexual change is difficult and takes 100 percent determination and commitment.

Once we have overcome resistance in the patient and the patient has changed, how do we sustain change?

1. The patient must become consciously aware of the degree and the amount of time and energy wasted on homosexual fantasies, impulses, and acts.

2. The most important way a therapist can help a patient to sustain change is to make the patient aware of the things which trigger his homosexuality.

3. All homosexual attractions, fantasies, or practices, whether masturbatory or overt contacts, must be traced back to their inception each day. A detailed inspection of each homosexual attraction, fantasy, or impulse that leads to an overt homosexual act results in a patient's better understanding of the one or many mechanisms that trigger his homosexuality.

4. The patient must constantly be on the alert for methods of short-circuiting attractions to people and situations which trigger his homosexuality.

5. The patient must be made to consciously recall and identify trigger mechanisms and to think about them.

Note: The above suggestions and recommendations are taken from the book *Changing Homosexuality in the Male* by Lawrence J. Hatterer. This is the most helpful and practical volume available in giving practical techniques to assist the homosexual. A chart contained in this book, "Treatability and Goals of Therapy," assists the therapist in knowing whether the person is highly treatable or if the prognosis is poor.

Counseling the Homosexual: Part III

In counseling a homosexual, it is very important to have adequate knowledge of the subject of homosexuality. Therefore, many facts and much information have been given in this paper prior to this presentation on counseling the homosexual.

Characteristics of the Mothers of Male Homosexuals

1. More frequently the homosexual child is the mother's favorite child.
2. The mother demanded to be the center of the homosexual's attention.
3. The mother was domineering.
4. The mother spent a greater-than-average amount of time with the child.
5. She did not encourage masculine activities and attitudes.
6. She discouraged masculine activities and attitudes.
7. She encouraged feminine activities and attitudes.
8. She tried to ally with the son against the husband.
9. She often openly preferred the son to the husband.
10. She was unduly concerned with protecting the son from physical injury.
11. In childhood, the son was excessively dependent on his mother for advice and direction.

Characteristics of the Fathers of Male Homosexuals

1. Another child was favored over the subject.
2. The patient was the least favored child.
3. The father spent very little time with the child.
4. The patient did not feel accepted by the father.

5. The father failed to encourage masculine attitudes.
6. The patient often knowingly hated and feared his father.
7. The patient had little respect for his father.
8. The patient did not accept his father.
9. The father did not express affection for the patient.
10. The father had less respect for the patient than other male siblings.
11. The patient did not side with the father in parental arguments.
12. The patient found it more difficult to cope with the father than with the mother.
13. The patient feared his assertiveness would hurt or anger the father.
14. The patient felt the father did not consider his needs.
15. The patient did not currently feel respected by his father.
16. The patient did not regard the father as admirable.
17. The patient was not excessively dependent on the father.[36]

These characteristics are not presented as an excuse for a child who has become homosexual, but they are to be of use in working toward a prevention of homosexuality by both the individual family and the church. These common causes of homosexuality must be known by the counselor in helping the counselee know what type of pressures he will still feel if he is involved with his parents while trying to overcome this temptation.

Some further arguments for the causes of homosexuality and how they affect the homosexual are presented by Clyde Narramore:

Glandular Disturbances. This occurs when the sex hormones, estrogen and androgen, are out of balance. Not all homosexuals have this imbalance. Many people who have this imbalance are not homosexuals. Furthermore, individuals who have this imbalance have changed from homosexuals to heterosexual.

Genetic Causes. Personality factors which lead to homosexuality occur subtly in childhood. This leads to the erroneous conclusion that they were born this way. Troy Perry's statement is an example of this.

Dominant Mother. She stifles and belittles her son's masculinity. The child then loses respect for his own sex.

Weak Father. The son loses respect for his father and his own sex. For a daughter, she loses respect for men in general.

Overindulgent Mother. The child develops a strong attachment to his mother which cannot be broken as he grows older. No woman or girl can match his mother, so he does not develop normal heterosexual friendships.

Cruel Parents. This may cause the child to develop ill feelings toward others of the same sex as the cruel parent.

Poor Parental Marriage Relationship. One of the most common causes. The child grows up with the attitude that marriage is an unhappy and frustrating institution. Avoiding marriage, he turns to homosexual activity to obtain needed sexual gratification.

Overly Close Relationship with a Parent of the Same Sex. The child is unable to develop healthy heterosexual attitudes. Since the child's early experiences have been almost totally with the parent of the same sex, he is unable to relate to those of the opposite sex.

Lack of Appropriate Sex Education. When parents treat sex as a taboo, the child often develops poor sexual attitudes.[37]

These causes are presented to show what factors influence the mental attitude of the homosexual. These factors cause him to find his sexual identity in a homosexual act or role.

Most children go through a period of "curiosity seeking" where many actions might be called homosexual. But usually these do not carry on past puberty. If they do carry on past puberty, then there is a high chance of homosexual identity being formed.

The best method for counseling a homosexual seems to be through the framework of Reality Therapy. The following are steps utilizing the principles of Reality Therapy:

1. Become involved! One of the homosexual's problems is that people who can help him won't listen to him.

   a. Do not overreact when he tells you he's "gay."

   b. Honor the trust that the person has placed in you.

   c. Separate the individual from the act.

   d. Be genuinely concerned for the individual and show hope in his ability to change. HE CAN CHANGE!

2. Evaluate the present behavior. Help him see and evaluate.

   a. Recognize that homosexuality is a sin. That's God's opinion, not just yours.

   b. Condemn the act, not the person.

   c. Stress the positive aspects of living according to God's standards.

   d. Stress the negative aspects of living as a homosexual.

   e. Show the homosexual that Christ holds the answer to sin. HE CAN CHANGE!

3. Plan. Let him make the plan.

   a. Show the homosexual that homosexuality is a total way of life and that if he really desires to change, he must learn a completely new way of life.

b. Emphasize the importance of breaking off past associations.

c. Pray with him for the Holy Spirit's guidance in restructuring his life so as to avoid his old ways and cut ties in order to discourage returning ("If it doesn't work out, I can always go back.").

d. Do not allow the person to isolate himself, but encourage participation in mixed group activities.

e. Encourage Scripture memorization.

4. Alternatives. Let him make the alternatives.

5. Commitments. DO NOT ACCEPT EXCUSES!

a. Part of the homosexual pattern is lying.

b. Beware of lies and excuses.

c. Expect, don't accept!

A counselor needs to encourage the counselee to change his sexual identity from that of homosexual to that of heterosexual. In order to do this, the counselor must provide motivation for the counselee by helping him plan for meeting his needs in a correct manner. The counselor must really spend time in prayer and in reliance upon the leading of the Holy Spirit for himself and for the counselee.

Counseling homosexuals is one of the hardest tasks in counseling. The acceptability of homosexual activity and attitudes of society today makes the job especially difficult. A counselor cannot expect quick change, but must be ready for a long-term process back to correct living.

FOOTNOTES

1. Merville Vincent, "A Christian View of Homosexuality," *Eternity* (August 1972), 23.
2. Paul Chance and Evelyn Hooker, "Facts That Liberated the Gay Community," *Psychology Today* (December 1975), 52.
3. M. Weinburg and C. Williams, *Male Homosexuals: Their Problems and Adaptations* (New York: Oxford University Press, 1974).
4. Alex Davidson, *The Returns of Love.*
5. Vincent, p. 23.
6. John R. Powell, "Understanding Male Homosexuality: Developmental Recapitulation in a Christian Perspective," *Journal of Psychology and Theology*, II (Summer 1974), 163.
7. Dave Griffiths, "Grace is for the Gay," *His*, XXIV (March 1974), 20-21.
8. The interpretations of the UFMCC are taken from two tracts and a taped interview provided by the Reverend Troy Perry.
9. H. Freeman and Maurice Simon, eds., *Midrash Rabbah*, I (London: Soncino Press, 1939), 437-38.
10. Clement of Alexandria, "The Instructor," *The Ante-Nicene Fathers*, Vol. II, ed. Alexander Roberts and James Donaldson (Buffalo: Christian Literature Publishing, 1855), p. 282.
11. Derek Kidner, *Genesis* (Chicago: Inter-Varsity Press, 1967), pp. 136-37.
12. Francis Brown, S. R. Driver, and Charles Briggs, *A Hebrew and English Lexicon of the Old Testament* (Oxford: Clarendon Press, 1974), pp. 12-13.
13. J. A. Thompson, "The Significance of the Verb Love in the David-Jonathan Narratives in I Samuel," *Vetus Testamentum* (July 1974), 334-36.
14. H. Meyer, *Critical and Exegetical Handbook of the Epistle to the Romans* (New York: Funk & Wagnalls, 1889).

15. William Arndt and Wilbur Gingrich, *A Greek-English Lexicon of the New Testament* (Chicago: University of Chicago Press, 1957), p. 489.
16. J. H. Thayer, *Greek-English Lexicon of the New Testament* (New York: Harper & Brothers, 1887), p. 75.
17. American Psychiatric Association, *Diagnostic and Statistical Manual of Mental Health*, 2d ed. (Washington, D.C.: American Psychiatric Association, 1968; rpt., 1975), vi.
18. American Psychiatric Association, p. 44.
19. Paul Chance, "The Darling of the Gay Community," *Psychology Today* (December 1975), 54.
20. Powell, p. 164.
21. Charles Wahl, ed., *Sexual Problems: Diagnosis and Treatment in Medical Practice* (New York: Free Press, 1967), p. 194.
22. Alfred Kinsey, Wordell Pomeroy, and Clyde Martin, *Sexual Behavior in the Male* (Philadelphia: W. B. Saunders, 1948), pp. 650-51.
23. Chance and Hooker, p. 101.
24. Harold Lindsell, "Homosexuals and the Church," *Christianity Today* (September 28, 1973), 8.
25. Kinsey, p. 657.
26. Wahl, p. 89.
27. Wahl, p. 158.
28. Armand Nicholi, "Homosexualism and Homosexuality," *Baker's Dictionary of Christian Ethics*, ed. Carl Henry (Grand Rapids: Baker Book House, 1973), p. 295.
29. Arno Karlen, *Sexuality and Homosexuality* (New York: W. W. Norton, 1971), pp. 340-41.
30. Wahl, p. 194.
31. Shirley Braverman, "Homosexuality," *American Journal of Nursing* (April 1973), 653.
32. Chance and Hooker, p. 55.
33. Peter Wyden and Barbara Wyden, *Growing Up Straight* (New York: Stein & Day, 1968), pp. 49-50, 62-63.
34. Nicholi, pp. 295-96.
35. Powell, pp. 165-66.
36. Irving Bieber and others, *Homosexuality: A Psychoanalytic Study* (New York: Basic Books, 1962).
37. Clyde Narramore, *Encyclopedia of Psychological Problems* (Grand Rapids: Zondervan, 1966), pp. 112-14.

BIBLIOGRAPHY
A. Books

Aaron, William. *Straight: A Heterosexual Talks About His Homosexual Past.* New York: Doubleday, 1972.

Arndt, William, and Wilbur Gingrich. *A Greek-English Lexicon of the New Testament.* Chicago: University of Chicago Press, 1957.

Bieber, Irving, and others. *Homosexuality: A Psychoanalytic Study.* New York: Basic Books, 1962.

Brown, Francis, S. R. Driver, and Charles Briggs. *A Hebrew and English Lexicon of the Old Testament.* Oxford: Clarendon Press, 1974.

Drakeford, John. *Forbidden Love.* Waco, Texas: Word Books, 1971.

Enroth, Ronald M., and Gerald E. Jamison. *The Gay Church.* Grand Rapids: William B. Eerdmans Publishing Co., 1974.

Evening, M. *Who Walk Alone.* Downers Grove: Inter-Varsity Press, 1975.

Freeman, H., and Maurice Simon, eds. *Midrash Rabbah*, Vol. I. London: Soncino Press, 1939.

*Hatterer, Lawrence J. *Changing Homosexuality in the Male.* New York: McGraw-Hill, 1973.

Henry, Carl, ed. *Baker's Dictionary of Christian Ethics.* Grand Rapids: Baker Book House, 1973.

Karlen, Arno. *Sexuality and Homosexuality.* New York: W. W. Norton, 1971.

Kidner, Derek. *Genesis.* Chicago: Inter-Varsity Press, 1967.

Kinsey, Alfred, Wardell Pomeroy, and Clyde Martin. *Sexual Behavior in the Male*. Philadelphia: W. B. Saunders, 1948.

Meyer, H. A. W. *Critical and Exegetical Handbook of the Epistle to the Romans*. New York: Funk & Wagnalls, 1889.

Perry, Troy D. *The Lord is My Shepherd and He Knows I'm Gay*. Los Angeles: Nash Publishing Co., 1972.

Philpott, Kent. *The Third Sex*. Plainfield, N.J.: Logos, 1975.

Roberts, Alexander, and James Donaldson, eds. *The Ante-Nicene Fathers*, Vol. II. Buffalo: Christian Literature Publishing, 1885.

Thayer, J. H. *Greek-English Lexicon of the New Testament*. New York: Harper & Bros., 1887.

Wahl, Charles, ed. *Sexual Problems: Diagnosis and Treatment in Medical Practice*. New York: Free Press, 1967.

Weinberg, Martin. *Homosexuality: An Annotated Bibliography*. New York: Harper & Row, 1972.

Weinberg, M., and C. Williams. *Male Homosexuals: Their Problems and Adaptations*. New York: Oxford University Press, 1974.

Wyden, Peter, and Barbara Wyden. *Growing Up Straight*. New York: Stein & Day, 1968.

*This is the most helpful book available for learning how to counsel male homosexuals.

B. Periodicals

Bockmühl, Klaus. "Homosexuality in Biblical Perspective," *Christianity Today*, September 28, 1973, pp. 12-18.

Braverman, Shirley. "Homosexuality," *American Journal of Nursing*, April 1973, pp. 652-55.

Chance, Paul. "The Darling of the Gay Community," *Psychology Today*, December 1975, pp. 52-55, 101.

Charles, Guy. "Gay Liberation Confronts the Church," *Christianity Today*, September 12, 1975, pp. 14-17.

Griffiths, Dave. "Grace is for the Gay," *His*, XXIV (March 1974), pp. 20-21.

I. M. "Metropolitan Community Church: Deception Discovered," *Christianity Today*, April 26, 1974, pp. 13-18.

Lindsell, Harold. "Homosexuals and the Church," *Christianity Today*, September 28, 1973, pp. 9-12.

McGinnis, Marilyn, with H. Norman Wright. "Ministering to the Homosexual," *Moody Monthly*, September 1973, pp. 82-87.

Powell, John R. "Understanding Male Homosexuality: Developmental Recapitulation in a Christian Perspective," *Journal of Psychology and Theology*, II (Summer 1974), pp. 163-73.

Scanzoni, L. "On Friendship and Homosexuality," *Christianity Today*, September 27, 1973, pp. 11-14.

Vincent, Merville. "A Christian View of Homosexuality," *Eternity*, Agusut 1972.

C. Annotated Bibliography

Davidson, A. *The Returns of Love*. Downers Grove: Inter-Varsity Press, 1970. This short book written in the form of letters between two Christian homosexuals portrays very realistically the frustrations and feelings of one who is attracted to a member of the same sex, but knows that it is wrong to act it out. The writer explores deeply into his own life and the answers that he has discovered in the Bible. The book should be read by any Christian who is a homosexual.

Adams, Jay E. *The Christian Counselor's Manual*. Grand Rapids: Baker Book House, 1973. In the chapter dealing with the counseling of homosexuals, Adams does a good job of presenting what needs to be done when one counsels a homosexual. He emphasizes the importance of completely restructuring the life of the homosexual such that the homosexual removes himself from temptations to return to his previous life of sin.

Narramore, Clyde M. *Encyclopedia of Psychological Problems*. Grand Rapids: Zondervan Publishing House, 1966. This is an excellent book in terms of providing information regarding homosexuality. It presents the causes of homosexuality, but it does not adequately deal with the "how to" of counseling.

Glasser, William. *Mental Health or Mental Illness?* New York: Harper & Row, 1960. In his chapter dealing with sexual neuroses, Glasser presents the dangers of homosexuality to society. He presents some of the mental attitudes of homosexuals, both male and female, and discusses the problems involved in searching for sexual identity.

Krafft-Ebing, Richard von. *Psychopathia Sexualis*. New York: Stein & Day, 1965. This work was written in the 1870s. It deals with the technical and physiological aspects of homosexuality by the use of many case studies. Both male and female homosexuality are discussed with case studies presented. This is an excellent technical book for those who wish to fully understand the problems of homosexuality. His treatment for homosexuals is through the use of hypnotism. Therefore, this book does not contain practical suggestions for counseling.

Hendricks, Howard. *Christian Counseling for Contemporary Problems*. Dallas: Dallas Theological Seminary, 1968. This is a fairly good book on dealing with problems but was weak on the area of counseling the homosexual. It did present the subject and gave a brief outline of a plan for treatment.

From The Marriage and Family Resource Newsletter, Vol. II, No. 6, June/July 1976. Editor — H. Norman Wright.

ORDER BLANK

for materials to use with this curriculum

QUANTITY	ITEM	AMOUNT*
	Premarital Counseling, Norm Wright	15.95
	Marital Counseling, a biblically-based behavioral, cognitive approach, Norm Wright.	17.95
	Biblical Applications for the TJTA Test	5.95
	Counseling with the TJTA Practical Applications	13.95
	The Pillars of Marriage, Norm Wright	7.95
	Beating the Blues, Norm Wright	7.95
	The Divorce Decision, Gary Richmond	8.95
	How to Speak Your Spouse's Language, Norm Wright	6.95
	Leading a Child to Independence, McKeon, Paul & Jeannie	7.95
	Overcoming Hurts and Anger, Dwight Carlson	5.95
	What to Say When You Don't Know What to Say, Lauren Littauer Briggs	5.95
	Damaged Emotions (tape)	5.95
	Sex Problems and Sex Techniques in Marriage (tapes), Dr. Wheat	19.95
	Before the Wedding Night (tapes), Dr. Wheat	19.95
Prepaid Orders Only	Subtotal	
California residents add 6% sales tax		
Postage and handling:		
$2.25 for the first item		
$ .35 for each additional item	Total	

Name _____

Address _____

City _____ State _____ Zip _____

Mail to:
Christian Marriage Enrichment,
1913 E. 17th Street, Suite 118,
Santa Ana, CA 92701

*Prices subject to change without notice.